UNLOCKING PYTHON

T0357610

Unlocking Python

A COMPREHENSIVE GUIDE FOR BEGINNERS

Ryan Mitchell

Published by John Wiley & Sons, Inc., Hoboken, New Jersey.
Published simultaneously in Canada and the United Kingdom.

ISBNs: 9781394288496 (Paperback), 9781394288519 (ePDF), 9781394288502 (ePub)

For general information on our other products and services or for technical support, please contact our Customer Care Department within the United States at (800) 762-2974, outside the United States at (317) 572-3993 or fax (317) 572-4002. For product technical support, you can find answers to frequently asked questions or reach us via live chat at https://support.wiley.com.

If you believe you've found a mistake in this book, please bring it to our attention by emailing our reader support team at wileysupport@wiley.com with the subject line "Possible Book Errata Submission."

Wiley also publishes its books in a variety of electronic formats. Some content that appears in print may not be available in electronic formats. For more information about Wiley products, visit our web site at www.wiley.com.

Library of Congress Control Number: 2024950121

Cover design: Wiley
Cover image: © CSA-Printstock/Getty Images

SKY10101277_041125

ABOUT THE AUTHOR

RYAN MITCHELL is the author of *Unlocking Python* (Wiley) and *Web Scraping with Python* (O'Reilly). She has six LinkedIn Learning courses, including *Python Essential Training*, the leading Python course on the platform. An expert in web scraping, application security, and data science, Ryan has hosted workshops and spoken at many events, including Data Day Texas and DEF CON.

Ryan holds a master's degree in software engineering from Harvard University Extension School and a bachelor's in engineering from Olin College of Engineering. She is currently a principal software engineer at the Gerson Lehrman Group, where she does back-end development and data science on the AI & Data Platform team.

ABOUT THE TECHNICAL EDITORS

PETER HENSTOCK is now a Senior Machine Learning Engineer at Incyte, after leading AI/ML efforts at Pfizer. His work has focused on the intersection of AI, visualization, statistics, and software engineering applied to drug R&D. Peter holds a PhD in artificial intelligence from Purdue University, along with seven master's degrees. He was recognized as being among the top 12 leaders in AI and pharma globally by the Deep Knowledge Analytics Group. He also currently teaches graduate AI and software engineering courses at Harvard.

DAVIN POTTS became a CPython Core Developer in March 2016. When he is not fielding questions about or helping folks do more with the Python language, he can be observed visiting large, dangerous snakes at the local zoo or watching episodes of *Monty Python's Flying Circus* on repeat.

ACKNOWLEDGMENTS

THE BEST TECHNICAL EDITORS ARE the ones you dread bringing onto a project because you know it's going to be a lot of work. My extreme gratitude to Dr. Peter Henstock and Davin Potts for their voluminous and accurate feedback chapter after chapter. If any errata are sent in for this book, it's almost certainly because I overlooked one of their notes.

Thanks to James Minatel at Wiley for suggesting this book and seeing the project through. Thanks to Elizabeth Britten for cracking the whip over many months of writing and editing. Her flexibility and occasional crisis management were crucial.

My thanks and love to Edson Lacerda, John Mitchell, and Valinda Mitchell. You all hold my life together because I apparently haven't developed the skill of doing it myself yet. Love also to Viola and Hazel, who are my life.

Finally, thanks to Jim Waldo, who started this whole project many years ago when he mailed a Linux box and a copy of *The Art and Science of C* to a young and impressionable teenager.

CONTENTS

PART I
Programming

1

Introduction to Programming

The computer programmer is a creator of universes for which he alone is the lawgiver. No playwright, no stage director, no emperor, however powerful, has ever exercised such absolute authority to arrange a stage or field of battle and to command such unswervingly dutiful actors or troops.

— JOSEPH WEIZENBAUM

The programming book has a curious place in the modern world. With Python documentation, tutorials, and entire courses available online, what is the purpose of long-form text on the subject?

Similarly, what is the purpose of, say, historian John Keegan's book *The First World War* when a straightforward timeline of battles is readily available? This question is, obviously (at least, I hope), rhetorical. Books convey the author's point of view, insights, colorful commentary, and perhaps even add a little entertainment to the mix. They present facts, expand on those facts, and bring them to life.

For most people, the concept of "bringing history to life" probably makes more visceral and immediate sense than the concept of "bringing programming to life." This is unfortunate.

The goal of this book is to teach you to write Python programs, yes, and also to discuss the history, culture, and context of Python, the machines that run it, and the people who write it. The first step to understanding a programming language isn't simply copying that first line of code and hitting the Go button—it's learning what the computer is doing while that first line of code is running.

Whatever your motivations for learning Python, I hope this text can inspire in you the same enthusiasm I have for Python, and programming in general. In some small way, perhaps it can bring it to life.

PROGRAMMING AS A CAREER

"If you could be anyone in King Arthur's court, who would you be?" was the question posed to me one weekend afternoon in the kitchen of my childhood home by my uncle, a software engineer visiting from Massachusetts.

As a teenager, my knowledge of King Arthur was mainly limited to the film *Monty Python and the Holy Grail*, so even thinking of suitable answers was difficult. There was Lancelot, Galahad, and all the rest of the knights, but none of them seemed especially worth becoming. "King Arthur" himself would have been a fun way to respond, but surely, there must be a more interesting character. What about the Lady of the Lake—the kingmaker herself?

Of course, in some versions, such as the 1963 Disney classic *The Sword in the Stone*, Arthur becomes king, not by women in ponds distributing swords, but by pulling Excalibur out of a stone. I thought about that movie, too.

And, certain that my answer was cheating somehow, I finally gave my uncle the snarky response: "Merlin."

This, of course, is the correct answer. Years later, my uncle said that it was because of this answer that he knew my future profession as a programmer was inevitable.

The association between programming and wizardry is a long one. And the association between programmers and snarky responses is even longer.

Programmers shape the world we view through our screens and create new realities seemingly out of thin air. They realize that the boundaries of the virtual world are artificially constructed. They either implement the rules passed down by kings or subvert them as they choose. They perform feats by mastering the arcane languages.

The power of King Arthur depends on external factors: his fame, wealth, political clout, and societal recognition of his authority. The power that Merlin has is intrinsic.

Of course, even if my response had been "King Arthur," I still would have become a programmer. Software engineers giving single-question personality tests to teenagers is no basis for career determination, just like yanking a sword out of a rock doesn't make you a king.

Myths About Programmers

Let's be honest: Many aspiring programmers get interested in the field tempted by big paychecks, job security, great benefits, and favorable working conditions. These things are all nice, to be sure. But getting hundreds of thousands of dollars a year from a big-name company is far more challenging than most programming bootcamps would have you believe. Also very common (but less lauded in the media) are entry-level programmers working long hours for small companies, nonprofits, and start-ups whose funding allows them a runway measured in months.

As a programmer you will experience both good times and bad times. Times when you are working from your couch on very easy and enjoyable projects for lots of money. And times when you are, perhaps volunteering (or working for so little in return that it's essentially volunteering), on stressful projects in an office with a long commute and a strict dress code.

So, what really differentiates programmers and nonprogrammers? The people who stick it out and have long, happy careers, and the ones who give up in frustration? I want to address a few industry misconceptions about what's "required" to be a programmer:

They Are Very Smart   I can't blame you if you think that programmers need to be very smart, based on typical media depictions of programmers. Programmers are not required to be geniuses, or even to be particularly nerdy.

For the vast majority of you learning to program, there are going to be certain problems you're not going to understand right away, certain concepts you're just not going to get. And these have nothing to do with some fundamental deficiency in your brain.

Programming is a marathon, not a sprint. Determination and consistency with always be more valuable in programing than genius.

They Work Very Hard   This stereotype is shifting somewhat thanks to an increase in remote work and contract jobs available for programmers. However, there is still a perception that programmers are glued to their computers all day, every day, working insane hours under lots of pressure to fix a bug or add a feature.

There is also the complicating factor that it can be difficult to estimate how much time is required to add a feature or fix a bug. If you are working for a small and/or mismanaged company, you may occasionally find yourself in a situation where a feature is *required* to be added by a certain deadline; complications arise, ballooning the hours required to add it; and you are the only one who can rescue the project.

But this is not a common situation, and if you find yourself doing this more than once or perhaps twice a year, consider finding new employment. In general, working as a programmer is the same as working anywhere else; in a well-managed company with good work-life balance, the hours are about the same as they are for any other profession.

Programmers do sometimes face pressure at "FAANG" companies: Facebook, Apple, Amazon, Netflix, and Google.[1] Depending on your team, company, position, and the current politics and/or economic environment, you may find yourself coasting into an easy retirement or under constant pressure to perform at the threat of losing your job. I have heard many versions of both stories, even from employees within the same company! But, again, a high-stress job is not a given, even at a large and competitive company while getting a large paycheck.

They Have Meticulous Attention to Detail   If a program is off by even a single character, it will not perform as expected. No typos or errant logic is allowed. Even an insignificant-seeming bug can bring down a system that people's lives depend on.

Technically, the above is all true. However, it's also a very disingenuous view of the realities of modern programming. For starters, we have software that finds and highlights errors as we write the code (for more information, see Chapter 12, "Writing Cleaner Code"). It's somewhat difficult to make a simple syntax error or to forget a character—the code must still be syntactically valid in order for it to run at all. At the very least, you should probably make sure it runs—not that it produces the correct output but merely runs at all—before it goes anywhere important.

---

[1] There are a variety of acronyms for these companies, and definitions of the "top" tech companies, and even the names of the companies themselves, change frequently. Some have also suggested replacing FAANG with MAMAA for Meta, Amazon, Microsoft, Alphabet, and Apple, reflecting the parent companies of Facebook and Google, as well as replacing Netflix with Microsoft. With this in mind, feel free to mentally replace "FAANG" with whatever definition of "popular tech giants" you see fit.

Programs are usually run in various testing environments over many scenarios. New features get multiple stages of testing and review before they go to production. And that's just for the code that doesn't have any lives depending on it!

I know many meticulous, detail-oriented programmers. But to be honest, I don't know anyone who would describe me similarly.

The great thing about computers is that, when something does go wrong, it will tell you what went wrong and where (at least to some extent). You see an error message, a stack trace, or at least an output that's different than what you were expecting. Nothing blows up, nobody dies, you're just sitting there at your computer with a puzzle to solve and something to fix.

Can extreme conscientiousness be an asset in programming? Absolutely! Is it required? Not at all.

They Are Good at Math   The nice thing about computers is that they do the math for you. If you frequently find yourself struggling with arithmetic, you can rest assured that "mental math" has no bearing on programming aptitude.

However, there is one intersection between programming and what most people may have encountered in a high school math class, and that is *word problems*. Programming is, in many ways, the art of modeling real-world scenarios with algorithms. If you had an aptitude for word problems, you may enjoy programming.

They Start Young   Many well-educated and affluent parents are flocking to programming toys, books, and games as a way to get their children—even toddlers—a leg up in programming and computer science. Toy manufacturers are, of course, extremely happy to meet this demand.

But is it necessary or even beneficial to give a three-year-old a Fisher Price Code-a-Pillar? Will your programming career suffer because you never learned Scratch in middle school or played with toy robots?

STEM (science, technology, engineering, and math)-branded toys are relatively new, rising in popularity in the early 2010's. Because of their relatively-recent appearance, there aren't any studies (at least none that I could find), that link early use of programming toys with successful programming careers in later life.

A study comparing groups of children playing with robot programming toys to groups playing with blocks[2] found that the "robot" group did slightly better on tests of computational thinking afterwards. However, both groups improved overall. You don't need robots to teach computational thinking—you can use wooden blocks.

When I think back on formative experiences that helped me become a better programmer, I think of volunteering at my school library. I had to reshelve books (where I invented the insertion sort), use a card catalog (a secondary index), and look up things in the giant dictionary (binary search).

It isn't surprising to me that some of the best programmers I know majored in library science, philosophy, and journalism rather than computer science or software engineering and only started programming as part of a career change in adulthood.

---

[2] Yang, W., Ng, D. T. K., & Gao, H. (2022). Robot programming versus block play in early childhood education: Effects on computational thinking, sequencing ability, and self-regulation. *British Journal of Educational Technology*, 53, 1817–1841. https://doi.org/10.1111/bjet.13215

Programming is simply applied logic, with a smattering of easy-to-learn syntax. This book will teach you the syntax (and a few best practices), but programming is really a skill that takes a lifetime to master. I think that childhood is better spent practicing logic, algorithmic thinking, and creative problem-solving outside the context of programming than it is spent learning some invented and infantilizing syntax for a nonsense programming language that will never be used again.

HOW COMPUTERS WORK

I do not know how computers work. I've met very few people who might know how they work, but I'm sure that even those rare individuals have blind spots. Computers work because of math, yes, but also because of physics and chemistry. Silicon impregnated with boron has interesting interactions with electrons, which ultimately allow us to do math.

As you might suspect, you don't need to know any of this to do programming, which is why not very many people know how computers work.

What this section is really about is the mental models that programmers rely on to understand what's appearing on the screen in front of us and how to control it. The shorthand, the analogies, and even the occasional lore. While none of these stories may be completely precise, my goal is that you find them useful.

The first computers were essentially calculators that took input in the form of switches and dials that could be set to one value or another. You input the numbers you want with the dials, and the operation you want performed on them (addition, subtraction, multiplication, etc.), press the "go" button, and the output is calculated.

Then, an innovation: What if, instead of setting these with switches and dials each time we wanted to use them, the computer could "write the numbers down" for later use? The numbers would be stored in some section of the computer's memory, and then we tell the computer to perform an operation on those stored numbers.

But what is an "operation"? Could that be written down as well, alongside the numbers and stored until we want to access it? Perhaps we could write down and save whole lines of numbers and operations and call them "instructions."

```
Retrieve value at memory location 31415
Retrieve value at memory location 27182
Add the two values together
```

It's important to understand these two concepts of storing and retrieving data as well as performing operations on that data. These two things are at the core of what computers do. In fact, they're really *all* that computers do. A computer is simply a machine that stores and retrieves values and performs operations on those retrieved values.

The values have changed significantly in the last 90 or so years that digital computers have been around. Instead of numbers we want to add, they may also be images, keyboard input, mouse clicks, streaming data from a remote server on the internet, and so on.

The operations have changed as well. Instead of adding two numbers together, we are compressing files, doing machine learning, or running Adobe Photoshop. However, at their core, computers and the programming languages that control them are still doing the same thing: setting values, retrieving values, and performing operations on those values. Take for example, this line of Python:

```
a = 2
```

The equals sign here is called an *assignment* in programming. It assigns values into variables. Here, the integer value 2 is being assigned to the variable a. The computer stores the value 2 in memory and then records the variable a as pointing to the location in memory where that value 2 is stored.

Not only is the value, 2, stored, but stored alongside it is information that tells us that it is a number, as opposed to a piece of text, or an MP4 file, or some other data. This tells the computer what things can be done with it, as an integer. We can use Python to perform addition and multiplication on the integer 2, but cannot, say, play it in a video player.

We can perform an operation:

```
a = a + 1
```

This tells the computer to retrieve whatever value the variable a is referencing, add the number 1 to it, and then store it back in memory so that the variable a is pointing to the new value.

As we're programming, we don't literally need to think about these things all of the time. But having this mental model does come in handy. Take this situation, for example:

```
a = [1,2,3,4]
```

The square bracket notation with comma-separated numbers denotes a *list* in Python. Rather than a single number, like 1 or 2, we can store a whole array of them. This entire list, [1,2,3,4], is assigned to the variable a.

Let's make another assignment:

```
b = a
```

This introduces a new variable, b, and assigns it to the same location in memory that a is pointing to. They both point to this same exact list of numbers. This is illustrated in Figure 1.1, which shows the variables a and b in a piece of Python code, pointing to a shared location in memory.

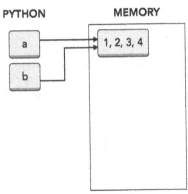

FIGURE 1.1: Variables a and b both point to the same location in memory when a is assigned to b.

Let's create a new instruction, written in the English language for the sake of example, and which we can pretend the computer understands how to execute:

```
append the number 5 to the end of list b
```

This adds the number 5 to the end of the list that variable b is referencing. Now, what happens when we view the list referenced by variable a? Because both variables are assigned to the same location in memory, both a and b now contain the list value:

```
[1,2,3,4,5]
```

This is because variables contain references, or *pointers*, to values rather than containing intrinsic values themselves. Every variable references a location in the computer's memory, and variables can also reference the same locations in memory if they're assigned to each other.

Files work in much the same way as values in memory. When you store a file, such as an image or text document, you may think that you are storing it at a "location" like C:\Users\RMitchell\ Documents or /Users/RMitchell/Documents.

However, what this file path directly references is not the file data itself, but a disk location for where that file data starts and also a file size—how many bits must be read past the starting point in order to load the entire file.

The contents of a file in your Documents folder might be mixed in on disk right next to a bunch of files from your Pictures folder or Downloads folder. It's only because of the organized way your computer tracks all of these references to disk locations and accurately retrieves them that gives the appearance of an orderly nested filesystem.

Although data in memory and files on a disk work in similar ways, using pointers and references, they are very different things. Files are stored on your computer's hard drive; this is often called *storage*. Files in storage persist when the computer turns off. Data in memory is faster to access and use, but it does not persist when the power turns off. Data in a running program is lost if the computer reboots and the program is not able to save it to storage.

Granted, as technology progresses, the line between "storage" and "memory" does get somewhat blurred. Some computers may have nonvolatile or persistent memory that does not get erased when the computers turn off. Some computers may have persistent file storage that is faster than the memory of most other computers. Hardware technicalities aside, most operating systems still carry these concepts of memory and storage forward, and so this is how we tend to think of them as programmers.

Importantly, the data that computers place into both memory and storage is in the form of binary values, 1s and 0s. If you open a computer, you're not literally going to see the character "1" and the character "0" written into a disk anywhere, but they're stored as an electrical or magnetic charge. You can think of a 1 as "high charge" and a 0 as "low" or "no charge."[3]

---

[3] As with many of the concepts we encounter in this section, exactly how these are stored with electricity, magnets, and silicon is highly dependent on the technology and is of little importance for our purposes. But it may be helpful to think of a 1 as "charged" and a 0 as "uncharged."

Human language is made up of more than just 1s and 0s, so if you want to store letters, books, or just about anything else, you're going to need some sort of substitution. The clever computer scientists came up with just that:

```
A - 01000001          a - 01100001
B - 01000010          b - 01100010
C - 01000011          c - 01100011
```

And so on. This is called the ASCII (American Standard Code for Information Interchange) alphabet, and it's how text files are stored.

Each one of these letters (or *characters* as computer scientists call them) is composed of 8 binary values, or 8 bits. The measurement 8 bits is so commonly used that it has its own special name: a byte. Count all the possible combinations you could make out of a byte: 00000000, 00000001, 00000010, 00000011, etc. You will arrive at the value 256. There are 256 possible combinations in 8 bits, which means there are 256 possible characters you can represent with an 8-bit block of memory.

It's not a coincidence that $2^8 = 256$, and the number of bits we are working with is 8. In general, if you have n bits there are 2^n possible combinations. This is because the first bit gives you two options (0 or 1), the second bit doubles that (0 or 1 with a 0 or a 1 in front of it), the third bit doubles it again, until you end up with $2 \times 2 \times 2 \times \ldots$ however many bits you have.

When computers store numbers, rather than characters or letters, they also have to use a binary representation of the number. When we write numbers, we use the base 10 or decimal system to do it.

In the decimal system, the number 1,234 has a 1 in the thousands place, a 2 in the hundreds place, a 3 in the tens place, and a 4 in the ones place. Or, more mathematically, it has a 1 in the 10^3's place, a 2 in the 10^2's place, a 3 in the 10^1's place, and a 1 in the 10^0's place (see Figure 1.2).

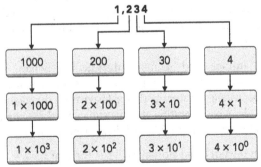

FIGURE 1.2: The number 1,234 broken down into the "ten to the thirds" place, "ten squareds" place, "ten to the firsts" place, and "ten to the zeroth" place

We can write decimal numbers like this because there are 10 possible characters for us to choose from for each "place." But what if there were only two possible characters, a 1 and a 0? In that case, we would have to use the binary or base 2 system. The number 10101 has a 1 in the 2^4's place, a 0 in the 2^3's place, a 1 in the 2^2's place, a 0 in the 2^1's place, and a 1 in the 2^0's place (see Figure 1.3). Therefore:

```
10101 (binary)  = 1 * 2⁴ + 0 * 2³ + 1 * 2² + 2 * 2¹ + 1 * 2⁰ = 21 (decimal)
```

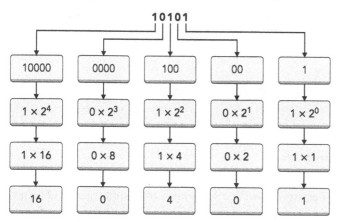

FIGURE 1.3: The binary number 10101 broken down into the "two to the fourths" place, "two to the thirds" place, "two squareds" place, "two to the firsts" place, and "two to the zeroth" place

In the same way that humans can write down any possible number with only the 10 digits 0 through 9, computers can store any possible number with just 2 bits (binary digits): 0 and 1. The bits just take up a little more space.

Very rarely do programmers need to actually do any of this binary math. But understanding exactly how the data is represented is invaluable. For example, the word four as text will take more room to store on disk than the number 4. The word four has four ASCII characters in it, where each character requires 8 bits, for a total of 32 bits:

```
01100110 01101111 01110101 01110010
   f        o        u        r
```

The number 4 can be represented simply as 100, for a total of 3 bits.

Theoretically, this is correct and important to understand. However, in practice, it's a little bit disingenuous. Although the number 4 only needs 3 bits, the number 1,000,000 needs 19 bits. And the computer doesn't know how big the number is we're trying to store or how to separate the numbers in memory. For instance, the sequence 100101 could be read separately as 100 and 101 (4 and 5 in decimal), or it could be read as a single number, 100101 (37 in decimal), or some other combination.

To solve this problem, integers in many programming languages are declared to be 4 bytes, or 32 bits, in length. This allows integer numbers up to 2^{32} or 4,294,967,296 to be stored.[4] Therefore, the integer number 4 would be:

```
00000000 00000000 00000000 00000100
```

This makes it just as long, in practice, as the ASCII word representation four. However, when dealing with larger numbers, you'll find that storing them as integers is far more efficient. Consider, for example, that 1,234,567 written out as "one million two hundred thirty four thousand five hundred sixty seven" is 69 bytes long!

A BRIEF HISTORY OF MODERN COMPUTING

There is a long and rich history of programming before 1970. However, the development of the languages and software that still impact us today began in the early 1970s with the release of the operating system Unix and the programming language C.

In fact, the date January 1, 1970, itself has important significance in modern computing. When computers store dates and times, they often store them as "the number of seconds since midnight on January 1st 1970." The time 0 is 01/01/1970 00:00:00, the time 3600 is 01/01/1970 01:00:00, and the time 1,000,000,000 is 09/09/2001 01:46:40. This is called *Unix time* or *epoch time* and it is a standard recognized by every computing system today.

So, for all intents and purposes, I like to think of the world as beginning at time 0 on midnight January 1, 1970. Back then, operating systems weren't much more than a command-line interface. You get a prompt, give it a command to execute, and the operating system interprets the command and executes it.

Operating systems themselves were varied and were often developed by computer manufacturers for their specific hardware. Therefore, the commands that were interpreted by these operating systems were also extremely varied, as were the programming languages they used and understood.

The Unix Operating System

Unix was originally developed by three programmers at Bell Labs in a relatively small-scale and modest project. Fortunately for the history of computing, an antitrust case in 1956 brought against AT&T by the Eisenhower administration meant that any non-telecommunications patents and documentation had to be licensed to all applicants at reasonable royalty rates. Because Bell Labs was a subsidiary of AT&T and Unix was definitely not a piece of telecommunications software, this meant that Unix had to be licensed and made open source and could not be kept as proprietary and expensive like many other operating systems of the time.

Unix quickly spread throughout academia, which welcomed a cheap and universal operating system. Academics, after graduating, spread it to the companies they worked at, where it gained popularity in the corporate world as well.

---

[4] This is an oversimplification and ignores the existence of negative numbers. In Python, the size of integers is complicated and not something you generally need to worry about. However, the concept of numbers being a relatively large default size (often 4 bytes) does hold true across programming languages.

A large part of Unix's appeal was that it was written in the C programming language, which was also gaining popularity. Although C was not the first high-level[5] modern programming language, or even the first high-level famous language (that would be FORTRAN), C has outlasted its predecessors and is still in common use today. C is also what most popular modern languages, such as C#, C++, Go, Haskell, Java, JavaScript, Perl, PHP, and Python, are derived from today.

Although modern operating systems are not derived from, or "based on" Unix in the sense that they directly use Unix, many of their principles of operation and the commands they use are based on Unix commands. In fact, many of the commands you'll learn and work with later in this book such as cd, ls, and mkdir, were developed for Unix and later adopted by many other operating systems.

Modern Programming

When you write a Python program, the Python code that you write gets translated by the computer into C code before being executed. In fact, much of the Python language itself is written in C. You can see an example of some of the C code that runs Python on the Python GitHub page: https://github.com/python/cpython/blob/main/Python/getversion.c

If the computer has to translate Python into C code before it can be run, why don't we simply write all programs in C? If written correctly and competently, a program written in C will usually be faster than the same program written in Python. However, C's syntax is much more complex. It also relies on the programmer to perform low-level tasks, such as allocating and releasing memory, that are taken care of in Python.

Prior to 1970, programming was very hardware-specific. A programmer might have to learn new languages or new ways to write those languages as new computers were released. The wide adoption and portability of C led to a flourishing of new programming languages that focused on style and architecture of the code, rather than the underlying hardware. Programming languages could be designed for specific types of applications and specific types of programming philosophies.

In the mid-1980s, higher-level languages like Objective-C and C++ were released. These languages used a programming style that focused on relationships between, and attributes of, objects or entities.[6] This style is called *object-oriented programming*, and it grew quickly in popularity over the next decades, led by languages like Java and C#, which came on the scene in the mid-1990s.

In 1995 JavaScript was introduced, which revolutionized a completely different area of computing: the internet. JavaScript allowed web pages to become dynamic and have programmable content for the first time.

---

[5] "High-level" and "low-level" languages will be discussed in more detail later; for now, know that a high-level programming language is, essentially, one that is written more like plain English. It has many abstractions and features that hide details of the underlying operating system and hardware, making it easier to write programs. Python is considered a high-level language, whereas assembly is considered a low-level language.

[6] Objects are values in computer science that have a complex structure to them. Unlike simple values like numbers or words, objects might have an elaborate schema with many attributes and functionality associated with them. For example, you might have a "user" object or a "blog post" object which contains all the information associated with that user or blog post. Don't worry about objects too much for now; we'll be revisiting them shortly and throughout the rest of the book!

Up until now, programs had to be executed by specialized software that the user purposefully installed and ran. Or it was compiled into an executable file that could only be run by a very specific operating system. Now, no special software or specific operating system was needed, the web browser itself executed JavaScript. If you had a web browser, you could run JavaScript on a web page.

This required cooperation from every company that had a web browser. The JavaScript code had to execute in the same way whether users visited a website with Internet Explorer or Netscape. However, it provided tremendous benefit to users, who could now use dynamic web applications powered by JavaScript.

Although the name "JavaScript" is similar to "Java," the two languages have nothing to do with each other. A popular saying in programming is that "Java is similar to JavaScript in the same way that a car is similar to a carpet." This isn't completely true, after all, Java and JavaScript are at least both programming languages. However, JavaScript was named after Java for marketing reasons, rather than any meaningful connection between the two languages.

Although several other languages attempted to compete with, or at least complement, JavaScript on the web (notably Java Applets and Flash Player), none succeeded in the long run. Today, JavaScript is the only in-browser language available for programming websites.

In 2009, Node JS was released; which allowed JavaScript to be run outside a web browser and power any code running on a computer. Now, it is one of the most popular general-purpose programming languages, alongside Python, Java, and C#.

TALKING ABOUT PROGRAMMING LANGUAGES

With so many programming languages in the world, a set of jargon was developed to help quickly describe and differentiate programming languages. If one programmer is trying to explain to another why they should learn Python, they might say, "It's a dynamically typed, garbage-collected multiparadigm language."

But what does this mean? Understanding these words doesn't just help us understand Python—it helps us understand how programmers think about programming languages in general.

This section, at first glance, may look more like a glossary to be used as needed than something to be seriously perused. However, I encourage you to read each term and try to understand it, at least in an abstract way. I've put the terms into logical groupings for ease of comparisons.

Open Source An *open source* programming language, like any piece of open source software, is one where you can read the source code. It's a popular misconception that open source necessarily means "free." This is usually the case; however, you must still check the software's *license*, which will dictate its terms of use.

If you cannot read the source code, the software is called *closed-source*. Java, .NET, and C++ are all closed-source programming languages.

Garbage-Collected Previously, we looked at how computers store values in memory. Before the values can be written in memory, that memory must be *allocated* for the values that will be stored. This allocation process makes sure that no other programs are using the memory (the memory is free) and then reserves the memory so that no other programs can use it.

When the memory is no longer needed, it is released, or *deallocated*. This does not mean that the data in the memory is deleted—that's not necessary and would simply waste time. However, any references to the memory are removed and the memory space is marked as available for the next program that needs it.

But, when you're working with variables in a computer program, how can you tell when values are no longer needed? How do you analyze a program and determine, for sure, that a variable will never be used again? This is a very complicated topic, but the automated tool responsible for determining which memory is and isn't needed is the *garbage collector*.

In the past, many programming languages required that you collect your own garbage. You had to explicitly allocate and deallocate memory. If you forgot to release memory and make it available for other programs, your program would have what's called a *memory leak*. Severe memory leaks could crash the program, or even the system.

Programming with a garbage collector is a bit like driving a car with an automatic transmission as opposed to a stick shift. Letting the computer take over is preferable in most circumstances and lets you focus your attention elsewhere, but there are those who prefer to chase efficiencies and do the garbage collection themselves.

Object-Oriented   Those new to programming often think of computer programs like recipes. If you follow a recipe step by step, you'll end up with cake or chicken alfredo, or whatever food the recipe was for.

True, some programs look like recipes. But as code repositories grow to millions of lines and software applications become increasingly complex, it just doesn't make sense to write programs as step-by-step lists like you would write a recipe (even a very complicated recipe with many parts!).

Some programming styles prefer to focus on defining objects that have certain properties, attributes, and behaviors. For example, if you're writing software for a poker game, you might create a "player" object that has a "hand" object. Each "hand" object contains "card" objects, and each card in turn has attributes like a suit, a face, and a value. A deck of cards is also a separate object, a "deck" object, and it might have behaviors that allow it to shuffle itself and deal cards to various players in the "game" object.

This style of programming is called object-oriented programming. It's a very popularly used style with Python, which we will explore in depth in Chapter 11, "Classes." Some people describe Python as an object-oriented language because it supports object-oriented programming so nicely. However, Python does not strictly require an object-oriented approach like some languages, such as Java.

Object-oriented programming has enjoyed steady popularity over the last couple decades, but some argue that it generates a lot of unnecessary overhead, leading to slow runtimes and bloated repositories.

Procedural   Unlike object-oriented programming, procedural programming is very similar to the recipe metaphor. Of course, most recipes we make are limited to a dozen ingredients and a similar number of steps (at the high end!). Some recipes might have "sub-recipes" where they instruct you to make the sauce, the frosting, the crust, or some other component of the final product. Similarly, procedural programs break out into many *functions* or *subroutines* that break the massive set of steps into more manageable chunks.

Procedural programming was once the only way available to write programs. All programs, and programming languages, were procedural. In recent years, procedural programming has fallen out of popularity in favor of object-oriented and functional programming styles. However, trends aren't always correct.

Functional In a functional recipe, you might define a process for creating sauces in general and simply pass in the ingredients. Functions can also be *composed*, or combined.

Functional programming is, unsurprisingly, a style that focuses heavily on functions. Rather than declaring variables and setting them to values, and then making decisions based on those values, functional languages apply the same set of functions to every input and simply map every input to its desired output.

Loops, `if` statements, and objects do not exist in functional programming. This may make things difficult, but in theory, no program written in a procedural or object-oriented style is impossible to write using only functions. For example, every loop that says "perform this operation 10 times in a row" can be replaced by a function that simply calls itself over and over again until exiting on the 10th self-referential call.

Functional programming is especially loved by academics and those who spend a lot of time pursuing "elegance" in their programs. In some situations—especially when taken to extremes—functional programs can be difficult to read and debug.

Multiparadigm A multiparadigm language is one that allows you to program in two or more programming *paradigms*, such as the object-oriented, procedural, or functional paradigms.

Low Level A low-level programming language is one that is closer to machine code. Machine code is binary numbers encoding instructions that can be directly executed by the computer's CPU. This is obviously not something that programmers write in directly, but something that programming languages are developed from.

High Level A high-level programming language is one that is very dissimilar from machine code. There are levels of abstraction, sometimes many levels of abstraction, separating a high-level language from a low-level one. High-level languages are often more "human readable" and closer to natural language. They are usually designed to be easier to read and write in.

The difference between high- and low-level languages is often relative. For example, if you were a programmer in the 1970s writing assembly code (a type of low-level language just one step removed from machine code) for many years you may think that the C programming language was very high level! Today, C is considered somewhat low level and the most popular languages—Python, Java, C#, and JavaScript—are high level.

Compiled Compiled languages are first built into low-level machine language before they can be run. These machine language files are called *executables*. The program is compiled into an executable file so that it can be run efficiently. However, you may need to create many different executable files for different operating systems and CPUs. Java and C# are compiled languages.

Interpreted Interpreted languages are languages that are not compiled but read and executed in their original form by a program called an *interpreter*. When a program in an interpreted language is shared, it is simply shared in the form it was originally written in by the programmer. Any computer that also has an interpreter for that language can run the program, and programs are exactly the same regardless of operating system and CPU. Python and JavaScript are interpreted languages.

Dynamically Typed   Dynamically typed languages allow you to declare a variable and store any type of data in it with no questions asked. For example, in Python we can do this:

```
a = 123
a = 'Alice'
```

Here, we're assigning the integer number 123 to the variable a, and then assigning the text "Alice" to that variable a in the next line. What type of data is the variable a "supposed" to contain? Python doesn't care. We tell Python that a is anything we want—a file, some media data, a decimal number, a whole list of numbers—and Python will happily accept that.

Statically Typed   Statically typed languages require that you declare what type of data a variable will hold before you store anything in the variable. An error will occur if you store anything other than the declared type in the variable. For example, in Java, you can declare a variable like this:

```
int a = 123;
```

The int means that the variable a is an integer and will be assigned an integer value. This declaration will cause an error:

```
int a = "Alice";
```

Java and C# are statically typed languages, whereas JavaScript and Python are dynamically typed languages.

PROBLEM-SOLVING AS A PROGRAMMER

Things will rarely go exactly the way you want them to. Documentation, even that found in this book, will be incomplete or out-of-date. You must read error messages and strive to understand them, not rely on others to do the problem-solving for you.

This is, perhaps, one of the greatest leaps you need to make when you go from being a mere user of software to being a creator of it. There is no one you can delegate responsibility to, blame, or ask for help—it's up to you to solve the problem.

That's not to say that help isn't available; there are a wide range of tools and resources you can use. But, importantly, you have to *use* them. You also have to be able to accurately assess your situation and use those tools appropriately.

There are some scenarios when copying and pasting the exact text of an error message you're getting into a search engine is the best course of action. The first link will give you exactly the solution that you need from someone else who has been in your shoes, saw what you're seeing, and solved the puzzle.

There are other times when the error message is only a very generic by-product of your underlying problem and searching for it isn't going to get you anywhere close to solving anything.

For example, let's say that you're writing a Python program that looks like this:

```
a = 1
a + b
```

You get the error message:

```
Traceback (most recent call last):
  File "<stdin>", line 1, in <module>
NameError: name 'b' is not defined
```

If you haven't programmed before, this might look intimidating. There's three lines of text and a lot of mysterious words and symbols going on (`<stdin>`? `Traceback`?). Copying and pasting this error message into a search engine also doesn't give you anything especially useful. Unfortunately, outside of hiring very expensive private tutors or consultants, there is no one to call and no one to swoop in and save you.

As it turns out, the first two lines of this error message are boilerplate and describe only where and in what context the error occurred, rather than anything about *what* the error is or how you might solve it. You can find this out by observing and reading other error messages you get as you program. You know that something about the last line `a + b` triggered the error, so you already know where it is and you only need to look at the last line of the error message to get a hint as to how to solve it.

```
NameError: name 'b' is not defined
```

You're not sure what `NameError` means, but you read the text after the colon, `name 'b' is not defined`. So could name be another word for "variable"? As in a "variable name"? If that's true, then this message is simply saying "variable b is not defined." Or, in other words, "Hey, I saw this variable b in the line `a + b`, but don't know what b means—you never defined it for me."

Looking again at the program, it looks like you remembered to set a to the value 1, but b was, indeed, not defined. You can fix the program by adding this line:

```
b = 2
```

This might seem like a trivial example—maybe even one that doesn't deserve such exhaustive discussion. But this is the type of problem that you will encounter over and over (and over) again as a programmer. Each time, you need to go through the same series of evaluation steps:

1. What is the important part of this error message?

2. What is the important part of the error message actually saying? You may need to replace some words with synonyms, look words up, ignore them and see if you can still make sense of it, or do some creative thinking to dig down into the meaning.

3. What might the underlying cause be that is triggering this message?

4. What should you do to fix the underlying cause?

As another example, consider this line of Python code:

```
1 + "cat"
```

This produces the error:

```
TypeError: unsupported operand type(s) for +: 'int' and 'str'
```

There's something called a `TypeError` with the message `unsupported operand type`. Looking up the word "operand," you see that it means "the quantity on which an operation is to be done." The operation, in this case, is addition (the + sign in the error message), and the quantities that we're doing addition (the operands) are the number 1, and the text `"cat"`.

So, another way of saying `unsupported operand type(s) for +:` might be: "You can't do addition on ___"

And what does the rest of this error message mean? What can't we do the addition on? We can't do addition on `'int'` and `'str'`. An int is short for integer, a number. The `str` stands for string, or a string of text characters. You will learn more about strings later, but for now, just keep in mind that a string is simply another word for text.

The error message `TypeError: unsupported operand type(s) for +: 'int' and 'str'` simply means "You can't do addition on numbers and text," which is exactly what we were trying to do by nonsensically adding the number 1 to the word "cat."

Other error messages might not tell you what the problem is at all, but need to be interpreted as a guide to where to look next. For example, later on we'll be working with a graphing and visualizations library in Python called `matplotlib`.

In order to use `matplotlib` in Python code, you need to first import it using the `import` function:

```
import matplotlib
```

While running this code, you might receive the error message:

```
ModuleNotFoundError: No module named 'matplotlib'
```

A *module*, here, is another name for a library, which we will be learning about later on. The important part is that `matplotlib` wasn't found. Why wasn't it found? As it turns out, it's a library that requires installation first before you can use it—it's not part of the *Python core* and must be installed separately. The solution, in your case, might be to install it.

Perhaps you did install `matplotlib` exactly according to the instructions you were given. However, what you might not have noticed is that, while you were installing the software, you got several repeated messages looking like this:

```
WARNING: Retrying (Retry(total=0, connect=None, read=None, redirect=None,
status=None)) after connection broken by
'NewConnectionError('<pip._vendor.urllib3.connection.HTTPSConnection object at
0x105812e00>: Failed to establish a new connection: [Errno 8] nodename nor servname
provided, or not known')': /simple/matplotlib/
```

followed by a final error message:

```
ERROR: Could not find a version that satisfies the requirement matplotlib (from
versions: none)
ERROR: No matching distribution found for matplotlib
```

Because you were following the instructions and weren't expecting anything to go wrong, you might not have even noticed this failure until much later when you run into `ModuleNotFoundError: No module named 'matplotlib'`. But `ModuleNotFoundError` is not your problem. The problem was your *installation*.

The important part of that was the repeated warning while the installation is being attempted.

It says, `Failed to establish a new connection`. What this means is that, for whatever reason, the installation software cannot connect to the internet. The root cause of the problem (you discover after doing some digging) is that your Wi-Fi is down.

A problem encountered while running a Python program later on was caused by a previous faulty software installation, ultimately because of internet connectivity issues during the attempted installation.

Developing your problem-solving prowess as a programmer will take time and patience. It's a skill that is complementary but still distinct from programming itself. Learning the language of programming will help greatly in interpreting the error messages. Even then, I still sometimes need to use "creative interpretation" and read them a few times to figure out what they're saying!

As you work through the exercises in this book, and work on projects of your own, you will run into problems you're not initially sure how to solve. You will run into problems that you weren't expecting and that I don't prepare you for in the text. However, with patience, critical thinking, reading and rereading, and the occasional well-placed Google search, I guarantee that every error is solvable.

Programming Tools

There are many types of software that programmers use. On top of that, there are countless modules, plug-ins, and configurations for that programming software that make understanding the programming tool landscape daunting for beginners.

While I encourage you to read about new tools, take recommendations from friends and colleagues, download them, and try them out when convenient, you also shouldn't stress too much about the "fear of missing out."

While the exact brand and type may change over the years, there are a few basic programming tools that every developer should be familiar with:

➤ Shell

➤ Version control system

➤ Integrated development environment (IDE)

➤ Web browser

Apart from the web browser, you may not have heard of any of these things before. In this chapter, we're going to go over each of these tools, what the most popular versions are for Python programmers in the industry today, and how to use them.

SHELL

Your computer's shell, also known as the terminal or, on Windows, the command prompt or PowerShell, is a sort of text-based interface to the operating system. Technically, the shell is simply a computer program just like any other program run by the operating system, but it allows you (assuming you have the correct permissions) to give extremely powerful commands and change far-reaching configurations on the computer that are not normally possible through just any third-party application. You must be careful, though; if you have admin privileges and are so inclined, you could break the computer.

Programmers usually refer to this program's user interface as the "terminal," rather than a "shell," and I will generally use the word "terminal" throughout the book.

As a programmer, you'll use the terminal throughout the day. After a while, you may find yourself using it to do even mundane tasks like creating and renaming files, editing text documents, and even getting data from the web.

You'll also be using the terminal to work with Python. It's useful for installing Python packages and running Python code. Another key use of the shell is to navigate your computer's directory structure.

To navigate your directory structure in the terminal, you first need to open the terminal. How to do this is dependent on your operating system:

> **Windows:** Click Start, search for **PowerShell**, and open the PowerShell.

> **Mac:** Go to Applications ⇨ Utilities ⇨ Terminal.

> **Linux:** There are many different types of Linux. In general, you should search your applications for a program called **Terminal**.

When you first open the program, you'll be greeted with (depending on your operating system and the exact terminal software you're using), your computer's name, username, and/or your current directory. Then there is some sort of symbol indicating that you should start typing. This symbol might be a tilde (~), greater than symbol (>), dollar sign ($), or percent sign (%). This default text that appears in the terminal is called your *command prompt*, or *prompt*.

Regardless of the symbol you see in your computer's prompt, it represents the same thing: a cue that you can type a new command. By convention, terminal commands are represented in instructional texts, like this book, as starting with a dollar sign:

```
$ echo "hello, world!"
```

You do not actually type this dollar sign, but the dollar sign indicates that what follows is a command you type in the prompt, rather than a line of Python code or something else. You type everything after the dollar sign and the space, and so would type only these characters:

```
echo "hello, world!"
```

The word echo here is the command. The echo command prints to the terminal the text in quotes that follow it. In this case, after you type echo "hello, world!" and press the Enter key, it will print out this:

```
hello, world!
```

There are many commands you can use in the terminal. Another important one is the cd command. The command cd stands for "change directory." It navigates to whatever directory you pass in after it. For example:

```
$ cd Documents
```

will take you to your Documents directory. It is important to know that every terminal session has a current location associated with it. Every time you run a command that interacts with files and folders, it will act on the files and folders in wherever your current location is. For example, you can create a new file using the touch command:

```
$ touch newfile.txt
```

That new file is created inside the directory where the terminal is currently located.

When you first open a terminal, by default, the terminal is located in the user's home directory. In Windows, this might be at C:\Users*username* and on a Mac it might be /Users/*username*. When the command cd Documents is run, the location changes from the default user home directory to the Documents directory within that home directory.

When you pass the directory Documents to the cd command, you're giving the command what's called a *relative path*. The command is only able to navigate to the Documents directory because it's currently inside the home directory, where Documents is located.

We can also give it an *absolute path*, which it will be able to navigate to no matter where the terminal is currently located. On Windows, you might type this:

```
$ cd C:\Users\username\Documents
```

and on Macs and Linux:

```
$ cd /Users/username/Documents
```

Once you're in your Documents folder, you can view all the files and folders within it. Unlike the cd command, the command for viewing all files and folders is different depending on your operating system. On macOS or Linux the command is ls (the list command). On Windows, the command is dir.

macOS and Linux:

```
$ ls
```

Windows:[1]

```
$ dir
```

This will print a list all the files and folders in the current directory.

Throughout the book, I will be defaulting to the Mac and Linux/Unix standard for writing commands. This means I will use ls rather than dir (although in some cases I will give separate commands for each operating system). This is because these commands are familiar to users of the widespread and popular shell programming language called *Bash*, released in 1989.[2] In addition, all commands are compatible with Windows PowerShell, so users of PowerShell should have no problem following along even though they're using non-native commands.

The ls command (as well as dir) can be followed by a file path or directory name. This directory name is an *argument* to the command ls. Rather than listing all the files in the current directory, passing this argument will cause it to list the files and directories within the provided directory:

```
$ ls myFolderInsideDocuments
```

Occasionally, you may get an error message, like this:

```
cd: myFolderInsideDocuments: No such file or directory
```

---

[1] The Windows program PowerShell has an alias (alternate command linked to another command) set up so that ls will also work.

[2] Bash has become somewhat of a *lingua franca* in computer science and programming and has a long and interesting history in the industry. I encourage you to read more about it. Even Windows users will find it difficult to avoid! https://en.wikipedia.org/wiki/Bash_(Unix_shell).

This error indicates that whatever file or directory you were trying to access doesn't exist. It might be because you mistyped the name, or because you're not in the location you think you are.

To check if you're in the correct location, you can use the pwd (print working directory) command:

```
$ pwd
```

This command will print the full, absolute path for your current location.

If you are in the right place, you may be misspelling the name. The easiest way to fix this is to get the computer to spell it for you! You can use the Tab key to autocomplete file and directory names while you type them. Simply type the first couple letters of the file or directory name, then press Tab, and it will complete the rest for you.

Now that you know how to navigate into subfolders within your current directory, how do you get back out? For example, if you're currently in your Documents folder, how do you go back to your home directory again? This is where the special filename .. (dot dot) comes in handy. The command

```
$ cd ..
```

will take you to the parent directory of the directory you're currently in. You can also combine this with other directory names to make a path. For instance, if you're currently in your Documents directory but want to go to Downloads, you can type the following:

```
$ cd ../Downloads
```

Navigating the filesystem via text commands might seem a little awkward at first, but it quickly becomes second nature with practice. I recommend spending time meandering around your computer's filesystem and poking into things using the commands cd and ls until they become muscle memory.

GOING HOME

The directory you start out in when you open a new terminal is called the *home directory*. The home directory is specific to your user account. Each account on the computer has its own home directory. For example, you may have a home directory at /Users/rmitchell, /Users/ajones, /Users/bsmith, etc.

On all operating systems, the notation for the home directory is a ~ (tilde). So you can navigate to the current user's home directory from anywhere on the machine by using the command:

```
$ cd ~
```

This is equivalent to typing:

```
$ cd /Users/username
```

Note that if you are using the Windows command prompt, rather than PowerShell, cd ~ will not work. Because PowerShell is officially replacing the command prompt, I recommend that you use it in Windows instead.

VERSION CONTROL SYSTEMS

You may have encountered a situation in which multiple parties are trying to share and make changes to a document, sending it back and forth over email. Very often you wind up with many different, and slightly different, copies of the file:

- `mydocument.doc`

- `mydocument_05012025.doc`

- `mydocument_05012025_bob_updates.doc`

- `mydocument_final.doc`

and so on.

Not only are there many copies of the file floating around, but tracking changes from version to version is extremely difficult. This is a mere annoyance in most situations, but what if you're dealing with long and complicated contracts being passed back and forth between opposing counsel and with tight signing deadlines? Changes slipping in without one party noticing could be extremely costly.

When it comes to programming, multiple people working on the same files at the same time is simply business as usual. In addition, there's the added pressure that computer code is somewhat sensitive to incorrect changes and mismatched logic. All changes need to be monitored and completely understood by all parties.

A version control system provides an easy way for changes to files to be tracked as parties make them. In some types of version control systems, such as *SVN* (Apache Subversion, `https://subversion.apache.org`), individual files must be "checked out," modified by a single person, and then "checked back in" with that person's changes. This is done to avoid two people making changes to the same file at the same time.

Other types of version control systems, such as *Git*, allow any number of people to make changes to the same file, or even the same line, at the same time. If the same segment of text is modified in two different ways by two different people, it will force them to decide which version of the line should be the accepted version when the file is "checked back in" and merged into the rest of the codebase. The process of deciding which version to accept is called "resolving merge conflicts."

By far, the most popular version control system today is Git. It is flexible, easy to use, and has broad support in the industry. Git is so popular that the second most popular version control system is SVN, with approximately 5 percent of market share (with the next competitor, Mercurial,[3] coming in at just 1 percent).

Even if you someday find yourself working for a company that uses SVN, you will almost certainly need to learn and use Git in order to get that job. In fact, I recommend that you create a free account on Git's most famous developer platform, *GitHub*, in order to keep track of your programming projects and have a record of consistent programming work that you can show off at job interviews!

---

[3] See `https://stackoverflow.blog/2023/01/09/beyond-git-the-other-version-control-systems-developers-use`

While Git is the simple open source command-line software originally created by Linus Torvalds (the creator of Linux), GitHub is a commercial platform that runs this software and runs the servers that developers upload their code to. It also offers a sort of social networking platform where people create profiles, display their code, comment on code changes, discuss bugs and issues, and do other important development work. Having a GitHub profile is simply essential for any developer.

To create a GitHub account, go to `https://github.com`. It's very straightforward: Provide an email address, password, and username. Most developers choose something based on their real name, but others pick a short and catchy nickname or programming "handle."

Each programming project starts with a *repository*. A GitHub repository contains all the code files, resources, and documentation for a single project. Once you've logged into GitHub with your new account, you can create a repository by going to `https://github.com/new` or by clicking the green New button on your home page.

Don't worry about creating the perfect first project or something you want to keep around long term. Repositories are just as easy to delete as they are to create, so I recommend creating one just to try out the GitHub features. You can, for example, create a repository called "testing" and give it the description "Just testing GitHub out!"

Once you've created this repository, its new "home page" is at `github.com/your-username/testing`. This is a shareable page, where people can go to read about your project, download its code, and potentially submit requests to modify the code (which you can review, approve, or reject).

Now that you have a GitHub account and repository set up, you need to be able to access the repository and modify the code from your own computer. This will require installing the `git` command-line tools locally.

Because Git is such a popular piece of open source software, there are many ways to install the command-line tools. However, the simplest way might be through installing the GitHub Desktop GUI (`https://desktop.github.com`), which will install the command-line software for you, regardless of your operating system.

In theory, GitHub Desktop is designed to replace the `git` command-line tools in the same way that Windows Explorer or the Mac Finder replaces navigating through files via the terminal. However, it is still valuable to know about and be able to use `git` commands directly.

To start, open a terminal and, to test your `git` installation, use this command:

```
$ git
```

You should see a large amount of text printed out, starting with this:

```
usage: git [-v | --version] [-h | --help] [-C <path>] [-c =<name>=<value>]
```

If you see an error message with something to the effect of "command not found," make sure that you've installed GitHub Desktop, and also try closing and reopening your terminal window. For more help with installation, try the GitHub install guide at `https://github.com/git-guides/install-git`.

Authenticating with GitHub with SSH Keys

Now that Git is installed locally, you need to let it know what your GitHub username and account is and be able to authenticate to that account. This allows you to add code and modify your new repository directly. Remember that you are the only one allowed to make changes to the repository. Others can only suggest changes. In order to change things, you need to, essentially, authenticate your local computer to GitHub.

The best way to do this is with SSH keys. An SSH key is a pair of documents that you create on your computer. It contains both a public key and a private key. The public key, as its name suggests, is one that you share publicly (including giving it to GitHub) and says, essentially, "The person who owns the corresponding private key is me."

You can think of a public key a bit like a lock, and a private key as, well, a key. You give GitHub the "lock" and say, "If someone comes along who can open this lock, that person is me."

To create a public/private key pair, open the terminal and type:

```
$ ssh-keygen
```

If you are running this command in Windows PowerShell, you may need to open PowerShell by right-clicking the PowerShell icon and selecting Run As Administrator.

This will open a prompt asking you which file you'd like to save the keys in:

```
Generating public/private rsa key pair.
Enter file in which to save the key (.ssh/id_rsa):
```

Use the default folder and key name .ssh/id_rsa by typing nothing and pressing Enter at the prompt. It will then prompt you for a passphrase:

```
Enter passphrase (empty for no passphrase):
```

This is an extra layer of security if attackers access your computer with its private keys. The passphrase makes the key unusable unless the private phrase is also known. It is considered an industry best practice to never use a blank passphrase, but for personal and learning purposes, you may not consider a passphrase to be necessary. You can add a passphrase or leave it blank and press Enter for no passphrase.

Finally, you will get a fingerprint and a "randomart" ASCII image that represents your new key pair. The randomart is essentially an easy way to visually compare and differentiate keys at a glance and does not need to be saved. The two important files that get generated are .ssh/id_rsa and .ssh/id_rsa.pub. The public key has the .pub extension, whereas the private key has no file extension.

HIDDEN FILES

The directory .ssh has a dot preceding its name. If you open File Explorer or Finder you won't see it. This is because a dot in front of a file or directory name makes it a *hidden file* or a *hidden directory*. These hidden objects do not get displayed by default in software like the File Explorer, or even when using the ls command in the terminal.

continues

continued

In order to see them using the `ls` command, you can add `-a` to the command like this:

```
$ ls -a
```

The `-a` (spoken as "dash a") is called a *flag* or a *command flag*. It's an extra option passed to the command that changes how the command behaves. In this case, the `-a` causes `ls` to list all the files, including hidden ones. For example, if you run the commands:

```
$ cd ~
$ ls -a
```

you should be able to see all files and directories in your home directory, including the `.ssh` directory where your public and private key pairs are stored.

Next, you need to let GitHub know about your key pair. Go to `github.com`, click on your profile picture in the top-right corner, and choose Settings ⇨ SSH And GPG Keys. Alternatively, you can navigate to `http://github.com/settings/keys`, which will take you to the same page. Click the New SSH Key button.

This will take you to a form to add a new SSH key. Create a title for your key; this can be anything to help you remember it, and it's really just for your own purposes. Leave the key type as Authentication Key. Next, you'll have to copy/paste the text from the public key file into the Key text field.

To do this, go back to your terminal and navigate to your `.ssh` keys directory:

```
$ cd ~/.ssh
```

Use the `ls` command to view your keys:

```
$ ls
```

You should see the file `id_rsa.pub`. Next, you're going to use a new command that prints the text of a file to the terminal. This command is called `cat`.

```
$ cat id_rsa.pub
```

Make sure that you are working with the public file ending in `.pub`, rather than your private key, `id_rsa`. You should *never* share your private key with anyone, including GitHub, and no software should ever ask you for your private key.

Highlight and copy the text of the entire key, starting with `id-rsa` and ending in your email address or username. For example, my public key is:

```
ssh-rsa AAAAB3NzaC1yc2EAAAADAQABAAABgQDTxXDFQ/EObuTkkd8vh+DaJEmtxv0FfNMlaaMFc+EmyIy
fzMoNP/+UpYscyDtcY/SVzqxKM97csTH43XXbHksyBNWctFi8qEYVR/341I9lt0iz/OmeVZsxIwyr/ZmeKf
+gyvJgBm6m1kge4eCqH4kcj6zzrgpBjwAVbmeC9js9at/SCqbggorsoiblEa3YU+Ptvb9mBvKOhe0FAIdLs
lRtrgk6hbwJASkGkG6rDf3I68AzNy7Qzxm1jJPddJzUJ0XFTM4R5+d0UDzAzb6RR36ED1JcHUpYfalbqiDA
5BtqnkT2HUML1L2UKaEyrWfZW1ck/fSsVj/zIC5Nqrmr1yZiNHoofUS61ZE2sCIDJ8REc/o5GNrnvL0KHfn
VNRNIS+opsMPwKjbOq4uzxkeraVdLUvIVOFXLNEJxhf3TuDts2PPNBXtRSgGiINs9CFrBEAH0w28U7ZLi2d
WuTXaZB4jII+aZ0dZLwUTfTzCzS5R4Rd6WWFAkImGP+KiDhmax6Yk=ryan.e.mitchell@gmail.com
```

Paste this into the key text box on GitHub and save it with the Add SSH Key button.

Finally, go back to your terminal and type the command **ssh-add** to add your newly generated keys as available identities:

```
$ ssh-add
```

You should see your identity added. It is now available for authentication with GitHub.

Because you may be working with many projects on GitHub, it is best practice to create a new directory called git (or similar) to store all of them. I will reference the git directory throughout the book, but feel free to call this directory whatever you want.

You can create a new directory from the command line using the mkdir (make directory) command. Make sure to navigate back to your Documents folder before making it, or the directory will be created inside your .ssh directory, which is not ideal:

```
$ cd ~/Documents
$ mkdir git
```

This creates a new directory git within your Documents directory. Navigate to it:

```
$ cd git
```

Then you need to use the git tool to *clone* your project from github.com. When you clone a project, you copy all of that project's files locally onto your computer. You also create some hidden files and settings that tell the git software exactly where this project came from, what versions of it are available, how to publish changes to it, and other information.

Go to your project's GitHub page at https://github.com/your-username/testing. Here you can find the URL you'll need to clone your project by clicking the Code button and copying the SSH URL, as shown in Figure 2.1.

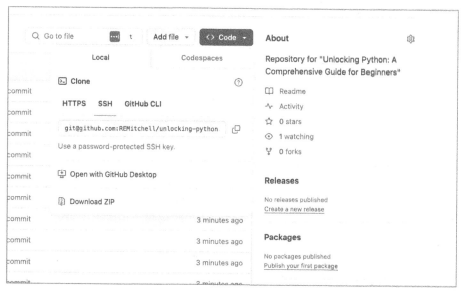

FIGURE 2.1: Cloning a project from GitHub

Use the command `git clone`, followed by this URL in order to clone the project:

```
$ git clone git@github.com:your-username/testing.git
```

Once you've done this, you should see a folder called `testing` at `~/Documents/git/testing` on your computer. Inside this should be a file called `README.md` located at `git/testing/README.md`.

`README.md` files are ubiquitous in GitHub projects. By default, they contain the project's name and the description that you wrote when creating the repository in GitHub. This is what gets displayed on the project's page, under the file listing.

Any type of information can be added to the `README.md` file, but it generally acts as documentation for the project (or a link to the documentation for larger projects), provides installation instructions, gives credit to authors and contributors, and more. For example, you can see all sorts of information for the official Python repository: `https://github.com/python/cpython`.

GITHUB MARKDOWN LANGUAGE

Markup languages aren't programming languages, but "formatting" languages. They're plain-text documents that describe how a document should appear when rendered. For instance, they can specify titles, headers, sidebars, italicized and bold text, links, and more.

If you've ever edited a Wikipedia page, or worked on an HTML file, you've used a markdown language. GitHub's markdown language makes it very easy to learn the basics.

To create a title, or heading, add a hash symbol and a space before the line:

```
# My title
```

You can add up to six hash symbols, with more hashes creating smaller titles:

```
## My smaller heading
###### My smallest heading
```

Bold text is surrounded in double asterisks: `**like this**`. Italicized text is surrounded by underscores: `_like this_`.

To insert a code block, use three backticks, with another three backticks after your code is done:

```
```
some code here
```
```

There are, of course, many ways to mark documents up and decorate them. Some READMEs are just plain beautiful! For more exploration, I suggest reading GitHub's documentation:

```
https://docs.github.com/en/get-started/writing-on-github/
getting-started-with-writing-and-formatting-on-github/
basic-writing-and-formatting-syntax
```

Using the text editor of your choice (such as Notepad or TextEdit), open the README file at ~/Documents/git/testing/README.md to edit it. Add something else about this repository, or perhaps a simple "Hello, world!" Do anything to modify the file, and then save it.

Back in the terminal, make sure that you're inside your project's repository directory:

```
$ cd ~/Documents/git/test
```

Use the git status command to check on the status of all the files:

```
$ git status
```

You should see that the README.md file has been modified. This lets you know that the file is changed from its state in the project on github.com. You have two options for publishing your changes to the project, or *committing* your changes.

First, you can commit your changes directly to the main project *branch*. A branch is like a version or a snapshot of the project. You can create multiple different branches or versions as you work on it, but the main branch is considered to be the official branch or the production branch.

The main branch is rarely committed to directly when working with multiple developers in industry because your commit must usually go through review and testing before it gets to the main branch. These checks are to ensure that your commit is safe and doesn't introduce any new bugs or crash the project.

However, because this is only a test project and you are a lone developer responsible for checking your own code, let's commit directly to the main branch:

```
$ git commit README.md -m "made some changes"
```

The -m flag with the message "made some changes" in quotes is called a *commit message*. This is displayed next to your change in GitHub, letting other developers on the project know why you made that change. In general "made some changes" is a terrible commit message because it's not very useful. It doesn't describe your changes or provide any explanation. Feel free to replace this with your own message—or don't, because it's a test project and the only person to read these is you!

Once the changes are committed, it's important to know that the changes are only committed locally on your computer. The server at github.com containing your public-facing project doesn't know about them yet. To let github.com know about the changes, you must *push* them. Both a commit and then a push are required to make changes to the project.

You can push changes with the git push command:

```
$ git push
```

This command will push the changes to the branch you're currently on, which is the main branch. After this, you should be able to see your changes on your GitHub project's repository page.

Next, create a new change in the README file. Add some text, remove some text, whatever you want, as long as the file is modified and saved. Here, we're going to pretend that we're developers working on a high-stakes project. We don't want to push any changes directly to the main (production) branch without getting a review of our changes from other developers first!

Create a new branch using the `git checkout` command:

```
$ git checkout -b new-feature
```

The `-b` flag is followed by a branch name, in this case `new-feature`. Branch names cannot contain spaces, but they can contain dashes. Best practice is to make them lowercase, with dashes separating words. Generally, you don't want branch names to be too long (more than three words is somewhat obnoxious) because you'll likely be typing the branch name a lot.

The `checkout` command with a new branch name will create a new branch with the given name and automatically switch your local environment to be using that branch. Depending on your operating system and configurations, you may see the new branch name appear in your terminal's command prompt—a handy reminder about which branch you're on. If the branch name doesn't appear, you can always check which branch you're on using the `git branch` command:

```
$ git branch
```

Now that you're on a new branch, you can commit your changes:

```
$ git commit -a -m "Worried about this feature and would like feedback"
```

Notice that I used a new flag `-a`, which indicates that all of the modified files should be committed. You can either name the file explicitly or pass in `-a` to commit all current changes. However, this will only commit changes to existing files that `git` knows about, such as `README.md`. If you create and want to add an entirely new file, you must explicitly add it with the `git add` command, followed by a `git commit`:

```
$ git add mynewfile.txt
$ git commit mynewfile.txt -m "Adding a new file"
```

Once you have your commits made on your new branch, push the branch to GitHub:

```
$ git push origin new-feature
```

Unlike the push that we did before to the main branch, which required only `git push`, this requires that you write `origin new-feature` (or whatever branch name you chose). The `origin` here is a shorthand that references the remote repository at `github.com` that the project came from. It's a substitute for the full URL that you passed into the `git clone` command earlier.

What this command is essentially saying is "push this to the `new-feature` branch at the `origin` repository."

Although there are ways to set your default branch so that you don't have to specify every time, it's good practice to specify `git push origin` *my-branch-name* whenever you're making a `git push`. This reminds you which branch you're pushing to and helps avoid errors.

After you've pushed your changes to your new branch, navigate to your repository at `github.com`. You should see at a yellow banner at the top, notifying you that there have been recent changes to your new branch and providing a button Compare & Pull Request. Click this button to see the page where you can create a `pull request`, or a request to pull your changes into the main branch.

The title is the branch name or commit message (if there is only one commit) by default, although you can change this to whatever you'd like. The description is optional, but you can fill this in with details of your new feature for other developers on the project to read.

Below this is a list of every commit you made, as well as changes to the files. Lines highlighted in red are things that have been removed and lines highlighted in green are things that have been added.

Click the green Create Pull Request button below the description box and you get a shareable page for other developers to view your request and either approve it or reject it. Because you are the repository owner and have full control over this repository, you are able to use the green Merge Pull Request button to merge your changes into the main branch whenever you want, however.

This has been a whirlwind overview of just a few of the most crucial features that GitHub has to offer. Like its name implies, it really is a hub of developer activity and a tool you will be using very often in the future. At the very least, I hope that you use it to get the code sample files for this book, at `https://github.com/REMitchell/unlocking-python`.

You can create a copy of this repository under your own GitHub account, also called a *fork*, by clicking the Fork button or going to `https://github.com/REMitchell/unlocking-python/fork`. If you see any errors in the code or have suggestions for changes, please make a pull request or submit an issue in the repository.

INTEGRATED DEVELOPMENT ENVIRONMENTS

In the section on Git, we used a text editor to make changes to the `README.md` file. In reality, programmers do not use text editors like Notepad or TextEdit—or, at least, the text editors that they use are fancier ones called *integrated development environments* (IDEs).

IDEs allow you to easily navigate code projects containing large numbers of files, have several files open at once, and make text changes to them. Similar to the autocorrect feature in English-language text editors, they also offer assistance with programming syntax, highlight errors, and provide suggestions.

Some IDEs are specific to the programming language. For example, *PyCharm* is a popular IDE that is specific to the Python programming language. These IDEs may work better "out-of-the-box" and require less configuration to do things with the language they were designed for.

Other IDEs can be used to work with any programming language—they are language agnostic. These IDEs can be good for programmers working with multiple languages, especially those switching back and forth between languages quickly, or working with code repositories written in multiple languages.

Visual Studio Code, also called just Visual Studio or VSCode, is an example of a very popular language agnostic IDE. Developed by Microsoft, it is completely free and does not have a paid version. This is in contrast to PyCharm, which requires a paid license for some commercial purposes.

Which IDE you decide to use is a personal decision that, to a large extent, doesn't matter very much. The code that results will be the same no matter what you write it with, and most employers do not have IDE requirements. I recommend that you try out both Visual Studio Code and the PyCharm Community Edition (the free version), at least, but which one you choose is up to you.

With that said, one of the most popular IDEs for Python today is the language-agnostic IDE Visual Studio Code. This is the one that I use, and you will see it in screenshots throughout this book.

If you download PyCharm, you will be prompted with the option Open A New Project. In Visual Studio Code, navigate to File ⇨ Open to open the same file-opening window. Unlike traditional file editors, IDEs are designed to work with entire directories of code at once. You can, for example, navigate to where you've downloaded the exercise files for this book (download them from `https://github.com/REMitchell/unlocking-python` if you have not done so already) and select the directory containing all the exercise files. Make sure that you are selecting the entire directory, and not just a single file.

In both IDEs, you will see your files in the navigation bar on the left, and be able to click on and edit individual files. As you click on files, they will open alongside all the other open files, and you can navigate back and forth between open files using tabs at the top.

IDEs will also allow you to run code inside them, and often include a mini-terminal tool that you can open as a sidebar to run code from the command line inside your IDE. Whether you choose to write code in the IDE and run it in a separate terminal or PowerShell window, or run it from the IDE itself, is a matter of personal style that you will develop over time.

WEB BROWSERS

You may not think that a web browser would be a primary tool of programmers. It's generally thought of as something used to view already developed web applications, rather than something used in the development process itself. However, a web browser is an essential tool in most programmers' kits.

Ten or 20 years ago, it was common to download and run lots of desktop software to do relatively trivial tasks. Almost everything you wanted to do was done through desktop software, and the internet was where you went simply to get information.

Today, many of these desktop software tasks are being moved to the internet—we use web applications to perform tasks that used to be done with native software. In addition, more and more things that used to be done "in the real world" are being done online. We can order food, do banking, edit photos, talk with friends, create documents, and store and view files all in a web browser.

This all requires lots and lots of web applications—software that is run in the web browser and that sends and receives data to and from a web server that is also running web application software. This also means that most programmers working today are, essentially, web developers.

When we think of "web developer," we might think of someone who designs and builds the graphics of a website that we see when we load a page. This type of web development is done in *HTML* (Hypertext Markup Language) and *CSS* (Cascading Style Sheets). However, most web developers today create the business logic that powers the interactions between a user's clicks and data in the database.

If you work as a programmer, the odds are that you're working on a web application, or will be very soon. For Python developers, the odds that their application is—directly or indirectly—used on the web is even greater. Python is an excellent language for retrieving data from a database, transforming it with business logic, and sending it across the web.

When data is sent across the web, it is generally sent in the form of HTTP requests and responses. HTTP will be covered in greater detail in Chapters 20, 21, and 22, when we deal with Python libraries specifically designed for sending and receiving with this protocol. However, you can see HTTP requests and responses in action in your web browser right now using the `developer tools`.

Developer tools are essentially the same from web browser to web browser, although most programmers prefer to use Firefox or Chrome. To open the developer tools in your web browser, use the following hot keys:

> **macOS:** Command+Option+I
>
> **Windows:** CTRL+Shift+I

If you prefer to use the menus to open the developer tools, you can use the following menu options:

> **Chrome:** View ➪ Developer ➪ Developer Tools
>
> **Firefox:** Tools ➪ Browser Tools ➪ Web Developer Tools

On most web browsers you can also right-click anywhere on the page and choose Inspect from the context menu.

By default, this will open a window at the bottom of the browser showing all the HTML elements on the page. This is a useful view to see how web pages are built, and we will use it in Chapter 22, "Web Scraping and Scrapy," in order to scrape data from web pages automatically using Python.

You can switch between different views using the top row of tabs. The Network tab shows data that is being sent between your browser and the remote web server over HTTP. If you open the developer tools and reload the page (only HTTP requests with the developer tools open will be recorded), you will see various requests being made in the Network tab, as shown in Figure 2.2.

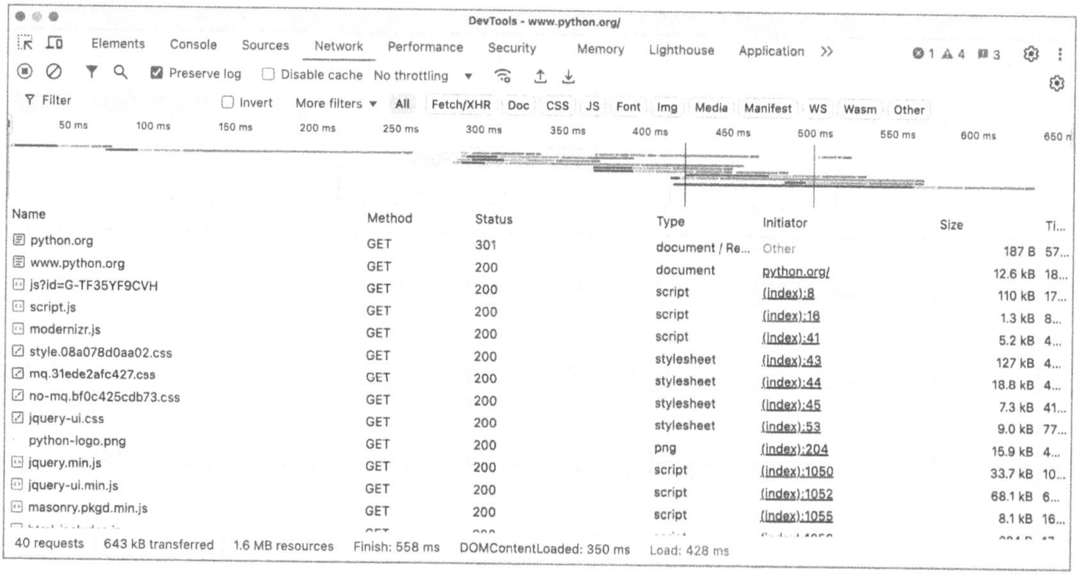

FIGURE 2.2: Chrome Developer Tools showing network requests when loading `python.org`

The Name column shows the name of the document being requested. The main document being loaded is www.python.org itself. This is an HTML document that requires many JavaScript, CSS, and image files in order to render correctly. The HTML page is loaded first, followed quickly by its other required files, which are sent across in separate HTTP requests and responses.

The Status column shows the integer *HTTP status* returned by the server for each request. Any status starting with a 2 indicates that the request was successful; it received an appropriate response from the server, if a response was expected. Other HTTP statuses include the famous 404, "document not found" and 500, "server error."

Clicking on each line, you can see the details of each HTTP request and response. This type of information is critical if you are writing software designed to generate and respond to these requests with HTTP.

For example, if you are writing a Python program on a web server designed to respond to HTTP requests, you can use your web browser to generate those requests. If an error occurs, you can use the Network tab to quickly examine the exact data that was sent to your web application, as well as any error messages the web application sent back.

Web browsers are not simply used to passively consume websites and applications. As a programmer you will frequently use browsers, and their developer tools, to really dig down into how applications are built and diagnose what might be going wrong with them.

3

About Python

Any fool can write code that a computer can understand. Good programmers write code that humans can understand.

— MARTIN FOWLER

Although there are thousands of people who have contributed to Python and its community in one way or another, the language is ultimately the brainchild of one man: Guido van Rossum.

Van Rossum started developing the language as a personal project in 1989. The name "Python" was chosen as a nod to Monty Python's *Flying Circus*, a bizarre and very dry British sketch comedy show that I highly recommend.

Unusually for such a popular and highly adopted programming language—indeed, a popular project of any sort—Van Rossum largely retained control as final decision-maker of Python until he prompted plans for a new governance structure in 2018. Although democracy is largely considered to be a good thing, there's also a reason the phrase "design by committee" exists. Python avoided the pitfalls of both fascism and bureaucracy by simply having a benevolent dictator. In fact, Van Rossum's official role at the Python Software Foundation was *Benevolent Dictator for Life* (BDFL).

Of course, Python got lucky in that Guido van Rossum was truly a benevolent dictator with an excellent vision for the language. In 2001 he founded the American nonprofit *Python Software Foundation* (PSF) as a way to organize a community around the language and source ideas and help for its continued development.

Today, Python is the most popular programming language in the world[1]—depending on what day it is, how you measure, and who you ask. Because of its popularity, it has a thriving community with several official organizations to help with development and education.

---

[1] See, for example, `https://spectrum.ieee.org/the-top-programming-languages-2023`. Other sources are less certain: `www.stackscale.com/blog/most-popular-programming-languages`.

THE PYTHON SOFTWARE FOUNDATION

The Python Software Foundation (PSF), founded by Guido van Rossum, is the official nonprofit organization for the Python programming language. Their mission statement reads as follows:

> *The mission of the Python Software Foundation is to promote, protect, and advance the Python programming language, and to support and facilitate the growth of a diverse and international community of Python programmers.*

The PSF also oversees other Python-promoting groups, such as *PyCon* and *PyLadies*.

It's easy to get involved in the PSF. To become a basic member, all you have to do is sign up at `https://python.org/psf/membership`. You can, of course, also donate financially (as a supporting member) or volunteer your time (contributing member). Joining the PSF is one of the best ways to stay informed about Python events and developments in the language.

Proposed developments in Python are communicated through a Python Enhancement Proposal (PEP). Members can vote on PEPs, according to PEP 10 (`https://peps.python.org/pep-0010`), but these votes are simply used to gauge interest, and the majority opinion is not necessarily implemented. As mentioned before, it's not a democracy.

When Van Rossum stepped down from his position as BDFL in 2018, it set off a flurry of PEPs to decide on the new government structure. This led to the adoption of PEP-13 (`https://peps.python.org/pep-0013`), defining a five-person steering council that, essentially, replaced the single-person BDFL.

An index of all PEPs can be found at `https://peps.python.org`. Many of these make for interesting reading as historical documents and provide insight into how things got to where they are today. Others are frequently used and referenced, such as PEP 8, discussed later in this chapter.

PyCon

PyCon, or the Python Conference, is the largest annual conference for Python. It's a weeklong event, usually held in the United States, but with occasional forays into Canada. Each year several thousand attendees enjoy dozens of talks and tutorials at a convention center. There are also sponsor booths with plenty of *swag* (free branded items such as t-shirts and beverage insulators, usually of poor quality) to be found!

Job seekers may also want to consider attending. Each PyCon has a large job fair where you can meet companies and learn about open positions.

In addition to the main Python Conference, the PyCon organization hosts and partners with many smaller conferences and events around the world. To learn more, visit `https://python.org/events`.

THE ZEN OF PYTHON

The `import` statement in Python makes libraries available for use. There's no sense in loading the whole universe of functionality if none of it is going to be used, so certain things need to be explicitly declared in order to make them available.

For example, if you want to do some trigonometry, there's Python's math library:

```
>> import math
```

This provides access to the constant π out to 15 decimal places:

```
>> math.pi
3.141592653589793
```

You can use this value inside a sine function to calculate the value of, say, $\sin(1.5\pi)$:

```
>> math.sin(1.5 * math.pi)
-1.0
```

One of my favorite packages, albeit one with less practical utility than math, is called `this`. It's one of Python's many Easter eggs—little surprises hidden in the language by developers. When imported, `this` prints out the guiding principles of Python, called "The Zen of Python," as written by software engineer Tim Peters:

```
>> import this

The Zen of Python, by Tim Peters

Beautiful is better than ugly.
Explicit is better than implicit.
Simple is better than complex.
Complex is better than complicated.
Flat is better than nested.
Sparse is better than dense.
Readability counts.
Special cases aren't special enough to break the rules.
Although practicality beats purity.
Errors should never pass silently.
Unless explicitly silenced.
In the face of ambiguity, refuse the temptation to guess.
There should be one-- and preferably only one --obvious way to do it.
Although that way may not be obvious at first unless you're Dutch.
Now is better than never.
Although never is often better than *right* now.
If the implementation is hard to explain, it's a bad idea.
If the implementation is easy to explain, it may be a good idea.
Namespaces are one honking great idea -- let's do more of those!
```

These lines were originally introduced as "Python Enhancement Proposal 20" in 2004 (https://peps.python.org/pep-0020). Jokingly, it states that there are 20 aphorisms to guide Python development (presumably in honor of the 20th PEP), "only 19 of which have been written down."

Some of these principles are obvious: "Beautiful is better than ugly," "Simple is better than complex," "Readability counts," among others. These may seem like trite maxims at first glance, but if you've spent significant time working in other programming languages, you'll realize that you can't always take them for granted.

Some of these principles may only make immediate sense if you've spent some time in programming or engineering already. "Special cases aren't special enough to break the rules" is one of my favorites. Edge cases define the shape of your problem and should never be ignored. If your rules ignore these cases, then the rules themselves were badly designed, or designed for the wrong situation.

These two lines are especially interesting:

```
There should be one-- and preferably only one --obvious way to do it.
Although that way may not be obvious at first unless you're Dutch.
```

The phrase "one obvious way to do it" refers to the *Pythonic* way to do it. The term "Pythonic" is used frequently throughout the PEPs and style guides. "Pythonic" is a concept that is difficult to explain succinctly, but is best built up as an instinct over time by studying examples and being conscientious about your own code.

PEP 8, published in July 2001, provides an early look at some very concrete and easily implemented style suggestions for writing Pythonic code: `https://peps.python.org/pep-0008`. But Pythonic code is not limited simply to things like "use spaces instead of tabs." It also encompasses more philosophical design decisions that can take decades of practice to master. The correct design is not always obvious, unless perhaps, like Guido Van Rossum, you are Dutch.

THE PYTHON INTERPRETER

In Chapter 1, "Introduction to Programming," we discussed compiled and interpreted programming languages. As a brief recap: Compiled languages are translated into low-level machine language before they are run. Programs written in compiled languages can be sent from computer to computer as executable files. Interpreted languages are read and executed on-the-fly by an interpreter and are sent around as human-readable source code, rather than obfuscated machine language.

So, what is Python? The most pedantic answer is that "Python" is a specification; it's defined by its documentation and PEPs. The Python Software Foundation's mission is not simply to support developers to write a piece of software. It supports developers to write the *specification* for that piece of software. Anyone can write either a compiler *or* interpreter that is capable of running Python programs as long as it follows the standards published by the PSF.

To be less pedantic: The most popular implementation of Python is called CPython. CPython is supported by the Python Software Foundation and is what you download and install from `https://python.org`.

CPython is written in a combination of C (hence the name) and Python itself. Yes, the Python implementation is written in Python! This is a marvel of modern computer science known as *bootstrapping*, when an implementation (usually a compiler) of a programming language can be written, at least partially, in the programming language it's implementing.

Although Python is often mistakenly described as an interpreted language, the CPython implementation is both interpreted and compiled. Python programs are distributed as source code, not executable files. During the first run of a Python program on a single user's computer, it is compiled into byte code. This byte code is then interpreted during each subsequent run, for improved performance.

Byte code is higher-level than machine code, although the differences between the two aren't of much practical use for modern software engineers writing high-level languages like Python. What's important to understand here is that most traditionally compiled languages compile code into lower-level machine code, whereas Python compiles into slightly higher-level byte code, which is then interpreted.

Another popular Python interpreter (although less popular than CPython by a long shot) is *PyPy*. This is a Python interpreter written in Python itself. It often has better performance than CPython, which it achieves through just-in-time compilation—compiling parts of the program to machine code at runtime. This provides another sort of hybrid approach between compiled and interpreted languages.

While PyPy started life as a research project and is designed as a complete replacement for CPython, other interpreters have more niche purposes. For example, *MicroPython* is written in C, like CPython, but it is optimized to run on microcontrollers.

In implementations like MicroPython, not all Python features are supported. The interpreter is optimized for speed and size, not necessarily keeping things up-to-date with the latest PEP standards.

Every time you run a Python program, there is a specific interpreter being invoked. You may have multiple interpreters installed on your computer. For example, on a Mac, your Python interpreter might be at /usr/local/bin/python3.13, but you might have an interpreter for an older version of Python at /usr/local/bin/python3.11.

When you use the command-line executable python, you are invoking the interpreter. You can pass it a file to interpret:

```
$ python hello.py
```

You can also pass it nothing and enter the Python command prompt, also called interactive mode:

```
$ python
```

This interactive mode allows you to pass one line of Python code to the terminal at a time, similar to commands in a command prompt.

THE PYTHON STANDARD LIBRARY

Some Python functions are available any time Python executes your code, without having to do anything. For example, you don't need to import anything to use the print function. These are called *built-in* functions (or simply "built-ins"). In addition to functions, there are also built-in types, classes, exceptions, and constants. If you don't know what these things are, that's fine! We'll see and work with many examples of these features starting in Chapter 5, "Python Quickstart."

Other Python features are not built-ins but require that you use an import statement. For example:

```
>> import math
>> math.pi
```

You cannot call math.pi directly without importing Python's math library first. However, you don't need to install any third-party tools in order to access the math library. The math library is not a built-in, but it is still a part of the Python Standard Library.

The standard library is large. It contains tools for networking and internet protocols, parallel computing, file handling, unit testing, data compression, cryptography, and so much more. In fact, up until Chapter 20, "REST APIs and Flask," we will rarely need to venture outside the standard library.

The Python Software Foundation is responsible for all documentation and definitions of the Python Standard Library. While the PSF may work closely with other groups that develop additional features and frameworks on top of the standard library, those third-party libraries are outside the jurisdiction of the PSF.

THIRD-PARTY LIBRARIES

Outside of the standard library are third-party libraries. These are Python programs that require a separate installation in order to use them. Usually, you install them with a package manager. We'll see an example of this in Chapter 4, "Installing and Running Python," when we use `pip` (the Python package manager) to install JupyterLab.

Third-party libraries can be large, well supported, have nonprofit organizations, run their own conferences, and work closely with the PSF. For example, Django, a web framework we'll use in Chapter 21, "Django," has all of these.

Third-party libraries can also be small. They might be as simple as a file called `hello.py` that contains a single line:

```
print('Hello, World!')
```

If I open my terminal, navigate to the directory where the file `hello.py` is saved, and then type **python** to enter a Python command prompt, I can do the following:

```
>>> import hello
Hello, World!
```

The `hello` in the line `import hello` literally refers to the name of the file `hello.py`, where the `.py` file extension is implied. Being in the current directory where the file `hello.py` is saved is important here. If I were in another directory, the Python interpreter wouldn't be able to find the file and wouldn't know what I meant by `import hello`.

However, Python doesn't just look in the current directory and give up if the file isn't found. There is a list of directories it will look in first. You can see this list of directories using these lines:

```
>>> import sys
>>> print(sys.path)
```

This will list all the locations the Python interpreter will look, in the order that it will examine them, stopping as soon as it finds a match. In this way, it can resolve a line like `import hello` to an actual piece of code to execute, the file `hello.py`.

The first item in the list of locations is always empty (with nothing between the single quotes `''`). This represents the directory where the program is currently being executed.

Although it's not considered to be best practice, you could, if you really wanted to, override the Python Standard Library. For example, you can create a file called `math.py` with the single line:

```
pi = 3.0
```

Then, in the same directory, run this:

```
>> import math
>> math.pi
```

This will redefine the value of `pi` to `3.0`.

I bring this up, not because it's a good thing to do, but because it's a potential pitfall that you should be aware of when naming files. Years ago, during a presentation, I forgot that I had a file named `random.py` in the same directory where I was importing the Python built-in library `random` in front of an audience. Awkward confusion ensued.

Fortunately, accidentally overriding the Python Standard Library by installing third-party software through a reputable package manager is more difficult to do. In general, the list of directories in `sys.path` will look like this:

- Current directory
- Python Standard Library
- Installed third-party libraries

Again, this is the order that files are searched for when you make an `import` statement. This means that standard library features will always be loaded first if there is a match to the import name, and third-party libraries will be searched only if a match cannot be found.

VERSIONS AND DEVELOPMENT

The Python version numbering scheme is similar to other software projects. For example, the latest version of Python, as of this writing, is Python 3.13.1.

The number "3" is the major version. When referring to a major version of Python, the notation 3.x (anything in major version 3) or 2.x (anything in major version 2) is often used.

A major version is a huge new release that happens only once every decade or two. It involves not just adding new features, but changing fundamental syntax and definitions in the language such that code written in the new version is incompatible with code written in the old version.

For example, in Python 2.x, this was the accepted way to print `Hello, World!` to the screen:

```
print 'Hello, World!'
```

In Python 3.x, this would cause an error. Parentheses are now required to use the `print` function:

```
print('Hello, World!')
```

The next number in Python 3.13.1 is "13," the minor version. Minor versions contain additional features, functions, and syntax. However, these new features will never break any code written in a previous minor version of Python within the same major version.

For example, Python 3.6 introduced the f-string. This allows you to embed variables into text using curly braces by adding the letter `f` in front of the string:

```
name = 'Ryan'
print(f'Hello, {name}!')
```

In this example, it prints out the text `Hello, Ryan!`

Although this code would not work in Python 3.5, any of the features of Python 3.5 (or preceding minor versions 3.4, 3.3, etc.) will work when run in Python 3.6 without any issues whatsoever. Only code from Python 1.x or 2.x will break when run in Python 3.x.

Finally, the number "1" in Python 3.13.1 designates the micro version. These versions do not contain new features or functions but are bug fixes and efficiency improvements. Occasionally they will add enhancements to existing functionality, but these are usually niche corrections to a prior oversight.

Unless there is a specific bug you have been tracking and are anxiously awaiting the fix of (a rare situation for most of us!), there is no reason to worry about the micro version. Developers working on the same piece of software can usually run different micro versions of Python without any trouble.

PART II
Python

Installing and Running Python

Python has wide support and a powerful volunteer community making its installation as smooth as possible. This large community also produces a large amount of other software, such as Python libraries and development environments, to enhance your Python experience.

Some of this software is nearly unavoidable. You'll want to install some sort of package manager, whether it's pip or conda. Other software, such as JupyterLab, is nice for some applications, but certainly not required for regular development.

For the purpose of working through this book, I recommend that you install the following:

- ➤ Python
- ➤ Pip
- ➤ JupyterLab

This chapter will also cover Python virtual environments as well as the popular Anaconda distribution. I welcome you to play around with both of those as well, with the caveat that installing multiple package managers (such as *both* pip and conda) or Python distributions from multiple sources (e.g., Anaconda, python.org, Microsoft) may lead to conflicts.

INSTALLING PYTHON

In some cases, Python installation is unnecessary. On most Linux distributions, a recent version of Python is installed already. Python does come preinstalled on Macs as well, although you may want to update it.

Before installing Python, I recommend checking to see if you happen to have it installed already. Open your computer's terminal or command prompt and test:

```
$ python --version
```

On a Mac, you may need to type:

```
$ python3 --version
```

If you have Python installed, it will print the current version. I recommend upgrading Python if your version number is more than one release behind the current minor release. You don't have to rush out and upgrade from 3.13 to 3.14 as soon as the next version is off the presses (wait a bit for a few rounds of bug fixing first!). However, if 3.14 is out and you're still at 3.11, you should strongly consider updating.

Regardless of your operating system, you can always install Python by going to www.python.org/downloads, downloading the installer, and running it. However, I do have some operating system–specific tips for both installation and updating.

Windows

As of this writing, no version of Python comes installed by default with Windows. On Windows 10 and 11, you can install Python by opening the command prompt and typing this command:

```
$ python
```

This will open a pop-up that asks if you'd like to install Python. Click "yes" and follow the instructions to install.

On other versions of Windows (or if you prefer not to go through the Windows installer), you install Python using the official installer at https://python.org/downloads.

On the Advanced Options page of the installer, make sure you select Add Python To Environment Variables. This option is not selected by default, but selecting it will ensure that the keyword `python` works from the command prompt, in addition to the Windows default keyword `py`.

After installation is finished, open Windows PowerShell and check your installation with the `$ python --version` command.

macOS

For a long time, the package manager Homebrew (or "Brew") was the preferred method of installing and managing Python, as well as Python's package manager `pip`. It is a very popular method, and I do recommend Brew as a package manager tool for applications other than Python. It can be found at https://brew.sh.

However, installing Python's package manager, `pip`, through the package manager Brew leads to conflicts and management issues that I prefer to avoid. I recommend installing Python through the Python installer for macOS available at www.python.org/downloads.

This will either install the latest version of Python or update your current Python 3.x version to the latest. Most users should be able to click through the installation dialog using the default settings. Afterwards, Python will be installed so that it can be used in your terminal with this command:

```
$ python3
```

Because older versions of macOS had Python 2.7 installed by default, the `python3` command would run Python 3.x while `python` ran Python 2.7. Although Python 2.7 no longer comes with the operating system, the `python3` command remains.

It may be somewhat inconvenient to remember to type `python3` instead of just `python` every time, or you may accidentally execute a script under an older Python version, which will lead to problems.

It's best practice to not uninstall languages that come with your operating system by default—other software could be depending on them. Rather than uninstall the Python version linked to the python command, you can add an alias to your terminal so that the command python is pointed at python3 instead.

As of 2019 the *Z Shell*, or *zsh*, has replaced Bash as the default terminal type on macOS. If you are unaware of the name of the software powering your Mac's terminal, it is probably zsh. You can add command name aliases to it in the configuration file at ~/.zshrc. If you are using Bash, this configuration file is at ~/.bashrc.

Add the following line to your .zshrc or .bashrc file:

```
alias python="python3"
```

If you have Visual Studio Code installed, you can use this command to open the file for editing, and add the alias to it that way:

```
$ code ~/.zshrc
```

Alternatively, Sublime is another excellent text editor that is ideal for editing small files in a Notepad-like environment. It can be downloaded from www.sublimetext.com. You can use it to edit your terminal shell's configuration file using this command:

```
$ subl ~/.zshrc
```

Linux

Congratulations, it is very likely that you already have some version of Python 3.x installed! Unfortunately, you will still want to update this version or at least know how to be able to update it in the future. As a reminder, you can check your Python version using this command:

```
$ python --version
```

Different distributions of Linux have different command-line package management tools that can be used to update Python. On Debian-based systems, such as Ubuntu, you can use apt to install Python:

```
$ sudo apt update && sudo apt upgrade
$ sudo apt install python3.13
```

On RedHat, you can use yum:

```
$ sudo yum update
$ sudo dnf install python3
```

As of this writing, the latest version of Python is 3.13. You should check at www.python.org/downloads for the latest version and update the version number in the command appropriately. As written, these commands will install Python 3.13, which you can use with this command:

```
$ python3.13
```

You do not want to disturb the system-installed version of Python, nor do you want to type out python3.13 every time you want Python. I recommend updating your ~/.bash_aliases file (or creating one if it does not exist) to include the following alias:

```
alias python=python3.13
```

This will alias the command python3.13 to simply python.

INSTALLING AND USING *PIP*

There are a plethora of third-party libraries, or packages, available for Python. It is possible, for each new project you want to use, to locate the GitHub page, download the project, and install it according to the instructions. Usually this will involve running the ubiquitous setup.py file located at the root directory of most Python packages:

```
$ python setup.py install
```

But what's easier than doing all of that is having a piece of software that takes care of everything for you. Most Python packages can be installed with pip, the package manager for Python. All you need is the keyword for the project that you want, and let pip do the rest:

```
$ pip install requests
```

This command installs a popular HTTP handling library called requests. If you want to uninstall the library afterward, it's similarly easy:

```
$ pip uninstall requests
```

Granted, the exact way you invoke pip may differ slightly depending on your operating system and programming environment. On macOS, if you use python3 to run Python you will want to use this:

```
$ pip3 install requests
```

If you have multiple versions of Python installed on your computer or if you have trouble with the pip command for whatever reason, you can execute the pip module directly from Python using this:

```
$ python -m pip install requests
```

COMMAND FLAGS

The -m (pronounced "dash m") in the command $ python -m pip install requests is called a flag. Flags modify the behavior of a command or allow you to pass options to it. The words following the flag, pip install requests, are arguments which are used by the flag.

Short flags, like -m, begin with a dash followed by a letter. In this case, the m stands for "module" and allows us to run modules, such as pip, through Python.

Long flags contain two dashes (--) followed by multiple characters or a word. An example of this is Python's --help flag:

```
$ python --help
```

This flag allows you to view information about the Python command, including other flags that you can use with it.

Flags are not a Python concept or unique to the python command. Flags are useful for most terminal commands. For example, the ls command, which is used to list files in a directory, can be used with the -l flag to list additional information, such as creation date and file size, for each file:

```
$ ls -l
```

Whichever method you use to invoke pip and install modules, note that you should use that method whenever you see a `pip install` command throughout this book.

Similar to Python, installing `pip` itself varies from operating system to operating system. Use the appropriate guide for your operating system, as follows.

Windows

If you followed the installation instructions for Python in the previous section, you should be fine. Open PowerShell and test that you have `pip` installed:

```
$ pip
```

You should see a list of `pip` command options printed to the terminal.

macOS

`pip` should already be installed with your Python installation. However, it may be installed under the command `pip3` rather than `pip`. You can add an alias to your `.zshrc` or `.bashrc` file, similar to the alias you added for the `python` command:

```
alias pip="pip3"
```

Test this out by opening a new terminal and typing this:

```
$ pip
```

You should see a list of `pip` command options printed to the terminal.

Linux

If you followed the Python installation instructions for Linux mentioned previously, you may have two different versions of Python installed on your machine. This can create confusion. It's recommended that you use a virtual environment when working with a specific Python version.

First, use `apt` to install the Python 3.13–specific version of the virtual environment library:

```
$ apt install python3.13-venv
```

Note that if you're using a Python version other than 3.13, you will need to use that version number instead. Then use `python` to create a new virtual environment folder at `.venv`:

```
$ python -m venv .venv
```

I recommend running this command from the home directory so that it is easily accessible when you open a new terminal. It's a hidden file, used only for the `activate` command, which starts your virtual Python environment:

```
$ source .venv/bin/activate
```

After this command is run, you should see the command prompt change to indicate that you're now in the `.venv` virtual environment. You can use `pip` to install Python packages and use them within a Python3.13 environment.

This `source .venv/bin/activate` command itself can be made into an alias in your `.bashrc` file:

```
alias startpython='source .venv/bin/activate'
```

This command will allow you to activate your Python virtual environment using the command `startpython`. You can even activate the environment by default every time you open a new terminal by putting the command directly into the `.bashrc` file.

There is a lot more to learn about creating and using virtual environments. See the section "Virtual Environments" later in this chapter for more information.

INSTALLING AND USING JUPYTER FOR IPYTHON FILES

Assuming that Python and `pip` are working now under the respective terminal commands `python` and `pip` (or possibly `python3` and `pip3` on macOS), the installation and configuration instructions are exactly the same regardless of operating system from here on out.

The exercise files for this book, at `https://github.com/REMitchell/unlocking-python`,[1] contain a variety of files with the file extension `.ipynb`. These are *IPython* files, also called *notebook* files or *Jupyter notebook* files. IPython, short for *Interactive Python*, is a type of file that lets you view, create, modify, and run short Python programs inside of cells.

Each Jupyter notebook file consists of many cells that share the same Python session. So a previous cell may declare some variables or functions, which are then used and referenced by subsequent cells. This breaks up code up into small chunks to demonstrate concepts one at a time, making notebooks an ideal Python learning tool.

Jupyter notebooks are also excellent at displaying graphics, such as charts, tables, and visualizations. They also help to break the code up into manageable pieces and show a logical workflow with printed results as you go. This makes them invaluable for the data science community, where code is often segmented into small chunks that need to be easily shareable and explainable and which often produce graphics that need to be displayed.

Although many IDEs can be used to edit and run these Jupyter notebook files (including Visual Studio Code), a popular piece of software used to work with them is called *JupyterLab*. It allows you to edit the files in your web browser by running a lightweight web server from your computer. JupyterLab is also purpose-built for notebook files and contains many advanced editing tools you won't find in most IDEs.

JupyterLab (not to be confused with the software called Jupyter Notebook, produced by the same company) is an application produced by Project Jupyter, a nonprofit dedicated to developing this software. The odd spelling of the name "Jupyter" comes from the three languages it originally supported: Julia, Python, and R. So, note this spelling when you install and run it:

```
$ pip install jupyterlab
```

This will install a command-line tool called `jupyter` that you can use to start the notebook server and work with IPython files. To do this, make sure you've downloaded the exercise files for this book. Use the terminal to navigate to where the exercise files are on your computer. Then start the Jupyter server:

```
$ cd path/to/exercise/files
$ jupyterlab
```

---

[1] *As an alternative to GitHub, you can go to* `www.wiley.com`, *search for this book's ISBN 9781394288496, and download a zip file of the code from Wiley.*

This should start the server and prompt your default browser to open a new window displaying the JupyterLab application. If a new window does not open, for whatever reason, you can copy the URL provided in the terminal under the line "Or copy and paste one of these URLs". For example:

```
http://localhost:8888/lab?token=b26cbd2255e42d2c4ed5266136966d8346b60c6b23584c99
```

The token provided in the URL here is a security measure for specific circumstances when multiple users are sharing the same computer system. It prevents others from modifying or running the notebook if you're working on a group server. Jupyter notebooks are not publicly accessible to anyone on the network by default, so you don't have to worry about working in a coffee shop and letting someone else on the Wi-Fi run Python code on your computer!

JupyterLab contains a list of all files in the current directory open in a menu on the left. You can open any of the files by double-clicking, and you can right-click to take certain actions like renaming and deleting the files.

You can create a new Jupyter notebook file in the top menu by choosing File ⇨ New ⇨ Notebook and selecting Python 3 for your kernel.

The file `03_01_Jupyter.ipynb` contains some example cells for you to work with. The first cell contains a title, "Introduction to Jupyter Notebooks," and some additional text in a markdown language. You can see this markdown by double-clicking inside the cell.

When you create a new cell, by default it is a Python code cell. Every Jupyter cell can be one of three types:

➤ **Code:** These contain runnable Python code.

➤ **Markdown:** These contain documentation, comments, or other formatted and readable text. They can even contain complex math equations (see the documentation for more information about how to do this: `https://jupyterbook.org/en/stable/content/math.html`).

➤ **Raw:** JupyterLab will skip these and not attempt to interpret or execute them. This cell type is usually only used in conjunction with additional tools that will interpret these cells as HTML or LaTeX markdown.

To change the cell type for a particular cell, first select the cell. Then, press the Esc key to enter *command mode*. Then, press "m" to switch the cell to markdown mode or "y" to switch the cell to code mode. There is also a drop-down menu immediately above the notebook page containing the options Code, Markdown, and Raw.

To execute a Python code cell, first select the cell you want to run, and use the keyboard shortcut Shift+Enter. This will also change the focus to the next cell in the notebook, which makes it convenient to quickly run down a page of cells by holding Shift and pressing Enter repeatedly. Alternatively, you can use the menu immediately above the notebook, which features Play and Stop buttons to run and halt execution, respectively.

Unless you are working in data science, it's unlikely that you'll use JupyterLab and notebook files every day. However, they are fantastic tools for learning Python and useful for organizing and viewing large numbers of small code samples. Even outside of education and data science, notebooks are useful in industry for running quick Python experiments, writing and sharing reports, and doing analytics.

This overview of JupyterLab and notebook files, plus a little exploration on your own, should allow you to get started running and modifying code in the exercise files accompanying this book. However, this is extremely powerful and flexible software about which an entire book could be written. For more information, Project Jupyter has very readable and easy-to-use documentation at `https://jupyterlab.readthedocs.io/en/latest`.

VIRTUAL ENVIRONMENTS

When you installed JupyterLab, you may have noticed extra stuff being installed. A lot of extra stuff. By my count, 89 separate packages are required as dependencies for JupyterLab to function. Each dependency has specific version requirements associated with it. For instance, one of the requirements that `pip` prints out during the installation is as follows:

```
ipython>=7.23.1
```

This means that it is fine with any version of the IPython package greater than or equal to 7.23.1. Other requirements are more specific. For example:

```
prompt-toolkit<3.1.0,>=3.0.41
```

This means that it requires a version of `prompt-toolkit` that is less than version 3.1.0 but greater than or equal to 3.0.41. But what happens if a different package is dependent on a version of `prompt-toolkit` greater than 3.1.0 or less than 3.0.41? This is known as a *dependency conflict* (a common cause of *dependency hell*; see `https://en.wikipedia.org/wiki/Dependency_hell`).

As the number of installed packages increases, the likelihood of a dependency conflict (and, thus, dependency hell) increases with it. If you installed JupyterLab according to the instructions for Windows or macOS, you installed this package, along with all its requirements, *globally*.

Sometimes when we talk about "globally installed software," we mean software that is installed for all users of the computer. Depending on how and where you installed Python, all users on the computer may not be able to access the Python installation. However, JupyterLab will be accessible globally to *all users of that Python installation*. If the users can access the Python installation, they can access the globally installed Python packages.

JupyterLab is installed alongside the Python installation itself. This means that when any user of that Python installation, running from any directory, runs the following line:

```
import prompt_toolkit
```

they will get the version of `prompt-toolkit` required by JupyterLab that was installed. If they decide they need a significantly different version of this `prompt-toolkit` library, it may break JupyterLab for all users of the Python installation.

A common practice to avoid this problem is to use a completely isolated, or *sandboxed*, set of third-party package installations for each project or type of environment you might want. Here, an "environment" means a set of installed packages with particular version numbers.

For example, you may have an environment where common machine learning and data science tools are installed for creating new machine learning models. You may have another environment for a web application you're building where only the packages that application needs are installed.

This is where virtual environments come in. Python's venv module, a core module that comes out-of-the-box with Python, allows you to create a new virtual environment or an environment from a predefined list of package requirements easily.

To create a new virtual environment, use this:

```
$ python -m venv my-environment
```

This command will create a new directory called my-environment. Inside the directory is a file pyvenv.cfg, which includes information such as the version of Python used to create the virtual environment, which will be the Python version used when the environment is activated. Because you may have multiple versions of Python installed, which one you use to create the environment is important. For example:

```
$ python3.9 -m venv environment_3_9
$ python3.10 -m venv environment_3_10
$ python3.11 -m venv environment_3_11
```

These commands all create different virtual Python environments you can use to easily switch between versions of Python. This may not seem particularly useful for personal development, but if you're working on several projects in a large company and each project requires a different version of Python, it would be very handy!

After creating the environment, activate it by running the following on macOS and Linux:

```
$ source my-environment/bin/activate
```

and, on Windows:

```
$ my-environment\bin\activate
```

After activating, your command prompt should display the virtual environment name, indicating that you are currently in that environment. While inside the virtual environment you will not have access to any globally installed packages and must reinstall everything from scratch. On the bright side, no packages means no dependency conflicts!

How does this magic work? You can see part of it if, while inside your virtual environment, you view the paths that Python is using to look for packages:

```
>>> import sys
>>> print(sys.path)
```

You'll see that the site-packages directory, where these third-party packages are stored, has been replaced with something like <path to your workspace>/my-environment/lib/python3.13/site-packages. Activating the environment updates your Python path so that it looks in a special place for these packages.

To return to your regular environment with all of its globally installed packages, simply type this:

```
$ deactivate
```

Virtual environments were designed to be disposable. Although you might keep the directories around for a long time, even using the same ones for years, it shouldn't be any great loss if they get destroyed.

The product that you care about isn't the virtual environment itself, but the settings and configurations that produce the environment. Rather than starting a new one from scratch, you can automatically populate all the dependencies in a virtual environment with a *requirements file*.

Requirements files usually have the filename `requirements.txt`. You often see them in the root directory of Python projects. To use them, activate a new virtual environment, and run the following:

```
$ pip install -r requirements.txt
```

Rather than installing packages one at a time with `pip`:

```
$ pip install jupyterlab
```

you can install any number of packages at once, populating the virtual environment with everything you need.

The format of a requirements file is straightforward, with each line containing a package name and a version number, or specified range of version numbers:

```
beautifulsoup4>=4.12.0
joblib==1.3.2
numpy==1.26.4
```

These requirements files are not usually created by hand, although they may be modified by hand after initial creation. You can use the `pip freeze` command to export your current environment (either the global environment or a virtual environment you have activated) to a `requirements.txt` file:

```
$ pip freeze > requirements.txt
```

Note that the greater than sign (>) here is an operator that means "export the output of this command to a file"—it does not describe some sort of relative magnitude. This command will create a requirements file with all of your currently installed Python packages. This will allow you to later create new virtual environments and populate them with `pip install -r requirements.txt`.

Some proponents of virtual environments caution to never install packages globally and to use virtual environments for absolutely everything. Personally, I'm not that much of a purist. If I like a package and use it frequently, I'll install it globally. This has almost never caused any issues. On the other hand, I also don't mind blowing away my entire Python environment from time to time. Absolutely everything is disposable, and all we are is dust in the wind.

ANACONDA

Anaconda is often thought of as just another package management system, like `pip`. This is because it is commonly used for its command-line package management tool, `conda`. Like `pip`, you can use `conda` to install packages:

```
$ conda install requests
```

Unlike `pip`, however, the Anaconda project itself has a much broader scope than just the package management system. It has its own Python distribution, installed set of packages (carefully chosen so that they all play well with each other), and repository that you can install thousands of new packages from.

Anaconda does have an excellent set of 250 preinstalled packages. In fact, most of the packages we work with throughout this book come bundled with the default Anaconda installation. The notable exception here is Django, which is an extremely large web application development framework. The fact that Django is so large and somewhat outside of Anaconda's target audience makes it unlikely to make the list. However, Django is available through Anaconda's repository as a separate download.

The Anaconda environment extends far beyond just the tools you use in your terminal. In fact, you don't have to use your terminal at all to use it. You can write your code in the Anaconda Navigator, host that code on the Anaconda Cloud, and then run and deploy your web applications all without leaving Anaconda's GUI environment.

The primary audience of Anaconda is those working in data science, machine learning, scientific computing, and other sciences. Their typical user does not necessarily have a strong background in software engineering, although they may write code on a daily basis. They want software that works out-of-the-box and don't want to spend a lot of time dealing with installation and dependency issues.

Often, when new programmers have installation issues, they start searching for solutions for those issues online. For example, they might get an error installing JupyterLab and see that someone has suggested they try installing Anaconda to use Jupyter through it. This works great! But what that programmer may not realize is that Anaconda works very well within its own environment but does not always play nicely with things outside of that environment.

It's important to understand that Anaconda is not simply an alternative package manager or another source of Python software. It is an ecosystem unto itself. It is a very well-maintained ecosystem curated by hundreds of employees at the for-profit company Anaconda Inc. Their pricing structure (https://anaconda.cloud/pricing) has a free tier available for personal use, but the fact that a pricing structure exists at all differentiates it from most of the other Python solutions out there.

With all of that in mind, let's look at installing and using Anaconda, if you choose to do so.

Navigate to www.anaconda.com/download and download and run the installer. The installation may take a few minutes to complete. After you run it, the default Python and pip installation on your computer will be pointed to Anaconda's version.

Some people refer to Anaconda as "conda," which is the name of its package management tool. To be clear, conda is just one piece of software created by the company Anaconda and is often bundled with its Python distribution. But they are separate concepts.

Anaconda's package management tool, conda, can be used like pip. As an example, you can install Django with this command:

```
$ conda install django
```

You can also create virtual environments:

```
$ conda create -n my-environment
```

These are similar to the environments created with the Python venv module. Instead of the directory being automatically created in the location that the command is run in, it will prompt you to choose a specific directory and default to the envs folder in your Anaconda installation.

The commands that activate and deactivate the environments are fairly intuitive:

```
$ conda activate my-environment
$ conda deactivate my-environment
```

Similar to Python virtual environments through the venv module, you can install packages using the conda install command while your Anaconda environment is active.

There are a variety of other tools that come with your Anaconda installation. The easiest way to view them is through the GUI application, Anaconda Navigator. This is an application that is installed automatically with the distribution installation, and you will find it wherever the rest of your software applications are.

This is a great way to see the full suite of Anaconda products, or products that are supported by Anaconda. For example, both PyCharm and Visual Studio Code, discussed in Chapter 2, "Programming Tools," are available here. JupyterLab (and its predecessor Jupyter Notebook) is also in the Navigator. Launching Jupyter from this application will start a new server running in your home directory.

You can also manage your virtual environments from the Navigator. Clicking the Environments tab in the left menu will show your base (global) environment as well as any Anaconda environments you've created. Clicking each environment will show all its installed libraries and allow you to add or remove libraries.

Installing Anaconda will effectively replace all of the other installation steps in this chapter. It's important to consider that installing the Anaconda Python distribution and conda alongside the standard Python distribution and pip may cause management complications in your programming environment that are outside the scope of this book.

5

Python Quickstart

By now, you should have your Python environment set up, your package manager working, the exercise files that accompany this book downloaded from https://github.com/REMitchell/unlocking-python and open in JupyterLab. There's only one thing left to do: actually write some code.

This chapter is intended to provide both a broad and a shallow overview of the Python programming language that will help provide context during the deeper dives that we'll take ahead. Each section here builds on the previous one and is intended to be read in order. However, as you progress, you may also want to refer back to specific passages in this chapter as needed to refresh yourself on a particular topic.

By the end of this chapter, you should have everything you need to start writing basic Python programs. I highly encourage you to do this! Exercises at the end of the chapters will give you some starting points, but it may also be helpful to come up with your own topics and programming challenges.

The best thing to cement your understanding of the concepts in each chapter is to write Python code that uses them.

VARIABLES

Variables are associated with data. They become associated with data using an equal sign (=), which can be used to write assignment statements. For example:

```
name = 'Ryan'
pi = 3.14
five = 5
```

This last line assigns the numeric value 5 to a variable with the name five. In Python, as with virtually every other programming language, the value being assigned (5) is on the right side of the equal sign and the variable the value is being assigned to (five) is on the left.

These are called "variables" because the data in them can be changed, or reassigned. The data is "variable." For instance, we can do this:

```
five = 6
```

In practice, of course, I wouldn't recommend assigning `five` to the value 6 because that would be confusing. When it comes to naming variables in Python, there's a difference between what you *can* do and what you *should* do.

Variable names in Python can be anything you want, with a few rules to keep in mind:

> ➤ They can only contain numbers, letters, and underscores.

> ➤ They must start with a letter or underscore (they can contain numbers, but cannot start with a number).

They are case-sensitive.

There are two additional rules that, while not enforced by Python, are very strange to not follow. It will raise more than a few eyebrows if you ignore these conventions for variable names:

> ➤ They should not start with an uppercase letter.

> ➤ They should not start with an underscore.

These rules can be broken without raising any eyebrows under special circumstances, which will be covered in more detail later. For example, you can create a variable name in all caps to indicate that it should not be changed:

```
VALUE_OF_PI = 3.14159
```

These special variables, called *constants*, are usually written at the top of a Python file and made available to the rest of the code for general use.

The following are valid and good variable names in Python:

```
my_name
aFunVariable
lonelygirl15
```

The following are invalid variable names:

```
3sCompany
excitingVariable!
dash-dash
```

The following variable names are technically valid in Python but should not be used:

```
AnotherVar
__s_n_a_k_e__
```

You may also see a variable name that consists of only a single underscore:

```
_
```

This is called a throwaway or temporary variable. It is used in places where a variable declaration is required by Python, but the variable will not be used. We will see examples of these later when working with loops.

In general, and especially while you're still learning, you should always start variable names with a lowercase letter. For variables containing more than one word, you can use underscores or capital letters to separate each word. Using underscores, as in my_variable_name, is called *snake case*. Using capital letters, as in myVariableName, is called *camel case*.

Snake case is the preferred convention for Python, as specified in "PEP 8 – Style Guide for Python Code," and will be used throughout this book. However, both styles are still commonly used in industry.[1]

Variables give you the opportunity to provide a label for your data and describe your code to others. A good variable name is short and descriptive. As you write programs and read code written by others, you'll get a sense of what separates the good variable names from the bad. For example:

```
var1 = 10
var2 = 5
```

The names var1 and var2 tell us nothing about how these variables should be used. Even if we do know what they are when we initially declare them, it can make it difficult to remember which is which later on. Much more effective might be something like this:

```
items_per_batch = 10
max_batches = 5
```

This tells us exactly what these numbers mean and how they should be used. When we see the variables used throughout the code, the variable names themselves aid in our understanding, rather than obfuscate the code.

Sometimes variable names aren't enough, and we need another way to provide commentary to help others understand what's going on. In these cases, you can use a *comment*. A comment is a piece of human language text that is completely ignored by the Python interpreter. Comments start with a hash symbol and end at the end of the line. Each new line with a comment must start with another hash. For example:

```
# Number of items to process in each batch
items_per_batch = 10

# Maximum number of batches to run before exiting
# If items are left in queue after processing the last batch
# this program will be restarted hourly to continue processing
max_batches = 5

done_processing = False # Set to True after last batch
```

Comments can provide information about the purpose of a piece of code, explanation for confusing aspects of it, attribution to the authors, and even suggestions for future improvement, called *TODO* comments:

```
# TODO: Add ability for program to restart itself after processing last batch
```

The effective use of comments and variable names will help make your code clean, readable, and Pythonic. This is useful, not just to others working on your team, but also to your future self reading the code months or years later!

---

[1] Snake case is mostly used by recovering developers who worked in other languages where that is the preferred convention, and who have not yet taken the time or given attention to what Python's style conventions are.

DATA TYPES

Every piece of data in Python has a *type*. This tells Python whether the data represents a number, some text, or even something more complex like a media file. Some basic Python data types are:

➤ Integers

➤ Floats

➤ Strings

➤ Booleans

An *integer* is, exactly like it sounds, a number that does not contain a decimal or fractional component. Here are some examples of integers:

```
123
0
-1276
```

If you're even in doubt about whether something in Python is an integer, you can use the `type` function to tell you:

```
>>> type(123)
int
```

In this case, it returns `int`, the Python type name for integers.

The *float* type is also a number, but one that represents rational numbers (both integers and numbers with a decimal component). Floats use decimal notation when displayed. Here are some examples of floats:

```
123.456
0.5
-0.5
4.0
```

Again, we can use the `type` function to confirm that they are floats:

```
>>> type(123.456)
Float
```

HOW THE FLOAT GOT ITS NAME

If you're not familiar with the computer science term "float," it might seem like an odd word to choose for something that, in plain English, might simply be called a "decimal number." The word "float" has to do with how computers encode this data in memory.

continues

continued

The value 0.123456789 has a great deal of information that it needs to store to the right of the decimal point (or *radix point* if you want to use the fancy computer science term for it). Yes, everything to the right of the decimal point represents less than an eighth, but it's a very, very precise "less than an eighth" that, when stored in binary notation, takes up a lot of space.

The value 123456789.0, in contrast, has a great deal of information to the left of the decimal point and very little stored to the right. Therefore, the decimal point itself "floats" back and forth in this sea of information. Sometimes it's shifted to the left, sometimes it's shifted to the right.

Floats can be turned into integers through a process called *casting*, which you might also hear referred to as *type conversion* or *type casting*. You can cast a float to an integer in the following way:

```
>>> int(2.718)
2
```

Notice that Python does not round the 2.718 up to 3, but simply cuts off anything after the decimal, leaving only the integer portion.

Integers can also be cast to floats:

```
>>> float(3)
3.0
```

This creates a float with the same value as the integer. Many Python data types are able to be cast from one to another, although you should be sure and test how this casting works, as it can occasionally have unexpected results.

Like the float, another data type with interesting etymology is the *string*. A string is simply text data. In Python, strings are surrounded by either single quotes or double quotes. Whether you choose to use single quotes or double quotes is a matter of personal preference, but you should be consistent. The following are examples of strings:

```
'Hello, World!'
"a"
'我不会说中文'
```

Using the type function, we see that the Python type name for string is simply str:

```
>>>type('Hello, World!')
str
```

Each Latin character in a string requires 1 byte to store, while non-Latin characters take more bytes, depending on their rarity. Therefore, the string "hello" requires 5 bytes of memory, and the string "a" requires only 1 byte because it is just a single character.

ASCII, UNICODE, AND BYTES

In Chapter 1, "Introduction to Programming," we discussed ASCII character encoding, where each capital and lowercase letter in the Latin alphabet is represented as a byte of binary data:

```
A - 01000001     a - 01100001
B - 01000010     b - 01100010
C - 01000011     c - 01100011
```

You might think that 8 bits, or a byte, would provide 256 possibilities for different characters that could be encoded in this way. In fact, only 7 bits are used in the ASCII character set. This allows for 128 characters, including capital and lowercase letters, punctuation, numbers, and many control characters such as backspace, escape, shift, and newline.

Although each ASCII character only needs 7 bits to encode itself, it still requires a full byte to store. The remaining leftmost bit is always 0 for every ASCII character. However, this is not a waste of space! If this leftmost bit is set to 1, that indicates that the character being encoded is not in the ASCII character set at all, but in the Unicode character set (of which ASCII is just a small subset). The first 4 bits of a Unicode character (excluding ASCII, which is a special case) tell you how many bytes are used to represent the character.

Unicode characters require anywhere between 1 and 4 bytes to encode. The first few bits of the first byte will tell you how many total bytes are required for each character:

➤ Characters starting with 0 are in ASCII and require only 1 byte.

➤ Characters starting with 110 require 2 bytes.

➤ Characters starting 1110 require 3 bytes.

➤ Characters starting with 11110 require 4 bytes.

Using Unicode, characters and symbols across many different languages, cultures, academic disciplines, and historical periods can be encoded efficiently within the same piece of text. Emoticons are also part of the Unicode standard.

One interesting character from the Unicode library is ꘏, from the Mende Kikakui script. This script was used briefly in the 1920s and '30s (but now replaced by Latin) for the Mende language, spoken by the Mende people in Sierra Leone. Its binary representation requires 4 bytes:

```
11110000 10011110 10100000 10010000
```

Less obscure is ⠺, the Braille letter "w." Its binary representation is:

```
11100010 10100000 10111010
```

The Greek lowercase omega, ω, has a 2-byte binary representation:

```
11001111 10001001
```

In general, the more common a character is, the shorter its Unicode representation. This makes Unicode both a flexible and concise format for writing any text document. When the data for each string is stored, the data for each character within that string is stored consecutively in memory or on the disk, one character byte after the other. The characters are then strung together to create "strings" of characters.

How many characters are in the string '\n'? Although it looks like this string contains two characters (a backslash and the letter n), this string is a type of special case known as an *escape character*. The string \n is just one character, a newline. It represents a line break. When inserted into a piece of text it forces the text to continue on the next line.

Most escape characters, like the newline, represent whitespace, or represent characters with no other visual way to display them. Other common escape characters are the tab \t and, on Windows, the carriage return \n.

You may also see the character \' used in strings. This is also a single character, escaped with a backslash. This is used to insert apostrophes into text that is surrounded by single quotes in Python, like so:

```
some_str = 'Monty Python\'s Life of Brian'
```

Without being escaped, the apostrophe in Python's would appear to be the end of the string, causing an error. The backslash is used to escape illegal characters in strings, forcing them to be inserted as their literal value.

Ideally, numerical values would always be stored as numbers and never treated as strings. However, you may occasionally find yourself in a situation where you're dealing with "numbers represented as strings." This might occur, for example, when you're using Python to read a CSV file and the incoming cell data read as strings. In that case, you can cast the data using either int or float as needed:

```
>>> int('1')
1
>>> int('-100')
-100
>>> float('1')
1.0
>>> float('3.141')
3.141
```

Finally, we have the *Boolean* data type. You may be familiar with the term "Boolean" from its use in mathematics, philosophy, and logic.[2]

In programming, when we're dealing with logic and control flow, we're often dealing with Boolean values. For example, take this programming scenario, written in plain English: "If we've collected 100 log records, write them to the database. Otherwise, keep storing log records in memory" The check for "we've collected 100 log records" has a definite Boolean value. You've either collected 100 log records or you haven't. The statement is either True or False.

---

[2] The word Boolean is, in most cases, capitalized as a proper noun because of its namesake, the mathematician George Boole.

Here are the only two Boolean values that ever existed and ever will exist:

```
True
False
```

These values are case-sensitive. `True` is a Python Boolean value, and `true` is not. Writing this would be valid, but confusing, in Python:

```
true = True
```

Writing this would be valid, but even more confusing, in Python:

```
false = True
```

The Python type name for Booleans is simply `bool`:

```
>>> type(True)
bool
```

Integers, floats, and strings can all be cast to Booleans in Python. Unsurprisingly, 1 is cast to `True` and 0 is cast to `False`:

```
>>> bool(1)
True
>>> bool(0)
False
```

It is important to know that 0 is the only integer that is considered `False` in Python. Every other integer is `True`:

```
>>> bool(2)
True
>>> bool(-1)
True
>>> bool(-1000000)
True
```

Floats behave similarly:

```
>>> bool(0.0)
False
>>> bool(1.0)
True
>>> bool(-1.0)
True
>>> bool(0.000000001)
True
```

If you consider the behavior of strings when cast to numerical values like ints and floats, the following makes sense:

```
>>> bool('True')
True
```

However, if you use that example to infer a general pattern, you will be in for a surprise:

```
>>> bool('False')
True
```

In fact, every single string will evaluate to a Boolean `True` except for one—the empty string:

```
>>> bool('')
False
```

This is because, under the hood, Python is actually testing the *length* of the string to see whether it should evaluate it to a Boolean `True` or Boolean `False`. The string length is then subject to the same rules used for integers when casting to a Boolean—only 0 is `False`.

Boolean values are rarely stored in variables directly, as in:

```
collected_100_logs = True
```

They are most often generated as a byproduct of some programmatic comparison. To make these comparisons, you need to perform an operation.

OPERATORS

There are a limited number of operators in Python, all of which are defined in the Python Standard Library. The operators are divided into groups:

➤ Arithmetic

➤ Comparison

➤ Boolean

➤ Identity

➤ Membership

➤ Bitwise

Like their name suggests, operators perform operations. They take values and do something with them. That "something" might be a modification, a decision, or a computation. Apart from *bitwise operators*, which are rarely used and outside the scope of this book, you will use all of these operators frequently.

Arithmetic Operators

Arithmetic operators do math. There are seven arithmetic operators; each one is shown here with a comment:

```
# addition
1 + 1

# subtraction
5 - 3

# multiplication
```

```
4 * 5

# division
20 / 5

# floor division
20//5

# exponent
2**5

# modulo
20 % 6
```

The first three operators—addition, subtraction, and multiplication—should all be self-explanatory. Division also looks straightforward; the first number is the numerator and the second number is the denominator so that the operation 20/5 would return a quotient of 4. If you run this operation in the Jupyter notebook file that accompanies this chapter (05_Quickstart.ipynb), you might notice that it returns the float value 4.0, rather than an integer 4 like the previous operations do.

Any operation that has the mathematical possibility of returning a float value will return a float value. Compare these two operations:

```
>>> 1 + 1
2
>>> 1.5 + 1
2.5
```

Adding two integers together will always result in an integer value. Adding a float to an integer will, as a rule, return a float value. Even if the float has a 0 in the decimal portion, because it is a float type, it will result in a float sum:

```
>>> 1.0 + 1
2.0
```

The rules for the type of the return value when performing multiplication and subtraction operations are the same: Two integers will always return an integer. Two floats, or an integer and a float, will return a float. Division is the outlier here because the division of two integers can result in a non-whole number. Therefore, any division operation in Python will return a float.

If you want to perform a division operation that will be guaranteed to return an integer, you can use *floor division* (//). This returns the lower integer value when it performs division, rounding down:

```
>>> 20//5
4
>>> -20//3
-7
>>> 99.9999//10
9.0
```

The exponent operator is represented by two asterisks (**). The number to the left is the base, and the number to the right is the exponent, meaning that 2**5 (two to the fifth power) returns 32.

In many other programming languages, the caret symbol (^) is used to indicate exponents, as in 2^5. But be careful not to use it to perform an exponent operation in Python:

```
>>> 2^5
7
```

In Python, this caret is actually a *bitwise operator*, performing an entirely different type of operation (a rarely used one, and one that is outside the scope of this book). However, accidentally using ^ when you intended to use ** will return a valid integer value and may lead to difficult-to-find bugs!

The modulo operator is one that you might not have encountered before. It was first introduced by mathematician Friedrich Gauss in 1801, but is today probably better known in computer science than in mathematics.

Modulo refers to the remainder after dividing one number by another number. For example, 6 goes into 20 three times, with a remainder of 2. Therefore, 20 modulo 6 is 2.

We can write this as:

```
>>> 20 % 6
2
```

You might also say that the *modulus* is 2. Just like "sum" is the returned value from addition and "quotient" is the returned value from division, "modulus" is the returned value from the modulo operation 20 modulo 6 has a modulus of two.

While modulo operators might seem mysterious if you haven't worked with them before, they're extremely common in programming. In fact, many of the code samples throughout this book will use a modulo!

Operators and Assignments

So far, we've looked at Python statements that use operators to return a new value. Sometimes, however, you want to perform a transformation on an existing value. A number may be incremented, decremented, multiplied by another number, or any number of other operations.

Of course, you can always write a transformation like this:

```
num = 5
# Add three to num
num = num + 3
```

This statement requires us to use the variable num twice, once in the operation (num + 3) and once to assign the new value to itself.

Python has a convenient shorthand that allows us to write these transformations more succinctly. In many cases, a mathematical operator can be combined with an equal sign to create a new type of assignment expression. This will update the value of the variable on the left with the result of the arithmetic operation performed on the original variable and the value on the right. For example:

```
num = 5
# Add three to num
num += 3
print(num)
```

This will result in the value 8 being printed. Note that, in order to use these new assignment operators, the variable being operated on must already have been *declared* (defined and have a value assigned to it). Simply writing this:

```
new_num += 3
```

will result in a `NameError` in Python, meaning the name of something was referenced (in this case, new_num) that Python doesn't know about yet:

```
NameError: name 'new_num' is not defined
```

Additional arithmetic operators can be used in assignment expressions as follows:

```
num = 5

# Subtract 2 from num
num -= 2

# Multiply num by 10
num *= 10

# Divide num by 2
num /= 2

# Set num to itself modulo 8
num %= 8

# Divide (floor division) num by 2
num //= 2

# Raise num to the fourth power
num **= 4
```

For those of you following along at home, or running the Jupyter notebook accompanying this section, the final value of num is `81.0`

Comparison Operators

Comparison operators compare two values and return a Boolean. You're probably familiar with most comparison operators already:

```
# Less than
1 < 5

# Greater than
5 > 1

# Less than or equal to
5 <= 5

# Greater than or equal to
1 >= 1
```

Each of these statements evaluate to the Boolean `True`.

There are two other comparison operators used to determine equality, or whether or not two values are equal to each other The *equality operator* is two equal signs in a row:

```
# Equality
1 == 1
```

Remember that a single equal sign is used in assignment expressions. To make a statement about the equality of two values, you must use -- instead of =. The following two lines do very different things:

```
num = 5
num == 5
```

The final comparison operator tests for inequality. It is the *inequality operator* and returns True when two values are not equal to each other:

```
# Inequality
1 != 2
```

The exclamation mark (!) is a common symbol in programming and computer science, even outside of Python. It is called a *bang*, and it means "not" or "opposite of." In this case, it is used alongside an equal sign to mean "not equals."

When reading code out loud, you should read 1 != 2 as "one bang equals two" rather than "one not equals two" or the even less direct "one is not equal to two." Using the word "bang" when the exclamation point is being read out loud is something of a shibboleth[3] in programming.

Identity Operators

Identity operators, like Boolean operators and membership operators (discussed later in this section), use English words instead of the symbols and punctuation that most other operators use.

Identity operators are concerned with whether two things are the "same" or not. These operators are, simply enough: is and is not. Identity operators are primarily used to compare variables holding data rather than comparing data directly. In fact, you will get a warning to use a comparison operator when making a statement like 5 is 5, for reasons you will see shortly.

On the surface, is and is not seem very similar to the equality and inequality operators. For example:

```
a = 1
b = 1

print(a == b)
print(a is b)
```

This produces the output:

```
True
True
```

However, if we change the type of one of the variables, making a a float, we get a different result:

```
a = 1.0
b = 1

print(a == b)
print(a is b)
```

---

[3] The term *shibboleth* comes from Hebrew. It is a word that, according to an account in the Hebrew Bible, one of the tribes of Israel pronounced differently than other tribes. After a war in which that tribe was defeated, surviving soldiers were identified by their pronunciation of the word *shibboleth* and executed. Today, shibboleth simply means any word or phrase understood by a group of people and that can be used to differentiate them from others by their use of it.

This produces the output:

```
True
False
```

The "value" of a and b is the same—1.0 and 1 are equal—however, they are not the "same." Unlike comparison operators, identity operators don't test value; they test whether the items being compared literally point to the same location in memory. (See Chapter 1 for more information about memory locations.)

With this in mind, you may question the results of the first test. If variable a points to a memory location with the stored integer value 1 and variable b points to a memory location with the stored integer value 1, why are they pointing to the same memory location? Why not store the value 1 in two different locations?

The answer has to do with how Python works under the hood. Currently, all integers between −5 and 256 are prepopulated as values in memory and made available for use. Pointing a variable at the integer 10 will simply point to this location in the prepopulated list of values. It's only when an integer outside of this −5 to 256 range is requested that a new section of memory is allocated and written to. You can see this in action in the following example, which demonstrates both the is and is not operators:

```
a_256 = 256
b_256 = 256

a_257 = 257
b_257 = 257

print('Testing 256:')
print(a_256 is b_256)
print(a_256 is not b_256)

print('\nTesting 257:')
print(a_257 is b_257)
print(a_257 is not b_257)
```

This produces the output:

```
Testing 256
True
False

Testing 257
False
True
```

Identity operators are easy to write and read like plain English: a is b. However, you must keep in mind the nature of the relationship that you're evaluating. If used incorrectly, identity operators can easily lead to misleading and unpredictable behavior.

Boolean Operators

Boolean operators are used to evaluate Boolean logic. There are three Boolean operators:

➤ and

➤ or

➤ not

Both and and or evaluate a result based on two Boolean values. The and operator returns True if both values are true. The or operator returns True if either value is true and will return False if both are false.

The only situation in which an and operator returns True is if both sides are true:

```
True and True # This is True
```

Everything else returns False:

```
True and False # False
False and True # False
False and False # False
```

The only situation in which an or operator returns False is if both sides are false:

```
False or False # This is False
```

Everything else returns True:

```
True or False # True
False or True # True
True or True # True
```

The not operator is unusual in that it only operates on a single argument. It "flips" the value of whatever it's given so that True becomes False and False becomes True:

```
not True # False
not False # True
```

Boolean operators can be combined into longer statements, using parentheses to dictate which operations should be evaluated first:

```
a = True
b = False
c = False
a and (b or not c)
```

The output of this statement is True.

Membership Operators

Membership operators evaluate whether an element on the left of the operator is a member of (is contained in) the elements on the right side of the operator. The operator in returns True if the element is found on the right, and not in returns True if the element is not found on the right. One common application of this is deciding whether a string is contained in another string:

```
# Returns True
'cat' in 'My cat is named Ash'
```

Of course, the concept of "words" here is meaningless to Python. While the word "cat" is found in the sentence "My cat is named Ash," it's worth noting that "cat" is also found in the sentence "The patient is catatonic."

Evaluating strings using a membership operator is also case-sensitive:

```
# Returns False
'cat' in 'Santa Catalina Island'
```

The most common use of membership operators is using them to decide if an element is present in a Python data structure such as a *list*. Lists will be covered in more detail later, but for now, know that they contain multiple elements and are defined with square brackets in the following way:

```
my_list = ['a', 'b', 'c', 'd', 'e', 'f']
```

You can use membership operators with lists just like you would with a string. Both of the following expressions evaluate to True:

```
'a' in my_list
'z' not in my_list
```

You cannot use membership operators to decide if an element is contained in a float, an integer, or a Boolean:

```
1 in 123
```

This statement will result in the error:

```
TypeError: argument of type 'int' is not iterable
```

The word *iterable* here means that it has multiple elements that can be iterated through. Strings are iterable because they contain multiple characters you can scan through one at a time. Lists are iterable because they contain multiple elements.

Integers may appear iterable because they contain multiple digits. However, in the world of Python, mathematics, and computer science the digits are merely used as a display to represent a magnitude or "value," which is the important thing. The fact that the digit 1 is in the first position of 123 is not considered an intrinsically important property of integer value 123. In Python, numbers do not contain multiple elements and are not iterable.

This concept of iterability is very important in Python and will come up again, including in the next section when we discuss control flow and loops.

CONTROL FLOW

So far, we've written Python programs that, essentially, have been only one line long. Sure, maybe there's some variable declarations at the top, but the important parts are still just single isolated lines that don't do very much. Here, we're going to expand into code blocks that span multiple lines and make "decisions" about where to go.

If and *Else*

The `if` statement in Python executes the code indented below it only if the Boolean expression it is given is true:

```python
if 1 == 1:
    print('One and one are equal')
```

The `if` statement is given some expression, or condition, to evaluate. In this case, the condition is `1 == 1`. This condition is followed by a colon (`:`), then some code indented below it. Any indented code following the `if` statement is considered to belong to the `if` statement and is only evaluated if the provided condition is `True`:

```python
if 1 == 1:
    print('One and one are equal')
    print('Another line under the if statement')
```

As soon as an outdented line is reached, that line no longer belongs to the `if` statement and will be printed regardless:

```python
if 1 == 1:
    print('One and one are equal')
    print('Another line under the if statement')
print('This line is always printed')
```

Everything under the `if` statement is said to belong to that statement's block. One can describe those two print statements as "the `if` block." As soon as you outdent (also called "dedent") you are no longer inside the `if` block.

Optionally, an `if` statement can be followed by an `else` statement with a corresponding `else` block. The `else` block is only executed if the `if` statement is false:

```python
a = 1
b = 2

if a == b:
    print('a and b are equal')
else:
    print('a and b are not equal')
```

An `else` statement must directly follow an `if` statement and its `if` block. If there are any other outdented lines between the two blocks, it is unclear to the Python interpreter what that `else` block "belongs" to. The following is invalid:

```python
a = 1
b = 2

if a == b:
    print('a and b are equal')
print('Another line')
else:
    print('a and b are not equal')
```

When run, this code results in a `SyntaxError`:

```
    else:
    ^
SyntaxError: invalid syntax
```

The caret pointing to the `else:` indicates that it is misplaced and Python isn't sure what to do with it. Although the error here is that the previous line wasn't indented (or perhaps the previous line was placed there by mistake), this error message still offers a clue about what the problem might be.

For

A `for` statement is a type of *loop*. Loops execute the same block of code repeatedly for either a predetermined number of repetitions or until some condition changes. If you've used `for` loops in other programming languages, you may find that Python's work a little differently. The `for` loop in Python iterates through some iterable, allowing you access to each element as you go through it:

```
for num in [1, 2, 3, 4, 5]:
    print(num)
```

Like the `if` statement, a `for` loop contains a colon followed by an indented line starting the `for` block. In this case, it iterates through each item in the list `[1, 2, 3, 4, 5]` and prints it in the `for` block below.

The concise syntax of Python's `for` loop reads like plain English: "For item in iterable . . ." It's important to note that the `in` here has nothing to do with the membership operator `in`, discussed previously. Here, it is a keyword used to declare a new variable used inside the `for` loop block.

By combining `for` loops, `if` statements, operators, and our knowledge of the ASCII character set, we can start to do some interesting things with Python:

```
for char in 'Ryan Mitchell':
    if char >= 'A' and char <= 'Z':
        print(char)
```

This prints only the uppercase letters in the string `Ryan Mitchell`. When letters are compared in Python, they are compared based on their numerical value. In the ASCII character set, all the uppercase letters are assigned sequential binary values, followed by some punctuation, and then the lowercase letters. Therefore, if the character has a value greater than or equal to `'A'` and less than or equal to `'Z'`, it must be a capital letter.

While

The `while` loop continues to execute the code inside its block until the condition it is given evaluates to `False`. It has a syntax similar to the `if` statement and the `for` loop:

```
num = 0
while num < 5:
    num += 1
    print(num)
print('num is now 6!')
```

Here, we are initializing a variable num to 0. The condition being evaluated is num < 5. While num is less than 6, we add 1 to num using the += operator and then print the value. Finally, num is no longer less than 5, the loop is exited, and the final print statement is called.

while loops can be dangerous. For example, if we forget to modify the variable being tested, the loop will run forever:

```
num = 0
while num < 5:
    print(num)
print('num is now 6!')
```

Because nothing is modifying the variable num, the loop will continue to print out 0 until it is forcibly stopped. It is important to always double-check your while loops to make sure you haven't accidentally created an *infinite loop*.

while loops that increment a variable and check to see if that variable has reached a certain size yet are often better written as for loops instead. You can do this using the range function. The range function creates an iterable sequence that starts at the first number you provide and ends before reaching the second number. For example:

```
for num in range(1, 6):
    print(num)
```

This prints the output:

```
1
2
3
4
5
```

A while loop can be used to wait until a specific event occurs, like a certain clock time. We can get the current computer clock time in seconds using the Python datetime module:

```
from datetime import datetime

print(datetime.now().second)
```

This will print the seconds portion of the current time, which will be a number from 0 to 59 unless you are experiencing a leap second.[4] If you want to wait until, say, a second that ends in a 0 or a 5 you can use the modulus operator.

```
while datetime.now().second % 5 != 0:
    print('Waiting!')
print(datetime.now().second)
```

---

[4] A *leap second* is an event that happens occasionally as needed to keep atomic time in sync with Earth's actual rotational speed, which may vary very slightly due to geologic and climate events. When it happens, a second is added to atomic clocks around the world so that the time will display 23:59:60 (following the more traditional day ending time of 23:59:59) before going to 00:00:00 starting the next day. I've seen a few of them myself at http://time.gov and it is truly a spectacle to behold.

The statement `datetime.now().second % 5 != 0` will only be false when the current time ends in a 0 or 5 (is divisible by 5 with a remainder of 0). While the time does not end in a 0 or 5, the `while` block will be executed and the word "Waiting!" printed to the screen.

Caution: I do not recommend actually running this program. Python runs very fast, and by the time the `while` loop exits you're likely to have a screen overflowing with the word "Waiting!" repeated, potentially, hundreds of thousands of times. What we want is a `while` loop that does nothing at all. It simply spins, waiting for its cue to exit. However, a `while` loop like this without an indented block under it would result in an error:

```
while datetime.now().second % 5 != 0:
print(datetime.now().second)
```

The solution is to use the `pass` statement. This is a statement that results in absolutely nothing happening but can serve as a placeholder in situations like this:

```
while datetime.now().second % 5 != 0:
    pass
print(datetime.now().second)
```

When run, this should print the seconds of the current clock time as soon as that time ends in 0 or 5.

FUNCTIONS

Loops allow us to execute the same piece of code multiple times in a row. *Functions* are similar in that they also allow us to encapsulate a block of code and execute it repeatedly. Unlike code blocks inside loops, functions are independent units of computation that accept values, called *arguments*, and return values. We can *call* a function (execute it) by using its name and, optionally, some arguments. If you took algebra in school, you learned about functions. This is a popular function you may be familiar with:

$$f(x) = x^2$$

Here, f is the name of the function. The function takes one argument: x. The function transforms x by squaring it, and the output, or return value, of the function is x^2.

This is the Python version of that function:

```
def f(x):
    return x**2
```

The keyword `def` is used to start a function definition. Then, a function name is provided. In this case, the function is called `f`. Parentheses surround the function arguments—here just the single argument x.

A colon (`:`) indicates that the next line will be indented and start the function block. This function consists of a single line. The `return` keyword indicates that it will be returning a value x squared. If we were to call this function we could use the returned value like this:

```
output = f(4)
print(output)
```

This prints the integer 16.

Unlike in algebra, functions do not necessarily have to return anything at all. This is a perfectly valid function:

```
def print_square(x):
    print(x**2)
```

Rather than returning the square of the argument passed in, print_square prints the value and returns nothing at all. When I say "returns nothing at all" I mean this somewhat literally. It returns a None value. None is a special Python keyword similar to *null* in other programming languages. It indicates the absence of any value.

If we store the output of the print_square function into the variable output, just like we did with the function f, you can see the None value:

```
output = print_square(4)
print(output)
```

This prints the integer 16 from within the print_square function, and then the output None is printed:

```
16
None
```

Printing None is just about the only thing you can do with it. For example, using an arithmetic operator on None will get you into trouble:

```
None + 2
```

This results in a TypeError, which is what happens when you try to do something with a value that is disallowed by its type:

```
TypeError: unsupported operand type(s) for +: 'NoneType' and 'int'
```

Let's say we want to add two numbers together, but there's a chance that one or both of the numbers may be None. We can write a function to safely handle this situation:

```
def safe_sum(a, b):
    if a is None or b is None:
        print('Cannot perform this operation')
    else:
        return a + b
```

The function safe_sum takes two arguments, a and b, separated by a comma. If either of these arguments is None, a statement is printed letting the caller know that the sum cannot be performed. Otherwise, a + b is returned.

Functions may also have labeled arguments, called keyword arguments. These can be found in the function definition with a name, an equal sign, and some default value:

```
def safe_operation(a, b, op='add'):
    if a is None or b is None:
        print('Cannot perform this operation')
    else:
        if op == 'add':
            return a + b
        if op == 'sub':
            return a - b
```

The function `safe_operation` performs either addition or subtraction on two values. If no operation is explicitly defined with the argument `op`, it will default to performing addition. `safe_operation` can be called in the following way:

```
safe_operation(4, 5)
safe_operation(5, 4, op='sub')
```

Functions allow us to save space and time by encapsulating and labeling logic that may need to be performed over and over again. If we had a lot of numbers to add at various points in a program, we could certainly make this check for `None` values each time. However, putting those checks into a function and calling that function instead may save some keystrokes.

CLASSES

While functions encapsulate a few lines of logic and label it with a name, *classes* encapsulate multiple functions and attributes into more complex named structures that can be used to create `objects`. These objects can have stored states, complex behaviors, and interact with each other.

When used effectively, classes can be used to translate even the most tangled business requirements into clean, elegant, and Pythonic code. Designing code around classes is known as *object-oriented programming (OOP)*.

Let's make a class called `Person`:

```
class Person:
    def __init__(self, name):
        self.name = name
```

Python classes start with the `class` keyword, followed by the name of the class (`Person`), and a colon indicating that the indented class block will start on the next line. According to PEP 8, class names should always be capitalized (with the exception of certain built-in classes that will be discussed in the next section). It's important to keep function and variable names lowercase in order to distinguish them from class names.

The line starting with `def __init__` defines a function that belongs to the class `Person`. Functions that belong to classes are called *methods*. In Python, `__init__` (note that there are two underscores before and after the `init`) is a special method name that is used by Python to initialize the class.

In Python, these special methods with two underscores before and after the name are also called `dunder methods`, or sometimes "`magic methods`." They allow you to define or override key functionality for your class. The special method `__init__` is called, appropriately enough, the *initializer*.

The initializer takes, as arguments, everything that it needs to initialize a new object from the class. Initializing an object includes setting class *attributes*, in this case, the name attribute. The name itself is passed in as the second argument to the initializer and represents a string name.

The first argument, `self`, is a little more complicated. It represents the *instance* of the class, or the particular object,[5] that we are operating on. It's a specific instance of a Person with their own name.

---

[5] The terms "instance" and "object" are often used interchangeably. We talk about instances when focusing on the class and the context of what class a particular thing belongs to. We might talk about "an instance of the class Person." The term "object" is used more generally and colloquially, especially when multiple types of things are involved. We might say "this function can handle any type of object."

To illustrate this concept, let's use the `Person` class to make a new instance of a person like this:

```
alice = Person('Alice')
```

The statement `Person('Alice')` might look like a function call, but what we're doing is creating, or *instantiating*, a new instance of the `Person` class, which is returned and stored in the variable `alice`. The only thing we're passing into the `Person` class is the string name, `'Alice'`. When the initializer method (`__init__`) is called, however, what it receives is the instance of our `Person` class (`self`) along with the string name, `'Alice'`.

This `self` argument in the initializer is the exact same thing that is represented by the variable `alice`—they are both the same instance of the `Person` class. For example, I can access the `name` attribute in this way:

```
alice.name
```

This line is read out loud as "alice dot name." This `dot notation` is used to call attributes or methods on the class instance. In this case, `alice.name` returns the string `'Alice'`.

We can also add a method to the class and access the `name` attribute using the `self` variable from within the class itself:

```
class Person:
    def __init__(self, name):
        self.name = name
    def print_name(self):
        print(self.name)
```

This `print_name` method has only one argument, `self`, which is the specific class instance. It uses this instance to print the name. Therefore, `alice.name` outside of the class is equivalent to `self.name` inside a class method. Again, `alice` represents exactly the same thing as `self` in this example.

To call the `print_name` method, we use the same dot notation that we previously used to access the attribute `name`:

```
alice = Person('Alice')
alice.print_name()
```

Notice that, while the `print_name` method definition requires the argument `self`, we never pass it in (at least not explicitly) when calling `alice.print_name()`. This is a nifty little trick of Python's syntax. It will pass the `self` instance for you, by using the class instance (`alice`) that the method was called on as the first argument for the method.

In fact, these two lines are equivalent:

```
Person.print_name(alice)
alice.print_name()
```

The first line references the class method `print_name` and passes the specific instance, `alice`, in explicitly. The second line calls the method `print_name` on the instance `alice` and relies on the inner workings of Python to do the rearrangement and pass the instance `alice` as an argument to the class method. While the second line is the preferred syntax in Python, it's important to keep in mind what's going on behind the scenes and what these things mean when we write them.

It's also important to emphasize that class attributes, such as name, are specific to each class instance. For example, we can make two class instances, each that prints out its own name:

```
alice = Person('Alice')
bob = Person('Bob')

alice.print_name()
bob.print_name()
```

We can even modify the class attributes after the class has been created:

```
alice = Person('Alice')
alice.print_name()
alice.name = 'Alice2'
alice.print_name()
```

This prints out the name, changes the name, and then prints out the new name:

```
Alice
Alice2
```

Whether or not you choose to focus on object-oriented programming, classes in Python are unavoidable. Understanding the language requires understanding the basic mechanics of classes and objects within the language.

Everything Is an Object

Recall from earlier in this chapter the way that strings are converted, or cast, into integers:

```
int('42')
```

This int looks a lot like a function. In fact, many Python resources refer to it as a function. However, it's not a function at all—int is a class with, confusingly, a lowercase class name. When we call int('42'), we are passing the string '42' into the constructor[6] of the int class, which is used to instantiate a new int instance.

When we refer to something as having a "type" in Python—such as an int type or a string type—what we really mean is that it is an instance of that class. Its "type" is simply its class name. The number 42 is an int type because it is an instance of the int class.

Essentially everything in Python is an object. Even functions are instances of function objects! This is important to keep in mind as you continue to work with more complex objects, including data structures in the next section. The syntax and behavior of these structures in Python make perfect sense when you view them as classes and class instances.

DATA STRUCTURES

For the most part, the data we've worked with has had only a single value. The exception to this is strings, which are very similar to the lists that were briefly mentioned in the section on loops. Both strings and lists contain multiple values. In the case of strings, they contain multiple characters and

---

[6] The constructor method, __new__, is similar to the initializer method, __init__, in that it is a Python-defined dunder method that triggers at the beginning of a class's life cycle. The constructor *creates* a new class instance, whereas the initializer populates that newly created object with values.

can be as long or as short as you want to make them. Unlike strings, the values in lists aren't limited to just characters and can contain any type of object:

```
my_list = ['apple', 3.14, -106, 'c']
```

Data structures, in Python and computer science, are structures that hold multiple values that conceptually belong to each other. This makes the data nice and organized for both humans and computers. There are four basic types of data structure in Python. From (approximately) the most used to least used, they are:

➤ List

➤ Dictionary

➤ Tuple

➤ Set

Each of these data structures will be discussed in greater detail in upcoming chapters. However, having a basic understanding of them now will allow you to start writing far more interesting code for the exercises at the end of this chapter, and interesting code is more fun than uninteresting code.

Lists

As mentioned before, lists can contain absolutely anything. They can also contain nothing:

```
# an empty list
my_list = []
```

They can even contain other lists:

```
my_list = [['a', 'b', 'c'], [1, 2, 3]]
```

This is an example of a list that contains two elements: the list ['a', 'b', 'c'] and the list [1, 2, 3]. How long is this list? Although it contains complex elements, the length of this list is 2 because it contains two lists.

We can show this using the len function, which gets the length of a list, or the number of elements it contains:

```
len(my_list)
```

This returns:

```
2
```

The first element of this list, the list ['a', 'b', 'c'], of course, contains three elements. But how do we show that? We saw earlier how you can use a for loop to access each element of the list, so it's possible to iterate through our list and print out the length of each element:

```
for item in my_list:
    print(len(item))
```

This prints out:

```
3
3
```

There is a more direct way to access a particular element in a list rather than scanning through each one, however, and that is to use an *index*. An index is a record of the integer positions of the elements within a list, starting with 0. Somewhat confusingly, the word "index" also commonly refers to a single integer position within the index. The first element (`['a', 'b', 'c']`) has an index of 0. The second element (`[1, 2, 3]`) has an index of 1.

For any iterable data structure in Python, you can access a particular element in that data structure using its index. The syntax for retrieving an element at index 0 is:

```
my_list[0]
```

The name of the data structure (`my_list`) followed by square brackets containing the integer index you're trying to access (0) will get the element at that index value. To get the length of the first sublist in `my_list` we would write the following:

```
len(my_list[0])
```

The element at index 0 is `['a', 'b', 'c']` which has a length of 3. So this line produces the output:

```
3
```

To get the third element, at index 2 of the sub-list, we can use this line:

```
my_list[0][2]
```

This retrieves the string `'c'`.

Indexes make it easy to update elements as well as retrieve them:

```
my_list[0] = 'a'
my_list[1] = 1
print(my_list)
```

This prints the list:

```
['a', 1]
```

Although indexes that start with 0 are common in programming, using them can take some getting used to if you haven't done it before. If it helps, you can think of this index value as an "offset from the starting position" rather than the first, second, third . . . elements of a list, which can be misleading

In addition to updating elements based on their index, you can modify the list by simply adding or appending elements to the end of it. This is done using the append method:

```
my_list = [1,2,3]
my_list.append(4)
print(my_list)
```

This will result in the output:

```
[1,2,3,4]
```

Dictionaries

If you remember back to the pre-internet age (or just imagine what it was like), you may recall a physical book that was used to look up the definitions of words. This was called a "dictionary." Each word was ordered alphabetically to make lookups fast and easy, and after looking up the word you would be rewarded with a longer string of text describing it.

What if you were presented with the longer description string and asked to find the word instead of the other way around. For example: "*transitive verb*. 1. To refuse to accept, to reject as unauthorized or as having no binding force. 2. To reject as untrue or unjust . . ." Find that word!

Can you use a physical dictionary to look up the word that matches the definition? Well, that's a much harder problem. Sure, you may have figured out or guessed the word: repudiate. However, the dictionary itself wouldn't have been helpful at all here, apart from a brute-force approach of going through every single definition until you find a matching one.

The word itself is a bit like a *key* to accessing a definition, which is a *value*. I don't think I'm stretching the metaphor too much when I say that the Python *dictionary* data structure acts in much the same way. After all, there's a reason they're called dictionaries.

A Python dictionary is defined using curly braces surrounding it. Colons separate key-value pairs, and commas separate each key-value pair:

```
my_dictionary = {
    'apple': 'A red fruit',
    'banana': 'A yellow fruit',
    'cantaloupe': 'A beige melon'
}
```

Similar to accessing a particular element of a list using its index, you can access a particular element (value) of a dictionary using its key:

```
my_dictionary['apple']
```

This returns the line:

```
'A red fruit'
```

Like strings and lists, dictionaries are also iterable. When you iterate over a dictionary, you iterate over just its keys:

```
for item in my_dictionary:
    print(item)
```

This prints out each key in the dictionary:

```
apple
banana
cantaloupe
```

If you want to get each value in the dictionary instead, you need to make sure to access that in the original dictionary using the key you're given during the iteration:

```
for key in my_dictionary:
    print(my_dictionary[key])
```

This prints out the values:

```
A red fruit
A yellow fruit
A beige melon
```

And, as you might suspect from the similarity of the syntax between accessing elements in a list:

```
my_list[0]
```

and accessing elements in a dictionary:

```
my_dictionary['apple']
```

you can use the same syntax that you would use to update elements of a list to update elements in a dictionary:

```
my_dictionary['apple'] = 'An American multinational corporation'
```

Tuples

Tuples are very similar to lists. They contain multiple elements of any type, they are iterable, and you can access elements within them using an integer index. Rather than being defined with square brackets, they are defined with parentheses:

```
my_tuple = ('a', 'b', 'c')
```

The important difference between a list and a tuple becomes clear if you try to update one of the elements:

```
my_tuple[0] = 'A'
```

This results in a `TypeError`:

```
TypeError: 'tuple' object does not support item assignment
```

Remember that "assignment" in Python refers to assignment expressions using an equal sign (=) to assign a value. In this case, we are trying to assign the uppercase 'A' to the first element of the tuple at index 0.

Tuples do not support item assignment, meaning they can't be updated. In fact, once a tuple is declared you cannot add, remove, or reassign the elements in any way.

Surely, tuples must offer some innovative new feature that makes them superior to lists in order to compensate for this, right? Not really. Tuples do exactly everything that lists do, except that they cannot be modified.

But this "disadvantage," when used correctly, can actually be an advantage. Recall how computers store data in memory. When a computer allocates memory for a list, it needs to account for the fact that the list may be modified, so it will allocate a larger space in memory than the list strictly requires.

Let's say you're working with a program that uses thousands or millions of cartesian coordinates containing x, y pairs. You're unlikely to ever need to add a third value to any of these or modify the existing values. By using a tuples to store the coordinates rather than lists you're essentially giving Python permission to pack them as efficiently as possible in memory, saving space.

Sets

Sets look a lot like lists and tuples, but with curly brackets instead of square brackets or parentheses:

```
my_set = {1, 2, 3}
```

You can also iterate through a set just fine. They are iterable data structures:

```
for item in my_set:
    print(item)
```

This produces the output:

```
1
2
3
```

This is approximately where the similarities between lists and sets end. While you can iterate through a set, they traditionally don't have a concept of "order" like lists and tuples do. Although iterating through the set produced the values 1, 2, 3 in that specific order, this is behavior that was only codified in Python in version 3.10. Prior to this, the order of items in sets could not be relied on.

In the broader field of computer science, sets aren't considered to have an order at all! A set is like a jumbled bag of elements. You can pull items out of the bag one by one, but the order you retrieve those items in isn't guaranteed. You can see this computer science concept reflected in Python by trying to access the element of a set at index 0:

```
my_set[0]
```

Just like when we tried to modify the tuple, we get a `TypeError`. This one says:

```
TypeError: 'set' object is not subscriptable
```

Subscriptable means able to be accessed through an index. Anything you can use the square bracket notation with (`my_dict['apple']`, `my_list[0]`, etc.) is subscriptable.

While you can add and remove items to and from sets, items within the sets must be unique. This uniqueness is enforced by the set class itself. For example:

```
my_set = {1, 2, 3}

my_set.add(1)
print(my_set)

my_set.add(2)
print(my_set)

print('And now for something completely different...')⁷
my_set.add(4)
print(my_set)
```

Adding something that already exists in the set won't cause an error, but it won't do anything to modify the set either. The previous code will print:

```
{1, 2, 3}
{1, 2, 3}
And now for something completely different...
{1, 2, 3, 4}
```

---

⁷ This is a reference to the sketchy comedy film by Monty Python, which the Python programming language was named after: https://en.wikipedia.org/wiki/And_Now_for_Something_Completely_Different.

There is an interesting relationship between sets and dictionaries. Like sets, the order of keys in a dictionary is not considered important. Dictionary keys are also required to be unique. We can update the value for an existing key, but doing this will overwrite the old one, not add a duplicate key with a separate value.

While the fact that sets and dictionaries are both denoted with curly braces is accidental, it may be a useful mnemonic that curly braces make collections unique!

EXERCISES

Exercises are designed as a check of your understanding of the chapter material. Also, for new programmers, it's a great way to strengthen your skills. Reading about programming is one thing—doing it is an entirely different muscle!

Exercises are ordered from easiest to hardest. If you disagree with my assessment of the difficulty level, please consider writing to me at author@unlockingpython.com with your own experience.

1. Print the text 'Hello, World!' to the screen. This is a traditional first exercise in programming (https://en.wikipedia.org/wiki/%22Hello,_World!%22_program).

2. Write a function that takes, as its argument, a string. It will print each character of this string, but only if the character is a vowel.

   Example input:

   ```
   'Ryan Mitchell'
   ```

   Example output:

   ```
   y
   a
   i
   e
   ```

   Your function definition will look something like this:

   ```
   def print_vowels(input_str):
   ```

   You can call it using something like this:

   ```
   print_vowels('Ryan Mitchell')
   ```

   You can decide how or if you want to handle capital letters. Whether or not "y" counts as a vowel is also a personal preference you can make up your own mind on.

3. Write a function that determines if a number is even. If it is even, return True. If it is odd, return False. Your function definition should look something like this:

   ```
   def is_even(num):
   ```

   It will be called like this:

   ```
   is_even(5)
   is_even(2)
   ```

There are many ways to determine if a number is even or not. One popular way to do this uses a modulo operator.

4. Print the numbers from 1 to 100. If the number is divisible by 3, print "Fizz" instead of the number. If the number is divisible by 5, print "Buzz" instead of the number. If the number is divisible by 15, print "FizzBuzz" instead of the number.

   Example output:

   ```
   1
   2
   Fizz
   4
   Buzz
   6
   ...
   ```

   This exercise, called "FizzBuzz," is based on a children's game and is somewhat famous as a programming interview question (https://en.wikipedia.org/wiki/Fizz_buzz). It's generally considered a simple problem that competent programmers should be able to easily solve (https://blog.codinghorror.com/fizzbuzz-the-programmers-stairway-to-heaven).

5. Create a class called UniqueList. This class will have a single attribute called internal_list, which starts as an empty list when the class is initialized. It also has two methods: append and print. The append method takes, as an argument, a new value to append to the list. When append is called, it will append the value only if that value does not currently exist in the list. That is, all elements in the list must be unique.

   The print method simply prints the existing values in the list.

   Example of UniqueList being initialized and used:

   ```
   unique = UniqueList()
   unique.append(1)
   unique.append(2)
   unique.append(1)
   unique.append(3)
   unique.append(2)

   unique.print()
   ```

   This prints:

   ```
   [1, 2, 3]
   ```

Lists and Strings

This chapter is about both lists and strings because they are very similar types in Python. For many purposes, you can think of strings as "lists of characters."

It's important to note that strings and lists are not literally the same data type in Python. A string is not a "specific type of list." However, they are both very commonly used ordered iterable types in Python and operations on them often share a similar syntax.

STRING OPERATIONS

Strings in Python are immutable. This means that you cannot add or remove characters to or from a string once it is declared. You can access the values of existing characters within the string like we saw previously:

```
my_string = 'Hello, World!'
my_string[0]
```

However, assigning anything to those characters will result in a syntax error:

```
my_string[0] = 'J'
```

For the most part, this doesn't matter that much. When we work with strings in Python, we tend to make a lot of copies of them and put them into new strings. Although there is no function or method that will modify a string *in place*, or directly in its original memory location, there are plenty of operations that create new strings from existing ones.

String *concatenation* uses the addition operator to combine strings:

```
'String 1' + 'String 2'
```

This returns a new string that can be stored in a new variable:

```
'String 1String 2'
```

Another way to combine strings is with the *f-string*, or formatted string. The f-string, introduced in Python 3.6, allows you to compose new strings with the following syntax:

```
name = 'Ryan'
introduction = f'My name is {name}'
```

This sets the value of introduction to the string:

```
'My name is Ryan'
```

The letter f outside of the string's quotes may look a little odd, but this simply indicates that it's an f-string. The letter "f" is not included in the final string. All values inserted into the string, like {name}, are enclosed with curly brackets.

The f-string can accommodate data types other than strings as well. Anything that can be cast to a string can be used in an f-string:

```
letters = ['a', 'b', 'c']
print(f'Here is a list of {len(letters)} letters: {letters}')
```

This prints the string:

```
Here is a list of 3 letters: ['a', 'b', 'c']
```

Generally, f-strings are preferable to string concatenation because of their elegance and readability. They're also just easier to write and can save you potential errors, especially when it comes to data type conversion. Consider this string concatenation, for example:

```
letters = ['a', 'b', 'c']
print('Here is a list of '+len(letters)+' letters: '+letters)
```

This will cause a TypeError because strings ('Here is a list of ') cannot be concatenated with integers (len(letters)). Similarly, strings cannot be concatenated with lists. This can be solved by casting each of these to a string before concatenating:

```
letters = ['a', 'b', 'c']
print('Here is a list of '+str(len(letters))+' letters: '+str(letters))
```

Not only is this more difficult to read, but you're also liable to inadvertently forget to cast a value at some point, creating an error. Although string concatenation has its uses, it's almost always preferable to use an f-string.

String Methods

There are a number of commonly used methods in the string class that are worth discussing. The first group of methods deals with converting strings to upper or lowercase and then deciding whether or not a string is entirely upper or lowercase.

These methods are lower, upper, islower, and isupper. Both lower and upper are used to convert a string to lower- and uppercase. Remember, because strings are not modifiable, a new string is created and returned rather than modifying the existing string directly:

```
my_string = 'Spam'
print(f'Lowercase Spam: {my_string.lower()}')
print(f'Uppercase Spam: {my_string.upper()}')
print(f'Original Spam: {my_string}')
```

This prints:

```
Lowercase Spam: spam
Uppercase Spam: SPAM
Original Spam: Spam
```

As a general pattern, any method starting with `is` will return a Boolean value. Therefore, `isupper` returns a Boolean `True` if the string is composed entirely of uppercase letters and `islower` returns a Boolean `True` if the string is composed entirely of lowercase letters:

```
uppercase_string = 'SPAM'
lowercase_string = 'spam'
mixed_string = 'Spam'

print(f'Uppercase is uppercase: {uppercase_string.isupper()}')
print(f'Lowercase is lowercase: {lowercase_string.islower()}')
print(f'Mixed is uppercase: {mixed_string.isupper()}')
print(f'Mixed is lowercase: {mixed_string.islower()}')
```

This prints the text:

```
Uppercase is uppercase: True
Lowercase is lowercase: True
Mixed is uppercase: False
Mixed is lowercase: False
```

Note that the string must be *entirely* upper- or lowercase for these methods to return `True`.

Next, stripping. *String stripping* refers to removing *whitespace*[1] (or sometimes other characters) from the beginning and end of a string. This whitespace at the beginning and end of a string is also called leading and trailing whitespace.

The most common method used to do this is `strip`:

```
whitespace_string = '  spam  '
whitespace_string.strip()
```

This returns the string:

```
'spam'
```

You can also use the methods `lstrip` to strip only the leading whitespace (to the left) and `rstrip` to strip only the trailing whitespace (to the right). For example:

```
whitespace_string.lstrip()
```

returns the string:

```
'spam  '
```

---

[1] *Whitespace* refers to any character that creates space but does not leave a visible mark. Whitespace characters most commonly include spaces, tabs, and newlines. There are a number of other, more exotic whitespace characters such as the vertical tab, carriage return, and feed. You can use the `isspace` string method to determine whether or not a string is entirely composed of whitespace characters.

If you want to strip something besides whitespace, you can, optionally, pass a string to the methods `strip`, `lstrip`, and `rstrip`. Any characters found in the argument string will be stripped. For example:

```
punctuation_string = '!!.,spam!!*'
punctuation_string.strip('!.,*')
```

returns the string:

```
'spam'
```

Just like the `strip` method, passing characters to strip to `lstrip` and `rstrip` will strip those characters from the left and right, respectively.

Another handy string method is `replace`. This replaces all instances of one substring with another substring. As a simple example:

```
my_string = 'spam spam spam'
my_string.replace('m', 'n')
```

returns the string:

```
'span span span'
```

The `replace` method is not limited to single characters or even substrings of the same length. For instance:

```
my_string = 'spam spam spam'
my_string.replace('m', 'malot')
```

returns the string:

```
'spamalot spamalot spamalot'
```

You can even use `replace` to remove substrings by replacing them with an empty string:

```
my_string = 'spam spam spam'
my_string.replace('sp', '')
```

This returns the string:

```
'am am am'
```

Finally, let's look at a method that allows us to turn strings into lists. The `split` method splits a string based on any substring that is passed in. By default, strings are split based on whitespace. If no substring is passed in, the string will be split into a list of words:

```
my_string = 'spam1 spam2 spam3'
my_string.split()
```

This produces the list:

```
['spam1', 'spam2', 'spam3']
```

Another common use case is to split a string based on commas, or a comma and a space:

```
my_string = 'spam1, spam2, spam3'
my_string.split(', ')
```

This produces the same list as before, but from the differently formatted string:

```
['spam1', 'spam2', 'spam3']
```

LIST OPERATIONS

Although Python has many list-specific methods, it is likely that you will routinely use only a few of them. Of the first two I want to focus on, you've already seen one of them, and that is append:

```
alphabet = ['a', 'b', 'c']
alphabet.append('d')
```

The append method, of course, adds the element that you pass in to the end of the list. It also has a less common but still very useful relative, extend:

```
alphabet.extend(['e', 'f', 'g'])
```

The argument for the extend method is always another list, rather than a single element. It concatenates the two lists so that the value of alphabet is now this:

```
['a', 'b', 'c', 'd', 'e', 'f', 'g']
```

Using the extend method as shown is also equivalent to this:

```
alphabet = alphabet + ['e', 'f', 'g']
```

Using extend instead of a list concatenation is, arguably, nicer looking. The extend method also has the benefit of being able to modify the original list, without returning another list which needs to be assigned to the original variable, in this case, alphabet.

In addition to adding items, there are various ways to remove them. The pop method removes an item from the end of a list and returns it:

```
alphabet = ['a', 'b', 'c', 'd', 'e', 'f', 'g']
g = alphabet.pop()
```

Here, the variable g is assigned to the string 'g'. Once this item has been removed, or "popped," it no longer exists in the original list. The value of alphabet is now this:

```
['a', 'b', 'c', 'd', 'e', 'f']
```

The pop method is commonly used in loops. For example:

```
while alphabet:
    print(alphabet.pop())
```

This will print the alphabet list backward. Recall that the Boolean value of an empty list ([]) is False, while any other list will evaluate to True. This while loop prevents pop from being used unless there are elements in the list to pop. If pop is called on an empty list, an IndexError will be raised:

```
IndexError: pop from empty list
```

Optionally, an index can be passed into pop to remove an item at any position in the list. For example, if we wanted to pop items from the list in left to right order, we'd use the following:

```
alphabet = ['a', 'b', 'c', 'd', 'e', 'f', 'g']
while alphabet:
    print(alphabet.pop(0))
```

This will remove items at index 0, the first item, from the list at every pass through the while loop. However, I don't encourage you to use this feature of pop unless it's truly necessary. Using pop to remove an item from the tail (end of the list) is fast. Passing an index to remove it anywhere else is measurably slower in Python.

If you've studied computer science in any depth, you'll know how complex the problem of *sorting* a list can be. Fortunately, Python makes it easy:

```
alphabet = ['d', 'f', 'g', 'c', 'a', 'b', 'e']
alphabet.sort()
print(alphabet)
```

This prints the letters, perfectly sorted by their ASCII value:

```
['a', 'b', 'c', 'd', 'e', 'f', 'g']
```

To reverse the sorted order, use the keyword argument reverse:

```
alphabet.sort(reverse=True)
print(alphabet)
```

This prints:

```
['g', 'f', 'e', 'd', 'c', 'b', 'a']
```

Python is able to sort letters because they have an established numerical value. However, not everything is sorted so easily. For instance, which of these dictionaries is biggest?

```
{'monty': 'python'}
{'spam': 'spam'}
```

I can try putting them in a list and sorting:

```
silly_list = [{'monty': 'python'}, {'spam': 'spam'}]
silly_list.sort()
```

Rightfully, I get an error:

```
TypeError: '<' not supported between instances of 'dict' and 'dict'
```

When Python sorts the elements of a list, it needs to use comparison operators such as < to decide which element is bigger than the other. Although the error here might be more obviously written as something like "Sorting is not valid for instances of 'dict' and 'dict,'" we can still read between the lines and figure out what's happening. Python is trying to sort a list containing dictionaries and encountering an error when it needs to compare them using <.

In some situations you need to sort a list and provide Python with the rules that define how the sorting should happen. One way is by using the sort method's key argument . The key argument requires a function as an argument. This function must be capable of taking any item in the list and returning a value that Python can use to sort that list. Here is an example of sorting a list of dictionaries:

```python
people = [
    {'name': 'Bob', 'age': 30},
    {'name': 'Diana', 'age': 20},
    {'name': 'Alice', 'age': 40},
    {'name': 'Charlie', 'age': 10},
]

def name_key(person):
    return person['name']

people.sort(key=name_key)
print(people)
```

Here, each `person` dictionary has both a string name and an integer age that can be sorted by. The function `name_key` allows us to sort by name. It takes in the person and returns the name, which can be sorted by ASCII value. The function itself is passed to the `sort` method as an argument in this line:

```python
people.sort(key=name_key)
```

It's important to note that we are not actually calling the `name_key` function. There are no parentheses after the function name. Calling the `sort` function with `key=name_key()` is incorrect and will result in an error. The function `name_key` is being provided so that it can be called in Python's `sort` function itself.

This results in the people list, alphabetically sorted by name:

```python
[{'name': 'Alice', 'age': 40},
 {'name': 'Bob', 'age': 30},
 {'name': 'Charlie', 'age': 10},
 {'name': 'Diana', 'age': 20}]
```

SLICING

Most programming languages have a concept of *list slicing*, or of extracting a sublist from a larger list based on an index range. What differentiates Python from other languages in this regard is the certain simplicity and elegance of its list slicing syntax.

Both list slicing and list comprehensions (discussed in the next section) are two excellent parts of Python's syntax that make the language a real pleasure to write in, especially for text and data processing applications.

Given a list:

```python
alphabet = ['a', 'b', 'c', 'd', 'e', 'f', 'g', 'h', 'i', 'j']
```

we can take "slices" of that list by specifying a start index and an end index. The list slicing syntax uses square brackets and two indexes separated by a colon:

```python
alphabet[2:5]
```

This example, `alphabet[2:5]`, produces a list that contains the elements at indices 2, 3, and 4 (up to, but not including 5):

```
['c', 'd', 'e']
```

Slicing can be done with any iterable object and is very commonly done with strings. For example, slicing can be used to remove or extract text:

```
greeting = 'Hello, Ryan'
name = greeting[7:11]
```

In this example, the variable `name` is set to the string `'Ryan'`. If we didn't know the total length of the string (`11`), there are a couple alternate ways to do this. We can use the length function (`len`) as the endpoint for our slice:

```
name = greeting[7:len(greeting)]
```

Or, we can use the fact that a missing index as the second argument defaults to the end of the string. This will also set `name` to the string `'Ryan'`:

```
name = greeting[7:]
```

Similarly, not including anything for the first index will default to the beginning of the string (in this case, this is the same as writing 0 for the first index). This will set the variable `hello` to the string `'Hello'`:

```
hello = greeting[:5]
```

Remember that strings cannot be modified, and slicing will always return a new string, leaving the original string unchanged. If we want to make a copy of the entire string, both indices can be left blank, so that the slice will contain everything from the very beginning to the end of the string:

```
greeting_copy = greeting[:]
```

In addition to the start index and the end index, Python's slicing syntax has an optional third argument, the "step size." By default, the step size is always 1 and every element is captured. If we want to capture every other element instead, a step size of 2 can be used:

```
alphabet = ['a', 'b', 'c', 'd', 'e', 'f', 'g', 'h', 'i', 'j']
print(alphabet[0:10:2])
```

This prints the array from index 0 to index 10 with a step size of 2. Because the array is 10 elements long, this is equivalent to this somewhat strange-looking statement:

```
print(alphabet[::2])
```

Both of these print every other element, starting with the first one (at index 0):

```
['a', 'c', 'e', 'g', 'i']
```

This slicing syntax is similar to the `range` function seen in Chapter 5, "Python Quickstart." We provide two indexes: one to start at and another index to go up to. Recall that the following produces an iterable range containing the numbers 1, 2, 3, 4, 5:

```
range(1, 6)
```

Like slicing, the `range` function can also take a third argument of step size. This will produce the numbers 1 through 50, with a step size of 5:

```
range(1, 50, 5)
```

When the "steps" are taken, the first number is always included (or, in the case of a list slice, the item at the first index is always included). To visualize what this range looks like, we can use the values in the range to construct a list:

```
list(range(1, 50, 5))
```

This returns the list:

```
[1, 6, 11, 16, 21, 26, 31, 36, 41, 46]
```

The power of slicing and ranges don't stop there, however. For both of these, each argument can be any integer, including negative integers. What does it mean to use a negative index or a negative range? In the case of a negative index, it represents the offset from the *end* of the string or array, rather than the offset from the beginning. For example:

```
numbers = [0, 1, 2, 3, 4, 5]
numbers[-2]
```

Here, `numbers[-2]` represents the number 4 because it is second from the end of the list. Conveniently, using an index of -1 will always give you the last item of a list, in this case, 5:

```
numbers[-1]
```

What happens if we use a negative index that is far greater than the length of the list? Will it simply circle back around and around until it lands on a value?

```
numbers[-20]
```

No. In a list of length 6, such as this one, any index less than -6 or greater than 5 will give us the error:

```
IndexError: list index out of range
```

Using the list slicing syntax, we can go from one negative index to another just like we go from one positive index to another:

```
alphabet = ['a', 'b', 'c', 'd', 'e', 'f', 'g', 'h', 'i', 'j']
print(alphabet[-5:-1])
```

This prints:

```
['f', 'g', 'h', 'i']
```

Notice that the first index (-5) is still smaller than the last index (-1). Because we are moving from the first index up to the second index in increments of the default step size (1), this makes sense. Our end goal must be greater than where we started if we want to be able to move forward.

But what if we move backward?

A negative step size accomplishes this and allows us to step backward through the list, collecting elements as we go:

```
alphabet = ['a', 'b', 'c', 'd', 'e', 'f', 'g', 'h', 'i', 'j']
print(alphabet[5:0:-1])
```

This prints the values:

```
['f', 'e', 'd', 'c', 'b']
```

The step function starts at the element at index 5 ('f'), moves backward one step at a time, and stops before reaching the element at index 0 ('a'). If we want to include the 'a' we can leave the second index unbounded by removing it entirely. Doing the same for the first index will allow us to encompass the entire list and reverse it:

```
alphabet = ['a', 'b', 'c', 'd', 'e', 'f', 'g', 'h', 'i', 'j']
print(alphabet[::-1])
```

This prints the full reversed list:

```
['j', 'i', 'h', 'g', 'f', 'e', 'd', 'c', 'b', 'a']
```

Slicing and rearranging strings and lists can take a little getting used to at first, particularly when working with negative indexes and step sizes. Don't feel pressure to get it exactly right at first—that's what practice and double-checking your work is for.

Getting an index wrong in particular can often result in an *off-by-one error* (https://en.wikipedia.org/wiki/Off-by-one_error). These errors can be easy to overlook if you're not familiar with the situations in which they commonly arise, but they're also easy to fix. Even experienced programmers will often run through an example in the Python command prompt to be sure that they're slicing what they think they are!

LIST COMPREHENSIONS

An extremely common scenario in programming is to loop through every element of a list or other iterable and transform it into a new list. For example:

```
numbers = [1,2,3,4,5]
doubled = []
for x in numbers:
    doubled.append(2*x)
```

This loops through every element of the numbers list and multiplies it by 2, resulting in the doubled list:

```
[2, 4, 6, 8, 10]
```

List comprehensions, one of the excellent parts of the Python language, are a syntactical shorthand for doing this same operation in one line:

```
doubled = [2*x for x in numbers]
```

A list comprehension is surrounded with square brackets ([]), declaring the new list. The syntax for x in numbers looks very much like the for loop, which is not a coincidence. It does the same thing: declares a new temporary variable x, which is used in the statement 2*x.

It's important to note that the original list, numbers, is not changed. A new list is unavoidably always created when a list comprehension is used. You don't have to do anything with the value of the new list, but the new list is still created. For example:

```
[print(2*x) for x in numbers]
```

This prints the values 2, 4, etc. while iterating through each item in numbers. The print function itself returns None, so this will, in fact, create the list:

```
[None, None, None, None, None]
```

Even if that list is never assigned to any values and nothing is done with it, the list will still be created. In situations like this, where the list comprehension itself is not used, it may be better to write out the statement with a for loop instead even if the list comprehension is technically fewer lines.

List comprehensions can be combined with if statements to add filtering:

```
numbers = [1, 2, 3, 4, 5]
evens = [x for x in numbers if x % 2 == 0]
```

Recall that the modulo statement x % 2 == 0 evaluates to True if x is even and False if it is odd. The if statement acts as a filter on the list of numbers, allowing only the even numbers to be included in the new list. This sets the value of evens to [2, 4].

List comprehensions make text processing especially easy as well. As an example, we'll use this text from the script for *Monty Python and the Holy Grail*:

```
text = '''
Strange women lying in ponds distributing swords is no basis
for a system of government. Supreme executive power derives
from a mandate from the masses, not from some farcical
aquatic ceremony.
'''
```

Here, the triple quotes ''' indicate a *multi-line string*. Normally, strings in Python cannot span multiple lines. However, using three single quotes (''') or three double quotes (""") in a row allows you to insert newlines in your string. The string continues until matching triple quotes are used at the end.

We can split this long string into individual sentences by splitting on a period (.) :

```
sentences = text.split('.')
print(sentences)
```

This produces the printed list:

```
['\nStrange women lying in ponds distributing swords is no basis \nfor a system of
government', ' Supreme executive power derives \nfrom a mandate from the masses,
not from some farcical \naquatic ceremony', '\n']
```

There are a few issues here. First, newline characters (\n) and whitespace surround the sentences and should be removed. Second, a new line character was broken off as its own "sentence" at the end of the list. Let's look at how we might clean this up with list comprehensions.

First, remove leading and trailing whitespace from each sentence using the strip function:

```
sentences = [s.strip() for s in sentences]
```

This creates a cleaner version of the sentences, although it's important to note that newline characters and extra whitespace may still be between each word within the sentences:

```
['Strange women lying in ponds distributing swords is no basis \nfor a system of
government',
 'Supreme executive power derives \nfrom a mandate from the masses, not from some
farcical \naquatic ceremony',
 '']
```

Finally, we can filter out any empty sentences:

```
sentences = [s for s in sentences if s]
```

Remember that an empty string (`''`) evaluates to a Boolean `False`. So the statement `if s` will reject any empty strings, leaving us with just the two sentences:

```
['Strange women lying in ponds distributing swords is no basis \nfor a system of
government',
 'Supreme executive power derives \nfrom a mandate from the masses, not from some
farcical \naquatic ceremony']
```

To clean individual words, we can split each sentence into words, then convert each word to lowercase and strip any whitespace around it. This will require a *nested* list comprehension:

```
sentences = [[w.lower().strip() for w in s.split()] for s in sentences]
```

This contains two list comprehensions. The outer one effectively looks like this:

```
[s for s in sentences]
```

But what do we do with that s to the left? We turn it into an inner list comprehension:

```
[w.lower().strip() for w in s.split()]
```

Recall that the `split` function, by default, splits on spaces. So `s.split()` here is splitting each sentence into individual words. Finally, each word is cleaned by converting it to lowercase and stripping whitespace using `w.lower().strip()`.

Printing `sentences`, we get the cleaned product:

```
[['strange', 'women', 'lying', 'in', 'ponds', 'distributing', 'swords', 'is', 'no',
'basis', 'for', 'a', 'system', 'of', 'government'], ['supreme', 'executive',
'power', 'derives', 'from', 'a', 'mandate', 'from', 'the', 'masses,', 'not', 'from',
'some', 'farcical', 'aquatic', 'ceremony']]
```

Note that this is two separate lists, each list containing its own collection of words. If we want to combine all words into the same list, we can create another type of nested list comprehension.

```
words = [w for s in sentences for w in s]
```

Although it's a little odd looking, this is valid Python syntax, with two `for` statements that are chained together. The order of this may be a little clearer if you think about it in terms of traditional `for` loops:

```
words = []
for s in sentences:
    for w in s:
        words.append(w)
```

If you start with the first `for` statement and imagine stretching the code horizontally, this reads "for s in sentences for w in s"—which is exactly how it reads when written out as a single list comprehension. We are telling Python, "I want a list that contains all elements, w . . ." then begin drilling down into describing what, exactly, w is: "`for s in sentences for w in s`."

This creates the single list of words:

```
['strange', 'women', 'lying', 'in', 'ponds', 'distributing', 'swords', 'is', 'no',
'basis', 'for', 'a', 'system', 'of', 'government', 'supreme', 'executive', 'power',
'derives', 'from', 'a', 'mandate', 'from', 'the', 'masses,', 'not', 'from', 'some',
'farcical', 'aquatic', 'ceremony']
```

There are a few duplicate words here. A common scenario in programming is removing duplicates from a list. In almost any programming language, you can use this nifty trick to get a list of only unique words:

```
words = list(set(words))
```

Remember that a Python set contains only unique elements. By casting the list to a set and casting that set back to a list again we get a list containing only unique elements. The list of unique words looks like this:

```
['supreme', 'is', 'executive', 'system', 'the', 'government', 'lying', 'farcical',
'basis', 'distributing', 'aquatic', 'no', 'some', 'ceremony', 'mandate', 'swords',
'not', 'derives', 'a', 'in', 'women', 'strange', 'from', 'for', 'of', 'power',
'masses,', 'ponds']
```

It's important to note that the original list of words starts with `'strange'`, `'women'`, `'lying'`, `'in'`, `'ponds'`. This order is lost when we convert it to a set, even if it's converted back to a list again. If it's important that the order of words be preserved when removing duplicates, you will want to use a different approach.

From here we can do things like get a collection of only short words:

```
[w for w in words if len(w) < 4]
```

or get words that start with vowels:

```
[w for w in words if w[0] in ['a', 'e', 'i', 'o', 'u']]
```

or any number of other fun things! For more fun things to do, see the exercises at the end of this chapter.

EXERCISES

Some of these exercises require some amount of starting data or setup to work with. Rather than typing everything by hand, keep in mind that you can use the exercise files in the GitHub repository accompanying this book: `https://github.com/REMitchell/unlocking-python`.

1. Generate a list of all numbers less than 100, divisible by 3, in descending order (99, 96, 93. . .).

2. Given a list of people:

```
people = [
    {'name': 'Bob', 'age': 30},
    {'name': 'Diana', 'age': 20},
    {'name': 'Alice', 'age': 40},
    {'name': 'Charlie', 'age': 10},
]
```

use Python to sort this list of people by length of their name.

3. Find a unique list of all words four characters long or less in this text from Monty Python's "Dead Parrot" sketch:

```
text = '''
It's not pining, it's passed on. This parrot is no more. It has ceased to be.
It's expired and gone to meet its maker. This is a late parrot. It's a stiff.
Bereft of life, it rests in peace. If you hadn't nailed it to the perch, it
would be pushing up the daisies. It's rung down the curtain and joined the
choir invisible. This is an ex-parrot.
'''
```

4. Write a function that takes an argument `text` and returns that same string but with every odd character in lowercase and every even character in uppercase.

Example:

Input: `'This is an ex-parrot.'`

Output: `'tHiS Is aN Ex-pArRoT.'`

Dictionaries, Sets, and Tuples

This chapter expands on many of the concepts introduced in Chapter 6, "Lists and Strings" with three new data structures: dictionaries, sets, and tuples.

Dictionaries, in particular, are invaluable in Python programming. When combined with lists, they can form any shape of data. In this chapter, we'll look at some of the more advanced forms of dictionary usage, including iterating over keys and values, working with dictionary comprehensions, and reducing dictionaries.

Although dictionaries are invaluable in Python, tuples are unavoidable. Even if you don't explicitly use this data type in your code, Python uses tuples under the hood to pass data to and from functions.

Finally, you'll learn about one of the lesser-used (and, I would argue, under-appreciated!) data types: sets. We'll work with these in both a programming and mathematical context and discuss how they can be used to solve common programming problems.

DICTIONARIES

Dictionaries contain sets of keys. Each key points to a value. Dictionaries are said to be composed of key-value pairs. This is a dictionary from Chapter 5, "Python Quickstart":

```
my_dictionary = {
    'apple': 'A red fruit',
    'banana': 'A yellow fruit',
    'cantaloupe': 'A beige melon'
}
```

Here, the keys are `'apple'`, `'banana'`, and `'cantaloupe'`. The values are `'A red fruit'`, `'A yellow fruit'`, and `'A beige melon'`.

As with lists, you can use the `len` function on dictionaries:

```
len(my_dictionary)
```

In this case, the length is 3. The length of a dictionary is always equal to the number of keys it has. You can access the keys of a dictionary using the `keys` method:

```
my_dictionary.keys()
```

This returns a `dict_keys` object containing the following keys:

```
dict_keys(['apple', 'banana', 'cantaloupe'])
```

Like sets, `dict_keys` objects are iterable but not subscriptable. You can iterate through them in a `for` loop:

```
for key in my_dictionary.keys():
    print(key)
```

However, you cannot access an individual key by index:

```
my_dictionary.keys()[0]
```

Similarly, you can access the values of a dictionary using the `values` method:

```
my_dictionary.values()
```

This returns a `dict_values` object containing these values:

```
dict_values(['A red fruit', 'A yellow fruit', 'A beige melon'])
```

Like `sets` and `dict_keys`, `dict_value` objects are iterable but not subscriptable. Along with keys and values, you can access the key-value pairs of a dictionary using the `items` method:

```
my_dictionary.items()
```

This returns, as you might have guessed, a `dict_items` object containing key-value pairs:

```
dict_items([('apple', 'A red fruit'), ('banana', 'A yellow fruit'), ('cantaloupe',
'A beige melon')])
```

And, if you're following the pattern, you've likely guessed this already, but this `dict_items` object is iterable but not subscriptable. Each element in the `dict_items` object is a tuple, consisting of the key and the value. You can iterate through items of a dictionary like this:

```
for item in my_dictionary.items():
    print(f'key: {item[0]}, value: {item[1]}')
```

You can also iterate through items of a dictionary like this:

```
for key, value in my_dictionary.items():
    print(f'key: {key}, value: {value}')
```

Both versions of this code do the exact same thing; however, the second version is somewhat easier to read because it extracts the values in the `item` tuple into two more descriptive variables: key and value. This is called *unpacking*, and it can be done with any iterable object. For example, you can unpack the elements of a string into three separate variables:

```
a, b, c = ['a', 'b', 'c']
```

This sets the variable a to the string `'a'`, the variable b to the string `'b'`, etc. A word of caution when you unpack values: You must make sure that the number of variables on the left-hand side of the assignment operator is equal to the number of elements in the iterable object to the right. If these counts don't match up, you'll get a `ValueError`. For example:

```
a, b, c = ['a', 'b', 'c', 'd']
```

results in the error:

```
ValueError: too many values to unpack (expected 3)
```

However, in our example with items in a dictionary, we know that there are always exactly two elements (the key and the value) to unpack in every tuple of the `dict_items` object, so we're safe from `ValueErrors`.

If `for key, value in my_dictionary.items()` looks a little strange at first, imagine it written like this:

```
for item in my_dictionary.items():
    key, value = item
    print(f'key: {key}, value: {value}')
```

Rather than making the assignment `key, value = item` in a separate line, we save a little space and make it more elegant by doing both the unpacking and assignment within the `for` statement.

The keys, values, and items methods are great for getting ahold of all the data from a dictionary, but what if we're interested in just a single value? Sure, you can do this:

```
my_dictionary['apple']
```

But you run into a problem if you attempt something like this:

```
my_dictionary['dragonfruit']
```

In this case, the key `'dragonfruit'` is not found in the dictionary and you get a `KeyError`:

```
KeyError: 'dragonfruit'
```

These `KeyErrors` can be avoided using the get method:

```
my_dictionary.get('dragonfruit')
```

The get method returns a `None` value if the key given does not exist in the dictionary. If the key does exist, it will return the corresponding value. If you don't want `None` to be returned, you can also provide it with a default value to return in the case of missing keys:

```
my_dictionary.get('dragonfruit', 'Missing definition')
```

All the methods we've seen so far read values from the dictionary. For modifying the dictionary, of course you can always add and modify individual values in the following way:

```
my_dictionary['apple'] = 'A red or green fruit'
my_dictionary['dragonfruit'] = 'Comes from a cactus'
```

In some situations, you may want to add several values to the dictionary at once. You can add the values from one dictionary to another dictionary using the update method:

```
additional_fruits = {
    'elderberry': 'Good for jam',
    'fig': 'Pollinated by wasps',
    'grape': 'Mostly grown for wine'
}
my_dictionary.update(additional_fruits)
print(my_dictionary)
```

This updates the keys and values in my_dictionary with the information in additional_fruits. After this update is performed, we can see that the new value of my_dictionary contains the new fruits:

```
{'apple': 'A red or green fruit',
 'banana': 'A yellow fruit',
 'cantaloupe': 'A beige melon',
 'dragonfruit': 'Comes from a cactus',
 'elderberry': 'Good for jam',
 'fig': 'Pollinated by wasps',
 'grape': 'Mostly grown for wine'}
```

It's important to note that, if you perform an update with a dictionary that contains an existing key, the value will be overwritten:

```
additional_fruits = {'banana': 'Likely originated from New Guinea'}
my_dictionary.update(additional_fruits)
print(my_dictionary['banana'])
```

This prints the new value:

```
Likely originated from New Guinea
```

When using the update method, you must be very careful about what keys the new dictionary contains and whether or not you're okay overwriting values if there's a match.

Dictionary Comprehensions

As with lists, you can create a dictionary from a *dictionary comprehension*:

```
names = ['Alice', 'Bob', 'Charlie']
names_dict = {n[0]: n for n in names}
```

With a list comprehension, we only needed to declare one element for each position in the list. Now, of course, we have to worry about two of them: the key and the value. Here, I'm using n[0] (the first character of each name) to represent the key and n (the name) for the value. This creates the dictionary:

```
{'A': 'Alice', 'B': 'Bob', 'C': 'Charlie'}
```

Just like list comprehensions, any iterable can be used to generate a dictionary. This dictionary uses integers as keys and maps every number from 0 to 99 onto a value that is two times that number:

```
doubles = {n: n*2 for n in range(0, 100)}
```

You can also use `if` statements to filter dictionaries:

```
doubles = {n: n*2 for n in range(0, 100) if n % 10 == 0}
```

This creates a dictionary containing only multiples of 10 as the keys.

One fundamental difference between dictionary comprehensions and list comprehensions is that a list comprehension without using any filtering will always create a list of equal size to its inputs. There is always a 1-to-1 mapping. For example:

```
ten_elements = [0, 1, 2, 3, 4, 5, 6, 7, 8, 9]
new_list = [any_function(e) for e in ten_elements]
```

Although `any_function` isn't defined, you can imagine it as any function at all. It might return a value; it might return `None`. Regardless, we can be certain that the length of the resulting list, `new_list`, will always be 10.

The same cannot be said for a similar dictionary comprehension:

```
ten_elements = [0, 1, 2, 3, 4, 5, 6, 7, 8, 9]
new_dict = {
    any_key_function(e) : any_val_function(e)
    for e in ten_elements
}
```

In this case, if `any_key_function` maps values in a one-to-one way, then the dictionary will have 10 unique keys and have a length of 10. This function definition creates a dictionary with length 10:

```
def any_key_function(e):
    return e
```

However, if `any_key_function` is defined such that different inputs can map to the same output (many-to-one), the dictionary is liable to have a shorter length because the keys will overwrite each other:

```
def any_key_function(e):
    return e % 2

def any_val_function(e):
    return e
```

Here, `any_val_function` simply returns the original number. This version of `any_key_function` returns a modulo of the input, mapping it to either a 0 or a 1. This will create a dictionary of length 2:

```
{0: 8, 1: 9}
```

Notice that the values in the dictionary are 8 and 9—the last two values created in the dictionary comprehension. Values set with existing keys will always overwrite the previous values at those keys.

Reducing to Dictionaries

There are certain situations where you may want to iterate over a list and then produce a dictionary as your output, but you do not want to use a dictionary comprehension to do that—for example, when you are creating counts out of a list of values, taking a list like this:

```
chars = ['a', 'b', 'a', 'c', 'a', 'a', 'b']
```

and producing a dictionary of counts representing how many times each character was seen in the list:

```
{'a': 4, 'b': 2, 'c': 1}
```

This operation is called a *reduction* in computer science because it reduces the elements of a long list into a shorter summary. Some other examples of reduction might be finding the sum of a list of numbers, or finding the largest value in a list.

Let's look at one way to solve the problem of counting characters in a list:

```
chars_count = {}
for char in chars:
    if char not in chars_count:
        chars_count[char] = 0
    chars_count[char] += 1

print(chars_count)
```

In every reduction problem there is always an accumulator. This is what holds the values (and, eventually, the final result) as you're working through the list. In this case, `chars_count` is the accumulator.

Then we iterate through the list `chars` using `for char in chars`. Each time we encounter a new character, it must be added to the `chars_count` dictionary. If the `char` is not in the `chars_count` dictionary, we add a new entry with an initial count of 0 using `chars_count[char] = 0`. Then, for all characters encountered (whether or not it was newly added), we can increment the count using `chars_count[char] += 1`.

There is one slightly clever optimization on this solution using the `get` method:

```
chars_count = {}
for char in chars:
    chars_count[char] = chars_count.get(char, 0) + 1
print(chars_count)
```

This eliminates the need to check each time whether or not `char` is in the `chars_count` dictionary.

Alternatively, you can use a Python object called a `defaultdict` to solve this problem. The `defaultdict` is in the built-in `collections` package. While it comes with Python automatically and you don't have to install anything, it must be specifically imported in your code before you can use it.

When a key is used in a `defaultdict` that does not currently exist in the dictionary, it does not raise a `KeyError` and terminate the program like a regular dictionary would. Instead, it adds the key to itself and creates a new value of a certain type. What type this value is must be declared when you create the dictionary.

For example:

```
dict_of_lists = defaultdict(list)
print(dict_of_lists['new_key'])
```

Here, we are creating a new `defaultdict` with the type `list` passed into its initializer. When we try to access a new key, `'new_key'`, that does not yet exist in the dictionary, it simply adds the key and sets its value to `list()` (calling whatever was passed into the initializer and instantiating a new object). This code will print an empty list `[]`.

Back to our original problem of reducing a list of characters to a dictionary containing characters and their counts, it's useful to know that when a new integer is created by calling the `int` type:

```
new_int = int()
```

that integer will have a default value of 0. This makes it easy to rewrite our reduction using the `defaultdict`:

```
chars_count = defaultdict(int)
for char in chars:
    chars_count[char] = chars_count[char] + 1
```

Next is a function that may not seem overly elegant at first glance but that is extremely powerful and can keep things tidy when reductions get more complicated. That is the `reduce` function in the built-in Python package `functools`. It provides everything you need to cleanly lay out your reduction algorithms:

```
from functools import reduce

def increment_count(chars_count, char):
    chars_count[char] = chars_count.get(char, 0) + 1
    return chars_count

reduce(increment_count, chars, {})
```

The function `increment_count` has the arguments `chars_count` (our count dictionary) and `char` (a single element from the list). Although you have the freedom to write your accumulation function however you want, it must take as its arguments an accumulator and an element from the list, in that order.

The function `increment_count` itself is passed to the `reduce` function, along with the list of `chars` and an empty dictionary (the starting point for the accumulator). The `reduce` function returns the expected output:

```
{'a': 4, 'b': 2, 'c': 1}
```

Finally, there is a fourth solution that, while not universally applicable to every reduction problem, has a certain appealing brevity when it comes to counting the appearances of items in a list. That is the `Counter`, again from the `collections` package.

```
from collections import Counter
Counter(chars)
```

This will return a `Counter` object, which can be used exactly like a dictionary and contains our counted characters:

```
Counter({'a': 4, 'b': 2, 'c': 1})
```

SETS

Sets contain values that are unique and unordered. We saw this in action when using a set to remove duplicates from a list:

```
letters = ['a', 'a', 'b', 'c', 'c', 'c', 'd', 'd', ]
letters = list(set(letters))
```

Converting a list to a set and then back again to remove duplicates is a nifty trick, but it does result in a list that may be out of order compared to what you were expecting:

```
['a', 'd', 'b', 'c']
```

One other side effect of unordered sequences is that comparisons can look a little funny:

```
{1, 2} == {2, 1}
```

This is `True`. Because the order of elements in a set doesn't matter, the set {1, 2} is equal to the set {2, 1}. Similarly, this is also `True`:

```
{1, 2, 1, 1} == {2, 1}
```

A set that contains only 1s and 2s is always equal to another set that contains only 1s and 2s. Adding a 3, of course, creates a different set, so this statement is `False`:

```
{1, 2, 1, 1} == {2, 1, 3}
```

The name "set" itself refers to the mathematical concept of a set. There are four operations in Python that are unique to sets and that you might recognize from their counterparts in set theory:

➤ Union

➤ Intersection

➤ Difference

➤ Symmetric difference

Each of these operations is performed on two sets and produces a third set as its result. A *union* of two sets is the set of all elements that are in either set. In mathematics, you might see this operation written as A ∪ B, where A and B are sets, and the ∪ is a union operator.

In Python, you can use the `union` method:

```
a = {1, 2, 3}
b = {3, 4, 5}
a.union(b) == {1, 2, 3, 4, 5}
```

Note that unions are *commutative*. "Commutative" is a fancy math word that means that the result will always be the same even if the operands (values to which the operator is applied) are reversed:

```
# True for any value of 'a' and 'b'
a.union(b) == b.union(a)
```

The next set-specific operation is the *intersection*. The intersection of two sets is the set of elements that are in both sets. In mathematics, this is represented by an upside-down union operator (∩), as in A ∩ B. In Python, you can use the intersection method:

```
a = {1, 2, 3}
b = {3, 4, 5}

a.intersection(b) == {3}
```

Or you can use the intersection operator:

```
a & b == {3}
```

The fact that an intersection is represented by an ampersand ("and symbol") is no accident. The intersection of sets a and b is the set of elements in a *and* b. Therefore, an intersection can be thought of as the set operation equivalent of the Boolean operation AND.

Similarly, if you've worked with other programming languages before, an OR operator is often represented by a pipe (|) or double pipe (||). In Python, a pipe acts as an operator for unions of sets—such as when an element is in set a *or* set b:

```
a | b == {1, 2, 3, 4, 5}
```

The next set-specific method is the *difference*. Unlike unions and intersections, differences are not commutative. The difference of two sets is the elements that exist in the first set that *do not* exist in the second set. In set theory, the difference between two sets A and B is written as either A \ B or A – B.

In Python, you can use the `difference` method:

```
a = {1, 2, 3}
b = {3, 4, 5}

a.difference(b)
```

This returns the set:

```
{1, 2}
```

As you might have guessed, there is another operator for the difference between two sets, the subtraction operator:

```
a - b
```

To illustrate the point that the order matters when it comes to using the difference operator, we can take the difference between these sets in two different ways:

```
a = {1, 2, 3}
b = {3, 4, 5}
print(f'a - b: {a - b}')
print(f'b - a: {b - a}')
```

This prints:

```
a - b: {1, 2}
b - a: {4, 5}
```

Difference is the only one of these four operations that is not commutative.

The final operation is the *symmetric difference*. The symmetric difference is often written in mathematics using a capital delta (Δ). The symmetric difference of two sets A and B, written as A Δ B, is a set containing all elements of set A and set B that do not exist in both sets.

A symmetric difference of two sets is equivalent to the union of both sets "minus" their intersection—or, rather, the difference between the union of both sets and their intersection. In mathematics:

$$A\,\Delta B = (A \cup B) - (A \cap B)$$

And in Python, we would write this as:

```
a = {1, 2, 3}
b = {3, 4, 5}
a.symmetric_difference(b) == (a.union(b)).difference(a.intersection(b))
```

Or, perhaps:

```
a ^ b == (a | b) - (a & b)
```

Note that the caret symbol (^) here is the symmetric difference operator. The reason the caret is used for symmetric difference is somewhat more obscure, and has to do with a little-used Boolean function called XOR, which stands for "exclusive or." An XOR operator returns True if exactly one of its operands is true, but will return False if both are false or if both are true. This is analogous to the symmetric difference of two sets, which contains an element if it "is true" (exists) in one set or another set, but not both.

In many programming languages, the caret is used as an XOR operator. Python also uses the caret as a *bitwise* XOR operator. However, as mentioned previously, bitwise operators are outside the scope of this book, and if you'd like to continue down this rabbit hole of Boolean logic and programming etymology (and I highly recommend that you do at some point!), you will have to look elsewhere.

TUPLES

As discussed before, tuples are, essentially, immutable lists. You can read data from them as you would a list, but you cannot add to, remove from, or modify data within them:

```
my_tuple = (1, 2, 3)
# This raises an exception
my_tuple[0] = 4
```

This lack of mutability may seem like a downside to tuples at first. Why would you want to use a data structure that is exactly like lists but lacks a key feature of lists?

The advantage of tuples is twofold. One, there is a slight improvement to memory efficiency when using tuples, particularly if you are using lots and lots of relatively small tuples in a program.

Second, there are cases where modifying data may be a bad thing. There may be cases where you want to make it very clear that data should be read and not modified, or cases where it doesn't make sense to modify the data. For example:

```
SCALING_VECTOR = (1.0, 2.5, 1.2)
```

This declares a constant vector, the values of which should not be modified. However, even if you feel that tuples are unnecessary in your own programs, you'll find that they're difficult to avoid in Python. In fact, we've used them without realizing it already in this chapter:

```
my_dictionary = {
    'apple': 'A red fruit',
    'banana': 'A yellow fruit',
    'cantaloupe': 'A beige melon'
}
for item in my_dictionary.items():
    print(f'key: {item[0]}, value: {item[1]}')
```

Instead of printing the individual elements of the dictionary item, let's print the type of this item itself:

```
for item in my_dictionary.items():
    print(type(item))
```

This type is a tuple! This makes sense, because dictionaries may have many, many entries in them. It's inefficient to create a great number of very small lists, but more efficient to create a great number of very small tuples. We know that these tuples will always have exactly two elements in them (dictionaries have keys and values and that's it—you're never going to get a third thing).

In addition, there's no real purpose to modifying the values returned from the items method. Modifying them won't modify values in the original dictionary, and it's far more common to unpack these values into individual named variables (such as key and value) anyway. In general, wanting to modify values in a function or method that returns a tuple is a sign of code smell.[1]

There are hidden tuples just about everywhere in Python. For example, you can declare multiple variables in a single line of code in this way:

```
a, b, c = 1, 2, 3
```

This assigns a to 1, b to 2, and c to 3. But what happens when we assign everything to a single variable? What is that type?

```
a = 1, 2, 3
type(a)
```

As you might have guessed, it's a tuple. You might think of tuples as the default data structure when no other data structure type is declared. This might have something to do with why they are declared with regular parentheses—a punctuation so common it's used across every other part of Python.

The widespread use of parentheses can cause some confusion as well. One common pitfall when trying to declare a tuple has to do with the use of parentheses as enforcement for order of operations. For example:

```
a = (2 + 3) * 3
```

---

[1] "Code smell" is a term used to describe structures or patterns in code that seem somewhat. . . off. A little funky. Code smell does not indicate a bug, but it may indicate that the code is difficult to work with and may cause technical debt down the road. The ability to smell code is developed with time and practice. Often, an experienced developer will catch a whiff of something rotten at a glance, and then spend several minutes digging down to pinpoint exactly what caused this immediate visceral reaction. It's considered impolite (and it's generally not useful) to tell someone "Your code smells." However, you should use "code smell" as a label for that feeling you get when you see code smell, which is a signal to investigate further and offer more concrete and helpful suggestions.

Without parentheses, the `3 * 3` would be calculated first, leading to a result of `11` rather than `15`. With that in mind, what is this?

```
a = (3)
```

Is this a tuple of length 1, or simply overzealous use of parentheses? Python has decided that it's the latter, and that the variable a is simply an integer 3. If you do need to declare a tuple with a single element, make sure you add a trailing comma to enforce that it's a tuple:

```
a = (3,)
```

EXERCISES

1. Without writing or running any code (unless you really want to), determine the resulting set from each of these lines:

   ```
   {'a', 'm'}.union({'p', 'm'})
   ```

   ```
   {'a', 'm'}.intersection({'p', 'm'})
   ```

   ```
   {'a', 'm'}.difference({'p', 'm'})
   ```

   ```
   {'a', 'm'}.symmetric_difference({'p', 'm'})
   ```

2. Write a function that converts a set of lowercase words into a dictionary that contains the original lowercase word as a key, with the uppercase version of the word as a value.

3. Using the excerpt from the "Dead Parrot" sketch in Chapter 5 (or some other piece of text that you prefer), create a dictionary where the keys are words in that text and the value is how many times that word appears.

   Be careful: Capitalized words that start a sentence should be counted as the same word as their lowercase version. In addition, you will want to ignore punctuation (such as commas and periods) that might cause words to be incorrectly counted. The string `'pining,'` is simply the word `'pining'`—not a unique word that ends in a comma. Consider using the `replace` or `strip` methods for this.

4. Write a function that takes, as its argument, a string, and returns a dictionary containing the first character of the string as its only key and its value is another dictionary with the second character as its key, pointing to another dictionary containing the third character as its key, and so forth.

   This is a data structure that is difficult to describe but easier to explain using examples. If the argument is the word `'ant'`, the returned dictionary is:

   ```
   {'a': {'n': {'t': None}}}
   ```

   If the argument is the word `'alice'`, the returned dictionary is:

   ```
   {'a': {'l': {'i': {'c': {'e': None}}}}}
   ```

   The value of the innermost dictionary is always `None`.

5. Write a function that takes, as its argument, a list of lowercase words, and returns a data structure of nested dictionaries similar to the data structure returned in question 4, but for multiple words.

Unlike the previous data structure, these dictionaries can contain multiple keys, if the multiple words contain multiple letters that go in that position.

That is, if the list of words is this:

```
['ant', 'and', 'act']
```

the nested dictionaries will look like this:

```
{
  'a': {
    'n': {
      't': None,
      'd': None
    },
    'c': {
      't': None
    }
  }
}
```

Test your function out with multiple word lists to ensure that it's working correctly.

6. Modify your function from question 5 to add an indicator when the end of a word is reached. This indicator will consist of the dictionary key 'STOP' pointing to the Boolean value True. If a dictionary contains 'STOP': True in it, you will know that a valid end of a full word has been reached.

For example, if we take the list of words in the previous problem and add the word 'ante' to it, we get the dictionary:

```
{
  'a': {
    'n': {
      't': {
        'STOP': True,
        'e': {'STOP': True}
      },
      'd': {'STOP': True}
    },
    'c': {
      't': {'STOP': True}
    }
  }
}
```

Once you have your dictionary generated from a set of words, verify that the following function correctly determines whether a word existed in the original word list, based on your dictionary and the word in question:

```
def word_exists(word, word_dict):
    current_level = word_dict
    for char in word:
        if char not in current_level:
            return False
        current_level = current_level[char]
    return current_level.get('STOP', False)
```

This data structure you created is similar to a *trie* in computer science; see https://en.wikipedia.org/wiki/Trie.

8

Other Types of Objects

So far in this book we've encountered many classes that let you create useful object instances. These include:

- ➤ `str` (String)
- ➤ `float`
- ➤ `int` (Integer)
- ➤ `dict` (Dictionary)
    - ➤ `Counter`
    - ➤ `defaultdict`
- ➤ `set`
- ➤ `tuple`

These are the real workhorses of Python and the types of objects you will be using day in and day out. But there a few others that are worth knowing about.

Some classes, like `datetime`, are crucial for building applications. You are almost certain to work with dates at some point in your career.

Other classes, like complex numbers, you may never use at all. But if you don't know about them, you're liable to occasionally run into confusing situations when working with square roots. They're also just fun, and, in my opinion, reveal interesting things about the inner workings of Python, computers, and mathematics.

OTHER NUMBERS

Between integers and floats, Python has everything on the number line covered. But what about numbers off the number line? If you remember from algebra, the square root of a negative number is an *imaginary number*. Imaginary numbers are often represented by the letter *i*. For example:

$$\sqrt{-1} = i$$

The square root of negative one is equal to *i*. Remember that everything in algebra has an invisible coefficient of 1, so this can also be read as:

$$\sqrt{-1} = 1i$$

Similarly:

$$\sqrt{-4} = 2i$$

In engineering, particularly electrical engineering, the imaginary number is represented by *j* instead of *i*. This is a convention that Python also follows.[1] When an issue was raised in 2011 to potentially change *j* to the more familiar *i*, Guido Van Rossum weighed in:

> *This will not be fixed. For one thing, the letter 'i' or upper case 'I' look too much like digits. The way numbers are parsed either by the language parser (in source code) or by the built-in functions (int, float, complex) should not be localizable or configurable in any way; that's asking for huge disappointments down the road. If you want to parse complex numbers using 'i' instead of 'j', you have plenty of solutions available already.*
>
> https://bugs.python.org/msg148083

This is an example of an imaginary number in Python:

```
imaginary = 2j
```

It's important to know that the letter j is not a *reserved word* (or *reserved keyword*) in Python. Some words, like None, for, and def are reserved and cannot be used as variable names. But j can be used as a variable name all you want. For instance:

```
for i, j in some_dictionary.items():
    print(i, j)
```

But this also means that you cannot simply type j and expect it to be recognized as an imaginary number. That will result in an error: NameError: name 'j' is not defined. If you want to declare an "imaginary 1" you need to explicitly write a number 1 in front of the j:

```
imaginary = 1j
```

---

[1] You may be surprised to learn that imaginary numbers are frequently used in electrical engineering. I don't want to imply that electricity is imaginary, but, suspiciously, imaginary numbers turn out to be a very useful tool for simplifying many electrical equations. However, electrical engineers can't use *i* for imaginary numbers because *i* is already used to represent electrical current. The electrical current "*i*," of course, represents *amperes*.

This is because of French physicist André-Marie Ampère, who used the symbol *i*—not for his own namesake unit (which would not be established until 50 years after his death)—but for the phrase *intensité du courant,* or "current intensity."

At any rate, using *i* for imaginary numbers would make the situation very confusing, so electrical engineers use its alphabetical neighbor *j* instead. Despite what Guido van Rossum claims about why he used *j* instead of *i*, I suspect that he, like British comedy troupe Monty Python, mostly wanted to highlight the silliness of the French.

Imaginary numbers have the type `complex` in Python because they support the mathematical concept of *complex numbers*, which have both a real and an imaginary component. Python handles complex numbers using a straightforward syntax:

```
cnum = 5 + 2j
```

It's important to note that, although `5 + 2j` looks like an expression with two distinct numbers joined by an addition operator, there is really nothing here to "calculate." This is the simplest representation of a single complex number. We can use the `type` function:

```
type(5 + 2j)
```

which returns the type `complex`.

Be careful when using Python to do calculations that result in complex numbers. For example, the `math` library does not do well with complex numbers:

```
import math

math.sqrt(-1)
```

This causes an error:

```
ValueError: math domain error
```

Instead, the Python `cmath` library should be used for complex math:

```
import cmath

cmath.sqrt(-1)
```

This returns the complex number:

```
1j
```

While there is no operator in Python for radical expressions or "roots," you may recall another fun math fact from algebra: The nth root of a number is equal to that number raised to the $\frac{1}{n}$ power. For example:

$$\sqrt{x} = x^{1/2}$$

So, in theory, we don't need the `cmath` library at all to get Python to return complex numbers. We can do something like this:

```
(-9) ** (1/2)
```

The square root of 9 is 3;[2] therefore, the square root of negative 9 should be 3*i*. Instead, Python returns this extremely complex number:

```
(1.8369701987210297e-16+3j)
```

The complex part of this number, at the end, is `3j` like we would expect, but the real (non-imaginary) part of the number is `1.8369701987210297e-16`. This is scientific notation, which Python uses when numbers get smaller than `0.0001`. That is, any number with 5 or more zeroes will get represented

---

[2] Technically, 9 has two square roots: -3, and 3. This fact is, rightfully, ignored by Python, but it seems worth at least acknowledging while we're talking about complex numbers.

using scientific notation. The e here is a shorthand meaning "10 to the power of" followed by a -16. So this number is approximately:

$$1.8 \times 10^{-16}$$

When written out without scientific notation, this number is:

$$.00000000000000018$$

That's 16 zeroes—a very small number. But why does it exist at all? The statement (-9)**(1/2) should evaluate to *exactly* 3j, not (very very small real number) + 3j.

The answer has to do with how Python calculates floats. It suffers from a problem that most programming languages do, which is *floating-point errors*. The easiest way to see a floating-point error is with a simple statement like this:

    1.1 + 2.2

which evaluates to:

    3.3000000000000003

Floating-point errors don't always add a tiny bit—sometimes they subtract it. For example:

    100.1 + 200.2

returns the sum:

    300.29999999999995

The exact values you get may differ based on your operating system and version of Python, but play around with floats for long enough and you'll see floating-point errors. This is because when Python stores the numbers to the right of the decimal point, it does not store them as literally the number 2 or the number 3, etc. Instead, it stores the values as sums of fractions.

Remember that Python stores whole integers like 123 as binary numbers. 123 becomes 01111011. However, 123 is not the same thing as 0.123 at all. For the decimal part of the number, Python encodes it as a sum of reciprocals of powers of 2. Summing reciprocal powers of 2 looks like this:

$$\frac{1}{2} + \frac{1}{4} + \frac{1}{8} + \frac{1}{16} + \frac{1}{32} + \frac{1}{64} + \frac{1}{128} + \frac{1}{256} \ldots$$

This is the first eight fractions that are reciprocal powers of 2. We can write binary numbers like 10101010 where a 1 turns a fraction "on" and adds it to our total, and a 0 turns a fraction "off" and does not add it to our total. Under this system, the binary number 10101010 would represent:

$$\frac{1}{2} + \frac{1}{8} + \frac{1}{32} + \frac{1}{128}$$

or 0.6640625 exactly.

If the decimal portion of the float is represented in 8 bits as 10101010, then the decimal it represents might have actually been 0.665. Representing 0.665 with 8 bits of reciprocal fractions is extremely space-efficient and easy for a computer to do mathematical operations with, but it does lead to results that can be slightly off.

As you might have guessed, Python uses far more than 8 bits to represent the decimal portion of a number. On my computer, it uses 53 bits by default. This provides numbers that are usually accurate enough for my purposes, especially if using the built-in `round` function:

```
round(100.1 + 200.2, 2)
```

This rounds the value `100.1 + 200.2` to 2 decimal places (without any trailing zeroes) to give the correct output:

```
300.3
```

Even with rounding there are some situations in which floating-point errors can creep into your calculations. And, of course, even programmers aren't perfect and may forget to round when it's required. If you're, say, working on a banking application you may want to avoid floats, and thus the possibility of floating-point errors, entirely. You can do this with the `decimal` module.

The `decimal` module contains the `Decimal` class, which can be used to store numbers as exact values. It has no problem, for example, adding 1.1 and 2.2:

```
Decimal('1.1') + Decimal('2.2')
```

This results in the `Decimal` number:

```
Decimal('3.3')
```

Notice that the numbers 1.1 and 2.2 are passed in as strings rather than floats, like `Decimal(1.1)`. That's because `Decimal`s will faithfully record the exact value of whatever you pass in. So, if you pass in a float, you're going to get the same floating-point errors! Not using strings, like this:

```
Decimal(1.1) + Decimal(2.2)
```

will return the same artifacts that come from summing reciprocals of the powers of 2 that we saw before—but now with far more precision!

```
Decimal('3.300000000000000266453525910')
```

By default, `Decimal`s have a precision of 28 significant figures. Here, significant figures include the numbers to both the left and the right of the decimal place. The number above has 27 digits in the decimal and 1 in the whole number portion, for a total of 28. The Decimal class will also round correctly (rather than truncating) if the precision of the values they're holding exceeds that limit.

To change the precision, you can use the `getcontext` function, which sets the context *globally* (for all uses of the `Decimal` class across the program). To do this, you need to import the `getcontext` function from the `decimal` module. You can do multiple imports on the same line from the same package by separating each import with a comma:

```
from decimal import Decimal, getcontext
```

Calling `getcontext` by itself will return a `Context` object:

```
Context(prec=28, rounding=ROUND_HALF_EVEN, Emin=-999999, Emax=999999, capitals=1,
clamp=0, flags=[Inexact, FloatOperation, Rounded], traps=[InvalidOperation,
DivisionByZero, Overflow])
```

To set any of the values, such as precision, simply assign it the new integer precision that you want:

```
getcontext().prec = 5
```

Each time you call `getcontext`, it will return the same `Context` object—it does not create a new one. This means that any time you need to modify a value in the context, just call `getcontext` again. By changing the precision to 5, we change the `Decimal` values that get returned:

```
Decimal('1.1111111') + Decimal('2.222222')
```

This returns a value with 1 integer digit and 4 decimal places:

```
Decimal('3.3333')
```

Computers have a reputation for being completely accurate in their mathematical calculations. In reality, computers may be very precise, but the accuracy is entirely up to the programmer, not the computer. Floats are extremely fast and lightweight to perform calculations with, but you must be careful about their limitations. Even the `Decimal` class can have its pitfalls.

Awareness of the kinds of numbers you're working with, what they'll be used for, and having an intuitive understanding of how the math impacts their precision and accuracy is crucial for programming with numeric values.

DATES

In 2015 I was asked to write a function that received the current date as a string and performed some operation using that same date as of last year. For example, if I received the current date string `'01-15-2015'` I would need to get last year's date string `'01-15-2014'`. This is easy enough to do in Python:

```
date_str = '01-15-2015'
month, day, year = date_str.split('-')
date_last_year = f'{month}-{day}-{int(year)-1}'
```

I wrote the function quickly and never thought about it again until some months later when I walked into the office only to find that the production application wasn't displaying data to our users. It was a Monday. Not just any Monday, but a very specific Monday: February 29, 2016.

You see, this function had dutifully calculated last year's date as `'02-29-2015'` and sent it to an upstream system to fetch some data based on a date that, in fact, did not exist at all. This upstream system received this nonexistent date and raised an error that caused the application to crash.

Being presented with a "trivial" task like finding today's date last year revealed my hubris. I had violated a cardinal rule of programing: Never, ever, deal with dates or times unless you're using a library designed specifically for that purpose.

To paraphrase Humphrey Bogart in *Casablanca*: If you try to manipulate `datetime`s yourself and you're not using a library, you'll regret it. Maybe not today, maybe not next daylight-saving time, but soon, and for the rest of your life.

The Python `datetime` library takes care of all sorts of easily overlooked considerations. It contains three classes in particular:

➤ date

➤ time

➤ datetime

The date class contains attributes that allow it to represent a date on the Gregorian calendar: year, month, and day. The time class contains hour, minute, second, microsecond, and (optionally) time zone information. The datetime class, reasonably enough, contains all the information from both the date class and the time class.

Because datetime combines all the features of both date and time, this section will focus on the datetime class for convenience. However, you may want to use date or time alone depending on the needs of your application.

The import statement for datetime is, admittedly, odd-looking:

```
from datetime import datetime
```

This is importing the datetime class from the datetime library of the same name. Once it's imported, the word datetime in your Python code refers to the class only, not the datetime library.

You can instantiate a new datetime instance like this:

```
python_release = datetime(1991, 2, 20, hour=9, minute=0, second=0, microsecond=0)
```

This represents February 20, 1991 (the date Python was first released) at 9 a.m. I'm unsure of the exact time Python was released, but start of business hours seems as good as any.

Using a datetime object, you can access all the attributes of it individually as integers:

```
python_release.day
python_release.month
python_release.year
python_release.second
```

There are also calculated values you have access to, such as the day of week. To get the day of the week you can use the weekday method:

```
python_release.weekday()
```

This uses a system where Monday is considered the first day of the week, represented by an integer 0, and Sunday is the seventh day of the week, represented by integer 6. Because Python was released on a Wednesday, python_release.weekday() returns a 2.

Sometimes you're given a string and need to convert it to a datetime before you can do anything with it. That string might look like this:

```
python_release = '02-20-1991 09:00:00'
```

To convert this string to a datetime object, you need to tell Python what the format of the string is. This involves using special format codes that indicate which characters in the string represent the years, months, days, etc.

For example, the format for the date `'02-20-1991 09:00:00'` is `'%m-%d-%Y %H:%M:%S'`. The following is a list of descriptions from the Python documentation for these characters:

➤   `%m`—Month as a zero-padded decimal number

➤   `%d`—Day of the month as a zero-padded decimal number

➤   `%Y`—Year with century as a decimal number

➤   `%H`—Hour (24-hour clock) as a zero-added decimal number

➤   `%M`—Minute as a zero-padded decimal number

➤   `%S`—Second as a zero-padded decimal number

Just about any date and time format you can think of can be represented with these format codes. For example, full month names, days of the week, and even names across multiple languages can be recognized. A full list of format codes can be found at `https://docs.python.org/3/library/datetime.html#strftime-and-strptime-format-codes`.

Once you've created the format code string, you can use the `strptime` method to convert strings into `datetime` objects:

```
datetime.strptime('02-20-1991 09:00:00', '%m-%d-%Y %H:%M:%S')
```

This returns the `datetime`:

```
datetime.datetime(1991, 2, 20, 9, 0)
```

You can go the other way as well, using the `strftime` method and convert the `datetime` objects back into strings. This is useful for displaying dates to users or converting them to a specific format required for storage. Notice that the `strftime` method is called on the `datetime` instance itself, rather than on the `datetime` class like with `strptime`. It takes only one argument, the format code string:

```
python_release.strftime('%A %B %d, %Y')
```

This returns a date formatted with the full day of the week, full month name, day of month, and year:

```
'Wednesday February 20, 1991'
```

To get the current `datetime`, you can use the now method:

```
datetime.now()
```

This returns a `datetime` object representing the current system time on your computer. Let's say we want to see how long ago Python was released. There are a few ways to do this. One way is to convert each `datetime` object to seconds and then do the math.

What does it mean to convert a `datetime` into seconds? As discussed in Chapter 1, "Introduction to Programming," most computers store time as the number of seconds from January 1, 1970 at 00:00:00. For dates before January 1, 1970, the time is stored as negative seconds. You can view these seconds using the `timestamp` method:

```
python_release = datetime.strptime('02-20-1991 09:00:00', '%m-%d-%Y %H:%M:%S')
python_release.timestamp()
```

This will provide you with the number of seconds after January 1, 1970 that Python was released at:

```
667058400.0
```

Using subtraction, we can get the number of seconds between the Python release date and today's date:

```
datetime.now().timestamp() - python_release.timestamp()
```

As of this writing, that would be `1050220142` seconds. How do you convert this number into something more useful, such as days or years? While theater buffs might know that there are 525,600 minutes in a year, this is not required knowledge for programming. The `timedelta` class[3] handles (some of) those details for you.

```
from datetime import timedelta

timedelta(seconds=1050220142.143286)
```

This returns a `timedelta` object:

```
datetime.timedelta(days=12155, seconds=28142, microseconds=143286)
```

Notice that it contains days, seconds, and microseconds but doesn't have years or months associated with it. That is because years and months are variable and somewhat ambiguous. If the current date is July 15, 2024, what does "0.5 years ago" mean? Does that mean 6 months ago on January 15, 2024, or does that mean 183 days before (remember, 2024 was a leap year with 366 days in it) on January 14, 2024?

The `timedelta` class ignores these details entirely and deals only with static, concrete units of time. "1 day" does not change, but "1 month" could be anything from 28 to 31 days long. If you want to get an approximate number of years from a `timedelta` object, you can always divide the days by 365.25 to account for leap years every fourth year:

```
td = timedelta(seconds=1050220142.143286)
td.days / 365.25
```

This returns approximately 33.28 years.

You can also create time deltas from two `datetime` objects directly, without needing to go through the intermediate step of creating epoch times. Subtraction is a supported operation between two `datetime` objects:

```
datetime.now() - python_release
```

This also returns a `timedelta` object showing how long ago Python was released.

Remember that the release date we used operated under the assumption that Guido van Rossum released Python at 9 a.m. This is a fine assumption to make, but it's important to note that he released it while living in Amsterdam, on Central European Time. I, personally, live in Boston which is on Eastern Time. These two time zones are, as of this writing, 6 hours apart. This means that when Guido released Python at 9 a.m., it would have been 3 a.m. in Boston and we should really be adding another 21,600 seconds to the `timedelta` for complete accuracy.

---

[3] The word "delta" in `timedelta` refers to the Greek letter delta, which is often used in science and engineering to mean "change" or "difference."

Well, not quite. Because right now it's summer in Boston and Python was released in the winter! Amsterdam operates on Central European Time (CET) from the end of October through the end of March, and then is on Central European Summer Time (CEST) for the rest of the year. Boston, similarly, is on Eastern Standard Time from early November through mid-March and then Eastern Daylight Time the rest of the year.

Different time zones shift differently at different times of year, and some don't shift at all. When you're comparing dates in different places across different seasons, you don't want to have to deal with any of this.

Python 3.9 introduced the zoneinfo module, which allows you to associate datetimes with IANA[4] time zones. As of this writing there are 529 of these zones, which designate regions where all the clocks have historically agreed with each other. This allows you to associate a datetime with a particular region and calculate its correct UTC offset.

For example:

```
from zoneinfo import ZoneInfo

python_release = datetime(1991, 2, 20, hour=9, tzinfo=ZoneInfo('Europe/Amsterdam'))
```

This creates a ZoneInfo object for Amsterdam and passes it to the datetime using the keyword tzinfo. To see the UTC offset associated with this datetime, you can use the utcoffset method:

```
python_release.utcoffset()
```

This returns the UTC offset in seconds as a timedelta object:

```
datetime.timedelta(seconds=3600)
```

In this case, the UTC offset is 3,600 seconds, or 1 hour. This is the offset UTC+1:00. If we use a datetime using the same ZoneInfo but at a different time of year, we may get a different offset:

```
dt = datetime(1991, 7, 20, hour=9, tzinfo=ZoneInfo('Europe/Amsterdam'))
dt.utcoffset()
```

With a datetime in July, the offset is 7,200 seconds, or UTC+2:00, because of Central European Summer Time.

You can see a complete list of time zones using the available_timezones function:

```
from zoneinfo import available_timezones

available_timezones()
```

As a reminder, there are 529 time zones, so it is a big list! If you prefer to set the UTC offset for a datetime directly yourself, you can do that as well using the timezone class:

```
from datetime import timezone

utc_1_timezone = timezone(timedelta(hours=1))
python_release = datetime(1991, 2, 20, hour=9, tzinfo=utc_1_timezone)
python_release.utcoffset()
```

---

[4] The Internet Assigned Numbers Authority (IANA) is responsible for tracking a great many things that helps the internet run. One of these things is time zones: www.iana.org/time-zones.

This returns the same offset that using the `ZoneInfo` class did:

```
datetime.timedelta(seconds=3600)
```

However, you should always be careful when setting the offset manually because it does not account for offset changes that might occur in the spring or fall.

BYTES

Every value in Python has a type associated with it. This type information tells Python what can and cannot be done with the value, and what different bits in the value mean. But what if we don't want to use the type data (at least not at the moment), and we simply want to treat it as a raw, meaningless expanse of 1s and 0s?

For this, you need a `bytes` object. Yes, technically, `bytes` objects do have the Python type `bytes`. And that type comes with instructions for how the values can be used and manipulated, just like every other Python type. However, it can be useful to think of the data values within bytes, on a less technical and more philosophical level, as being "typeless." You don't care what bytes are, you don't want to perform math operations on them or check if they're vowels—it's all just data.

To create a `bytes` object, you can instantiate it with the built-in class `bytes`:

```
bytes(4)
```

This looks a lot like we're converting the integer 4 into bytes. With most other classes in Python, that would be true! For example, `str(4)` creates the string `'4'` and `float(4)` creates the float `4.0`. However, bytes behave a little differently. The statement `bytes(4)` instantiates an empty series of bytes that is 4 bytes long:

```
b'\x00\x00\x00\x00'
```

HEXADECIMAL AND BYTES

"Hexadecimal" is base 16. That's "hex" like "hexagons" (6 sides, right?) and "decimal" like our good old-fashioned base 10. Stick those two together and you have 16!

In binary, or base 2, every position in the number has two possible characters: either a 0 or a 1. That's it.

In decimal, or base 10, every position in the number has 10 possible characters: the digits 0 through 9.

In hexadecimal, or base 16, every position in the number has 16 possible characters! Technically, these characters can be anything at all, but computer scientists like to use the numbers 0 through 9 followed by the first six letters of the alphabet. In this system each of the decimal numbers represent themselves, followed by a (10), b (11), c (12), d (13), e (14), and f (15).

continues

continued

As an example, let's convert the hexadecimal number fab to decimal. Starting from the smallest (least significant) position, the b is in the 1's place. A b corresponds to the decimal value 11.

Next, the a is in the 16's place. Remember that binary has the twos place and decimal has the tens place. Hexadecimal has the corresponding sixteens place! An a represents the decimal number 10, so we multiply 10 × 16 and add it to our 11 from the ones place. In Python, it looks like this:

```
10 * 16 + 11
```

Finally, the f is in the 256's place. In binary, the third position from the right is the 2^2, or fours, place. In decimal, it's the 10^2, or hundreds, place. In base 16, this is the 16^2, or 256ths, place. Because the character f corresponds to 15, our final statement for determining the decimal value of fab is:

```
15 * 256 + 10 * 16 + 11
```

Therefore, hexadecimal fab is decimal 4011. Great! But what does hexadecimal have to do with bytes? Well, a single hexadecimal character has 16 different possibilities. This is equivalent to 4 bits, or four binary characters. Therefore, we can represent four binary characters with a single hexadecimal character.

If we add on a second hexadecimal character, you can represent 256 possibilities with everything from 00, 1f, b4, all the way up to the largest two-character hexadecimal number: ff. This is equivalent to 8 bits of binary data, or 1 byte (remember that 1 byte also has 256 possible combinations).

Displaying byte data might be . . . a bit much if it's displayed in binary. For example, 4 bytes of binary data looks like this:

```
11110000 10011111 10010000 10001101
```

The same 4 bytes of hexadecimal data looks like this:

```
f0 9f 90 8d
```

The second version is much less likely to make your eyes glaze over and fill your screen up if printed out. This is why Python, like just about every other programming language and computer system, displays binary data as hexadecimal.

This looks a little like a string surrounded with single quotes; however, the b in the front gives it away as a bytes object. The \x indicates a set of two hexadecimal characters representing a byte.

If we want to create a bytes object with populated data, we need to instantiate the bytes object with both our value and the method used to encode that value so that Python can correctly extract the bytes. For example, we can convert strings to bytes objects:

```
floppy = bytes('💾', 'utf-8')
```

Here, I have a string of length 1, containing only the emoji for an obsolete magnetic storage device known as a "floppy disk." In the utf-8 (or Unicode Transformation Format – 8-bit) character encoding, most of the English characters we use every day are only 1 byte in length. However, emojis take more bytes per character to encode (for more information about this see Chapter 5, "Python Quickstart"). We can see that the floppy variable is a `bytes` object 4 bytes in length:

```
b'\xf0\x9f\x92\xbe'
```

To go the other way and turn a `bytes` object back into a string, we can use the `decode` method:

```
floppy.decode('utf-8')
```

Although the default encoding for the `decode` method is `'utf-8'` and this is equivalent to calling, simply, `floppy.decode()`, I prefer to explicitly pass `'utf-8'` so that it's clear what's going on. Regardless of what you choose to do, this returns the original emoji:

'💾'

If you want to manipulate and create bytes by hand, one useful tool is the `int` class. You can create a new integer from any base numbering system by providing your number as a string, followed by the integer indicating the base the string should be interpreted as. For example, this creates an integer from the base 16 number `fab`:

```
int('fab', 16)
```

If we look at the value of the resulting integer (regardless of the base they were instantiated from, all integers are printed to the screen in base 10) we see the correct value:

```
4011
```

Back to the floppy example, let's try to replace the last byte of data `'\xbe'` with the byte `'\xbf'`. `bytes` objects can be accessed one element at a time and printed:

```
for b in floppy:
    print(b)
```

Unfortunately, `bytes` objects are immutable. Trying to modify the values directly, as in this:

```
floppy[3] = int('bf', 16)
```

results in the error:

```
TypeError: 'bytes' object does not support item assignment
```

However, the Python type `bytearray`, which has much the same interface and syntax as `bytes`, does support modification:

```
floppy = bytearray('💾', 'utf-8')
floppy[3] = int('bf', 16)
floppy.decode('utf-8')
```

By incrementing the data in our floppy emoji and decoding it back to utf-8, we find that we have upgraded to the CD-ROM:

'💿'

For the most part, you will not be performing these sorts of operations on `bytearrays` or closely examining the contents of bytes. For many programmers, `bytes` objects are something they might stumble across when using a third-party library, say, to transmit data across SSH. They might print out a response, see that it has a b in front of it, and be alerted to the fact that this data requires an encoding to interpret.

Other programmers may enjoy generating bytes objects and strive to squeeze just a few more bits of storage efficiency out of every output.

Understanding the purpose of bytes and knowing a few tricks for working with them will serve you well regardless of where your programming journey takes you.

EXERCISES

1. Recall that I once caused a bug in production by using a suspect method of subtracting one and passing the invalid date February 29, 2015 to an upstream service. What would be a better way to do this? If it's currently February 29, 2016, what does "one year ago" mean? (Note: There are two right answers, and you can do whatever makes sense for you).

    Use `timedelta` to write a function that subtracts one year from a `datetime` object and returns the new `datetime`.

2. Quadratic equations are equations of the form:

$$ax^2 + bx + c = 0$$

    There are usually two possible solutions for x that make this equation true (unless both solutions are the same, in which case there is just one solution). Both solutions can be found using this formula:

$$x = \frac{-b \pm \sqrt{b^2 - 4ac}}{2a}$$

    Here, the sign $\pm$ indicates that you can either add or subtract the square root statement to get a solution, so one of the solutions is:

$$x = \frac{-b + \sqrt{b^2 - 4ac}}{2a}$$

    And the second solution is:

$$x = \frac{-b - \sqrt{b^2 - 4ac}}{2a}$$

    It's important to note that if the value of $b^2 - 4ac$ is negative, then both solutions will have an imaginary component.

    Write a function that takes in the arguments a, b, and c and returns two solutions for the quadratic equation they represent.

3. Write a function that takes, as an argument, a hexadecimal string of any length and returns its integer value.

Hint:

▶ The rightmost hexadecimal character is in the ones place, or 16^0ths, place (remember that any number raised to the power 0 is 1).

▶ The second hexadecimal character from the right is in the sixteenths place, or 16^1ths, place.

▶ The third hexadecimal character from the right is in the 256ths place or 16^2ths place

▶ In general, the nth hexadecimal character from the right is in the 16^nths place.

Iterables, Iterators, Generators, and Loops

In this chapter, we're taking a deep dive into the complex relationship between iterables (like lists and strings) and loops, as well as the wide variety of both looping and iterating techniques that Python has to offer.

Obviously, we can use a loop to iterate over a list or string. That is, we might say that loops use iterables. In Python, however, we can also use loops to *define* iterables. We can encapsulate loops into iterable objects, which are iterated over in other loops. It's loops all the way down![1]

Understanding iterables and loops, and how they're handled in Python, is critical to writing clean and concise code. While your algorithm might require repetition, your code should not. You might also think about this chapter as the art of defining and using "patterns."

ITERABLES AND ITERATORS

A Python *iterable* is anything that has multiple elements in a defined order so that those elements can be traversed (or iterated across) one at a time. This includes (obviously), lists, sets, and tuples. Somewhat less obviously, it also includes strings and dictionaries.

Technically, any class that implements the `__iter__` method is an iterable. The `__iter__` method is surrounded by double underscores, like another one we've seen previously, `__init__`. Methods surrounded by double underscores are called *special methods*. Special methods are defined by the Python specification and used to implement certain core Python behaviors, like initializing a new object (in the case of `__init__`) or iterating over data (in the case of `__iter__`).

---

[1] A play on the phrase "Turtles all the way down"; see https://en.wikipedia.org/wiki/Turtles_all_the_way_down.

The __iter__ method is required by the Python specification to return an *iterator*, which is an object we use to actually perform the iteration over the iterable object.

The iterator object, returned by the __iter__ method, contains a __next__ method. This __next__ method is what's repeatedly called to retrieve the next element in the iterable itself.

If the distinction between iterable and iterator is all a little confusing, I promise you're in good company. Let's look at a concrete example using a list, which, as an iterable, has an __iter__ method:

```
numbers = [1,2,3,4,5]
numbers.__iter__
```

Normally, the __iter__ method would be called using parentheses, but by leaving off the parentheses, we can simply confirm that it exists and get a little note returned telling us what and where this thing is:

```
<method-wrapper '__iter__' of list object at 0x10631e680>
```

In this case, it's a method on the list object and its location in memory is 0x10631e680 (astute readers might recognize that as a hexadecimal value!).

Let's call the __iter__ method and examine the object that gets returned:

```
iterator = numbers.__iter__()
type(iterator)
```

The returned type is a list_iterator, which is the corresponding iterator for the iterable list. Our new iterator object has a __next__ method. When this next method is called, it will return the first value of the list:

```
iterator.__next__()
```

This returns the value 1. On subsequent calls it will return 2, 3, 4, and 5. On the sixth call, it will raise a StopIteration error:

```
StopIteration:
```

There's no message here after the name of the error because this is usually an expected error that is handled internally and does not require explanation to the user.

We can write our own iterables and iterators as well, by creating two classes and implementing the appropriate methods. Let's create a class called Fibonacci_Iterable that will allow us to iterate over the Fibonacci[2] sequence:

```
class Fibonacci_Iterable:
    def __init__(self, stop):
        self.a = -1
        self.b = 1
        self.stop = stop

    def __iter__(self):
        return Fibonacci_Iterator(self)
```

---

[2] The Fibonacci sequence is an infinite sequence starting with 0, 1, 1, 2, 3, 5, 8, 13. . . where the next number is the sum of the previous two numbers. Its invention is often credited to 13th-century Italian mathematician Leonardo Fibonacci. However, Fibonacci simply popularized the sequence in Europe from its origins in Indian mathematics as early as the 3rd century BC.

The attributes a and b will be used to keep track of the last two items of the sequence and return their sum. Here, they're initialized to –1 and 1 so that the first two elements in the sequence will be 0 (which is –1 + 1) and 1 (which is 0 + 1), not because —1 is part of the Fibonacci sequence. This is a little bit of a hack to avoid special cases with the first two elements of the sequence.

The stop attribute is set based on a number passed into the constructor and defines how long the sequence should be. The __iter__ method returns a new Fibonacci_Iterator instance with self (the Fibonacci_Iterable instance) passed into its constructor.

Here is Fibonacci_Iterator:

```
class Fibonacci_Iterator:
    def __init__(self, fib):
        self.fib = fib

    def __next__(self):
        if self.fib.stop <= 0:
            raise StopIteration()
        self.fib.stop -= 1
        temp = self.fib.b
        self.fib.b = self.fib.a + self.fib.b
        self.fib.a = temp
        return self.fib.b
```

The initializer is fairly straightforward. It takes, as an argument, a Fibonacci_Iterable instance and sets it to the attribute fib. The __next__ method is more complicated.

First, if self.fib.stop has reached zero, we should raise a StopIteration exception. The keyword raise will be covered in more detail later, but for now just know that it is the thing that makes an error happen.

At this point, we want to compute the next value in the sequence. The new value of b (which gets returned) will be the old versions of a + b. The old b becomes the new a. All of this switching around requires a temporary variable, temp, which holds the old value of b until it can be put into a.

Finally, we can iterate through our sequence of Fibonacci numbers:

```
[f for f in Fibonacci_Iterable(10)]
```

This creates a list containing the first 10 Fibonacci numbers:

```
[0, 1, 1, 2, 3, 5, 8, 13, 21, 34]
```

GENERATORS

Iterators and iterables have a lot of moving parts involved in them. There's a lot of infrastructure to support, essentially, a function that returns the next element every time you call it (the __next__ method). Infrastructure isn't a bad thing—it's often necessary and makes your code clearer. However, other times, all you need is a single function. In these cases, Python has the generator function.

The key to a generator is the yield statement. Any function with a yield statement is automatically a generator function. For example:

```
def powers_of_two(n):
    for i in range(0, n):
        yield 2**i
```

A `yield` behaves a bit like a `return` statement. The difference is that a return halts the execution of the function—you don't go back to finish the function after the `return` statement is hit. A `yield` statement, in contrast, simply pauses execution of the function until it is called again and we pick up exactly where we left off, after the last `yield` statement. This means that all variables hold the same value they did before. Nothing is "reset" between yields.

In the generator function `powers_of_two`, a number n is passed that determines how many values the function will generate or yield. For each number i between 0 and n (up to, but not including n), we yield `2**i`.

If you call `powers_of_two` directly, like this:

```
powers_of_two(10)
```

you'll only get the resulting generator object:

```
<generator object powers_of_two at 0x1087d5230>
```

This generator object has an `__iter__` method in it:

```
powers_of_two(10).__iter__
```

Although the `generator` object may not be directly viewable in full in the same way that a list or string is, the presence of an `__iter__` method means that it can still be iterated over. You can use generator objects in a `for` loop or similar:

```
[x for x in powers_of_two(10)]
```

This results in a list containing the first 10 powers of two:

```
[1, 2, 4, 8, 16, 32, 64, 128, 256, 512]
```

You can also pass generators to a list directly and get the same result:

```
list(powers_of_two(10))
```

Here, the initializer for the `list` class is essentially doing the same thing we were doing before and iterating over the generator until it is exhausted, using the yielded values to build a new list. However, the syntax is cleaner and more readable using `list` than it is using a list comprehension.

Sometimes sequences are more easily written using a yield format. For example, we can rewrite the Fibonacci iterable and iterator using a generator:

```
def fibonacci(n):
    a = 1
    b = 0
    for _ in range(0, n):
        yield b
        temp = b
        b = a + b
        a = temp


list(fibonacci(10))
```

Note that the underscore is used as a variable name in the statement `for _ in range(0, n)` to indicate that the value is not used. This function generates the same sequence that we saw before:

```
[0, 1, 1, 2, 3, 5, 8, 13, 21, 34]
```

On a side note, it is a common pattern in programming to use a temporary variable when you want to, essentially, switch the value of two variables like we're doing here. For example:

```
a = 1
b = 2
# Switch a and b
temp = a
a = b
b = temp
print(f'Now a is {a} and b is {b}')
```

This prints:

```
Now a is 2 and b is 1
```

Because Python allows you to unpack assignments, you can write this somewhat more concisely:

```
a = 1
b = 2
# Switch a and b
a, b = b, a
print(f'Now a is {a} and b is {b}')
```

This produces the same result as the previous code, but without the need to use a temp variable. We can apply this same principle to the fibonacci generator to simplify it further:

```
def fibonacci(n):
    a = 1
    b = 0
    for _ in range(0, n):
        yield b
        b, a = a + b, b
```

Both generators and custom iterators are useful when you want to produce large sequences of data, but don't want to have to store the entire sequence in memory at once. The fibonacci generator can generate a (theoretically[3]) infinite number of Fibonacci numbers, while only storing a few values at any given time.

LOOPING WITH PASS, BREAK, ELSE, AND CONTINUE

Previously, we encountered for and while loops as separate entities with different properties. Here, we are going to cover some more advanced features of these loops that apply to both.

---

[3] There is, as always, a limited number of atoms available in the universe to represent the information needed for the larger numbers in the Fibonacci sequence. More practically, though, you will be constrained to the amount of memory on your computer available for your Python program to use. In many inferior (non-Python) programming languages, integers are allocated a reasonable amount of memory, such as 32 bits (4 bytes). One of these bits is used for differentiating negative or positive numbers, so if you want a number that's smaller than -2,147,483,648 (-2^{31}) or larger than 2,147,483,648 (2^{31}), you need to use a different type of integer that gets even more space allocated for it.

Python makes this whole thing very easy and will automatically allocate more and more memory for your integer as the size of the number gets bigger and bigger. Still, there are limits when Python itself runs out of space.

If you find yourself running into this problem, you might consider the following: There is more to life than calculating Fibonacci numbers. Please don't make them that big.

Consider the following Python statement:

```
from datetime import datetime

two_seconds_from_now = (datetime.now().second + 2) % 60
```

This extracts the "seconds" portion of the current datetime, adds two to it, and uses a modulus so that we can't end up with values like 60 or 61. That is, if the current value of datetime.now() .second is 59, we will add two to it to get 61, take the modulus and end up with a final value of 1. Therefore, two seconds from a current second count of 59 is 1.

We can use this in a while loop to print out a message after approximately[4] two seconds has passed:

```
two_seconds_from_now = (datetime.now().second + 2) % 60

while datetime.now().second != two_seconds_from_now:
    pass
print('Done!')
```

The pass statement means "Ignore this line and do nothing." You might think that a statement that explicitly does nothing is useless. On the contrary, the program fails without it:

```
while datetime.now().second != two_seconds_from_now:

print('Done!')
```

This raises the error:

```
IndentationError: expected an indented block after 'while' statement
```

Without *something* there, Python assumes that you've made a mistake and have forgotten to add a code block under the while statement. Every time you write a colon, you have to have some sort of indented code filling in a new block under it.

This is what the pass statement is for. It preserves indentation and allows you to write a code block that literally does nothing.

There's another way to write this logic as well:

```
two_seconds_from_now = (datetime.now().second + 2) % 60

while True:
    if datetime.now().second == two_seconds_from_now:
        break
print('Done!')
```

I'm not going to argue that this is a *better* way to write the same logic, but it is *another* way. This uses the break statement, which breaks out of the current loop regardless of what the evaluated statement in the loop says.

The loop in this case says while True. Personally, I get a little nervous when I see something like that. Continuing forever might be a good thing in, say, a web server, but iPython Notebook cells are difficult to stop when they're in the middle of running forever and are just not designed for this sort of thing.

---

[4] I say "approximately" here because we will be executing the program and setting the value of two_seconds_from_now at some point partway through the current second. Then Python will exit the loop as soon as it's able after the computer's clock ticks over into the appropriate second (likely very quickly). This program will most likely take between 1 and 2 seconds to execute.

There is rarely a good reason to write while True in a situation like this. And if you do choose to raise everyone's blood pressure with a while True, you should follow it up relatively quickly with a break statement, and perhaps a reassuring comment like this:

```
while True: # This looks bad, but I'm using a break statement to exit the loop
```

Note that, along with everything else in this section, you can use break in for loops as well:

```
for n in range(2, 100):
    for factor in range(2, int(n**0.5) + 1):
        if n % factor == 0:
            print(f'{n} is divisible by {factor}')
            break
```

Here, the outer/first loop iterates through all the numbers from 2 to 99. For each number, it loops through each potential factor `factor`, up to the square root of the number. If a number is divisible by a factor, that is, if n % factor == 0, it prints a message about a factor being found and then breaks out of the inner loop (the inner loop only; it will still remain in the outer loop) without testing for any other factors.

If it hasn't found a factor after reaching the square root, we can be certain that the number does not have any other factors[5] and there is no need to continue searching.

You may notice that there are some numbers, such as 2, 3, 5, and 7, that don't get printed out at all. These don't have any factors (except for 1 and themselves). They are *prime numbers*.

We can print out a list of prime numbers by removing the print statement announcing found factors and adding one beneath an else statement:

```
for n in range(2, 100):
    for factor in range(2, int(n**0.5) + 1):
        if n % factor == 0:
            break
    else:
        print(f'{n} is prime!')
```

So far, we've only seen an else statement used in conjunction with an if statement, like this:

```
if datetime.now().second == 42:
    print('42 seconds!')
else:
    print('Not 42 seconds')
```

However, else statements can be used with loops as well. If a break statement is never reached in the loop, the else statement will be entered. In the case of our prime-finding logic, the break statement

---

[5] I leave it as an exercise to the reader (https://en.wikipedia.org/wiki/Proof_by_intimidation) as to why we only need to search for factors up to, and including, the square root of the number.

If the reader is tired of this exercise, here's a brief explanation: Factors come in pairs. For example, 18 has the factors 3 and 6. One member of the pair will always be *less* than the square root of the number and one member will always be *greater* than the square root of the number. In this case, the square root of 18 is approximately 4.2, so the 3 is less than 4.2 and the 6 is greater than 4.2. Remember: if both factors in the "factor pair" are greater than the square root, the product of those factors would necessarily have to be greater than the number we're dealing with!

The edge case here is with square numbers, like 25, which have factor pairs where each factor is the same, like 5 and 5. Matching factors are guaranteed to be the square root of the number, so we must test up to and including the square root.

However, if we haven't found any factors after reaching the square root, it's guaranteed that there won't be hidden ones lurking on the other side of that square root.

is reached only if we've found a factor for the number, n, being tested. If no factor is found, then the `else` statement announces that the number is prime.

Next, we have the `continue` statement. When reached, the `continue` statement will skip all the rest of the code in the loop and go to the next iteration of the loop.

A `continue` statement is unlike a `pass`, because it causes the rest of the code in the loop to be skipped—it has an effect—whereas the `pass` statement is ignored entirely. It is also unlike `break`, which skips the rest of the code and exits the loop entirely. However, like a `break` statement, `continue` is usually wrapped in an `if` statement so that it is only executed in certain circumstances within the loop.

```python
two_seconds_from_now = (datetime.now().second + 2) % 60

while True:
    if datetime.now().second != two_seconds_from_now:
        continue
    break

print('Done!')
```

Here we have the same scary-looking `while True`, but the `if` statement is checking that the current second is *not* equal to `two_seconds_from_now`. This will not be true until we've traveled into the future, so the `continue` statement causes the `break` statement to not be reached until then.

If you can follow this logic, congratulations! This is not the most Pythonic code in the world, but good for working through in order to check your understanding. A more common situation for `continue` statements to be used is at the beginning of `for` loops, say, in order to avoid extra checks for special cases.

For example, we can create a function `is_prime`, which returns a Boolean that indicates whether or not the number n is prime:

```python
def is_prime(n):
    for factor in range(2, int(n**0.5) + 1):
        if n % factor == 0:
            return False
    return True
```

Using this, we create a `for` loop, which first checks to see if a number is prime and, if it is prime, does not bother creating a list of its factors:

```python
for n in range(2, 100):
    if is_prime(n):
        continue

    factors_list = []
    for factor in range(2, n):
        if n % factor == 0:
            factors_list.append(factor)
    print(f'Factors of {n}: {factors_list}')
```

While there are certainly more mathematically efficient ways to solve this problem, the `continue` statement keeps the code organized and lays it out in a readable way.

There is one operator we haven't covered that is especially useful when used in conjunction with a `while` loop.

ASSIGNMENT EXPRESSIONS

The assignment expression, introduced in Python 3.8, allows you to assign a value to a variable and evaluate that variable at the same time. Although not commonly used in a `print` statement like this, we can see the assignment expression in action in the following lines:

```
print(a := 100)
print(a)
```

This will print the value `100` twice. It makes the assignment to the variable and returns the value of the variable at the same time.

If you ask another Python programmer about assignment expressions, they will most likely have no idea what you're talking about. This isn't just because they're relatively new to Python—it's because the only people who use the phrase "assignment expression" are the people who write the Python documentation. Everyone else knows them by another name entirely.

WALRUS OPERATORS

That's better.

"Assignment expressions" are actually called *walrus operators*. If you don't know why, turn your head sideways:

`:=`

The walrus operator is useful in a variety of situations, and especially useful with `while` loops. It's very common in a `while` loop to retrieve some data, evaluate the data to see if we should keep looping, and also do something with the data inside the `while` loop. For example, if we're batch-processing a list of records we might get the records, make sure there are still records in the list, and then process them. That would look something like this:

```
records = get_records()
while len(records):
    process records here
    records = get_records()
```

Note that this is not runnable code—the function `get_records` is not defined and the line `process records here` isn't Python code at all. This is pseudocode (https://en.wikipedia.org/wiki/Pseudocode) and is intended to be used for discussion of the general pattern only.

The problem with writing things like this is that `records = get_records()` needs to be written twice—once to fetch the records initially, and then again at the end of the `while` block on each subsequent fetch. This might not seem like a big deal, but what if you want to change how the records are fetched or update the function name? The risk is that you might update one line but forget about the other. It's certainly happened to me before!

In general, it's just better to not have to write the same thing twice—especially when it can be rewritten far more elegantly using a walrus operator:

```
while len(records := get_records()):
    process records here
```

Outside of loops, the walrus operator can often help clean up `if` statements as well:

```
from random import randint

if (n := randint(1, 100)) < 50:
    print(f'{n} is less than 50')
else:
    print(f'{n} is greater than or equal to 50')
```

This uses the *random* module and imports the `randint` function. This function returns a random integer between (and including) the two numbers passed in as arguments. In this case, it returns a number between 1 and 100 inclusive. If this number is less than 50, it prints one message, and if it's greater than 50, it prints another message.

By using the walrus operator, we can avoid an extra line of assignment above the `if` statement. It's also worth noting that the variable n can be accessed inside the `else` block as well. In fact, n will be defined from that point forward and can be used anywhere in subsequent code. The use of n is not limited to the block inside the `if` statement, even though that's where it's assigned.

RECURSION

> *To iterate is human, to recurse divine.*
>
> —L. PETER DEUTSCH

In the 1993 film *Groundhog Day,* weatherman Phil Connors (played by Bill Murray) finds himself magically repeating the same day over and over (and over) again. He awakens to the same Sonny & Cher song every morning. On the street, he passes the same people doing the same activities, encountering the same events that happened before. At midnight everything resets completely and he wakes up the previous morning to the same song on the radio.

In the 2019 Netflix TV series *Russian Doll,* software engineer Nadia Vulvokov (played by Natasha Lyonne) is in a similar predicament. Her loop starts at her 36th birthday party, with the same songs playing, the same guests greeting her with the same greetings. As the loops progress, however, they seem to retain echoes of the loops that came before. Gradually, people and things start popping out of existence and the world looks barer and barer. The universe itself starts losing memory, crashing under the weight of all the previous iterations.

Whereas Phil Connors is stuck in an iterative loop like a `for` or `while` loop, Nadia Vulvokov is stuck in *recursion.*

Recursion is caused, essentially, when a function calls itself. Here is an example of a recursive function that takes, as an argument, an integer greater than 0:

```
def recursion(i):
    if i <= 0:
        return
    print(i)
    recursion(i-1)
```

If i is less than or equal to 0, we return from the function without doing anything. Otherwise, print the number that was passed in, then call that same function, recursion, with i-1.

When the function is called with the number 5:

```
recursion(5)
```

it prints a countdown and then exits:

```
5
4
3
2
1
```

In Python, as well as many other programming languages, function calls are kept track of on a *stack*. When one function calls another one, information about that new function is added to the stack. When we return from the new function, it is removed from the stack and we return to the old function that called it.

This is why the output of a program when an error is raised is called a *stack trace*. For example:

```
def a():
    b()

def b():
    c()

def c():
    return 1/0


a()
```

Here, there are three functions chained together. Function a calls b, which calls c, which causes an error by dividing by 0. When run, the complete resulting stack trace looks like this:

```
---------------------------------------------------------------------
ZeroDivisionError                       Traceback (most recent call last)
Cell In[12], line 10
      7 def c():
      8     return 1/0
---> 10 a()

Cell In[12], line 2, in a()
      1 def a():
----> 2     b()

Cell In[12], line 5, in b()
      4 def b():
----> 5     c()

Cell In[12], line 8, in c()
      7 def c():
----> 8     return 1/0

ZeroDivisionError: division by zero
```

The arrows (---->) indicate lines that are in the path or stack where the error originated. At the very top, we can see where a() was originally called on line 10. Then inside function a, b() was called, then c() was called, and finally the error was triggered by the line return 1/0.

These are called stack traces because they trace the stack of function calls that existed at the time of the error all the way down to where the error occurred. In a large, complex program, you might be confused if only the line that caused the error was displayed. How did your program get there? The stack trace explains everything.

Popping back up to our recursion example:

```
def recursion(i):
    if i <= 0:
        return
    print(i)
    recursion(i-1)
```

in the line recursion(i-1), another function call is added to the stack. Often, programmers think of adding to the stack as "descending" and returning from a function as "ascending" or "popping" up the stack. Every time recursion (i-1) is called, we descend and descend until, finally, the value of i reaches 0, the return statement is hit, and we immediately pop back up out of all the instances of the recursion function added to the stack.

You can visualize this "popping out" by adding a print statement to the recursion function:

```
def recursion(i):
    if i <= 0:
        return
    print(i)
    recursion(i-1)
    print(f'Popping out of recursion where i is {i}')


recursion(5)
```

The resulting print statements show Python removing function calls from the stack in the reverse order that they were added on:

```
5
4
3
2
1
Popping out of recursion where i is 1
Popping out of recursion where i is 2
Popping out of recursion where i is 3
Popping out of recursion where i is 4
Popping out of recursion where i is 5
```

Clearly, recursion creates loops. But they're fundamentally different sorts of loops than we saw with iterators like for and while statements.

We could, of course, write this same thing with a `while` loop:

```
def loop(i):
    while i > 0:
        print(i)
        i = i - 1
```

This produces the same output, but with less overhead. Adding to the stack takes time and memory. In fact, calling the `recursion` function with numbers greater than 1,000 will raise an error:

```
RecursionError: maximum recursion depth exceeded in comparison
```

Python, quite wisely, places a limit on the allowed size of the stack. Although the default maximum size is 1,000, that limit can be modified using the `sys` module:

```
import sys
print(sys.getrecursionlimit())
sys.setrecursionlimit(2000)
```

However, because of the memory required to support recursion, I strongly recommend against raising the recursion limit. In fact, I cannot recall ever needing to modify the recursion limit in practice.

So why use recursion? Some problems are easier to solve and simpler to write with a recursive solution. For example, a function that calculates factorials[6] can be written this way:

```
def factorial(n):
    if n == 1:
        return 1
    return n * factorial(n-1)
```

If written with an iterative loop, the function is somewhat more complicated:

```
def factorial(n):
    f_val = 1
    for i in range(1, n+1):
        print(i)
        f_val = f_val * i
    return f_val
```

Although an iterative solution is always possible, it turns out that there are many algorithms in computer science that are much easier to write and visualize when written recursively. These are generally algorithms that don't require a huge number of loops or go very "deep." Remember: If you're tempted to increase Python's default recursion limit, that's generally a sign that you should rethink your code and consider an iterative solution.

---

[6] In mathematics, a factorial is indicated by an exclamation point, and represents that number multiplied by all the positive integers less than or equal to it. For example:

$$5! = 5 \times 4 \times 3 \times 2 \times 1$$

The 5! Is read as "five factorial." It is a very useful operation when calculating how many combinations or arrangements of things you can make. For example, five different objects (such as playing cards) can be arranged in 5! or 120 different ways.

1. This is a recursive function that returns the factorial of a number passed in:

    ```
    def factorial(n):
        if n == 1:
            return 1
        return n * factorial(n-1)
    ```

    Modify the function to do the following:

    ➤   Check the type of the argument passed in. If it is a non-integer, return `None`.

    ➤   If the integer is negative, return `None`.

    ➤   If the number is `0`, return `1` (mathematicians have decided that 0! is 1).

2. Write a recursive function that returns the corresponding triangular number (`https://en.wikipedia.org/wiki/Triangular_number`) for the positive integer passed in.

3. Write a generator function, using `yield`, that generates prime numbers up to some number, `n`, passed in as an argument.

4. The `input` function prompts the user to enter some input (into the terminal, or into a text input box in Jupyter). You can see it in action using this example:

    ```
    name = input('What is your name?')
    print(f'Hello, {name}!')
    ```

    Write a function that will keep prompting the user for numbers to add together. As soon as the user enters a key word (such as `stop` or `done`), the program will print the sum of all the numbers entered up to that point and exit.

    You can assume, for the purpose of this exercise, that the user is benevolent and competent and will only either enter valid numbers or the correct key word to exit the program when they're done.

    Here is an example of the program output:

    ```
    Enter a number:  4.5
    Enter a number:  36.97
    Enter a number:  103
    Enter a number:  stop
    The sum of the numbers entered is: 144.47
    ```

    Use the walrus operator so that you only need to use the `input` function at a single point in the code.

10

Functions

We've used and written a lot of functions so far in this book. In fact, the very first program we wrote involved the print function:

```
print('Hello, World!')
```

When it comes to programming in Python (or any modern programming language), functions are nearly unavoidable. Because of this, you've already used and even written many functions while learning about other aspects of Python. But don't let your familiarity with functions make you complacent! There are many features and complexities of functions that are important to master.

In this chapter, we'll look at different ways to write function arguments, passing variable functions around in code, wrapping functions with Python decorators, and the various subtleties and pitfalls of how functions interact with their namespaces.

POSITIONAL ARGUMENTS AND KEYWORD ARGUMENTS

As you've seen, you can define a function to have any number of arguments:

```
def add(a, b, c):
    return sum([a, b, c])

add(1,2,3)
```

These arguments are called *positional* arguments because the order that they're passed into the function is very important. In general, the following function calls are liable to produce different results:

```
some_function(1, 2, 3)
some_function(3, 2, 1)
```

Regardless of how you call some_function, it appears clear that it takes three arguments. But can we create a function that has a *variable* number of arguments? Let's rewrite the add function to take in one, two, or more (or even zero?) positional arguments and add them together.

Of course, we could always use the built-in function sum and do something like this:

```
def add(list_of_values):
    return sum(list_of_values)
```

```
add([1,2,3,4,5])
```

Although we're achieving our goal from a certain functional perspective, we're still passing in a single argument, list_of_values, rather than any number of arguments.

It's worth noting here that the sum function takes in a single iterable sequence of things to sum, and passing arguments like the following will not work:

```
sum(1, 2, 3, 4, 5)
```

While creating a new function add that takes in a variable number of arguments and almost directly calls the sum function with them isn't the most useful thing you can do with Python, it does illustrate the challenge. Also, if we were fine with simply passing a list of values to our add function, we could do this:

```
add = sum
add([1,2,3,4,5])
```

To define a function that truly accepts any number of arguments (as opposed to a single list), we can use an asterisk in the function definition:

```
def add(*args):
    return sum(args)
```

```
add(1, 2, 3, 4, 5)
```

This asterisk allows us to *pack arguments*, and it automatically interprets anything passed into the function as members of a single tuple with the name args. We say that the multiple values passed into the function are "packed" into a single variable.

If we print the value of args, we can see the tuple containing all the arguments passed into the function:

```
def add(*args):
    print(args)
    return sum(args)
```

```
add(1, 2, 3, 4, 5)
```

This prints the tuple:

```
(1, 2, 3, 4, 5)
```

and then returns the value 15.

The variable name args is often used by convention, and is not enforced by Python.

This asterisk is not technically an operator in Python, in the same way that +, %, and += are operators. Regardless, you will often see this asterisk referred to as the "packing operator," "unpacking operator," or "star operator." For this reason, we will occasionally refer to it as an unpacking operator, which is one of the more popular and well-recognized names for it.

When multiple values are compressed into a single variable, it's called packing. When a single variable (containing multiple values in an iterable like a tuple or list) is assigned to multiple values it is called unpacking. We've seen an example of unpacking before:

```
for key, value in my_dictionary.items():
    print(f'key: {key}, value: {value}')
```

This unpacks the key and value of a dictionary item into the key and value variables.

A QUICK POINTER

If you're familiar with languages such as C, C++, or Go, you may have a sense of recognition when seeing this asterisk syntax in a function definition. These languages use an asterisk as a *pointer*.

Because many modern programming languages (including Python) derive from C, and because pointers are a fundamental concept in computer science, I think the syntactical similarities are worth a brief discussion.

A pointer is a type of variable that stores the computer's *memory address* of a value, rather than the value itself. This can be used inside a function to modify the value where it is stored. For example, in Python, this code will print out the value 5, not 6:

```
def add_one(val):
    val += 1

val = 5
add_one(val)
print(val)
```

That's because we're essentially modifying a copy of the value passed into the function, rather than the original variable. If we were to write this function in C, using a pointer, we could increment the value where it's stored in memory directly and the corresponding C code would print the value 6 instead.

With that said, unpacking in Python, as seen here:

```
def add(*args):
    return sum(args)
```

should not be confused with the similar-looking pointer syntax in other languages.

Not all the arguments of the function must be part of this args group, however. For example, we can write a function that prints greetings for a variable number of names:

```
def greet(salutation, *names):
    for name in names:
        print(f'{salutation} {name}')

greet('Bienvenue', 'Pierre', 'Marie', 'Louis')
```

The first value passed into the function call is assigned to the variable `salutation`, then the remaining values are assigned to `*names`.

The most common use of the unpacking operator is in functions declarations to handle a variable number of arguments. However, you can use them outside of function declarations as well. For example:

```
one, two, *the_rest = [1, 2, 3, 4, 5]
```

This assigns the value 1 to one, 2 to two, and `[3, 4, 5]` to the_rest. You can unpack these in a variety of ways, as long as there is only one variable containing an unpacking operator to avoid ambiguity:

```
one, *middle_stuff, five = [1, 2, 3, 4, 5]
*beginning_stuff, four, five = [1, 2, 3, 4, 5]
```

This same flexibility is not afforded to function definitions, however. The unpacking operator must always be last in the list of positional arguments. So, something like the following will cause an exception when the function is called:

```
def greet(salutation, *names, suffix):
    for name in names:
        print(f'{salutation} {name}{suffix}')

greet('Bienvenue', 'Pierre', 'Marie', 'Louis', '!')
```

While the Python programming language *could* support this feature, there are a few lines from The Zen of Python that are worth remembering:

```
Readability counts.
...
In the face of ambiguity, refuse the temptation to guess.
There should be one-- and preferably only one --obvious way to do it.
```

Python provides a nice bit of syntactic sugar[1] that allows you to cleanly write function definitions that contain complexities like `def greet(salutation, *names, suffix)`, and that is: *keyword arguments*. A keyword argument contains a variable name key and a default value if that key is not provided in the function call.

We've seen this before with the `sort` method on lists:

```
people.sort(key=name_key)
```

Here, the variable name is literally called `key`, although it doesn't have to be. We also saw keyword arguments in action in the `datetime` class declaration:

```
datetime(1991, 2, 20, hour=9, minute=0, second=0, microsecond=0)
```

Here, the `1991`, `2`, and `20` are values for the year, month, and day positional arguments. The keyword arguments are `hour`, `minute`, `second`, and `microsecond`.

---

[1] "Syntactic sugar" is a phrase for anything in a language that makes it easier (or "sweeter") to read and write the code. These things are not strictly required (any function with keyword arguments could be rewritten without them) but allow you to express yourself more cleanly or concisely. List comprehensions in Python are another good example of syntactic sugar.

We can rewrite our greet function to use keyword arguments like this:

```
def greet(*names, salutation='', suffix=''):
    for name in names:
        print(f'{salutation} {name}{suffix}')

greet('Pierre', 'Marie', 'Louis', salutation='Bienvenue', suffix='!')
```

Keyword arguments have default values. In this case, the default values for salutation and suffix are the empty string (''). Because these default values are provided, it's not necessary to pass values in for keyword arguments when calling the function. For example, we could also write and call the greet function like this:

```
def greet(*names, salutation='Dear', suffix=','):
    for name in names:
        print(f'{salutation} {name}{suffix}')

greet('Pierre', 'Marie', 'Louis')
```

This prints the output:

```
Dear Pierre,
Dear Marie,
Dear Louis,
```

Arguments specified with keywords must always come after positional arguments. The following is not a valid function definition:

```
def greet(salutation='', *names, suffix='')
```

As long as the positional arguments are first, the order of the keyword arguments themselves during function invocation is mostly unimportant. You can call the greet function with any order or combination of keyword arguments. These are all valid calls:

```
greet('Pierre', 'Marie', 'Louis', suffix='!', salutation='Bienvenue')
greet('Pierre', 'Marie', 'Louis', salutation='Bienvenue', suffix='!')
greet('Pierre', 'Marie', 'Louis', salutation='Bienvenue')
greet('Pierre', 'Marie', 'Louis', suffix='!')
```

However, the order *does* matter if you choose to omit the key names altogether. For example:

```
def division(numerator=1, denominator=2):
    return numerator/denominator

division(2, 10)
```

This returns the float 0.2, just as if it were called like this:

```
division(numerator=2, denominator=10)
```

Calling a function using keyword arguments as if they were positional arguments like this can be somewhat dangerous and lead to bugs down the road. Take for example, the previous greet function:

```
def greet(*names, salutation='', suffix=''):
    for name in names:
        print(f'{salutation} {name}{suffix}')

greet('Pierre', 'Marie', 'Louis', 'Bienvenue', '!')
```

Without using the keyword arguments, all strings passed in are assigned to the `names` tuple and the output of the function looks like this:

```
Pierre
Marie
Louis
Bienvenue
!
```

While this kind of output may be an obvious error here, I promise that in large enterprise systems with many moving parts not all errors will be so obvious or easily spotted and diagnosed. Ambiguous argument assignments are best avoided entirely by explicitly labeling all keyword arguments when calling the function.

Naming the keyword arguments also improves backward compatibility and the robustness of your code should the function definition change in the future. If, for whatever reason, someone decides to switch the order here:

```
def division(denominator=2, numerator=1):
    return numerator/denominator
```

this will return the same value as it did with the previous definition:

```
division(numerator=2, denominator=10)
```

while this one will not:

```
division(2, 10)
```

You will probably not be surprised to learn that Python has a very convenient feature for keyword arguments: *keyword argument unpacking*. Similar to using `*args` to allow for a variable number of position arguments, you can use `**kwargs` to allow for a variable number of keyword arguments.

```
def multilingual_greetings(**kwargs):
    print(kwargs)

multilingual_greetings(de='Willkommen', fr='Bienvenue', en='Welcome')
```

This prints the dictionary:

```
{'de': 'Willkommen', 'fr': 'Bienvenue', 'en': 'Welcome'}
```

As with positional argument unpacking, predefined keyword arguments can be combined with unpacked keyword arguments, as long as the defined arguments are first:

```
def multilingual_greetings(name='', **kwargs):
    for _, greeting in kwargs.items():
        print(f'{greeting} {name}')

multilingual_greetings(name='Ryan', de='Willkommen', fr='Bienvenue', en='Welcome')
```

This prints the output:

```
Willkommen Ryan
Bienvenue Ryan
Welcome Ryan
```

Although all four of these will rarely be used in the same function, the order of the types of arguments should be:

➤ Defined positional arguments

➤ Packed positional arguments (`*args`)

➤ Defined keyword arguments

➤ Packed keyword arguments (`**kwargs`)

Using positional and keyword arguments appropriately can make functions easier to use and understand. Explicitly passing 20 different settings into a function each time it's called is difficult to read. Only passing in the two settings that have changed from defaults during that particular call makes it much easier to see what's going on.

Through argument packing, more abstract functions can be written that can be reused for a variety of specific applications. Although using a variety of types of arguments in your functions isn't necessary, it makes life much easier in the long run.

FUNCTIONS AS FIRST-CLASS OBJECTS

In programming, a *first-class object* (also known as a first-class citizen or first-class entity) is one that generally has the following properties:

➤ It can be returned from a function.

➤ It can be assigned to a variable.

➤ It can be passed as an argument.

Integers, for example, can be returned from functions, assigned to variables, and passed as arguments to functions. Therefore, we would say that integers are first-class objects in Python. Really, any object or value is first-class.

An example of something that is *not* a first-class object would be an operator. You cannot pass an operator into a function or assign it to a variable.[2]

Functions in Python are first-class. They can be assigned to variables, returned from (other) functions, and passed as an argument. Functions can be thought of as values or objects just like any other. For example, take the function `some_function`:

```
def some_function(a, b):
    return f'a is {a} and b is {b}'
```

When this function is declared, Python associates it with the variable name `some_function`. You can think of a function definition statement using `def` as essentially an assignment operator for functions.

If we print the value of `some_function`, we get this:

```
<function some_function at 0x1073371a0>
```

---

[2] If you have a desperate need to treat operators as first-class objects, there are operator functions you can use. See the Python documentation for more information: `https://docs.python.org/3/library/operator.html`.

indicating that it's a function object with a particular location in memory. Function objects have properties that allow Python to execute the instructions they're associated with. For example:

```
print(some_function.__code__.co_varnames)
print(some_function.__code__.co_code)
```

prints this:

```
('a', 'b')
b'\x97\x00d\x01|\x00\x9b\x00d\x02|\x01\x9b\x00\x9d\x04S\x00'
```

This shows the function's argument names as a tuple of strings and the source code of the function as binary data. Knowing how to access the properties like __code__.co_varnames and __code__ .co_code is not very useful in day-to-day programming. I don't suggest that you memorize this or incorporate it into your own code. Accessing the source code of a function is not only a code smell, but is also more easily accomplished using the inspect module if you really have to do it:

```
import inspect

inspect.getsource(some_function)
```

What all of this shows is that functions are simply objects with various properties that tell Python how they should be interpreted. They are associated with code, represented by binary data, that should be executed if they are called.

This allows us to do many nifty and flexible things with functions. For example, you may have a variety of small processing or transformation tasks where the selection and order of those tasks is liable to change.

Here are five text processing functions that can be implemented in any combination or order on a piece of text:

```
def lowercase(text):
    return text.lower()

def remove_punctuation(text):
    punctuations = ['.', '-', ',', '*', '\'']
    for punctuation in punctuations:
        text = text.replace(punctuation, '')
    return text

def remove_newlines(text):
    text = text.replace('\n', ' ')
    return text

def remove_short_words(text):
    return ' '.join([word for word in text.split() if len(word) > 3])

def remove_long_words(text):
    return ' '.join([word for word in text.split() if len(word) < 6])
```

We may, for instance, only want to transform the text to lowercase, remove punctuation, remove newlines, and remove long words. The following code accomplishes that in a flexible way:

```
processing_functions = [
    lowercase,
    remove_punctuation,
    remove_newlines,
    remove_long_words
]

for func in processing_functions:
    text = func(text)
```

Simply by adding, removing, and changing the order of functions in the list, you can change how these functions are applied. This program is also self-documenting. Each available text processing function is clearly labeled with a function name that describes what it does. The processing_ functions list shows which ones are currently being used.

Functions can also be passed in as arguments to functions. For example:

```
def apply_text_processing(processing_functions, text):
    for func in processing_functions:
        text = func(text)
    return text
```

The function apply_text_processing takes in some text and a list of functions to apply to it. Here, I'm setting the text to *The Zen of Python* and applying some transformations:

```
text = '''
Beautiful is better than ugly.
Explicit is better than implicit.
...
Namespaces are one honking great idea -- let's do more of those!
'''
def apply_text_processing([
    lowercase,
    remove_punctuation,
    remove_newlines,
    remove_long_words
],
text)
```

This produces the output:

```
'is than ugly is than is than is than flat is than is than dense cases to break the
rules beats never pass in the face of the to guess there be one and only one way to do
it that way may not be at first dutch now is than never never is often than right now
if the is hard to its a bad idea if the is easy to it may be a good idea are one great
idea lets do more of'
```

Even in the best companies with the most brilliant and highly skilled project managers, programmers will need to deal with changing requirements. Software is rarely "done"—it will always need to be modified and fixed. New ideas come in; new use cases are discovered.

It is your responsibility as a software engineer not to anticipate these exact changes per se, but to anticipate the scope of all *possible* changes. A request for a specific type of text processing may be followed up with requests for other types of text processing. This may be followed up with a request for custom text processing that sources its steps from user settings or some other place.

This isn't to say that you should immediately implement all possible features or future features whenever you start working on a specific ticket. This violates the principle of YAGNI.[3] But programs should generally be written in a flexible, modular way that allows for future modification and expansion without huge rewrites.

In addition, new features will not always be written by the original author of the code. You may be modifying a feature in someone else's program, or a program you wrote yourself two years ago and have very little memory of today. Adding comments helps, but writing small modular functions with clear names can often be more useful than comments.

LAMBDA FUNCTIONS

In Python, I can write the value:

```
5
```

This is a valid line of Python code. It is the integer 5. It doesn't have a variable name, it's not assigned anywhere, it just exists. Of course, it doesn't do anything, but that's okay—it doesn't need to do anything useful to be valid Python!

I can take that value and pass it into a function:

```
def print_number(number=0):
    print(number)

print_number(number=5)
```

Outside of the function, there's still no variable name associated with the integer 5. It only exists as it's being used.

Compare that to the way we called the `sort` method on a list of dictionaries:

```
people = [
    {'name': 'Bob', 'age': 30},
    {'name': 'Diana', 'age': 20},
    {'name': 'Alice', 'age': 40},
    {'name': 'Charlie', 'age': 10},
]

def name_key(person):
    return person['name']

people.sort(key=name_key)
print(people)
```

---

[3] "You aren't gonna need it."

Here, we're declaring a function and assigning it to the name name_key before we can pass it in as a keyword argument to the sort method. But what if we want a function that only exists where it's being used, as we need it, like we did with the integer 5? For that, there are *lambda functions*, also known as *anonymous functions* in computer science.

The term "lambda function" comes from "lambda calculus," a branch in mathematics and computer science that uses the Greek letter lambda (λ) to denote a function definition. In lambda calculus, we might write the following:

$$\lambda x.x^2$$

This defines a function that takes in a variable, x, and returns x^2. The λ starts a new function definition, the x is the argument, and everything following the period (.) is the body of the function. In Python, we would write this as:

```
lambda x: x**2
```

The keyword lambda starts a new function definition, followed by an argument x, then a colon (:) and a function body, x**2. Absent from this function definition is the word `return`. Lambda functions evaluate a single expression, with only one line to write the function body (no `if` statements or `while` loops here!). Therefore, these functions have an *implied return* in that one-line statement, without needing to actually write the word `return`. Writing `return` will, in fact, cause a syntax error.

This lambda function is not assigned to a variable name, and does absolutely nothing if written on its own, just like writing the integer 5 does nothing on its own. However, declaring a lambda creates a proper function object, and it can be called:

```
(lambda x: x**2)(5)
```

Parentheses surround the function to avoid ambiguity and syntax errors. This returns the value 25.

The most common use of lambda functions is as arguments for other functions. For example, the call to the list sort method from above can be rewritten in this way:

```
people.sort(key=lambda person: person['name'])
```

Variables names in lambda functions are frequently shortened to single letters to save space (particularly in function calls with lots of arguments), so this could also be written as:

```
people.sort(key=lambda p: p['name'])
```

Lambda functions can also be written with multiple comma-separated arguments:

```
lambda x, y, z: x * y * z
```

This function returns the product of three arguments: x, y, and z.

You can also use lambda functions as a default for keyword arguments:

```
def apply_transformation(num, transformer=lambda n: n * 3):
    print(f'Applying function {transformer.__name__} to {num}')
    return transformer(*args)

apply_transformation(2)
```

The function `apply_transformation` uses the special attribute `__name__` to print the function name and the positional arguments being passed to that function. If no `transformer` function is specified, it will default to multiplying the argument by 3. Hopefully there's only a single argument and it's able to be multiplied!

Lambda functions are great for writing short one-off functions, especially as an argument when calling another function. However, you do lose the opportunity to name the function. Function names can be useful for describing what the function does. Lambda functions do not have any such useful labeling (unless you add a comment).

When and how to use lambda functions is a matter of developing a personal style—within the bounds of good taste and Pythonic best practices.

NAMESPACES

By now you hopefully have some sense of the concept of *namespace*. A namespace is a collection of variable names that all point to values. If I define the variable:

```
val = 5
```

and then later reference the variable `val` again, Python will look up the name `val` in the namespace and return the value 5.

But Python programs do not usually have just a single namespace. For example, the following is modified slightly from the code in the discussion earlier in this chapter about pointers:

```
def add_one(val):
    val += 1
    print(f'Value of val in the add_one function: {val}')


val = 5
add_one(val)
print(f'Outside value of val: {val}')
```

It prints these lines:

```
Value of val in the add_one function: 6
Outside value of val: 5
```

Even though the name of the variable `val` is the same both inside and outside the function, the values are different. The variables are, in fact, completely different and point to different locations in memory. There are two different namespaces involved here: one for outside the function, and a separate namespace for inside the function.

We could rewrite the function add_one to use a different variable entirely, calling it `function_val`, and this code would behave the same way:

```
def add_one(function_val):
    function_val += 1
    print(f'Value of function_val in the add_one function: {function_val}')
```

The difference now, is that the variable val is usable inside the function and remains untouched:

```
def add_one(function_val):
    function_val += 1
    print(f'Value of function_val in the add_one function: {function_val}')
    print(f'Value of val in the add_one function is: {val}')

val = 5
add_one(val)
print(f'Outside value of val: {val}')
```

This prints the lines:

```
Value of function_val in the add_one function: 6
Value of val in the add_one function is: 5
Outside value of val: 5
```

So, there are two different namespaces involved, but they are not entirely independent. Whenever you enter a function, Python has the ability to look up variables outside of that function in the *global namespace*. If the variable is not found, Python will look for that variable in the function's own namespace, the *local namespace*.

```
val = 5

def some_function():
    print(f'val is: {val}')

some_function()
```

This function accesses val in the global namespace and prints:

```
val is: 5
```

It's important to note that each function gets its own local namespace that lasts only as long as the function is being executed during that function call. Nothing is preserved from the local namespace of the function after a value is returned and the function exits. In Python you can see all the available variables in both the local and global namespace by using the functions globals and locals. They return all data in a dictionary containing variable names and values. Be careful; running the function globals() in JupyterLab will result in a *lot* of data! There is a lot of overhead and metadata in the Jupyter notebook file, including every variable encountered in every cell run in the current session.

Even from a terminal, starting with a brand-new Python command prompt, there's a fair amount of stuff already there:

```
>>> globals()
{'__name__': '__main__', '__doc__': None, '__package__': None, '__loader__': <class
'_frozen_importlib.BuiltinImporter'>, '__spec__': None, '__annotations__': {},
'__builtins__': <module 'builtins' (built-in)>}
```

If we call locals outside of a function, it will always be the same as globals:

```
>>> locals()
{'__name__': '__main__', '__doc__': None, '__package__': None, '__loader__':
<class '_frozen_importlib.BuiltinImporter'>, '__spec__': None, '__annotations__':
{}, '__builtins__': <module 'builtins' (built-in)>}
```

Not only do these two dictionaries have the same keys and values, but they are, in fact, the exact same dictionaries stored at the same location in memory. Outside of a function, the local namespace is equivalent to the global namespace, and Python, appropriately, returns the global namespace dictionary when calling `locals()`.

Let's look at a somewhat more complicated example of local namespaces using nested functions:

```python
def function_one(a, b, c):
    def function_two(a, b):
        d = 7
        print(f'function_two locals: {locals()}')

    function_two(5, 6)
    print(f'function_one locals: {locals()}')

function_one(1, 2, 3)
```

Here, `function_one` is a function that contains an inner function called `function_two`. This syntax might look a little odd if you haven't seen a nested function before, but it's perfectly reasonable. Remember: Functions can be declared and used just like anything else. If you can define a variable within a function, you can define a function within a function!

This code prints out the following:

```
function_two locals: {'a': 5, 'b': 6, 'd': 7, 'c': 3}
function_one locals: {'a': 1, 'b': 2, 'c': 3, 'function_two': <function
function_one.<locals>.function_two at 0x1073e72e0>}
```

The first line of `function_one`, after the `function_two` declaration, is the call `function_two(5, 6)`. This sets the value of a and b inside `function_two` to 5 and 6, respectively. You can see this in the local variables that are available inside `function_two`: {'a': 5, 'b': 6, 'd': 7, 'c': 3}.

Note that the variable c is available inside `function_two`, because it was copied from the locals of the outer function, `function_one`. Of course, if we were to reassign c or change the value in any way inside of `function_two`, it would no longer be the same variable as the one in `function_one`.

Also note that the variable d, declared only inside `function_two`, is not available in `function_one`. Similarly, the `function_two` itself is not available in the global namespace because it is only declared within `function_one`.

If we were to add the line:

```python
print('function_two' in globals())
```

it would print `False`.

One final feature to help you navigate and use namespaces effectively: the *global* keyword. In a previous example, we printed the value of a global variable from inside the function `some_function`:

```python
val = 5

def some_function():
    print(f'val is: {val}')

some_function()
```

While this example technically works, you'll find that it's not exactly robust. Although you can *access* the value of the variable val, trying to reassign it results in an error:

```
UnboundLocalError: cannot access local variable 'val' where it is not
associated with a value
```

In general, it's bad practice to use global variables at all from within functions. The global data should be passed in explicitly as an argument and then returned and updated outside the function instead. However, there are occasionally cases where it's cleaner to use and modify global values from within functions. In those situations, you can explicitly declare that you're accessing the global version of the variable using the global keyword:

```
val = 5

def some_function():
    global val
    val += 1
    print(f'val is: {val}')

some_function()
print(f'val outside the function is also {val}')
```

This prints the following:

```
val is: 6
val outside the function is also 6
```

Although global declarations can be made at any point before the variable is actually used, they are usually made as the first line under the function declaration.

DECORATORS

Decorators are an extremely powerful tool in Python that can have seemingly magical properties when first encountered. Decorators are used above a function, method, or class definition and are denoted with the at sign (@):

```
@some_decorator
def some_function
    pass
```

Decorators act as wrappers around functions and modify the behavior of functions. For example, a decorator may modify a function's arguments, modify its return values, or handle any exceptions that the function raises, among other things. Decorators can also "register" functions so that a call to that function can be triggered by other function calls and events.

For example, the atexit module has a decorator called atexit.register, which allows you to create a function that is called automatically when a program exits:

```
import atexit

@atexit.register
def say_goodbye:
  print('Goodbye!')

print('Hello!')
```

Note that, while this program is included in the accompanying Jupyter notebook files, it will not work in a Jupyter notebook for the simple reason that Python doesn't actually exit after a cell is executed. The Python kernel will keep going, waiting for you to run another cell. However, you can see this in action by entering it in the Python command prompt and then exiting the terminal:

```
>>> import atexit
>>>
>>> @atexit.register
... def say_goodbye():
...     print('Goodbye!')
...
>>> print('Hello!')
Hello!
>>> ^D
Goodbye!
```

Creating a Python file with this in its contents and executing it from the command line will work as well.

Decorators can do just about anything. In many programming languages, for example, you can define multiple versions of the same function to handle different types or numbers of arguments. This feature is commonly found in strongly typed languages where you can declare the required type of the arguments of a function. Although this feature is not available automatically in Python without using a decorator, it might look something like this:

```
def friendly_type(var: list):
    print(f'{var} is a list!')

def friendly_type(var: dict):
    print(f'{var} is a dictionary!')

def friendly_type(var: str):
    print(f'{var} is a string!')

friendly_type([1, 2, 3])
```

Here, I'm using the *type annotation* notation var: list to mean "this function expects an argument, var, of type list." These type annotations are an optional feature in Python that will be discussed in more detail in Chapter 12, "Writing Cleaner Code."

While the previous code is valid Python code that does run, it prints this result:

```
[1, 2, 3] is a string!
```

Although our argument is a list, it calls the version of friendly_type that takes string arguments. This is because functions with the same name overwrite each other in Python, even though they might have different argument types. In addition, while the type annotations like :str, :list, and :dict are useful for humans to understand functions, they are not enforced out-of-the-box by Python.

This results in the last `friendly_type` function to be declared being the one that gets called. However, this can be remedied using the singledispatch decorator:

```
from functools import singledispatch

@singledispatch
def friendly_type():
    pass

@friendly_type.register(list)
def friendly_type_list(var):
    print(f'{var} is a list!')

@friendly_type.register(dict)
def friendly_type_dict(var):
    print(f'{var} is a dictionary!')

@friendly_type.register(str)
def friendly_type_str(var):
    print(f'{var} is a string!')
```

Here, the decorator `@singledispatch` is used above a "stub function" (a short placeholder function) called `friendly_type`. There's nothing inside the function because the function name is all we really need. It creates a new decorator for us to use: `@friendly_type.register`.

Just like functions, decorators can take arguments. We use the `@friendly_type.register` decorator with an argument of the type of variable we want that function to handle (in this case, `list`, `dict`, or `str`). Then we define the function to handle that type. These function names, like `friendly_type_list`, don't matter—they won't be called directly. It's actually the seemingly empty `friendly_type` function that will be called directly. However, any calls to `friendly_type` will be passed off to the appropriate function (such as `friendly_type_list`) registered to actually handle that call.

We can see this in action by calling the `friendly_type` function:

```
friendly_type([1, 2, 3])
```

And it successfully prints:

```
[1, 2, 3] is a list!
```

So, what explanation is there for decorators besides "magic"? Technically, you don't need to know how they work in order to use them! However, knowing what's going on behind the scenes is valuable for debugging and understanding how to use many decorators. In addition, the arcane knowledge of decorators will allow us to write custom decorators, which can reduce code complexity in many situations.

Decorators are essentially wrappers for functions. Here is a new decorator called `custom_decorator`:

```
def custom_decorator(func):
    def inner_func(*args, **kwargs):
        print('You called a function with a custom_decorator!')
        return_val = func(*args, **kwargs)
        print('Done executing the function. That was fun!')
        return return_val

    return inner_func
```

We can use it on any function like this:

```
@custom_decorator
def any_func(a, b):
    return a + b
```

The `custom_decorator` function takes in a single argument: `func`. This is the function being decorated, `any_func`. The `custom_decorator` returns a function, `inner_func`, which gets called any time the decorated function, `any_func`, is called.

Most of the body of `custom_decorator` is simply a definition for the `inner_func` function. The function name, `inner_func`, doesn't matter at all and won't be used outside of `custom_decorator`. The only thing that matters is that `inner_func` accepts the arguments that will be passed to the decorated function (`any_func`) and that it's returned from the outer `custom_decorator` function.

Inside `inner_func` is where we can call our `func` with its arguments however we want. It's very important to make sure you're actually calling the function and returning the arguments inside `inner_func`! Otherwise, calls to the decorated function wouldn't work quite as expected. Consider this example:[4]

```
def hal(func):
    def inner_func(*args, **kwargs):
        print('I\'m sorry, Dave, I\'m afraid I can\'t do that.')
        print('''This mission is too important for me to allow you to jeopardize
it.''')
    return inner_func

@hal
def any_func(a, b):
    return a + b

any_func()
```

By not calling the function `func` at all, the `@hal` decorator essentially nullifies any function that it decorates. Note also that calling `any_func` without any arguments here is just fine, even though this would ordinarily result in a `TypeError` error. Because the decorator never calls the function, no error is raised.

Creating a decorator with arguments requires three nested functions:

```
def decorator_with_arguments(message):
    def decorator(func):
        def inner_func(*args, **kwargs):
            print(f'This function is decorated with {message}')
            return func(*args, **kwargs)
        return inner_func
    return decorator

@decorator_with_arguments('some message here')
def any_func(a, b):
    return a + b

any_func(3, 4)
```

---

[4] If you haven't seen the 1968 science fiction classic *2001: A Space Odyssey*, you really should!

First, the outer function, `decorator_with_arguments`, serves only as the vehicle for the decorator arguments, in this case, the single argument `message`. Unlike the previous decorator, the decorated function does not get passed in here. However, because this is the only globally available function name, as you might guess, it's also the name of the decorator itself: `@decorator_with_arguments`.

Next, the `decorator` function has the argument `func`, representing the decorated function (in this case, `any_func`). From here on out, it's very similar to the previous decorator example.

Finally, as usual, `inner_func` takes in any arguments for the particular function call and is responsible for any logic surrounding the call as well as actually calling the function and returning any values.

Note that `decorator_with_arguments` returns the function `decorator`, which, in turn, returns the `inner_func`. It's very common when writing decorators to forget to add return values! If something's not working right with your decorator, checking all the return values (including returning the value from `func(*args, **kwargs)` in the inner function) is a good first step!

Finally, it's important to note an odd side effect of using decorators. Because these decorated functions are, behind the scenes, wrapped with another function, these decorated functions, as far as Python is concerned, *are* the inner function returned by the decorator.

You can see this by accessing the __name__ attribute of a decorated function:

```
print(any_func.__name__)
```

Assuming that `any_func` is the one in the previous example, this will print the string `"inner_func"` rather than `"any_func"`. Other properties of the decorated function (such as docstrings, covered in Chapter 12) will also be those of the inner function.

This confusion can be avoided by using `functools.wraps`. Yes, this is a decorator within a decorator, but its usage is straightforward. Simply add the `@wraps` decorator to the function returned from the decorator:

```
from functools import wraps

def custom_decorator(func):
    @wraps(func)
    def inner_func(*args, **kwargs):
        print('You called a function with a custom_decorator!')
        return_val = func(*args, **kwargs)
        print('Done executing the function. That was fun!')
        return return_val

    return inner_func

@custom_decorator
def any_func(a, b):
    return a + b

print(any_func.__name__)
```

This prints the function name `any_func` rather than `inner_func`.

EXERCISES

1. Write a function that takes an arbitrary number of string position arguments and returns their concatenation.

2. Write a function that takes another function (`func`) as an argument. Your function should print `func`'s name, along with the variables it expects in some friendly descriptive message.

3. Using the `datetime` package and a lambda function, sort the following strings in ascending chronological order:

   ```
   ['01/01/1970', '02/20/1991', '10/29/1969', '12/20/1990', '11/03/1971',
    '01/23/1996', '04/03/1975', '08/17/1979']
   ```

   Tip: Use the format code `%m/%d/%Y`.

4. This is the Python logo rendered as ASCII art:

```
                    . . :-++**********+=-. . .
                 . .+******************* **-.
               .=****==+*****************:.
              .***=.     .=***************:.
              .***+.    .+***************:
              .****************************:
              .****************************:
              . . . . . . . . . . . .+**********:. . . . . . . .
        . :+**********************************:. :------:. .
       .+**********************************:. :---------. .
      ;**********************************:. :---------:
     .+**********************************:. :----------:. .
    .-**********************************+. .:------------:.
    .+**********************************+. .:------------:.
    .****************************** *=.  .:--------------.
    .****************-. . . . . . . . . . . . . ..:----------------.
    .***************. . . .::---------------------------.
    .+*************+. . .----------------------------------:.
    .=************:. .---------------------------------:.
    .************. .:-------------------------------:. .
     -**********. .:-----------------------------.
     .-*********. .:-----------------------------. . .
      .=********. .:---------------------------:.
          . . . . . . . . .:----------:.
              .:---------------------:.
              .:--------------------:-.
              .:---------------:. . . .:---.
              .:--------------:.    .---.
              .--------------:. .:---:.
              .:------------------::.
              . . .::!----------::::. . .
                  . . . . . . . . . .
```

This image, which can be found in the exercise files, is 81 characters wide (80 characters plus a newline character) and 34 lines long, making its total size 2,754 bytes (assuming 1 byte per character).

However, this image can be compressed using *run-length encoding*. Run length encoding attempts to compress a sequence by replacing consecutive copies of a symbol with that symbol and then how many times it occurs.

For example, the sequence:

```
AAAABBCCCCCCD
```

can be encoded as:

```
[('A', 4), ('B', 2), ('C', 6), ('D', 1)]
```

Write a function, `encode`, that takes a string as an argument and returns a list of character/count tuples as shown in the example.

Then, write a function `decode` that takes in the list of character/count tuples and returns the original string.

Test your function by encoding and then decoding the Python logo ASCII art. How many tuples can 2,754 characters be compressed to?

5. Write a decorator that checks to make sure all position and keyword arguments of a function are integers. If any of them are not integers, print a warning message and do not run the function.

6. Write a set of decorators that can handle functionality similar to that of the `@singledispatch` decorator. In particular, you should be able to declare a function that will have multiple "handlers" using the `@customdispatch` decorator, and then register each of several handlers using the `@register` decorator like so:

```
@customdispatch
def friendly_type(arg):
    pass

@register('friendly_type', list)
def friendly_type_list(var):
    print(f'{var} is a list!')

@register('friendly_type', dict)
def friendly_type_dict(var):
    print(f'{var} is a dictionary!')

@register('friendly_type', str)
def friendly_type_str(var):
    print(f'{var} is a string!')

friendly_type([1, 2, 3])
```

This should print the string

```
[1, 2, 3] is a list!
```

In this simple example, you do not need to worry about registering or handling functions with more than a single positional argument.

Tips:

- ➤ You may want to create a global dictionary to keep track of registered functions and use the `global` keyword to access it.

- ➤ You can get a simple string representation of a type or class (such as `list`, `str`, `dict`) using `some_type.__name__`.

- ➤ Feel free to modify the example code and experiment with different decorator syntax for declaring functions and registering handlers. There is more than one way to do this!

11

Classes

Show me your flowchart and conceal your tables, and I shall continue to be mystified. Show me your tables, and I won't usually need your flowchart; it'll be obvious.

—FRED BROOKS, *THE MYTHICAL MAN MONTH*

Show me your code and conceal your data structures, and I shall continue to be mystified. Show me your data structures, and I won't usually need your code; it'll be obvious.

—ERIC RAYMOND, *THE CATHEDRAL AND THE BAZAAR*

Spend a lot of time programming and you will almost certainly encounter the age-old debate between functional programming and object-oriented programming.

Functional programming seeks to interpret algorithms as a series or combination of functions. Functional programming minimizes stored state and moving parts. All problems are solved through applied transformations.

Object-oriented programming interprets algorithms as interactions with and between stateful structured objects. All problems are solved by creating objects with states and behaviors, and then passing them to other objects.

Both tribes have their stereotypes. Functional programming is for snobby purists in academia who make unusable software for other academics. Object-oriented programming is for corporate sellouts who spend more time writing documentation than writing code.

As often happens in these situations, the best path lies somewhere in between. Classes are good and useful. Functions are also good and useful. Recognizing when to use one or the other is a key skill to develop as a software engineer.

For example, physical objects containing stateful information that can be interacted with, and whose state and interactions influence the state of other physical objects in the world, are obvious candidates for a class.

Consider the standard deck of playing cards. There are 52 cards; they have a specific and meaningful order. When a new deck is opened (or instantiated, if you will), it's grouped by suit, ordered from Ace to King. Then we can shuffle those cards, creating a brand-new order. When cards are dealt, cards are removed from the deck and put into a player's hand, creating a "hand object" that is distinct from the deck they originated from.

In Python, we might write it up as something like this:

```python
import random

SUITS = ['SPADES', 'HEARTS', 'DIAMONDS', 'CLUBS']
FACES = ['A', '2', '3', '4', '5', '6', '7', '8', '9', '10', 'J', 'Q', 'K']

class Deck:
    def __init__(self):
        self.cards = [(f, s) for s in SUITS for f in FACES]

    def shuffle(self):
        random.shuffle(self.cards)

    def deal(self, num):
        if len(self.cards) < num:
            print(f'Not enough cards to deal {num} cards')
        else:
            dealt = self.cards[0:num]
            self.cards = self.cards[num:]
            return dealt
```

Here we're using the random package to shuffle cards with random.shuffle. Note that it shuffles the list in place and modifies the original list, rather than returning a shuffled list.

A stylistic choice here is the use of variable names in all capitals to represent the suits and face values of the cards. This is common to do when the data being stored in the variable is a *constant* and shouldn't be modified. For example:

```python
PI = 3.14159
```

Unless the value of pi changes, no one needs to mess around with this value, and we shouldn't expect it to be reassigned or modified in any way. Similarly, because suits and face values of playing cards have been the same since they came about in the 15th century in France, we can consider these to be constant as well.

Using this Deck class, we can create a new deck, shuffle it, and deal five cards like so:

```python
deck = Deck()
deck.shuffle()
deck.deal(5)
```

This returns five random cards, or at least tuples containing a suit string and a face value string that represent cards. Try it and see if you get a good hand!

Now, astute readers may have noticed an oversight in my rationalization for using constants to represent the suits and face values of cards. And that is: English was not commonly spoken in 15th century France. What France exported to the world was not spades, hearts, diamonds, and clubs, but *piques*, *cœurs*, *carreaux*, and *trèfles*.

This isn't to say the decision to use constant lists of strings like this was "wrong"—our Deck example works great for playing around with in the English-speaking world. But how do we expand on it and write additional functionality, such as multilanguage support, without the whole thing turning into, well, a house of cards?

In this chapter we'll explore advanced uses of classes and objects in Python and, more importantly, strategies for using those classes cleanly.

STATIC METHODS AND ATTRIBUTES

In the Deck class, the attribute cards is created when the new Deck instance is created. The order of cards within it is unique to every deck. This is called an *instance attribute* because it is only available in that particular class instance and may differ from instance to instance.

However, there may also be attributes of a class that do not change from instance to instance. For example, suit and face values are the same in every deck of cards (ignoring possible future multilanguage features, of course). We could easily rewrite the class initialization so the suits and faces are attributes of the class itself:

```
class Deck:
    def __init__(self):
        self.SUITS = ['SPADES', 'HEARTS', 'DIAMONDS', 'CLUBS']
        self.FACES = [
            'A', '2', '3', '4', '5', '6', '7', '8', '9', '10', 'J', 'Q', 'K'
        ]
        self.cards = [(f, s) for s in self.SUITS for f in self.FACES]
```

While these values are hard-coded in the __init__ method of the class, there's another way to define values like this:

```
class Deck:
    SUITS = ['SPADES', 'HEARTS', 'DIAMONDS', 'CLUBS']
    FACES = ['A', '2', '3', '4', '5', '6', '7', '8', '9', '10', 'J', 'Q', 'K']
    def __init__(self):
        self.cards = [(f, s) for s in self.SUITS for f in self.FACES]
```

When attributes are defined outside of a method and in the class itself, they are called *static attributes*. Static attributes are unchanging, inherent properties of a class. They are something important to the definition of the object itself. An essential attribute of a deck of cards is that it has these four suits and 13 face values.

The exact list of cards in the deck is an instance attribute because it changes from instance to instance. This particular deck has this many cards in it, and they are in this particular order. When we deal from the deck instance, the list of cards is modified to remove cards. Static attributes, in contrast, are typically not modified.

But the difference between static and instance attributes is not merely philosophical. Because static attributes are the attributes of the class itself, they can be referenced from the class. This provides the list of suits:

```
Deck.SUITS
```

This raises an attribute error because, by definition, the class Deck does not contain instance attributes:

```
Deck.cards
```

We can also access methods on the class Deck. For example, given the class with a shuffle method:

```
class Deck:
    SUITS = ['SPADES', 'HEARTS', 'DIAMONDS', 'CLUBS']
    FACES = ['A', '2', '3', '4', '5', '6', '7', '8', '9', '10', 'J', 'Q', 'K']
    def __init__(self):
        self.cards = [(f, s) for s in self.SUITS for f in self.FACES]

    def shuffle(self):
        random.shuffle(self.cards)
```

The fact that the Deck *has* a shuffle method is part of the definition of what a Deck "is":

```
Deck.shuffle
```

This tells us that it's a function on the Deck class:

```
<function __main__.Deck.shuffle(self)>
```

However, we cannot actually call the shuffle method:

```
Deck.shuffle()
```

This raises the error:

```
TypeError: Deck.shuffle() missing 1 required positional argument: 'self'
```

We're missing the self argument, the specific deck instance we want to shuffle. This tells us that you cannot shuffle the "theoretical definition of a deck of cards"; you can only shuffle an *actual* deck of cards.

However, there may be times when a method doesn't require a self or an instance argument at all. For example, we might have a method that returns a string containing a formatted list of suits:

```
class Deck:
    ...
    def get_suits_str():
        return f'The suits are: {', '.join(Deck.SUITS)}'
```

When called using Deck.get_suits_str(), this returns the string:

```
'The suits are: SPADES, HEARTS, DIAMONDS, CLUBS'
```

This method doesn't need to know anything about a particular instance of a deck of cards. In fact, it doesn't contain a `self` argument at all. Methods like this are *static methods*; they don't change from class instance to class instance. This method is perfectly fine, except if we want to do something like this:

```
deck = Deck()
deck.shuffle()
deck.get_suits_str()
```

This raises the error:

```
Deck.get_suits_str() takes 0 positional arguments but 1 was given
```

Remember that when you call a method on a particular class instance that Python automatically passes that instance in as the first argument to the method. Therefore, these two lines are equivalent:

```
deck.get_suits_str()
Deck.get_suits_str(deck)
```

The problem is that `get_suits_str`, as a static method, doesn't take any arguments at all, and we certainly don't want to pass an instance into it. To solve this problem, use the `@staticmethod` decorator:

```
class Deck:
    ...
    @staticmethod
    def get_suits_str():
        return f'The suits are: {', '.join(Deck.SUITS)}'
```

Then create a new deck with this updated class `Deck` and try calling the method again:

```
deck = Deck()
deck.get_suits_str()
```

Not only does the `@staticmethod` decorator remove any class instances that might be passed in, but it acts as documentation of sorts, making it immediately clear which methods are static.

INHERITANCE

> *"One day, my lad, all this will be yours."*
>
> *"What, the curtains?"*
>
> —MONTY PYTHON AND THE HOLY GRAIL

An important principle in software engineering is DRY: Don't Repeat Yourself. Avoiding repetition is a good thing, not only to keep codebases small and clean but to prevent errors that might arise from modifying code in one area but forgetting to modify its duplication somewhere else. The more places a function or value is written in, the more places that function or value needs to be maintained.

One powerful tool for accomplishing this is *class inheritance*. If you need to create a similar class to one that already exists, you can automatically inherit the parent class's methods and attributes, only specifying what needs changing in the derived child class.

For example, recall the full `Deck` class:

```
class Deck:
    SUITS = ['SPADES', 'HEARTS', 'DIAMONDS', 'CLUBS']
    FACES = ['A', '2', '3', '4', '5', '6', '7', '8', '9', '10', 'J', 'Q', 'K']
    def __init__(self):
        self.cards = [(f, s) for s in self.SUITS for f in self.FACES]

    def shuffle(self):
        random.shuffle(self.cards)

    def deal(self, num):
        if len(self.cards) < num:
            print(f'Not enough cards to deal {num} cards')
        else:
            dealt = self.cards[0:num]
            self.cards = self.cards[num:]
            return dealt

    @staticmethod
    def get_suits_str():
        return f'The suits are: {', '.join(Deck.SUITS)}'
```

This is a lot of code to rewrite if we want to create a `FrenchDeck` class, which contains French suit names and face value characters. However, using inheritance, we only have to specify the part that differs from the `Deck` class:

```
class FrenchDeck(Deck):
    SUITS = ['PIQUES', 'CŒURS', 'CARREAUX', 'TRÈFLES']
    FACES = ['A', '2', '3', '4', '5', '6', '7', '8', '9', '10', 'V', 'D', 'R']

french = FrenchDeck()
french.shuffle()
french.deal(5)
```

Here, we're passing the class `Deck` into the class declaration: `class FrenchDeck(Deck)`. This tells Python that we want to make a new class, `FrenchDeck`, which *extends* (or inherits from) the `Deck` class. Afterward, we simply write a class definition consisting only of the things we want to change from the parent `Deck` class.

In the case of the FrenchDeck, we have different suit names, as well as `'V'`, `'D'`, and `'R'` (*valet, dame, and roi*) substituting for the English face values `'J'`, `'Q'`, and `'K'`. Running this and dealing five random cards returned, for me:

```
[('7', 'PIQUES'),
 ('D', 'CARREAUX'),
 ('6', 'CARREAUX'),
 ('6', 'PIQUES'),
 ('V', 'CŒURS')]
```

Of course, it will, very probably, return a different hand when you run it.

Although it appears that this FrenchDeck class is relatively empty, it is fully populated and simply inheriting its method and attribute definitions from elsewhere, such as the parent Deck class. If we reference the method `FrenchDeck.__init__`, we find that it exists:

```
<function __main__.FrenchDeck.__init__(self)>
```

Unfortunately, the parent Deck class doesn't always do the correct thing in the context of a French-Deck class. Calling `french.get_suits_str()` results in this string:

```
'The suits are: SPADES, HEARTS, DIAMONDS, CLUBS'
```

Remember that the line inside `get_suits_str` that returns this is:

```
Return f'The suits are: {', '.join(Deck.SUITS)}'
```

It does not use `self.SUITS`; it specifically uses `Deck.SUITS` in the parent class. This references the original English suits that get printed out. There are a few ways to handle situations like this and make sure that the `FrenchDeck` class prints out the French version of the suits. The first is, of course, to add a get_suits_str method to the `FrenchDeck` class:

```
class FrenchDeck(Deck):
    SUITS = ['PIQUES', 'CŒURS', 'CARREAUX', 'TRÈFLES']
    FACES = ['A', '2', '3', '4', '5', '6', '7', '8', '9', '10', 'V', 'D', 'R']

    @staticmethod
    def get_suits_str():
        return f'Les enseignes sont: {', '.join(FrenchDeck.SUITS)}'
```

This has the benefit of allowing us to substitute "*Les enseignes sont*" for "The suits are," enhancing the translation. The drawback, of course, is that we have to duplicate some of the logic of formatting and joining the strings.

Another possible solution is to convert this from a static method to a *class method* in the parent Deck class. A class method is a bit like a static method in that it describes logic that is relevant to the definition of the class itself, rather than a particular instance of the class. Unlike a static method, it gets access to the `cls` argument, which represents the current class:

```
class Deck:
    ...
    @classmethod
    def get_suits_str(cls):
        return f'The suits are: {', '.join(cls.SUITS)}'
```

Now we can make an English deck:

```
deck = Deck()
deck.get_suits_str()
```

This returns the string:

```
'The suits are: SPADES, HEARTS, DIAMONDS, CLUBS'
```

And a French deck:

```
class FrenchDeck(Deck):
    SUITS = ['PIQUES', 'CŒURS', 'CARREAUX', 'TRÈFLES']
    FACES = ['A', '2', '3', '4', '5', '6', '7', '8', '9', '10', 'V', 'D', 'R']

french = FrenchDeck()
french.get_suits_str()
```

This returns the string:

```
'The suits are: PIQUES, CŒURS, CARREAUX, TRÈFLES'
```

Just as the `self` argument in instance methods represents the current instance, the `cls` argument in class methods always represents the current class. This can be extremely useful when working with class inheritance, where the "current class" may not always be the one you're writing the code in!

MULTIPLE INHERITANCE

The card game pinochle is played with an unusual deck. It uses only the face values A, 9, 10, J, Q, K, but every card appears in the deck twice. So, there are eight aces (two of each suit), eight 9s, etc. for a total of 48 cards.[1]

We can create a `PinochleDeck` class like this:

```
class PinochleDeck(Deck):
    def __init__(self):
        faces = [self.FACES[0]] + self.FACES[8:]
        self.cards = [(f, s) for s in self.SUITS*2 for f in faces]
```

Notice that `self.SUITS` is effectively iterated through twice by multiplying it by 2. I am also making a potentially controversial design decision here: The variable `faces` is a temporary variable in the constructor designed to keep track of only the faces in `self.FACES` that we actually want to use in the deck. In this case, we're using the first face (`'A'`) and the faces starting at index 8 through the end of the list (`'9'`, `'10'`, `'J'`, `'Q'`, `'K'`).

Another way to write this class might be:

```
class PinochleDeck(Deck):
    FACES = ['A', '9', '10', 'J', 'Q', 'K']
    def __init__(self):
        self.cards = [(f, s) for s in self.SUITS*2 for f in self.FACES]
```

Some might argue that this is "more correct." After all, the only face values used in a pinochle deck are A, 9, 10, J, Q, and K. Therefore, shouldn't any references to `PinochleDeck.FACES` reflect that fact? However, astute readers may have realized that I'm carefully setting up an illustrative example to demonstrate an aspect of Python programming. We will discuss additional "more ideal" approaches to this problem later, but for now, the first version of the `PinochleDeck` class will be used.

In the previous section we created a French language deck. Now we have a pinochle deck. How might we create a French pinochle deck? Using *multiple inheritance*, Python classes can use the attributes and methods of two or more classes.

---

[1] Although Pinochle-specific decks are sold, you can also create them by combining two decks of cards and simply removing every card with a value of 2 through 8.

While multiple inheritance can lead to a great deal of complexity and confusion if used thoughtlessly, it's undeniably an extremely powerful tool. Our `FrenchPinochleDeck` class requires no code at all, other than a class definition containing two parent classes, `FrenchDeck` and `PinochleDeck`:

```
class FrenchPinochleDeck(FrenchDeck, PinochleDeck):
    pass

fp = FrenchPinochleDeck()
print(len(fp.cards))
fp.shuffle()
fp.deal(5)
```

Printing the length of the cards confirms that there are 48 in the deck. Shuffling and dealing the first five result in:

```
[('10', 'CŒURS'),
 ('9', 'PIQUES'),
 ('9', 'CARREAUX'),
 ('A', 'CARREAUX'),
 ('J', 'CARREAUX')]
```

The order that the parent classes are passed to the class definition in is important. There may be cases where an attribute or method is defined in both parent classes (or *all* of the parent classes if there are more than two parents!), in which case a decision needs to be made about which version to use. Python chooses the version from the parent that defines it first in the list.

For example:

```
class A:
    name = 'A'

class B:
    name = 'B'
    another_attr = 'B'

class C:
    name = 'C'
    another_attr = 'C'

class Child(A, B, C):
    pass

print(Child.name)
print(Child.another_attr)
```

This prints the following:

```
A
B
```

All three classes define the static attribute `name`, so the first class in the list, `A`, gets its name used by the `Child` class. The attribute `another_attr` are only defined by `B` and `C`, so the value `'B'` is chosen for `another_attr`.

The order the classes are listed in also affects which version of the methods is used, including the __init__ method. So be very careful when using multiple inheritance and make sure that the version of the method you want in the child class will be the one actually getting used.

There is another multiple inheritance subtlety in cases where a grandparent (parent of a parent) class defines a method but the parent class itself does not. Take this simplified example of our deck classes:

```
class Deck:
    def __init__(self):
        print('Deck constructor!')

class FrenchDeck(Deck):
    pass

class PinochleDeck(Deck):
    def __init__(self):
        print('PinochleDeck constructor!')

class FrenchPinochleDeck(FrenchDeck, PinochleDeck):
    pass
```

Here, I've removed all the internal code from each class except for the initializers, which contain only a print statement to make it easy to tell which initializer was called. Remember that there are only two defined initializers: FrenchDeck defines only static attributes and FrenchPinochleDeck defines no code at all.

This does not mean that the FrenchDeck class doesn't have an initializer. It uses the parent constructor, Deck.__init__. We can see this when we instantiate a new FrenchDeck object:

```
french = FrenchDeck()
```

It prints this line:

```
Deck constructor!
```

However, in cases of multiple inheritance, Python will use the first version of the method that it finds, starting with the first direct parent, then using a somewhat complicated algorithm called *method resolution order (MRO)*.

You can view the MRO for any class using the __mro__ method:

```
FrenchPinochleDeck.__mro__
```

This returns the tuple:

```
(__main__.FrenchPinochleDeck,
 __main__.FrenchDeck,
 __main__.PinochleDeck,
 __main__.Deck,
 object)
```

This means that a search for an initializer for the FrenchPinochleDeck class will start with (of course) FrenchPinochleDeck, then the first parent class FrenchDeck, then the second parent class PinochleDeck, where it finally finds an initializer it can use. It stops there and never looks in the Deck class.

However, you should be cautious. Let's modify `PinochleDeck` so that it no longer extends `Deck` and look at the MRO again:

```
class Deck:
    def __init__(self):
        print('Deck constructor!')

class FrenchDeck(Deck):
    pass

class PinochleDeck():
    def __init__(self):
        print('Pinochle constructor!')

class FrenchPinochleDeck(FrenchDeck, PinochleDeck):
    pass

FrenchPinochleDeck.__mro__
```

By removing `Deck` as a parent class, we've actually moved it up in the order of precedence!

```
(__main__.FrenchPinochleDeck,
 __main__.FrenchDeck,
 __main__.Deck,
 __main__.PinochleDeck,
 object)
```

In fact, if we instantiate a `FrenchPinochleDeck` now, it will print this:

```
Deck constructor!
```

Because `PinochleDeck` no longer contains a `Deck` class in its ancestry, the MRO algorithm will examine `Deck` only as part of its examination of the `FrenchDeck` class first, before moving on to the orphan `PinochleDeck`.

In some situations, this might be very bad. Perhaps the pinochle deck doesn't extend `Deck`, but you still want to use its constructor. In that case, you can simply change the order of the parent classes. Let's call this new class `PinochleFrenchDeck`:

```
class PinochleFrenchDeck(PinochleDeck, FrenchDeck):
    pass

PinochleFrenchDeck.__mro__
```

This returns the MRO:

```
(__main__.PinochleFrenchDeck,
 __main__.PinochleDeck,
 __main__.FrenchDeck,
 __main__.Deck,
 object)
```

The algorithm that Python uses to decide the MRO is called *C3 linearization*. It's designed to be consistent and deterministic, but not intuitive or easy to use. For this reason, I encourage you not to rely on the subtleties of its workings when using multiple inheritance. Even if you understand what's going on, it's unlikely that your coworkers (or even future versions of yourself debugging the code later) will have the same understanding.

This isn't to say that you shouldn't use multiple inheritance! However, when you use multiple inheritance, you must be careful and explicit about what is being inherited.

If you rely on one class's methods and attributes to be preferred, list that class first. If you're unsure of what will happen, make sure you test! There's also nothing wrong with specifying what you want to happen explicitly:

```
class PinochleFrenchDeck(PinochleDeck, FrenchDeck):
    SUITS = FrenchDeck.SUITS
    FACES = FrenchDeck.FACES
    __init__ = PinochleDeck.__init__
```

Even if these definitions are redundant—and would have happened anyway according to the rules of C3 linearization—it makes the class definition easier to read and understand for others.

ENCAPSULATION

Here's a fun piece of code:

```
Deck.SUITS = ['spam', 'spam', 'spam', 'spam']

deck = Deck()
deck.cards
```

This produces a lot of spam. In fact, it will cause every deck of cards instantiated from that point forward to have all 52 cards labeled with a 'spam' suit.

When object-oriented programming is used in large codebases with multiple developers, it's not unheard of for these sorts of things to happen unintentionally. One developer may update a static attribute of a class that another developer uses without knowing about the update, leading to bugs.

Encapsulation is a practice designed to prevent this. It hides the parts of your class that shouldn't be touched and provides a sort of "user interface"[2] for the class that allows it to be used safely.

Rather than allowing the SUITS attribute to be modified directly, it can be marked as a *private attribute*. Private attributes and *private methods* should not be modified outside the class. They start with a leading underscore to indicate that they are private:

```
class Deck:
    _SUITS = ['SPADES', 'HEARTS', 'DIAMONDS', 'CLUBS']
    _FACES = ['A', '2', '3', '4', '5', '6', '7', '8', '9', '10', 'J', 'Q', 'K']
    def __init__(self):
        self.cards = [(f, s) for s in self._SUITS for f in self._FACES]
```

You shouldn't modify or call attributes or methods with a leading underscore. In fact, you shouldn't read or access them at all outside the class! In the Deck constructor, of course, we use the values of

---

[2] It's more common to hear the term "user interface" referring to the pretty user-facing side of web applications (such as forms and login pages). Here, when we're talking about the design of class interfaces, we mean "users" as other software engineers using the classes. The "user interface" of a class (or any other piece of code meant to be imported and used by other software engineers) is its methods and attributes and how those methods and attributes can be used.

`self._SUITS` and `self._FACES` to instantiate the cards, but their usage is fine inside the class (or derived child classes) However, outside the class, this sort of thing is frowned upon:

```
deck = Deck()
print(deck._SUITS)
```

To be clear, there is nothing actually preventing anyone from writing something like this:

```
Deck._SUITS = ['spam', 'spam', 'spam', 'spam']
```

This does not raise an error or even a warning. Python will happily execute it. The leading underscore is simply a convention introduced in PEP 8 that is generally best to follow.

What if those private attributes need to be accessed? This is where *getters and setters* come in. These are methods that start with the word `get_` or `set_` and allow you to interact with the private attributes in a safe way.

For example, we may decide that the `Deck` class needs a way for people to update the suits so that they can create fun novelty decks. However, the suits passed in need to meet certain criteria for them to be valid:

➤ Must be a list of strings.

➤ There must be four of them.

➤ Lists must not contain duplicate strings.

➤ Strings must be reasonably sized (10 chars or fewer).

Because we are now explicitly allowing the `_SUITS` attribute to be updated, we must also make it lowercase, following PEP 8 guidelines:

```
class Deck:
    _suits = ['SPADES', 'HEARTS', 'DIAMONDS', 'CLUBS']
    _FACES = ['A', '2', '3', '4', '5', '6', '7', '8', '9', '10', 'J', 'Q', 'K']
    def __init__(self):
        self.cards = [(f, s) for s in self._suits for f in self._FACES]

    @classmethod
    def set_suits(cls, suits):
            if cls._suits_are_valid(suits):
                cls._suits = suits

    @staticmethod
    def _suits_are_valid(suits):
        if type(suits) != list:
            print('Suits are not a list')
            return False
        if any([type(s) != str for s in suits]):
            print('Must be strings')
            return False
        if len(set(suits)) != 4:
            print('Must be four unique suits')
            return False
        if any([len(s) > 10 for s in suits]):
            print('Must be 10 chars or less')
            return False
        return True
```

Here I've added two methods: the externally facing `set_suits` and an internal `_suits_are_valid`. The method `set_suits` is also labeled with the decorator `@classmethod` to make it clearer that this updates the suits for the entire class moving forward, rather than a particular deck instance.

The method `_suits_are_valid` is an internal utility method that is not part of the "user interface" of the `Deck` class and so has a leading underscore to make it a private method. There's also a new list function used here: `any`. This returns `True` if any of the items in the list are `True`; otherwise, it returns `False`.

Assuming we also have the same `shuffle` and `deal` methods in this class as used previously, you can create a new deck with custom suits like this:

```
Deck.set_suits(['PYTHON', 'JAVA', 'LISP', 'RUST'])
deck = Deck()
deck.shuffle()
deck.deal(5)
```

This returns five cards:

```
[('7', 'JAVA'), ('Q', 'RUST'), ('Q', 'LISP'), ('K', 'RUST'), ('7', 'LISP')]
```

We've seen a getter method already in this chapter with `get_suits_string`. Often, getters are very thin wrappers and simply return a value:

```
@classmethod
def get_suits(cls):
    return cls._suits
```

However, they can also be more elaborate and provide formatting, like `get_suits_str`:

```
@classmethod
def get_suits_str(cls):
    return f'The suits are: {", ".join(cls._suits)}'
```

Getters can also be used internally and provide important business logic. Recall the `PinochleDeck` class and that one of the issues was that we couldn't modify the static `self.FACES` without breaking language translation, but picking out a subset of faces in the `__init__` method was also somewhat awkward and might be difficult to notice:

```
class PinochleDeck(Deck):
    def __init__(self):
        faces = [self.FACES[0]] + self.FACES[8:]
        self.cards = [(f, s) for s in self.SUITS*2 for f in faces]
```

This might have more clearly been written as:

```
class PinochleDeck(Deck):
    FACES = ['A', '9', '10', 'J', 'Q', 'K']
    def __init__(self):
        self.cards = [(f, s) for s in self.SUITS*2 for f in self.FACES]
```

However, this would break the ability of child classes to override the face values of the cards without causing general chaos and lots of bugs.

One solution in this case might be to rewrite using a getter:

```
class PinochleDeck(Deck):
    def __init__(self):
        self.cards = [(f, s) for s in self.get_suits()*2 for f in self.get_faces()]

    @classmethod
    def get_faces(cls):
        return [cls._FACES[0]] + cls._FACES[8:]

deck = PinochleDeck()
deck.shuffle()
deck.deal(5)
```

This makes it clearer that, while we have access to the full 13 face values defined by the current class, only a subset of them are considered in a pinochle deck.

Another technique that makes this even clearer uses the super function. The super function is used to access methods in the parent class (or classes). It returns an object that represents an instance of the parent class with the methods of the parent class but the attributes of the current child class instance.

The key word here is *represents*. The object that is returned from super is not actually an instance of the parent class, it's a special object that contains a reference to both the child class instance and its parent class definition.

The super function is commonly used to call a parent's __init__ method inside the __init__ method of the child class. The following demonstrates how this can be used to make class-specific data transformations (modifying the elements in the faces and suits) before calling the parent to initialize other attributes (the set of cards):

```
class Deck:
    SUITS = ['SPADES', 'HEARTS', 'DIAMONDS', 'CLUBS']
    FACES = ['A', '2', '3', '4', '5', '6', '7', '8', '9', '10', 'J', 'Q', 'K']
    def __init__(self, suits=None, faces=None):
        suits = suits or self.SUITS
        faces = faces or self.FACES
        self.cards = [(f, s) for s in suits for f in faces]

class PinochleDeck(Deck):
    def __init__(self):
        faces = [self.FACES[0]] + self.FACES[8:]
        suits = self.SUITS * 2
        super().__init__(suits, faces)
```

The __init__ method in the Deck class is modified so that it can, optionally, accept a custom set of suit and face values, but defaults to the static SUITS and FACES. The PinochleDeck class uses the static SUITS and FACES, which allows for the possibility of a different language translation, say, from a FrenchDeck class.

The last line of PinochleDeck.__init__ makes a call to the super function, returning an object that references the parent class Deck. When super().__init__ is called, we are passing the new values of suits and faces to the __init__ method in the Deck class.

Although this approach may be overkill in this particular example, calling super().__init__ in a child __init__ method is useful as a general pattern. This also has the benefit that any future business logic (for example, if we wanted to shuffle all decks as soon as they're created) only needs to be written in the __init__ method of the parent class, and does not need to be copied to each child's initialization method.

Class inheritance, especially multi-class inheritance, means that you must make many design decisions when writing classes that are similar or share properties. While the obvious way to write the classes may not seem so obvious at first (unless you're Dutch), these class inheritance patterns do become easier with practice.

POLYMORPHISM

Polymorphism comes from the Greek and means, literally, "many forms." In object-oriented programming, it refers to the practice of using templating to enforce common method and attribute names across many similar types of objects.

For example, we've seen several different types of card decks in this chapter. However, they all have common methods and attributes that allow us to use them in the same way as each other. We can write a method deal_cards, for example, that will allow us to deal equally well with both a FrenchDeck and a Deck:

```
def deal_cards(deck, num_cards, num_hands):
    return [deck.deal(num_cards) for _ in range(num_hands)]

deck = FrenchDeck()
deck.shuffle()
deal_cards(deck, 5, 2)

deck = Deck()
deck.shuffle()
deal_cards(deck, 5, 2)
```

The function deal_cards does not care what class the deck object is, as long as it has a deal method that takes, as an argument, a number of cards to deal. The deck argument doesn't even have to be a child of the Deck class!

In large programming projects, it may be necessary for a developer to create a new class to produce objects that will be used by code that they have not written or even seen. A well-known design approach for navigating this situation is called *design by contract (DbC)*, which outlines techniques for enforcing consistency between classes.

In Python, it is common to create "templates" or *base classes* that developers can use and reference when designing new classes of a certain type. Sometimes these templates can be used directly—the Deck class might serve as a standard for all sorts of card decks, but you can also instantiate a new Deck object and play with it just fine!

Other times, these templates exist only to act as parent classes, and it doesn't make sense to instantiate them directly. These are called *abstract base classes*. We can make an abstract base class called DeckBase that serves as a template for other types of decks:

```
class DeckBase:
    def deal(self, num cards):
        raise NotImplementedError()

    def shuffle(self):
        raise NotImplementedError()

    def get_cards(self):
        raise NotImplementedError()

    def set_cards(self, cards):
        raise NotImplementedError()
```

Here I'm using the `raise` keyword we'll discuss in more depth in Chapter 13, "Errors and Exceptions." This raises a new error, `NotImplementedError`. This is commonly used in abstract base classes that should be used for templates but not instantiated.

Notice that we don't explicitly reference suits or faces here, which are specific features of the 52-card playing deck and a few variations of it. You might use this `DeckBase` class to play any game from poker to Monopoly (which has decks of "chance" and "community chest" cards on the board).

While the `DeckBase` class might be extended by other classes, like the `Deck` class, we cannot implement it and use it directly:

```
deck = DeckBase()
deck.shuffle()
```

If we try this, of course, we get a `NotImplementedError`.

The `DeckBase` class is great for making sure that everyone follows the template. If we forget to implement something, it will let us know:

```
class Deck(DeckBase):
    _SUITS = ['SPADES', 'HEARTS', 'DIAMONDS', 'CLUBS']
    _FACES = ['A', '2', '3', '4', '5', '6', '7', '8', '9', '10', 'J', 'Q', 'K']
    def __init__(self):
        self.cards = [(f, s) for s in self._SUITS for f in self._FACES]

    def shuffle(self):
        random.shuffle(self.cards)

deck = Deck ()
deck.shuffle()
deck.deal(5)
```

Here, I've forgotten to implement the `deal` method and another `NotImplementedError` is raised.

For most projects, this strategy is great for creating class templates that everyone can agree on and use. There are cases, though, where a more formal and rigorous approach is needed for creating and extending abstract base classes. Some organizations may require the use of the `abc` module (Abstract Base Classes module) in Python: `https://docs.python.org/3/library/abc.html`.

Although the `abc` module is outside the scope of this book, I encourage you to look into it if you're interested in furthering your study of polymorphism and design by contract.

1. Create a Card class that has the attributes suit and face that can be passed into its construc-
    tor. Modify the Deck class to use a list of Card objects as cards, rather than a list of tuples.

2. Add a method called __str__ to the Card object in the first exercise. The __str__ method
    allows Python to know how to format the objects as strings and will be used automatically if
    populated. Use it to create a string representation of the card.

    Keep in mind you can use the Unicode symbols ♠, ♡, ◊, and ♣ in your string representations
    of the card.

3. Design an abstract base class for a hand of cards in a game called AbstractBaseHand. Think
    about what sorts of features a hand might have. Some methods you might require implementa-
    tion for might be:

    ➤ get_cards

    ➤ set_cards

    ➤ add_card (add card passed into the hand)

    ➤ remove_card (remove card matching value and suit passed in

    ➤ __str__

4. Extend your AbstractBaseHand class to create a specific Hand class with all methods imple-
    mented. At a minimum, you should be able to deal cards to it from the deck and display the
    resulting hand values.

12

Writing Cleaner Code

Bad code rots and ferments, becoming an inexorable weight that drags the team down. Time and time again I have seen teams grind to a crawl because, in their haste, they created a malignant morass of code that forever thereafter dominated their destiny.

— Robert C. Martin, *Clean Code*

We've covered many best practices so far. For example, starting class names with a capital letter is not enforced by Python, but doing so is a "best practice" that you can choose to follow, or not.

Some of these best practices aren't specific to Python at all but are good to follow regardless of the language you're writing in.

Things like choosing descriptive function and variable names will serve you well no matter where your programming journey takes you.

In this chapter, we'll take a deeper dive into some of the conventions, tools, and practices that can help you write clean, readable, and usable code.

PEP 8 AND CODE STYLES

The term *PEP 8*, or the Python Enhancement Proposal 8, is frequently mentioned when talking about coding style in Python. It is the canonical reference guide for coding styles. It's also surprisingly short: https://peps.python.org/pep-0008. In fact, rather than me rewriting its contents here, you should just go ahead and read it yourself.

This comprehensive guide to styling is one of the things that makes Python such a great language. In other programming languages, there might be debates about whether to use two, four, or even eight spaces per tab—and everyone is right, it's just a matter of personal preference. In Python, there are four spaces per tab because of PEP 8.

Although PEP 8 guidelines should always be followed (unless you have a really compelling specific reason not to), there are a few cases where they allow for personal freedom. For example:

> *In Python, single-quoted strings and double-quoted strings are the same. This PEP does not make a recommendation for this. Pick a rule and stick to it. When a string contains single or double quote characters, however, use the other one to avoid backslashes in the string. It improves readability.*

> *For triple-quoted strings, always use double quote characters to be consistent with the docstring convention in PEP 257.*

Throughout this book, I use single-quoted strings. You may choose to use double-quoted strings. In this chapter, we'll look at some ways of enforcing both PEP 8 and personal styles, as well as using the docstrings to document code.

COMMENTS AND DOCSTRINGS

Comments are designed to make code more quickly understandable for others and also future versions of yourself who might come back to the code and wonder what past versions of yourself have done. The presence of comments is usually a sign of good code.

Often, after hearing that comments are a good thing, new programmers will write something like the following:

```
# Set interest rate to 0.06 or 6%
interest_rate = 0.06
# Set principal to 100
principal = 100
# Set interest amount equal to interest rate times principal
interest_amount = interest_rate * principal
```

This is too many comments. No one needs to *read* `Set interest amount equal to interest rate times principal`; they can see that you're doing it when they read the line:

```
interest_amount = interest_rate * principal
```

Ideally, code is *self-documenting*. That is, it is cleanly written with consistent and well-chosen variable and function names so that it's immediately obvious, without comments, what it's doing and why it's doing that. Adding comments to clarify obvious lines simply makes that line twice as long, ironically, hindering readability.

There are a few major types of comments in Python:

➤ Explanatory comments for potentially confusing lines or sections of code.

➤ Code itself that has been commented out to prevent it from running. Done often during development, this is a sign of code smell.

➤ Docstrings that describe each function, class, and/or file.

There are multiple ways of writing explanatory comments themselves. In addition to placing them on their own line above the code they reference, you can write inline comments:

```
class ApplicationProtocolPorts:
    FTP = 21 # File Transfer Protocol
    SSH = 22 # Secure Shell (22 can also be SFTP)
    HTTP = 80 # Hypertext Transfer Protocol
```

Inline comments are placed next to existing code rather than above or below it on their own line. Because of this, they are usually shorter, or at least placed next to shorter segments of code. It is common to use them for detailed variable or value descriptions.

Longer comments are called multiline comments:

```
class ApplicationProtocolPorts:
    FTP = 21
    # Protocols such as SFTP can run over SSH
    # If packets are on port 22, further examination
    # must be done to determine the application protocol
    # being used
    SSH = 22
    HTTP = 80
```

Other languages may have specific symbols that start and end multiline comments (also called block comments). That way, comments can run on for several lines without needing to include a special character at the start of each line—simply provide the closing character when you're done. Although Python doesn't technically have this feature, you may see multiline strings used like this:

```
class ApplicationProtocolPorts:
    FTP = 21
    """
    Protocols such as SFTP can run over SSH
    If packets are on port 22, further examination
    must be done to determine the application protocol
    being used
    """
    SSH = 22
    HTTP = 80
```

Technically, this is not a "comment" but a string being inserted in the code, assigned to nothing and never used. However, it does work as a comment. It won't impact the code[1] and it provides plain-English documentation that everyone can read.

Multiline strings are also used as *docstrings* in Python. These are strings that are inserted as the first line of a function, class, module, or method and serve to document that entity.

---

[1] It's often touted that multiline strings won't impact code, but you really can't insert them anywhere at all like you can with an actual comment. This was pointed out in replies to Guido van Rossum in 2011 when he posted on social media: "Python tip: You can use multi-line strings as multi-line comments. Unless used as docstrings, they generate no code! :-)" (https://twitter.com/gvanrossum/status/112670605505077248). For example, if used in the middle of data structure definitions that span multiple lines, multiline strings will not be ignored in the same way that comments will.

Docstrings are described in PEP 257 (`https://peps.python.org/pep-0257`). Multiline strings can be written with single quotes:

```
'''Some text
is here'''
```

However, docstrings are always written with double quotes by convention:

```
"""This is a multi-
line docstring
"""
```

To be clear, regular multiline strings can be written with double quotes as well:

```
my_str = """Here is a
multi-line string that I
am storing in the variable
my_str.
"""
```

However, docstrings *must* use double quotes.

Here is an example of a docstring in a simple User class with __init__ and validate_email methods:

```
import re

class User:
    """This class represents a User object for our corporate
    web application. It can be extended into other classes
    such as SuperUsers or Employees
    """
    def __init__(self, name, username, email):
        """User initialization has the following arguments:
        name - real-world name for the user
        username - unique string, can contain underscores or numbers
        email - email address for the user
        """
        self.name = name
        self.username = username
        self.email = email

    def validate_email(self):
        """Raises an exception if email is invalid"""
        email_regex = r'^\S+@\S+\.\S+$'
        if not re.match(email_regex, self.email):
            raise Exception('Email address is invalid')
```

This contains two multiline docstrings, one for the User class itself and one for the initialization method __init__.

The validate_email method has only a one-line docstring, which is used for simple cases where a lot of explanation isn't needed. In one-line docstrings, putting opening and closing quotes on the same line as the docstring is allowed.

Docstrings can easily be used to create documentation for the entity they're documenting. The help function in Python will show you all docstrings for the class:

```
help(User)
```

This returns a string showing formatted docstrings:

```
Help on class User in module __main__:

class User(builtins.object)
 |  User(name, username, email)
 |
 |  This class represents a User object for our corporate
 |  web application. It can be extended into other classes
 |  such as SuperUsers or Employees
 |
 |  Methods defined here:
 |
 |  __init__(self, name, username, email)
 |      User initialization has the following arguments:
 |      name - real-world name for the user
 |      username - unique string, can contain underscores or numbers
 |      email - email address for the user
 |
 |  validate_email(self)
 |      Raises an exception if email is invalid
 |
 |  ----------------------------------------------------------------------
 |  Data descriptors defined here:
 |
 |  __dict__
 |      dictionary for instance variables
 |
 |  __weakref__
 |      list of weak references to the object
```

Some of the attributes, __dict__ and __weakref__, are inherited from the Python object class, which all objects are children of. Even if they don't explicitly extend anything, they still inherit from object. You can see that the User class extends object from the generated documentation:

```
class User(builtins.object)
```

The help function uses the __doc__ attribute to do this. Every object in Python has a __doc__ attribute. If the docstring isn't included, that attribute will be None, but it still exists:

```
def test():
    print('foo')

print(test.__doc__)
```

By iterating through all methods and in the class and collecting their docstrings, the help documentation is created.

The help function can also be used with modules and packages, like the re (*regular expressions*) package used in the validate_email method earlier:

```
import re

help(re)
```

This package allows you to write pattern-matchers called regular expressions to match characters in text, like an email address. Regular expressions look like strings but start with an r to indicate that they are raw strings. Raw strings are used in several places in Python (such as to represent file paths) and store strings without a particular encoding, like utf-8. Raw strings start with an r, much like bytes data starts with a b, and f-strings start with an f:

```
r'^\S+@\S+\.\S+$' # regular expression
f'Hello, {u.name}' # f-string
b'\xf0\x9f\x98\x86' # bytes
```

Although regular expressions are outside the scope of this book, learning how to write and use the regular expression strings to identify, filter, or validate text is a useful skill. More information about these strings and the re module can be found at https://docs.python.org/3/library/re.html.

DOCUMENTATION

When it comes to public and open source programming libraries, documentation can often make or break a project. The documentation for Python itself, at https://docs.python.org, is fantastic. But with some third-party Python libraries, I've had to look for alternatives simply because the documentation couldn't answer my questions about the library's usage.

If you're working on an internal project for your company, you might create documentation in the README.md file of the GitHub repository. Don't be too disappointed if this documentation isn't as widely read throughout the organization as you think it should be. In my experience, the value of documentation often comes from organizing your thoughts while writing it, even if it doesn't lead anywhere else. At the very least, you can link coworkers to the relevant section of your documentation when they ask you questions that have been answered there!

Documentation of a Python project often has sections like:

➤ **Introduction:** An introduction to or description of the project. What is it used for, or what problem does it solve?

➤ **Requirements:** Minimum Python version. Any other services required, such as a database.

➤ **Installation:** How to install the software.

➤ **Basic usage, or a tutorial:** Basic usage of the code or API with a few examples.

➤ **License:** What rights users have to share, alter, and use the work for commercial purposes.

➤ **TODO:** A list of features or fixes that need to be done.

➤ **Changelog:** A record of changes, or large changes, made to the project by version number.

Smaller projects may have just a simple "Usage" section with a few examples, while larger projects might have more involved tutorials, quickstart guides, a comprehensive API reference, and other resources. Larger projects usually outgrow their README files and may use another service for documentation such as Read the Docs (https://readthedocs.io).

Even when the code itself is cleanly written and well commented, it is still important to write documentation for it. This is because documentation is usually written for people who will never read the code.

In some cases, documentation may even be written for project managers or other nonprogrammers with an interest in the project. It might contain statistics about its performance, test results, and information about how it interacts with other projects in the company.

Usually, though, documentation is aimed at programmers who intend to use the project for their own purposes and want to do so in the fastest and most efficient way possible.

For public projects, license information is important to include in the documentation. Licenses determine several things about a project:

➤ If it can be used for commercial purposes

➤ If and how it can be shared and modified to create derivative works

➤ For derivative works:

   ➤ How attribution is managed

   ➤ If a similar license must be attached

➤ Any liability a creator has for the use of the product (Generally, open source licenses absolve a creator of all possible liability.)

Here are some types of popular open source licenses:

➤ Permissive licenses that allow unrestricted modification and distribution. Example licenses are:

   ➤ MIT license

   ➤ BSD license

   ➤ Apache license

   ➤ PSF (Python Software Foundation) license

➤ Copyleft (a play on the term "copyright") licenses, which grant users the right to modify and share the software, but require that any derived works have the same license:

   ➤ Creative Commons Share-Alike license

   ➤ GNU licenses, such as GNU Free Documentation License and GNU General Public License

➤ Public domain, which places no restrictions on use of the software:

   ➤ Creative Commons Zero (CC0) license

   ➤ WTFPL

   ➤ Unlicense

Although writing documentation for your Python projects might seem intimidating or even unnecessary for smaller personal projects, it's easy to add at least a few components to a GitHub README file to get started. Something as simple as a brief description, installation instructions, usage examples, and a license can be extremely helpful for fellow developers. Quality documentation also helps to highlight your projects for potential employers or clients.

LINTING

A *linter* is a funny word for a program that checks code and flags (or even fixes) potential issues. While they might seem very modern and high tech, the term was first introduced in 1978 as the name of a Unix command, `lint`, that checked C code.

A linter doesn't actually execute the code in order to do its job. It scans the code as a text file and looks for patterns that violate the linter's rules. If you've used an IDE such as Visual Studio Code, you've seen a linter at work.

In the figure 12.1, line 2 shows the argument `arg1` in a lighter gray style because it is not used. On line 3, the `for:` has an underline (red, in e-books with color images) indicating a syntax error because there's no Boolean statement or indented block of code below it. On line 5, `arg2` has an underline (yellow, unless the image is grayscale) because it is not previously declared. Finally, on line 6, the entire `print` statement is grayed out because it is impossible to reach.

```
1    # Caution: It's a bit buggy
2    def do_something(arg1):
3        for:
4
5        return arg2
6        print('This is not reached')
7
```

FIGURE 12.1: Four different types of errors shown in Visual Studio Code

Linters might detect several types of errors:

➤ Syntax errors

➤ Stylistic errors:

    ➤ Anything that doesn't conform to PEP 8

➤ Additional configuration of your own style preferences, or those of the company you're working for

➤ Logical errors:

    ➤ A `return` statement in a function followed by unreachable code

    ➤ A function that is declared but never called

➤ Some types of security issues:

    ➤ Passwords stored in plain text in Python files

    ➤ Outside data being loaded and executed as code

One popular linter is called `pylint`. You can install it with this command:

```
$ pip install pylint
```

This allows you to lint Python files using this command:

```
$ pylint my_file.py
```

The exercise files for this book include an example file called `12_pylint_before.py` to practice using the linter with. This is a bit of code I wrote for fun that generates and scores poker hands. You can run it from the command line with:

```
$ python 12_pylint_before.py
```

It produces outputs like the following:

```
3♠, 10♣;, 4♡, K♠, K♣
8♢, 2♢, 9♢, 6♠, 2♠
HAND 1 WINS!
```

This program was never designed to be used for any serious applications and so makes an excellent test subject when scanning for errors and style mistakes (of which there are many). You can run `pylint` against it using this command:

```
$ pylint 12_pylint_before.py
```

You should see many lines print out. The first few involve whitespace:

```
12_pylint_before.py:2:1: C0303: Trailing whitespace (trailing-whitespace)
```

The first part, `12_pylint_before.py`, is the filename. This is followed by the line number (2) and column number (1). Next is an alphanumeric code, `C0303`, indicating the error, and finally, a human-readable explanatory note for the same error indicated by the code.

The column number of the error indicates where, within the line, the error arose. Keep in mind that with some errors, like mismatched parentheses or quotes, the linter may have a different idea of where the error "occurs" than you do. Although a line and column number exists in the linter logs, you should sometimes take it with a grain of salt. The location you need to modify to fix the error may be different than the location the linter reports the error as being in.

The alphanumeric error codes, like `C0303`, begin with one of six different letters. From the PyLint documentation:

- ➤ [I]nformational messages that PyLint emits (do not contribute to your analysis score)
- ➤ [R]efactor for a "good practice" metric violation
- ➤ [C]onvention for coding standard violations
- ➤ [W]arning for stylistic problems, or minor programming issues
- ➤ [E]rror for important programming issues (i.e., most probably bug)
- ➤ [F]atal for errors which prevented further processing

The analysis score at the bottom of the list of errors is a general score out of 10 that tells you how well formatted and error free the linter thinks your code is:

```
Your code has been rated at 6.19/10
```

It's important to understand that a score of 10 does not mean your code is "good" (nor does it mean that it's "bad"). It simply means that it passes all of the linter checks.

Some linters will automatically fix errors for you, but PyLint does not have that feature at this time. However, there are other packages, like *autopep8*, that can help it conform to the PEP 8 standard automatically. You can install autopep8 with this command:

```
$ pip install autopep8
```

Once it's installed, you should be able to use it with the autopep8 command:

```
$ autopep8 12_pylint_before.py > 12_pylint_after.py
```

This automatically formats the file 12_pylint_before.py to at least some PEP 8 standards and saves it to a file called 12_pylint_after.py.

This new file can be run through PyLint again, and the new analysis score is a slight improvement over the previous 6.19:

```
Your code has been rated at 7.09/10
```

By default, autopep8 only fixes whitespace errors that are guaranteed not to affect functionality of the program. You'll notice that the C0303: Trailing whitespace errors have now disappeared.

The autopep8 command can also be used more aggressively by adding the --aggressive modifier to the command:

```
$ autopep8 --aggressive 12_pylint_before.py > 12_pylint_after.py
```

This approach can be somewhat risky because it implements changes that potentially impact the behavior of the code, such as replacing x == None with x is None.

In this case, the remaining linting errors are simply things that need to be fixed by hand. For example:

```
Argument name "indexVal" doesn't conform to snake_case naming style (invalid-name)
Missing function or method docstring (missing-function-docstring)
Either all return statements in a function should return an expression, or none of
them should.
Redefining name 'hand1' from outer scope (line 189) (redefined-outer-name)
```

The variable name *indexVal* could likely be replaced programmatically with index_val, but this would be dangerous if a variable by the name of index_val already existed in the code. Really, it's better to let the programmer fix it themselves.

Similarly, docstrings *could* probably be automatically generated. But how useful would those automatically generated docstrings really be? It's best to let the programmer take a look first, and let them add their own autogenerated or stub docstring as appropriate, rather than covering up the errors and violating the spirit (if not the letter) of best practices in Python.

FORMATTING

Linters concern themselves with, among other things, programmatic errors or warnings in the code. You may have unused variables, unresolved variables, or unreachable code. Formatters, on the other hand, only concern themselves with style of the code. For example, a formatter can recognize and fix issues such as the following:

➤ **Trailing spaces:** Extra spaces accidentally left in after a line of code. Lines should not end with a space character.

➤ **No newline at the end of a file:** All Python files should end with a single newline character.

➤ **Line length:** PEP 8 recommends lines of code that are a maximum of 79 characters. Although formatters cannot shrink lines in all situations, they can do some things to help, such as breaking lists across multiple lines.

A formatter project from the Python Software Foundation that has gained widespread adoption in recent years is *Black* (`https://github.com/psf/black`). The name is a reference to the Henry Ford quote: "Any customer can have a car painted any color that he wants, as long as it is black."

Black is a lightweight autoformatting tool that takes a heavy-handed approach in enforcing PEP 8. Every file that it formats will conform to PEP 8 standards without any way to circumvent that behavior.

Black can be installed with `pip`:

```
$ pip install black
```

It comes with a command-line tool, `black`. A full list of formatting rules and options can be seen in the help file:

```
$ black --help
```

You can run Black from the command line to format any Python code. To format a specific file or files within a directory, provide that file or directory name:

```
$ black myfile.py
```

Using a dot (`.`) will format everything within the current directory:

```
$ black .
```

Although Black will always apply PEP 8 formats, there is some wiggle room for personal style within PEP 8. Black provides options for applying those more specific rules as well. Optionally, you can add a file called `pyproject.toml`, written in the markup language *TOML*, to add rules.

The `pyproject.toml` file was introduced in PEP 518 and provides a centralized place for project configurations. It can be used as an alternative or a replacement for the `requirements.txt` file, discussed in Chapter 4, "Installing and Running Python."

Special configurations that are of concern only to a particular library in the project, like Black, can be written in `pyproject.toml` under that library-specific header:

```
[tool.black]
```

Configurations are written using the TOML format as key-value pairs separated by an equals sign:

```
[tool.black]
skip-magic-trailing-comma = true
line-length = 80
```

Black looks for this file in the base of the project, then ascends to parent directories if no file is found. Once it's found a `pyproject.toml` file, it will stop looking, even if no configurations for Black formatting are found in the file.

The setting `skip-magic-trailing-comma` uses the Black-specific concept of a *magic trailing comma* to write data structures with one element per line, rather than force them into a single line (default behavior) if they fit. For data structures that are frequently referenced or modified in code, it can be more visually pleasing to write them with one element per line. For example:

```
supported_currencies = [
    'USD': 'US Dollar',
    'EUR': 'Euro',
    'GBP': 'British Pound',
]
```

The trailing comma, at the end of `'British Pound'`, isn't required by Python, but indicates to Black that this list may be frequently modified. It's easier to keep track of changes to a data structure in versioning software, such as Git, if that data structure is written across multiple lines. This expanded form also has the benefit of being more readable to humans, in contrast to:

```
currencies = ['USD': 'US Dollar', 'EUR': 'Euro', 'GBP': 'British Pound',]
```

Black is guaranteed, through means of fancy computer science, to never modify the functionality of Python code. This means that it will not break your code. On the flip side, it also won't fix errors or suggest more extreme changes like a linter might.

TYPE HINTS

Type hints are optional annotations in Python that allow you to describe the types that each variable, argument, or return value is supposed to have when it is declared. When used to annotate a variable assignment, type hints come after the variable name, separated by a colon:

```
name: str = 'Ryan'
```

When used in a function declaration, type hints can describe the types of both the arguments and the return value:

```
def multiply_and_round(a: float, b: float) -> int:
    return round(a * b)
```

Here, I'm defining a function `multiply_and_round` that takes in two float arguments, a and b. It returns an integer, as indicated by the arrow (`->`) following the parenthesis and before the colon.

We can declare two variables and call our function just like any other function:

```
num1: float = 3.5
num2: float = 8.2
multiply_and_round(num1, num2)
```

Note that declaring variables with type hints is not very useful as the type (float) can be inferred from the value being assigned to it (3.5). In general, when type hints are used, they are used for functions and methods, rather than variable assignments like this.

It's also important to note that, by default, I can call the function multiply_and_round with anything I want, regardless of what I've declared with the type hints:

```
multiply_and_round(4, 5)
```

This returns the integer 20 without complaint.

If you've worked with a strongly typed programming language before, the Python type hint syntax may seem familiar. For example, this is the same function written in C++:

```
int multiply_and_round(float a, float b) {
    return (int)round(a * b);
}
```

Here, the int preceding the function name multiply_and_round indicates that it returns an integer. The arguments float a and float b indicate that the variables a and b are both floats. Unlike in Python, however, if you were to call this C++ function with integers instead of floats, an error would occur.

Even though we're adding the type hint notation to our Python programs, Python is still a weakly typed language (see Chapter 1, "Introduction to Programming," for more information about strongly and weakly typed languages). The type hints serve as documentation, rather than rule enforcement.

However, there are packages and plug-ins that you can use that take advantage of the formal syntax of the type hints. These can provide anything from warnings in the IDE when you're passing an inappropriately typed argument, to a runtime error when a bad type is used—effectively turning Python into a strongly typed language.

The popular third-party package *Mypy* checks code as you're writing to make sure that type hints are being complied with. It can be installed with this command:

```
$pip install mypy
```

This allows you to check Python files for errors from the command line. In the exercise files, there is a file called 12_type_hints.py, which contains the following code:

```
class User:
    def __init__(self, name):
        self.name = name

def process_user(user: User):
    print(f'processing {user.name}')

alice = User('Alice')
process_user(alice)
process_user(1)
```

This defines a User class and a function process_user that takes in a User object as an argument. Then process_user is called with both an appropriate User object and an integer.

This file can be checked using this command:

```
$ mypy 12_type_hints.py
```

This results in the error:

```
12_type_hints.py:17: error: Argument 1 to "process_user" has incompatible type
"int";
expected "User"  [arg-type]
```

Of course, writing code and then periodically checking it from the command line every so often is an inconvenient process at best. It's easier to be alerted directly as you're typing in the IDE. Fortunately, there are Mypy plug-ins for every major IDE. For Visual Studio, you can install the Mypy Type Checker found at https://marketplace.visualstudio.com/items?itemName=ms-python.mypy-type-checker.

Simply download the plug-in, open it with Visual Studio Code, and installation should be straightforward. Once installed, type checking is enabled and errors should be highlighted automatically as shown in Figure 12.2.

```
 12_type_hints.py > ...
 1    class User:
 2        def __init__(self, name):
 3            self.name = name
 4
 5    def process_user(user: User):
 6        print(f'p
 7                   Argument 1 to "process_user" has incompatible type "int"; expected
 8    alice = User(   "User" Mypy(arg-type)
 9    process_user(   View Problem (⌥F8)    No quick fixes available
10    process_user(1)
11
12
```

FIGURE 12.2: Arguments of the wrong type are underlined (in red, in editions with color images). Hovering over them displays the error.

Mypy is intended to reduce bugs and programming errors by alerting you to problems while writing the code. However, if you choose to ignore these alerts, Mypy will not prevent the code from being run. If you choose to ignore Mypy, of course, this will still result in an error:

```
AttributeError: 'int' object has no attribute 'name'
```

To prevent runtime errors like this one, it's best to use type hints consistently and fix any errors from Mypy when they occur, even if you understand the error and think it's ignorable. Here's an example:

```
def multiply(num1: int, num2: int) -> int:
    return num1 * num2

multiply(1.5, 2.3)
```

In this case, we're using the function `multiply` to multiply floats together, rather than integers, which is a perfectly reasonable thing to do. However, if you want `multiply` to accommodate this new use case, the function definition should be changed, rather than simply ignoring the error and assuming it will work at runtime:

```
def multiply(num1: float, num2: float) -> float:
    return num1 * num2

multiply(1.5, 2.3)
```

In the Python type system, certain types of numbers are considered compatible substitutions for other number types. For example, all integers can be interpreted as floats without any loss of data. Similarly, all floats can be interpreted as complex numbers. This concept is formalized in PEP 3141 (https://peps.python.org/pep-3141), "A Type Hierarchy for Numbers."

The type hint system allows number type substitutions according to this hierarchy, so any function that takes in float arguments will work with integers as well:

```
multiply(1, 2)
```

However, there are some cases where functions do need to accommodate multiple types. In situations like this, you can use an or operator (|):

```
def multiply(var1: str | int, var2: int):
    return var1 * var2
```

This allows you to pass either a string or an integer as var1, allowing function calls like the following:

```
multiply(4, 5)
multiply('hello ', 5)
```

Type hints can also be used to describe data structures:

```
def remove_larger(elements: list, size: int) -> list:
    return [e for e in elements if len(e) <= size]
remove_ larger(['apple', 'bear', 'cat', 'dogmatic'], 5)
```

In this case, the function remove_larger expects a list, elements, and an integer, size, to filter them. Of course, problems arise if we call remove_larger with something like this

```
remove_ larger([1, 2, 3, 4, 5], 5)
```

While we specify that elements must be of type list, we don't specify the type of the items *contained* in that list. For this, we can use a *composite type hint* by providing the type of element the data structure should consist of inside square brackets:

```
def remove_larger(elements: list[str], size: int) -> list[str]:
    return [e for e in elements if len(e) <= size]
```

In this case, only a list of strings is allowed. Of course, the len function also works with lists themselves, so we could allow lists of both strings and lists to be passed using a pipe operator:

```
def remove_larger(elements: list[str|list], size: int) -> list[str|list]:
    return [e for e in elements if len(e) <= size]

remove_larger(['apple', 'bearable', [1,2,3]], 5)
```

Other types of collections and composite types can be defined using type hints as well:

```
unique_names: set[str] = {'Alice', 'Bob', 'Charlie'}
number_values: dict[str, int] = {'one': 1, 'two': 2, 'three': 3}
```

Type hints can be nested even further to create arbitrarily complex objects:

```
words_by_character: dict[str, list[str]] = {'a': ['ant', 'apple', 'and']}
```

Although all the example functions shown so far have used positional arguments, type hints can also be used with keyword arguments:

```
def remove_larger(elements: list[str|list], size: int = 5) -> list[str|list]:
    return [e for e in elements if len(e) <= size]
```

If type hints are used with a variable number of arguments (like *args and **kwargs), the type hint will dictate the type for all arguments:

```
def remove_larger(*args: str, **kwargs: int) -> list[str] | None:
    if 'size' not in kwargs:
        return None
    return [e for e in args if len(e) <= kwargs['size']]

remove_larger('apple', 'bear', 'cat', 'dogmatic', size=5)
```

Here, the function remove_larger returns None if the size keyword argument is not provided.

It is rare that you will find a company that strictly enforces type hints, docstrings, and PEP 8 compliance, and that has guidelines for documentation and code comments. FAANG companies (Facebook, Amazon, Netflix, and Google) and other large tech companies frequently have many of these, or their equivalents, in place, but they are the exceptions in industry rather than the rule.

Most often, it is up to the developers themselves to create and enforce their own coding standards. Sometimes deadlines are rushed and quick-and-dirty fixes are critical, but I encourage you to take the time when and where possible to clean things up. Whether this means writing the README file, going through and applying type hints, adding docstrings, or doing some linting, keep in mind that even small actions can dramatically improve quality and prevent bugs.

PART III
Advanced Topics

13

Errors and Exceptions

It's hard to write Python without running into exceptions at some point. In fact, we've seen them a lot so far. The following statement raises, or "throws," an exception:

```
1/0
```

In this case it raises a `ZeroDivisionError` because we're attempting to divide by 0. As you might suspect, `ZeroDivisionError` is the name of the Python class. Exceptions, like everything else in Python, are first-class objects. As such, they can be handled, raised, and transformed based on their type or content.

In fact, exceptions in Python are a large and elegant system of first-class objects, which often require careful consideration. `ZeroDivisionError` extends class `ArithmeticError`, which extends `Exception`, which extends `BaseException`. Each class can be extended for custom functionality.

You may notice as we go through that some of these classes are called `Error` and some are called `Exception`. You may read various theories like "Errors are fatal and non-retriable, whereas exceptions should be . . ." or "Exceptions derive directly from `BaseException`, whereas errors derive from `Exception`. . ."

In my experience, the difference between errors and exceptions in Python is blurry and best not examined too closely lest you get bogged down in the . . . well, exceptions. In this spirit, I use the words "error" and "exception" interchangeably throughout the book. It's no error, so please don't take exception to it, but let's move on and focus our attention on exceptional programming instead.

HANDLING EXCEPTIONS

When an exception is raised from a Python program, the program prints a *stack trace* indicating where the error occurred, prints a message indicating what the error was, and then exits the program.

The following calls a function that raises an exception:

```
def make_an_error():
    1/0

make_an_error()
```

And here is the full stack trace and message that results:

```
- - - - - - - - - - - - - - - - - - - - - - - - - - - - - - - - - - - - - - - - - - - - -
ZeroDivisionError                           Traceback (most recent call last)
Cell In[10], line 4
      1 def make_an_error():
      2     1/0
----> 4 make_an_error()

Cell In[10], line 2, in make_an_error()
      1 def make_an_error():
----> 2     1/0


ZeroDivisionError: division by zero
```

However, a stack trace isn't an inevitable result of an exception being raised. If an error could possibly occur in a section of code, it's best to *handle* that exception. This is done with a `try` block followed by an except block:

```
try:
    make_an_error()
except:
    print('Something bad happened!')
print('Program continues')
```

This prints the lines:

```
Something bad happened!
Program continues
```

If an exception is raised anywhere in the `try` block, the code in the except block will be executed and then the program will continue to run. It's important to note that the code within the `try` block exits immediately after the exception, so subsequent lines will not execute:

```
try:
    make_an_error()
    print('This will not print')
except:
    print('Something bad happened!')
print('Program continues')
```

Being able to salvage our program is a huge improvement over it simply crashing, but we are losing information about what the error was. "Something bad happened" just isn't as descriptive as "division by zero," which was being printed to the screen earlier.

You can handle specific types of errors and get access to the actual exception object by naming that specific exception class in the except declaration followed by the keyword as and a new variable for the exception object:

```
try:
    make_an_error()
except ZeroDivisionError as e:
    print(f'A ZeroDivisionError was raised: {e}')
print('Program continues')
```

This prints the lines:

```
A ZeroDivisionError was raised: division by zero
Program continues
```

Although exceptions can seem a little scary—like a grenade being lobbed at a program in order to blow it up—when they're handled (or "caught"), they're just regular objects that do no harm and that can be printed and used just like any other object. Casting the exception to a string or using it in an f-string, like we're doing here, will simply print the exception message without causing the program to exit.

If it's possible for code within a `try` block to throw multiple types of exceptions, you may want to write multiple `except` statements to catch different errors and handle them appropriately. For example, we can rewrite the `make_an_error` function to throw random exceptions of different types:

```python
import random

def make_an_error():
    rand_num = random.randint(0,3)
    if rand_num == 0:
        return 1/0 # ZeroDivisionError
    elif rand_num == 1:
        [0, 1, 2][5] # IndexError
    elif rand_num == 2:
        {'a': 'apple'}['b'] # KeyError
    elif rand_num == 3:
        this_function_does_not_exist() # NameError
```

The four possible error types it can throw are `ZeroDivisionError`, `IndexError`, `KeyError`, and `NameError`. We can catch each of these four independently:

```python
try:
    make_an_error()
except ZeroDivisionError as e:
    print('ZeroDivisionError')
except IndexError as e:
    print('IndexError')
except KeyError as e:
    print('KeyError')
except NameError as e:
    print('NameError')
```

For every error, there is a separate `except` block and a separate action to take (in this case, simply printing out the name of the corresponding error).

Errors can be caught, not only by their specific class name, but by the name of any of the classes they derive from. Here is a list of the current errors we are catching in **bold**, and how they derive from the `Exception` class in Python (for example, `KeyError` is a child of `LookupError`, which is a child of `Exception`):

➤   Exception

       ➤   ArithmeticError

           ➤   **ZeroDivisionError**

➤ **NameError**

➤ LookupError

    ➤ **KeyError**

    ➤ **IndexError**

Both `KeyError` and `IndexError` can be caught by handling a `LookupError` in the except statement:

```
try:
    make_an_error()
except LookupError as e:
    print('Either an IndexError or a KeyError occurred')
except ZeroDivisionError as e:
    print('ZeroDivisionError')
except NameError as e:
    print('NameError')
```

`ZeroDivisionError` and `NameError` have the shared parent `Exception`, which is the same shared parent that `KeyError` and `IndexError` also have. However, we can take advantage of the fact that, when an exception is raised, the except statements are checked in the order they occur and only the first one that matches the raised exception is executed. This means that, if `Exception` is caught last, it will simply get the "leftovers" that didn't match anything above it:

```
try:
    make_an_error()
except LookupError as e:
    print('Either an IndexError or a KeyError occurred')
except Exception as e:
    print('Either a ZeroDivisionError or NameError occurred')
```

This is, obviously, a contrived example. Usually when you're catching the `Exception` class (often referred to in programming as "catching the general exception"), something very bad has happened and your program doesn't know how to deal with it. It's gone through all the known problems and now has to deal with some bad unknown—often by alerting and logging with detailed information about the error.

ELSE AND FINALLY

There may be times when you want to execute code only if an exception *wasn't* raised. If everything went smoothly, execute the code, otherwise, abort the mission. There are a couple of ways to do this. The first is to simply add the code to the `try` block, following the risky section:

```
data = reliable_data_fetching()
try:
    data = risky_data_processing_1(data)
    data = risky_data_processing_2(data)
    data = risky_data_processing_3(data)
    reliable_data_uploading(data)
except:
    print('Something bad happened and the data shouldn\'t be uploaded')
```

Here, we're fetching data from a reliable source that is unlikely to throw an exception (hence not surrounding it in `try`/`except` statements). Then, we have some risky data processing steps that must be completed before the data can be uploaded to a remote server.

We don't want to take the risk that something goes wrong during the processing and let half-processed data get uploaded. This can be accomplished by placing the `reliable_data_uploading` function call inside the `try` block itself, even though it's unlikely that anything will go wrong with the data upload. By placing it inside the `try` block, `reliable_data_uploading` will only be reached if the previous steps don't raise any errors.

Another way to do this is with an `else` block. An `else` block will only execute if nothing within the previous `try` block raised an exception and must follow all except blocks:

```
data = reliable_data_fetching()
try:
    data = risky_data_processing_1(data)
    data = risky_data_processing_2(data)
    data = risky_data_processing_3(data)
except:
    print('Something bad happened and the data shouldn\'t be uploaded')
else:
    reliable_data_uploading(data)
```

There is no great advantage to using one style over the other. Some argue for readability and say that the try/except/else is clearer than just a try/except. Personally, I use the former approach, without the `else` block, because it's a pattern more familiar to programmers in other languages. However, which you choose is not especially important and is a matter of personal preference.

Another common issue that programmers deal with is *cleanup*. This doesn't refer to "clean code" like we've often talked about, but refers to cleaning up data structures, upstream connections, open files, or any other things that a program might need to take care of before it exits.

For example, let's write a data processing function that requires a database connection for all steps involved (fetching, processing, and uploading). Creating a connection to the database is relatively expensive and we want to create only a single connection and then reuse that connection for all steps in the process. However, if our function crashes in the middle of processing, we need to make sure that connection closes—otherwise, we'll be left with too many open connections sitting around doing nothing, which could lead to worse problems (this is called a *connection leak*).

Our function, `process_data`, looks something like this:

```
def process_data():
    conn = create_connection()
    try:
        data = data_fetching(conn)
        data = data_processing(data, conn)
        data = data_uploading(data, conn)
        close_connection(conn)
        return data
    except:
        print('Something bad happened')
        close_connection(conn)
```

Because the function `close_connection` itself can raise an exception, it also needs to be put inside the `try` block. Notice that this means we need to call the function `close_connection` twice—once if there's an error and once if there's no error. There are certainly many ways to write this function with only a single call to close_connection, but perhaps the cleanest and most readable way is with a finally block:

```
def process_data():
    conn = create_connection()
    try:
        data = data_fetching(conn)
        data = data_processing(data, conn)
        return data_uploading(data, conn)
    except:
        print('Something bad happened')
    finally:
        close_connection(conn)
```

Where the except block is reached only if an error occurred and the else block is reached only if an error didn't occur, the finally block is guaranteed to execute whether or not an error occurred.

No matter what happens inside the try block, the finally block will always execute. Even when a value is returned from a function (in the earlier example, the result of data_uploading is returned), the finally block is executed before exiting the function process_data.

It's worth noting that a finally block can be used even without handling any exceptions:

```
def process_data():
    conn = create_connection()
    try:
        data = data_fetching(conn)
        data = data_processing(data, conn)
        return data_uploading(data, conn)
    finally:
        close_connection(conn)
```

If an exception is raised inside the try block here, the program will halt execution and a stack trace will print out, but the code inside the finally block will be executed before that is done and the database connection will still be closed.

Although else blocks are a neat feature of the Python programming language, they are not strictly necessary when it comes to exception handling. However, the finally statement is crucial for improving the readability of cleanup code and indicating procedures that must be executed regardless of any errors that occurred.

RAISING EXCEPTIONS

So far, we've been treating exceptions as if they're merely something for us to deal with when something goes wrong. However, Python isn't the only one that gets to complain; you can write and raise your own exceptions as well.

The function say_hello has a type hint that says it only accepts strings as inputs. Unlike most type hints, this one is enforced:

```
def say_hello(name: str):
    if type(name) != str:
        raise TypeError('name must be a string')
    print(f'Hello, {name}!')
```

Here, the keyword `raise` is used to raise a new `TypeError` exception. A message is passed that tells the user of the function exactly what they did wrong (`'name must be a string'`). When called with `say_hello(1)`, it prints the following stack trace and message:

```
--------------------------------------------------------------------------
TypeError                                 Traceback (most recent call last)
Cell In[76], line 1
----> 1 say_hello(1)

Cell In[74], line 3, in say_hello(name)
      1 def say_hello(name: str):
      2     if type(name) != str:
----> 3         raise TypeError('name must be a string')
      4     print(f'Hello, {name}!')

TypeError: name must be a string
```

This keyword `raise` is a bit like the keyword `return`. It automatically exits the function at that line[1] and pops out at the line where the function was called. Unlike `return`, however, `raise` doesn't gently proffer a value; it attempts to halt program execution entirely unless it's forcefully handled with an appropriate `except` block.

In some rare situations, you may want to return an exception rather than raise one:

```
def get_type_error(message):
    return TypeError(message)

get_type_error('some message')
print('Still alive!')
```

This prints the string:

```
'Still alive!'
```

indicating that the program continues to execute after the exception was merely returned rather than raised.

Although exceptions can be returned, non-exceptions cannot be raised. If you try to do that, you'll certainly get *something* raised:

```
def raise_something():
    raise 1

raise_something()
```

However, that something will always be a `TypeError`:

```
TypeError: exceptions must derive from BaseException
```

Although I've raised objects of type `TypeError` as an example in this section, it's rare that you'll be raising any built-in Python exception objects from your own code. For the most part, these classes are

---

[1] Unless there is a `finally` block following it, in which case the code inside that block will be executed before the exception is raised. Essentially, `raise` follows the same rules as `return` as a function-exiting statement.

used and raised by Python and merely handled by you.[2] Usually, the exceptions you raise will be ones that you design yourself.

CUSTOM EXCEPTIONS

When working on large programming projects, especially those meant to be used as a tool by other developers, you'll often write your own classes that derive from the Exception class. These custom exception classes can be used throughout your project and describe situations that are unique to the code you're writing and enforce the appropriate usage of that code.

While exception classes can be very elaborate and contain complex data about their origination and advice for handling them, they can also be extremely simple:[3]

```
class DeadParrotError(Exception):
    pass
```

The class DeadParrotError consists of nothing but a name and the fact that it is a child of the Exception class. However, it is still capable of providing a descriptive exception in the appropriate situation:

```
def purchase_bird():
    raise DeadParrotError('This parrot is no more')

purchase_bird()
```

This displays the error message:

```
DeadParrotError: This parrot is no more
```

There is nothing wrong with defining an exception class that is essentially just a name. Sometimes the name is all you need to tell you what you did wrong! Another common use case is to provide a default error message or otherwise modify the error message that gets passed in:

```
class DeadParrotError(Exception):
    def __init__(self, message):
        super().__init__(f'{message}. This is a late parrot!')

purchase_bird()
```

This uses the super function, covered in Chapter 11, "Classes," and appends the text 'This is a late parrot!'. This results in the exception:

```
DeadParrotError: This parrot is no more. This is a late parrot!
```

As a more practical example, consider a Python program responsible for generating HTTP responses for an API. A user might request a document by its document ID and, if that document isn't found, a "404 Not Found" message should be returned.

---

[2] One common exception to this rule of thumb is the NotImplementedError, which, as discussed in Chapter 11, should be raised in methods of a parent class that are intended to serve as templates for the child classes that actually implement them.

[3] The name DeadParrotError is a reference to a Monty Python sketch that is so famous it has its own Wikipedia article: https://en.wikipedia.org/wiki/Dead_Parrot_sketch. If you have not had the pleasure of enjoying the Dead Parrot Sketch already, I encourage you to drop this book and watch it immediately.

Other HTTP responses might include "502 Bad Gateway" if an error was received from an upstream service while requesting the document, or "401 Unauthorized" if the user does not have permissions to access the document.

We can create a general HTTPError that contains static attributes for an HTTP code (like 404, 502, 401) and a description ("Not Found," "Bad Gateway," "Unauthorized").

```python
class HTTPError(Exception):
    code = None
    description = None
    def __init__(self, message=None):
        if message:
            super().__init__(f'{self.code} {self.description}: {message}')
        else:
            super().__init__(f'{self.code} {self.description}')
```

The code and description attributes aren't populated in the HTTPError class itself because this class is intended to be extended into more specific child classes. However, it does contain logic for formatting the error message using that code and description.

Using this base class, it's trivial to create and organize all the HTTP exceptions that you might want to raise from your application:

```python
class Unauthorized(HTTPError):
    code = 401
    description = 'Unauthorized'

class NotFound(HTTPError):
    code = 404
    description = 'Not Found'

class BadGateway(HTTPError):
    code = 502
    description = 'Bad Gateway'
```

Raising an HTTPError exception in Python does not require an error message if no further information is needed. In the case of Unauthorized, we may not want to provide a specific message to avoid unnecessary information being provided and causing a security risk:

```python
raise Unauthorized()
```

This gives an austere error message:

```
Unauthorized: 401 Unauthorized
```

However, more information can, optionally, be provided:

```python
def get_document_stub(doc_id):
    raise NotFound(f'Document ID {doc_id} was not found on the server')


get_document_stub(123)
```

This function call raises the error with our message:

```
NotFound: 404 Not Found: Document ID 123 was not found on the server
```

In addition to informational messages intended to be shown to the end user, custom exception classes might also contain information about what should be done with them.

For example, a Bad Gateway error may be retriable (that is, even if it failed the first time, it could succeed if the same request is sent again). Authorization errors and Not Found errors are not considered retriable. If someone is not properly authenticated[4] to view the document, they should take action to fix that, and not keep asking to see it.

There are a couple of ways to encode information in our HTTP errors about whether or not they are retriable. One is to simply add a Boolean `retriable` to the base `HTTPError` class and populate it appropriately in the child exceptions:

```
class Unauthorized(HTTPError):
    code = 401
    description = 'Unauthorized'
    retriable = False

class NotFound(HTTPError):
    code = 404
    description = 'Not Found'
    retriable = False

class BadGateway(HTTPError):
    code = 502
    description = 'Bad Gateway'
    retriable = True
```

Another way to create a set of retriable exceptions is to make an `HTTPRetriableError` class that extends `HTTPError` and from which all retriable errors derive:

```
class HTTPRetriableError(HTTPError):
    pass

class Unauthorized(HTTPError):
    code = 401
    description = 'Unauthorized'

class NotFound(HTTPError):
    code = 404
    description = 'Not Found'

class BadGateway(HTTPRetriableError):
    code = 502
    description = 'Bad Gateway'
```

---

[4] In programming and computer science, "authentication" and "authorization" are two very different concepts. If someone is authenticated, that means you know who they are. This is often the result of logging in with a valid username and password combination or some other authentication procedure. Authorization, in contrast, refers to the specific permissions that an authenticated user has. Someone can be authenticated but still not authorized to view a particular document.

It may seem obvious then that the HTTP error "401 Unauthorized" should be raised when a known, authenticated user is overstepping their permissions and trying to view something they don't have the authorization for. If you think this, you'd be wrong. In fact, the original 1996 specification for the HTTP error code "401 Unauthorized," found in RFC 1945 (https://datatracker.ietf.org/doc/html/rfc1945#autoid-47) reads: "The request requires user authentication."

For actual authorization errors, the HTTP error "403 Forbidden" should be used.

Please do not ask my why this is. Ask the Internet Engineering Task Force member who wrote the paper in 1996.

You may prefer the former layout, with its clearly written Booleans and lack of an additional HTTPRetriableError class. Or you may prefer the latter structure, which centers around the concept of "retriability" as a core feature rather than just another bit of messaging.

However, you can't decide on an architecture for an exception hierarchy based only on what the classes look like, or even how they'll be instantiated and raised. Another important aspect to consider is how the exceptions will be handled by the caller.

EXCEPTION HANDLING PATTERNS

Although web applications and APIs won't be covered in great detail until Chapter 20, "REST APIs and Flask," it's useful to know how they work in broad strokes. When a request is made to a web server, that request is sent to the Python application on that server as some sort of "request" object. We can create a stub Request class to model this:

```
class Request:
    pass
```

In reality, these request objects have all sorts of information associated with them—the requested URL, data, cookies, session information, and so forth. Every piece of information needed for the server to fulfill the request and return a response should be included in that request.

Let's make a simple response object that the server sends back:

```
class Response:
    def __init__(self, http_code, data):
        self.http_code = http_code
        self.data = data

    def __str__(self):
        return f'{self.http_code} {self.data}'
```

If a Response is good, the http_code will be 200, letting the user making the request know that everything went well and they can use the data in the response. If the http_code is something else, say, a 404, then the data might contain some sort of error message rather than the data they were hoping for.

The Response class also implements the Python method __str__, which returns a string representation of an object when that object is printed or cast to a string. This allows us to print responses for easy viewing.

Finally, we have a function that handles the request and returns a response. Let's call it handle_request:

```
def handle_request(request: Request) -> Response:
    pass
```

There are a lot of moving parts involved in handling a request and returning a response. The user must be authenticated and authorized. In order to confirm their identity and permissions, the upstream services (like databases or other web servers) need to be running and returning responses correctly. Then we need to check what the user wants. Perhaps their request can't be fulfilled because the data they want is missing or their request for that data was malformed.

Because so many things can go wrong, there are a variety of errors that might be raised. Here are the two base classes, seen in the previous section, for all of these specific HTTP errors:

```python
class HTTPError(Exception):
    code = None
    description = None
    def __init__(self, message=None):
        if message:
            super().__init__(f'{self.code} {self.description}: {message}')
        else:
            super().__init__(f'{self.code} {self.description}')


class HTTPRetriableError(HTTPError):
    pass
```

Here are five HTTP errors that extend them:

```python
class Unauthorized(HTTPError):
    code = 401
    description = 'Unauthorized'


class Forbidden(HTTPError):
    code = 403
    description = 'Forbidden'


class NotFound(HTTPError):
    code = 404
    description = 'Not Found'


class BadGateway(HTTPRetriableError):
    code = 502
    description = 'Bad Gateway'


class GatewayTimeout(HTTPRetriableError):
    code = 504
    description = 'Gateway Timeout'
```

Let's design a web application that has a variety of useful utility functions: do_authentication, do_authorization, and do_get_data. The first two have a 20 percent chance of throwing an exception when called. The function do_get_data can throw one of three possible exceptions, each one with a 20 percent chance of being thrown:

```python
from random import randint


def do_authentication(request: Request) -> None:
    if randint(0, 4) == 0:
        raise Unauthorized()


def do_authorization(request: Request) -> None:
    if randint(0, 4) == 0:
        raise Forbidden()


def do_get_data(request: Request) -> str:
    r = randint(0, 4)
```

```
    if r == 0:
        raise BadGateway()
    if r == 1:
        raise GatewayTimeout()
    if r == 2:
        raise NotFound()
    return 'some data'
```

Finally, we modify the `handle_request` function to call each one of these tasks and (hopefully) return the data:

```
def handle_request(request: Request) -> Response:
    do_authentication(request)
    do_authorization(request)
    data = do_get_data(request)
    return Response(200, data)
```

If the request does manage to get through this gauntlet without an exception being thrown, a `Response` object with a 200 and `'some data'` will be successfully returned. The more likely scenario, of course, is that an uncaught exception will be raised and the end user will see a default "500 Server Error" when our web server software crashes.

You can try it out yourself:

```
print(handle_request(Request()))
```

The naïve approach to handling the many exceptions that this code can produce is to catch each one of them individually from the functions they're thrown from:

```
def handle_request(request: Request) -> Response:
    try:
        do_authentication(request)
    except Unauthorized as e:
        return Response(e.code, e.description)
    try:
        do_authorization(request)
    except Forbidden as e:
        return Response(e.code, e.description)
    try:
        data = do_get_data(request)
    except BadGateway as e:
        return Response(e.code, e.description)
    except GatewayTimeout as e:
        return Response(e.code, e.description)
    except NotFound as e:
        return Response(e.code, e.description)
    return Response(200, data)
```

Not only is this repetitive (the line of code in each `except` block is the same), but in the real world, it would also be overly fragile. Even if they don't do it right now, the authentication and authorization methods might be rewritten to, say, throw a `BadGateway` or `GatewayTimeout` exception in the future.

By handling *only* the exceptions that a method currently throws, we're implicitly encoding business logic about what each method does and how it does it in the outer handle_request function. Now, handle_request is responsible for "knowing" that do_authentication can only throw an Unauthorized exception, or that do_get_data can never throw a Forbidden exception. If anything ever changes, we need to rewrite handle_request.

This isn't necessarily a bad thing. In some situations, you may want the calling function to be a little smarter and keep track of what's going on. You may also want to enforce the fact that, say, do_authorization should never ever throw a GatewayTimeout and you would want that error to be raised and not caught if that ever happened.

However, if you have a web application with a lot of moving parts, and perhaps unpredictable and often-changing behavior coming from upstream services, you may consider a more robust approach:

```
def handle_request(request: Request) -> Response:
    try:
        do_authentication(request)
        do_authorization(request)
        data = do_get_data(request)
    except HTTPError as e:
        return Response(e.code, e.description)
    return Response(200, data)
```

In software engineering, this is an example of *decoupling*, where changes in one part of the system are isolated and do not require changes in another part.

Another thing we can do to make this web application more robust is to catch the general exception, or the Exception class, if something is raised that isn't an HTTPError:

```
import traceback

def handle_request(request: Request) -> Response:
    try:
        do_authentication(request)
        do_authorization(request)
        data = do_get_data(request)
    except HTTPError as e:
        return Response(e.code, e.description)
    except Exception as e:
        print(f'Something very unusual happened: {e}')
        print(''.join(traceback.format_exception(e)))
        return Response(500, 'Server Error')
    return Response(200, data)
```

Although we presumably don't want our web application to raise an exception and crash if something goes wrong, it's still a concerning event that we might want to log in a special way for review later. The *traceback* module can be used to get a stack trace from an exception object. The function format_exception takes, as an argument, an exception and returns a list of stack trace lines that can be joined into a single string.

Finally, we return a new Response object with a 500 HTTP code, which is the code for a generic server error when a more specific one is not available.

Recall that the errors BadGateway and GatewayTimeout are children of the class HTTPRetriableError. If one of these is thrown, it would make sense to retry the operation. However, we don't want to retry an infinite number of times in case the error is not actually retriable, or the problem isn't fixed quickly.

In this case, we can do something like this (with HTTPError and Exception handling blocks omitted for brevity):

```python
def handle_request(request: Request, retries=3) -> Response:
    try:
        do_authentication(request)
        do_authorization(request)
        data = do_get_data(request)
    except HTTPRetriableError as e:
        if retries > 0:
            print(f'Error: {e}, retries: {retries}')
            return handle_request(request, retries=retries-1)
        else:
            return Response(e.code, e.description)
```

The keyword argument retries has been added to the handle_request function with a default value of 3. If an HTTPRetriableError is raised, we check how many retries are left and, if the number is greater than 0, print a brief logging message before recursing and trying the request again with one fewer retry than we had before.

If the number of retries has reached 0, we simply give up and return a Response object with the appropriate code and description.

Although it might take a few runs to get an output that retries multiple times, this program produces output that looks like this:

```
Error: 504 Gateway Timeout, retries: 3
Error: 504 Gateway Timeout, retries: 2
403 Forbidden
```

While this error handling is getting very robust and full-featured, it's also very long. Currently, there are 13 lines of error handling alone. This isn't such a big deal, but in web applications there are usually multiple functions that handle requests for all sorts of purposes. For example, on a social media site we might have the following:

```python
def handle_profile_view(request: Request) -> Response:
    pass

def handle_comment_post(request: Request) -> Response:
    pass

def handle_add_friend(request: Request) -> Response:
    pass
```

Each one of these has its own business logic for handling its specific type of request, but the error handling should be essentially the same.

Obviously, copying and pasting those 13 lines of error handling creates a lot of extra code. It also creates management problems if we ever want to make a change to the error handling—someone needs to ensure that the change was correctly copied to each spot where the error handling copy exists.

Decorators, seen in Chapter 10, "Functions," are an excellent solution for this problem. Wrapping functions in an exception handling decorator isolates exception handling concerns to one area and makes each request handler clean and easy to write:

```
@handle_http_errors(3)
def handle_add_friend(request: Request) -> Response:
    do_authentication(request)
    do_authorization(request)
    return do_get_data(request)
```

Here, the decorator @handle_http_errors takes a single argument representing the number of retries. The decorator itself looks like this:

```
def handle_http_errors(retries):
    def decorator(func):
        def inner_func(*args, current_retries=retries, **kwargs):
            try:
                return func(*args, **kwargs)
            except HTTPRetriableError as e:
                if current_retries > 0:
                    print(f'Error: {e}, retries: {current_retries}')
                    return inner_func(
                        *args,
                        current_retries=current_retries - 1,
                        **kwargs
                    )
                else:
                    return Response(e.code, e.description)
            except HTTPError as e:
                return Response(e.code, e.description)
            except Exception as e:
                print(f'Something very unusual happened: f{e}')
                print(''.join(traceback.format_exception(e)))
                return Response(500, 'Server Error')
        return inner_func
    return decorator
```

where retries represents the starting number of retries and the variable current_retries represents the current retry value, which is decremented and passed around.

On the first pass through inner_func, the keyword argument current_retries gets set to its default value of the outer retries argument (the argument passed into the decorator). The argument current_retries is followed by other **kwargs that need to get sent to the decorated request handling function, func.

If a retriable error is raised from the call to func(*args, **kwargs), it recursively calls inner_func (not func) with a decremented number of retries that will be used, along with the *args and **kwargs that were originally passed in.

This results in the same types of output we saw previously, but without needing to reinvent the wheel each time a new request handler is added:

```
Error: 502 Bad Gateway, retries: 3
Error: 504 Gateway Timeout, retries: 2
Error: 502 Bad Gateway, retries: 1
some data
```

I don't think it would be a stretch to say that `handle_http_errors` is the most complex program encountered so far in this book. It brings together concepts of recursion, decorators, position and keyword arguments, variable scope (note that the outer `retries` argument can't be modified directly inside `inner_func`), and more.

I encourage you to work through this example in the Python notebooks accompanying this book. Add `print` statements, modify it, break it, and understand how it works as needed.

While exception handling is often treated as a trivial afterthought in Python (and programming in general!), it can also be challenging and, hopefully, rewarding.

EXERCISES

Programming should not be done in a vacuum! The first three questions may require outside research and resources to answer.

1. Write an exception class for the HTTP error code 400 Bad Request.

2. Write an exception class for the HTTP error code 308 Permanent Redirect.

3. Given `some_function`, which is capable of raising any error, determine which `except` block is not needed and explain why it will never be reached.

```
try:
    some_function()
except OSError:
    print('Caught OSError')
except BrokenPipeError:
    print('Caught BrokenPipeError')
except UnboundLocalError:
    print('Caught UnboundLocalError')
except MemoryError:
    print('Caught MemoryError')
```

4. Write a function `sneaky_python_wrapper` that calls any error-prone function, such as `make_an_error`, defined here:

```
def make_an_error():
    rand_num = random.randint(0,3)
    if rand_num == 0:
        return 1/0 # ZeroDivisionError
    elif rand_num == 1:
        [0, 1, 2][5] # IndexError
    elif rand_num == 2:
        {'a': 'apple'}['b'] # KeyError
    elif rand_num == 3:
        this_function_does_not_exist() # NameError
```

The `sneaky_python_wrapper` function should take any error raised and turn it into a new custom error: `SneakyPythonError`. The message passed to `SneakyPythonError` should be the string representation of the original error (e.g., `"ZeroDivisionError: division by zero"`).

Your function `sneaky_python_wrapper` must raise an error if the function it's calling does, but should be incapable of raising anything except for a `SneakyPythonError`.

5. Replicate the functionality of `sneaky_python_wrapper`, but as a decorator: `@sneaky_python_decorator`.

Any function decorated with this will only be capable of raising errors of type `SneakyPythonError`.

14

Modules and Packages

Libraries, packages, and modules—there are a lot of words in Python used to describe a "collection of Python code."

The definition of a module is easy. A module is a single Python file. It has a filename, and you can import it using that filename.

Packages are simply collections of modules, commonly organized as a directory containing multiple files. A package can be said to contain submodules, referring to those modules within a package's directory.

Whereas we associate modules with files and packages with directories of files, the definition of a Python library is a bit looser. Libraries can contain many packages. The Python Standard Library is a library that contains many packages.

Individual packages can also be referred to as "libraries," especially if they are large and complex. For example, scikit-learn (see Chapter 24, "Machine Learning with Matplotlib and Scikit-Learn") is, technically, a single package, but it would be a bit strange to refer to it as anything other than "the scikit-learn library."

Whatever you call them, they're a great way to keep your code organized and reusable. In this chapter, we'll create and use all of these various Python collections, as well as discuss ways to help others find and use your code.

MODULES

Every time you create a new Python file, you're creating a module. Let's create a module in a file called shapes.py. It consists of a single function, square:

```
def square(n=5):
    for _ in range(n):
        print('#'*n)
```

When called, this prints a square.[1] We can call this function by entering the Python command prompt in the same directory as shapes.py, importing it, and calling it:

```
>>> import shapes
>>> shapes.square()
```

You can also create a new Python file or Jupyter notebook file and, as long as it exists in the same directory as shapes.py, the shapes module can be imported and used in the file.

When a module is imported, the contents of that module file are read and executed. We can see this in action by adding a line to shapes.py that prints the module's name:

```
def square(n=5):
    for _ in range(n):
        print('#'*n)

print(f'Module name is: {__name__}')
```

The __name__ attribute was used in Chapter 10, "Functions," to print the name of a function, like:

```
some_function.__name__
```

Here, it is not an attribute on an object, but being used by itself. __name__ is a special variable in Python that contains the name of the current module. Now, when the shapes module is imported, the following line is printed:

```
Module name is: shapes
```

If the module file is not imported but run directly from the command line by calling:

```
$ python shapes.py
```

we see something different print:

```
Module name is: __main__
```

We are not, in fact, in a module, but in the top-level Python environment, so the variable __name__ is set to the string __main__ by Python. This feature is often used to modify behavior if a file is run directly rather than imported as a module. For example:

```
if __name__ == '__main__':
    print('This should be imported, not run directly!')
```

If the file shapes.py is run in the main code environment, rather than as a module, it will print a warning to the user.

There are a variety of ways to import items from modules. You can import the square function from shapes and use it directly:

```
from shapes import square

square()
```

---

[1] Or, at least, an n-by-n collection of hash symbols whose square-ness depends on the font your terminal uses, but is likely more rectangular than square. Use your imagination.

In addition to functions, you can add other things to modules and import them. In shapes.py, we can add a constant:

```
PI = 3.14159
```

We can also add a new class, Circle:

```
class Circle:
    def __init__(self, radius):
        self.radius = radius

    def draw(self):
        for i in range(-self.radius, self.radius + 1):
            y = math.sqrt((self.radius ** 2) - (i ** 2))
            y = round(y)
            print(' ' * (self.radius - y) + '#' * (y*2))
```

Then use both PI and Circle in a separate file that exists in the same directory as the shapes.py file:

```
from shapes import Circle, PI

c = Circle(5)
c.draw()

print(f'The area of this circle is {PI * c.radius**2}')
```

This produces the following output:

```
   ######
  ########
 ##########
 ##########
 ##########
 ##########
 ##########
  ########
   ######

The area of this circle is 78.53975
```

In addition to importing each value from a module individually, like in this line:

```
from shapes import square, Circle, PI
```

it is possible to import everything from the file using an asterisk:

```
from shapes import *
```

This asterisk is known as a *wildcard* import and is often read out loud as "import all." This imports all items found in the module and allows you to use them directly, like this:

```
print(PI)
c = Circle(10)
square()
```

However, using a wildcard is discouraged to avoid confusion. Normally when items are imported, the `import` statement itself acts as a sort of documentation. We can see that the shapes module contains `PI`, `Circle`, and `square`. When we see those used in code, we can easily look up where they came from.

This, however, is less clear:

```
from shapes import *

c = Circle(10)
```

One might assume that the class `Circle` was imported from the shapes module, but without running the code or manually examining the content of the `shapes` module, it's impossible to tell.

Something like this is even more ambiguous:

```
from shapes import *
from math import *

square()
```

Did the function `square` come from the `shapes` module or the `math` module?

While importing everything from a module with a wildcard might make writing Python easier in some ways, explicitly importing what you need as you need it will make your code much easier to understand in the long run.

Import This

Although most modules are designed to hold importable data, not all of them do! Consider the first module we encountered in this book:

```
>>> import this
```

The purpose of `this` is to print a message as soon as it's imported, and that's it. If you're interested in viewing the contents of this module (or, rather, `this` module), you can locate it using the `__file__` attribute:

```
>>> import this
>>> this.__file__
```

This will return the actual location of `this.py` on your computer. On my computer, this is at:

```
/Library/Frameworks/Python.framework/Versions/3.13/lib/python3.13/this.py
```

You can use whichever method you like to open and view this file. One option is to exit Python and use the `cat` command (the get-content command in Windows PowerShell) from the terminal:

```
$ cat /Library/Frameworks/Python.framework/Versions/3.13/lib/python3.13/this.py
```

This prints the file contents to the screen, which begins with some encoded text, reading, in part:

```
s = """Gur Mra bs Clguba, ol Gvz Crgref

Ornhgvshy vf orggre guna htyl.
Rkcyvpvg vf orggre guna vzcyvpvg.
...
"""
```

Then, the file contains an algorithm for decoding the string:

```
d = {}
for c in (65, 97):
    for i in range(26):
        d[chr(i+c)] = chr((i+13) % 26 + c)

print("".join([d.get(c, c) for c in s]))
```

This uses a simple substitution cipher to decode the string into the more familiar "The Zen of Python." While there's nothing like a decoding function available for import, the dictionary d can be imported:

```
from this import d
```

Running this import will still print "The Zen of Python," because the file this.py is being loaded by the import. It will also give you access to the dictionary d, which can be used to decode your own secret messages.[2]

With just a little module investigation, you might find that even the Easter eggs contain hidden surprises!

PACKAGES

When the functionality of a module outgrows a single file, it makes sense to split it up into multiple files, or even multiple directories and create a package. This allows for greater code readability and organization and also allows for longer and more descriptive import statements.

Although any Python file is automatically a module, not all directories of Python files are automatically packages. To tell Python that you'd like to use a directory of Python files like a package, start by creating a file in the directory called __init__.py.

Although the file __init__.py and the class function __init__ don't have anything to do with each other programmatically, they are somewhat philosophically related. Like the class initialization method, the __init__.py file serves as a starting point for a package. Python searches for it each time a package is imported and executes anything inside.

However, the __init__.py file doesn't have to have anything at all inside it. In fact, most of them are completely empty. Its mere presence, with the filename __init__.py, clearly communicates to everyone that this directory is a fully qualified Python package and serves as a placeholder for anything that needs to be defined or executed immediately upon import.

Let's create a package used for drawing shapes called draw. This package is located inside the directory 14_packages in the exercise files accompanying this book and has the following structure:

> draw

> > __init__.py

> > base.py

---

[2] Using the more traditional import this will give you access to d using this.d.

> ➤ circle.py

> ➤ rectangle.py

> ➤ square.py

The base.py file contains a very simple base class:

```
class Shape:
    def draw(self):
        raise NotImplementedError
```

This can be implemented by the Circle class previously seen in the shapes module. We can also create a Rectangle class in rectangle.py:

```
from draw.base import Shape

class Rectangle(Shape):
    def __init__(self, height, width):
        self.height = height
        self.width = width

    def draw(self):
        for i in range(0, self.height):
            print('#' * self.width)
```

Although the base class Shape is located in the base.py file right next to (i.e., in the same directory as) rectangle.py, it must be imported starting from the root directory name in the package. It cannot be imported like this:

```
from base import Shape
```

Because base is now part of the package draw, rather than a module of its own, it must be imported like this:

```
from draw.base import Shape
```

The existence of the Rectangle class makes the Square class extremely easy to write:

```
from draw.rectangle import Rectangle

class Square(Rectangle):
    def __init__(self, size):
        self.height = size
        self.width = size
```

Previously, when we imported modules that we wrote ourselves, Python needed to be running in the same directory to find those modules. The same is also true for packages. Make sure that, when attempting to import the draw package, that you are in the 14_packages directory within the exercise files directory.

When a module is imported in Python, the file will be read into memory and everything within it will be loaded. When a package is imported in Python, only the __init__.py file for that package is read and loaded into Python as the package.

These import *modules* within the package and are module imports:

```
from draw import rectangle
import draw.rectangle
```

This imports the *package* and is a package import:

```
import draw
```

When we import a module in Python, we are able to access all attributes in that module using dot notation, like this:

```
>>> import shapes
>>> shapes.square()
```

Trying this with the draw package is less successful:

```
>>> import draw
>>> draw.rectangle
Traceback (most recent call last):
  File "<stdin>", line 1, in <module>
AttributeError: module 'draw' has no attribute 'rectangle'
```

When we import the package, the __init__.py file is read, and it's blank. Nothing is loaded aside from the package name, draw, itself. To use the modules from the top-level package in code like draw.rectangle, we need to populate __init__.py:

```
from . import rectangle
from . import square
from . import circle
```

This dot notation is called a *relative import* and imports the package rectangle assuming that it is within the current directory of the file. The dot (.) is an *alias* (a stand-in that acts as) for the current directory. The statement from . import rectangle is the same as from draw import rectangle, but it allows for changes in the package name without modifying the code, which may or may not be important to you.

```
>>> import draw
>>> draw.rectangle
<module 'draw.rectangle' from '/Users/RMitchell/Documents/unlocking-python/draw/
rectangle.py'>
```

Note that, if you are doing this at home, you will need to exit Python and then load the interface again to re-import the changed version of the package. If using a Jupyter notebook, restart the kernel.

Adding these lines also allows us to import the Rectangle class and use it directly. This is probably the cleanest way to write the import, and how I chose to do it in the code for the package itself, earlier:

```
from draw.rectangle import Rectangle
```

Of course, you can also choose to use the Rectangle class from the rectangle module import:

```
from draw import rectangle
r = rectangle.Rectangle(4, 5)
```

The Python keyword **as** can be used to define an alias for the import. Instead of the predefined package and module names, you can use whatever name you like:

```
import draw as d
r = d.rectangle.Rectangle(4, 5)
```

Or:

```
from draw.rectangle import Rectangle as Rect
r = Rect(4, 5)
```

Using an alias for the import is handy if you've, say, already defined a `Rectangle` class and don't want the name of the imported class to conflict with that. Or the package name may be very long and it's more convenient to use as a shorter form.

Some of the libraries we'll work with in later chapters are traditionally imported under shorter names:

```
import matplotlib.pyplot as plt
import pandas as pd
import numpy as np
```

These shortened names are so common, you will often see `pd` or `np` used in code samples, instead of `pandas` or `numpy`, even without explicitly showing the imports. It's generally understood, in certain contexts, that `np` is the numpy package.

If you want to create more user-friendly import names for users so that they don't need aliases in the first place, the __init__.py file can come in handy again. We can populate the __init__.py file of our draw package with aliases like this:

```
from draw.rectangle import Rectangle
from draw.square import Square
from draw.circle import Circle
```

You may get a warning in your text editor because the classes are simply imported, without being used, but this is safe to ignore. Recall that the __init__.py file is loaded each time the package is first imported. We can see this in action by adding a `print` statement to __init__.py:

```
from draw.rectangle import Rectangle
from draw.square import Square
from draw.circle import Circle
print('Importing draw!')
```

Now when the package draw is first imported, this statement will print the following:

```
>>> import draw
Importing draw!
```

This means that all the `import` statements were also read, and that `Rectangle`, `Square`, and `Circle` are now directly available inside __init__.py. Whatever is available inside __init__.py is also directly available from the top-level package import. This means we can structure imports like this:

```
from draw import Rectangle, Square, Circle
```

The __init__.py file can be useful for structuring and organizing your packages, when packages get large and nested.

The package cdraw, alongside draw in the directory 14_packages in the exercise files, is an example of a nested package. It has a structure like this:

➤ cdraw

    ➤ __init__.py

    ➤ colors

        ➤ __init__.py

        ➤ colors.py

        ➤ printer.py

    ➤ shapes

        ➤ __init__.py

        ➤ base.py

        ➤ circle.py

        ➤ rectangle.py

        ➤ square.py

Notice that every directory within the package contains an __init__.py file, not just the top-level directory. Each subdirectory is essentially treated as a smaller package within the package.

This new package is named cdraw ("color draw") because it allows us to print shapes to the terminal in multiple colors. It takes advantage of the fact that colored text can be printed to the terminal using certain *ANSI escape codes*.[3] For example, the following prints Hello, World in red text:

```
print('\u001b[31mHello, World!\u001b[0m')
```

The ANSI code \u001b[31m makes text red and the ANSI code \u001b[0m sets it back to the default terminal color. Sandwiched in between is the string 'Hello, World!', which will appear red.

There are ANSI color codes for both the text color and the highlight color behind the text, which are catalogued in the file colors.py:

---

[3] American National Standards Institute (ANSI) escape codes have an interesting history. Early computer terminals in the 1960s used escape sequences transmitted in text to determine where to position text, where to place the cursor, what color the text should be, etc. This allowed the software to control the user interface to some extent, but the problem was that video terminal manufacturers couldn't agree on which escape sequences to use. The software became extremely dependent on, essentially, the manufacturer of the monitor it was hooked up to.

In 1976, a standardized set of escape codes were adopted by the American National Standards Institute. Unfortunately, this was slow to catch on because there were so many other popular competing standards, such as the European Computer Manufacturer's Association (ECMA) standard. Eventually ANSI and ECMA merged standards in 1983 and more widespread adoption followed. Despite this, Windows did not support ANSI escape codes until 2016, preferring the Cygwin standard.

```
DEFAULT = '\u001b[0m'

class TextColors:
    BLACK = '\u001b[30m'
    RED = '\u001b[31m'
    GREEN = '\u001b[32m'
    YELLOW = '\u001b[33m'
    BLUE = '\u001b[34m'
    MAGENTA = '\u001b[35m'
    CYAN = '\u001b[36m'
    WHITE = '\u001b[37m'

class BackgroundColors:
    BLACK = '\u001b[40m'
    RED = '\u001b[41m'
    GREEN = '\u001b[42m'
    YELLOW = '\u001b[43m'
    BLUE = '\u001b[44m'
    MAGENTA = '\u001b[45m'
    CYAN = '\u001b[46m'
    WHITE = '\u001b[47m'
```

This allows us to use the color codes from the package like this:

```
from cdraw.colors.colors import BackgroundColors, TextColors, DEFAULT

print(f'{TextColors.RED}{BackgroundColors.YELLOW}Hello, World!{DEFAULT}')
```

This prints the text `'Hello, World!'` in red on a yellow background. The module `printer.py` contains a class `ColorPrinter` that handles this task for us:

```
from cdraw.colors.colors import DEFAULT

class ColorPrinter:
    def __init__(self, text_color='', background_color=''):
        self.text_color = text_color
        self.background_color = background_color

    def print(self, string):
        print(f'{self.text_color}{self.background_color}{string}{DEFAULT}')
```

Using a `ColorPrinter` class, we can print the `'Hello, World!'` text again in red on a yellow background:

```
from cdraw.colors.colors import BackgroundColors, TextColors
from cdraw.colors.printer import ColorPrinter

cp = ColorPrinter(
    text_color=TextColors.RED,
    background_color=BackgroundColors.YELLOW)
cp.print('Hello, World!')
```

Although this technically requires more imports and more code to write a single line, the `ColorPrinter` object has an advantage in that it can be passed around and reused. We can rewrite the draw method of each shape class to, optionally, take a `printer` function as an argument:

```
def draw(self, printer=print):
    for _ in range(0, self.height):
        printer('#' * self.width)
```

By default, the `printer` function is simply the standard Python function `print`. If we pass the `print` method from a `ColorPrinter` object, however, the shape will print in color:

```
from cdraw.colors.printer import ColorPrinter
from cdraw.colors.colors import TextColors, BackgroundColors
from cdraw.shapes.square import Square

cp = ColorPrinter(
    text_color=TextColors.BLUE,
    background_color=BackgroundColors.GREEN)

s = Square(5)
s.draw(printer=cp.print)
```

We have some options here for cleaning up the imports and creating a nice "user interface" for our package. We write import statements in `cdraw/__init__.py` to make everything immediately available for the user:

```
from cdraw.colors.colors import BackgroundColors, TextColors
from cdraw.colors.printer import ColorPrinter
from cdraw.shapes.rectangle import Rectangle
from cdraw.shapes.square import Square
from cdraw.shapes.circle import Circle
```

This allows us to rewrite the imports for our program that prints the blue and green square as:

```
from cdraw import ColorPrinter, TextColors, BackgroundColors, Square
```

However, it may be desirable to separate concepts like "colors" from concepts like "shapes" and make these two distinct groups of functionality within the same package. We can do this by removing all imports from `cdraw/__init__.py` and writing the imports in `cdraw/shapes/__init__.py`:

```
from cdraw.shapes.rectangle import Rectangle
from cdraw.shapes.square import Square
from cdraw.shapes.circle import Circle
```

and the imports in `cdraw/colors/__init__.py` as:

```
from cdraw.colors.colors import BackgroundColors, TextColors
from cdraw.colors.printer import ColorPrinter
```

This changes the imports in our blue and green square printing program to:

```
from cdraw.colors import ColorPrinter, TextColors, BackgroundColors
from cdraw.shapes import Square
```

There are many considerations that must go into designing package structures, their imports, and their user interfaces. Whatever decisions you make for your own packages, make sure they're documented in your project's README file so that others can use them!

INSTALLING PACKAGES

Previously, we've used homemade packages and modules only when they're in the same directory as the code that's using them. This might do okay for experimentation and development, but it's very inconvenient in the real world. We want packages to be installable and usable by any Python program anywhere on the computer.

Recall from Chapter 3, "About Python," that, when an import is made, Python looks for that module along the module search path, which can be viewed using sys.path:

```
import sys
print(sys.path)
```

On my computer, this results in the following list:

```
['', '/Library/Frameworks/Python.framework/Versions/3.13/lib/python312.zip', '/
Library/Frameworks/Python.framework/Versions/3.13/lib/python3.12', '/Library/
Frameworks/Python.framework/Versions/3.13/lib/python3.12/lib-dynload', '/Library/
Frameworks/Python.framework/Versions/3.13/lib/python3.12/site-packages']
```

When a package is installed, it goes into the site-packages directory, where it is discoverable by Python.

There are many ways to make packages installable. So far in this book, we've installed a lot of packages with pip. To install a package with pip, you only need to give it the name of the package. For example:

```
$ pip install requests
```

This installs a very popular HTTP package called requests. pip is able to look up the package by the name, requests, because that is its unique identifier in the *Python Package Index* (PyPI). pip fetches the files from pypi.org, downloads them, and then installs them on your computer.

Making a package available through PyPI is a fairly involved process, which requires you to create an account at pypi.org, create a unique package name, and upload it to the index.

If you want to create a widely distributed Python package, uploading it to PyPI so that it can be installed through pip is a must. Unfortunately, this process is outside the scope of this book, but there is an excellent official walkthrough available here: https://packaging.python.org/en/latest/tutorials/packaging-projects.

For many purposes, such as distributing a package to friends or within a company, it doesn't need to be available in the Python Package Index at all. You can download the files and install it in one of several different ways as long as it's packaged correctly and has an installation script called setup.py.

In the exercise files accompanying this book, I've created a sample package ready for distribution called cdraw2. It is a copy of the cdraw package created earlier, renamed to avoid conflicts. It also has an extra layer of packaging and files:

- ➤ cdraw2
  - ➤ cdraw2
    - ➤ colors
    - ➤ shapes
    - ➤ __init__.py
  - ➤ LICENSE
  - ➤ README.md

➤ `requirements.txt`

➤ `setup.py`

Inside the outer `cdraw2` directory is an inner `cdraw2` directory containing the actual package. Alongside the package are a variety of files that provide information about the package and instructions for its installation.

Chapter 12, "Writing Cleaner Code," discussed both the LICENSE file and the README.md file. The `requirements.txt` file is useful if you want to do development on the package. It contains a list of all the package dependencies required to run the development environment, including any tests for the package.

The `requirements.txt` file is called a *requirements file*. The listing of the libraries it contains can be installed with pip using the `-r` flag and a filename:

```
pip install -r requirements.txt
```

In a requirements file, the package names are listed one per line with, optionally, specific required versions or version ranges that must be used. For example, the requirements for the Python library `flask` (discussed in Chapter 20, "REST APIs and Flask") are, in part:

```
alabaster==0.7.16
asgiref==3.8.1
babel==2.14.0
```

The `flask` package needs to import those libraries at some point during its operation and requires those specific versions of `alabaster`, `asgiref`, and `babel` to guarantee success. Alternatively, it might specify an `alabaster` version of *at least* 0.7.16, but allow for a higher version to be used as well:

```
alabaster>=0.7.16
```

Or perhaps it could specify any version of `alabaster` greater than 0.7.16 but less than version 1.0.0:

```
alabaster>=0.7.16,<1.0.0
```

Requirements files can often be lengthy. For this reason, developers will often use a Python virtual environment (see Chapter 4, "Installing and Running Python") specifically for working on a package and run `pip install -r requirements.txt` within that virtual environment to keep their work isolated.

Although `requirements.txt` is handy for development, testing, and reference, it's not required for installation. The `setup.py` file is responsible for installation, including installation requirements.

The `setup.py` file in the `cdraw2` package looks like this:

```
from setuptools import setup

setup(
    name='cdraw2',
    version='0.1',
    description='Makes colorful shapes',
    author='Ryan Mitchell',
    author_email='ryan@ryanemitchell.com',
    packages=['cdraw2'],
    install_requires=[],
)
```

The package `setuptools` is not technically part of the Python Standard Library, although it is so commonly installed by default with some Python installers that one might think that it is. It is also included with `pip`, so if you have `pip` installed, you will have `setuptools`.

The Python Standard Library did contain its own packaging library called `distutils`, which `setuptools` was originally built on top of. However, `distutils` was deprecated and removed in Python 3.12, leaving `setuptools` as the officially recommended packaging and installing tool: `https://docs.python.org/3.10/library/distutils.html`.

Although there are many ways to package and distribute Python libraries today, using the `setup` function in `setuptools` is generally considered to be the most straightforward and bare-bones approach. It allows users to install your package *from source*, by downloading the source code, navigating to the directory, and running an installation script.

The setup function requires the following:

- ➤ library name
- ➤ version number
- ➤ description
- ➤ author information
- ➤ listing of packages in the library (important if there are multiple packages, but usually just a list containing a single package)
- ➤ installation requirements

The `install_requires` field is very similar to the `requirements.txt` file; however, it defines only the libraries needed to install, import, and use the package, rather than develop it. For example, if there are requirements to run unit tests associated with the package, those will not be included in `install_requires` because they are not installation requirements.

Let's say we wanted to enhance our `cdraw2` package with a feature that makes it clear to the user how much work is going on behind the scenes to draw shapes to the screen. A progress bar with informative messages would do nicely here:

```
configuring angles...      :  42%|
███████████████████████
| 42/100 [00:01<00:01, 41.54it/s]
```

This progress bar was created with the `tqdm` package (`https://tqdm.github.io`), which can be installed with `pip`:

```
$ pip install tqdm
```

The method `do_loading`, in the base `Shape` class, creates the loading bar:

```
def do_loading(self):
    messages = [
        'loading hashes...        ',
        'configuring angles...    ',
        'queuing euclidean axioms...',
```

```
                        'defragging edges...        ',
                        'Done!                      '
                    ]
                    loading_bar = tqdm(range(0,102))
                    for i in loading_bar:
                        m = messages[int(i/25)]
                        loading_bar.set_description(m)
                        time.sleep(0.02)
```

Then, each child class adds it to their `draw` method—for example, in the `Rectangle` class:

```
        def draw(self, printer=print):
            self.do_loading()
            for _ in range(0, self.height):
                printer('#' * self.width)
```

This displays a loading bar for two seconds, spending half a second on each message before ending on the message `'Done!'` as the shape is printed out. While this pomp and circumstance may not be necessary for our drawing program, it does add a certain professional flourish. (In all seriousness, I highly recommend the `tqdm` package whenever a progress bar is needed!).

When our package is installed, we need to make sure that the `tqdm` library is installed with it. If the `tqdm` package is missing, then `cdraw2` will fail when the end user tries to run it.

You can view the current version of any package using the `__version__` attribute:

```
>>> import tqdm
>>> tqdm.__version__
'4.66.4'
```

This allows us to update the setup file appropriately:

```
setup(
    name='cdraw2',
    version='0.1',
    description='Makes colorful shapes',
    author='Ryan Mitchell',
    author_email='ryan@ryanemitchell.com',
    packages=['cdraw2'],
    install_requires=[
        'tqdm==4.66.4'
    ],
)
```

If we trust that the library will follow the rules of major and minor versions and that any version of `tqdm` with a major version of "4" will be backward compatible with previous 4.x.x versions, then we might specify the following:

```
    install_requires=[
        'tqdm>=4.66.4,<5.0.0'
    ],
```

The more flexible you can be with the version numbers (i.e., the larger the ranges of versions you accept), the greater are the chances of compatibility with other packages installed on the same machine.

For example, if another package is using the same `tqdm` loading bar, but with a slightly different version specified:

```
install_requires=[
    'tqdm==4.66.3'
],
```

Then these two packages will be incompatible with each other, leading to potential headaches for the end user.

Whatever packages and version numbers you decide on, of course, you should also put them in your `requirements.txt` file if you choose to have one. If you have a lot of requirements in your package and you're starting to lose track, a good practice is to develop in a virtual environment, install only what's needed, and then use `pip freeze` to create your requirements file:

```
$ pip freeze > requirements.txt
```

Here, the greater than sign (`>`) is a terminal command, which takes the output of the left side (`pip freeze`) and writes it to a file on the right (`requirements.txt`). This automatically creates a `requirements.txt` file for the libraries and versions that are in your current Python environment.

Finally, we're ready to install the `cdraw2` package. Navigate to the outer `cdraw2` directory. If you use the `ls` command to list the files, you should see the following:

```
$ ls
LICENSE          README.md          build          cdraw2      requirements.txt setup.py
```

From here, there are two ways to install it. The first is to call `setup.py` with the `install` command:

```
$ python setup.py install
```

The second way is to use `pip` and pass a period (`.`) to it instead of the usual package name. This indicates that pip should install the package located in the current directory, rather than attempting to locate a package in the Python Package Index:

```
$ pip install .
```

If you want to experiment with package installation it may be wise to uninstall the package between installs. You can do that from anywhere on your computer (it does not have to be within the `cdraw2` directory):

```
$ pip uninstall cdraw2
```

EXERCISES

1. Use the `cdraw` package to make a rainbow consisting of stacked rectangles, each having a height of 2 and a width of 80.

2. Write a function that uses the dictionary, `d`, from `this` to decode this message:

```
Ybofgre Gurezvqbe nhk perirggrf jvgu a Zbeanl fnhpr, tneavfurq jvgu gehssyr cngr,
oenaql, naq n sevrq rtt ba gbc, naq Fcnz. - Gur "Fcnz" fxrgpu
```

This string is also provided in the exercise files accompanying this book, which I suggest using instead of copying the string by hand!

3. Add a class `Triangle` to `cdraw2`. It should have, as attributes, a height and a width. It should be fairly easy to draw a right triangle (essentially, a rectangle cut in half diagonally), but for an added challenge, you can draw an isosceles (symmetric) triangle.

4. Add a new directory to `cdraw2` called `text`. Add a module to it that contains a function that takes, as arguments, a short string message and a `ColorPrinter` object. It then prints the text as ASCII art using the `ColorPrinter` object.

   Use the package at `https://pypi.org/project/art` to transform text into ASCII art with the `text2art` function. Make sure you add this package to the `requirements.txt` file and the `install_requires` in `setup.py`!

5. Add functionality to the `text` addition of the `cdraw2` package from Exercise 4 so that the text can, optionally, be drawn with multiple colors. Each character must be displayed horizontally in line with the others (side by side), but adjacent characters have the ability to be printed in completely different colors.

   You will likely want to retrieve the ASCII art representation of a character from the `text2art` one character at a time, and then carefully concatenate characters row by row while changing the colors within the concatenated lines.

   Also, you will want to consider the user interface for your new module or set of modules in the package. Will the user pass in multiple `ColorPrinter` objects, or perhaps `ColorPrinter` can be modified to have multiple colors? Will each character be explicitly assigned a specific color, will colors simply alternate through the list, or something else?

15

Working with Files

For the entirety of this book, the only output of every Python program we've written has been text in a terminal. Whether that text is a prime number, some ASCII art, or a poker hand, it's still just characters on a screen.

In this chapter, we'll build Python programs whose spheres of influence aren't limited to the terminal but that can read and write files on your computer. If this doesn't seem especially exciting, consider that the goal of many pieces of desktop software—Adobe Photoshop, MySQL, and most of the Microsoft Office Suite—is, ultimately, to create, read, and edit files. At the end of the day, the tools simply create files on a disk.

The ability to manipulate files in code not only lays the groundwork for powerful standalone functionality but also allows for collaboration between software applications via files.

READING FILES

To read the contents of a text file, you must first open the file:

```
f = open('15_test.txt', 'r')
```

The open function takes two arguments: the string filename (or path, if the file is not in the same directory) and a short string that indicates the mode we want to open the file in. In this case, we are passing `'r'`, meaning we are opening the file for reading.

This returns a file object, f, which can be used to read all the lines of the file:

```
f.read()
```

In this case, the file contains the lines of all five Monty Python films separated by newline characters:

```
"And Now for Something Completely Different\nMonty Python and the Holy Grail\
nMonty Python's Life of Brian\nMonty Python Live at the Hollywood Bowl\nMonty
Python's The Meaning of Life"
```

Finally, we must close the file:

```
f.close()
```

This is the first time we've dealt with data that does not originate from the Python software application itself. This text file might have been created by any number of other software applications and saved to our computer's filesystem. It has nothing to do with Python, and its permissions and access are controlled by the operating system.

When we open the file with the open function, a request is made to the operating system to access its contents, and information about that file and the Python application accessing it is loaded into memory. When we close the file, we are telling the operating system that we no longer need to access it, and that memory is released. If we try to read from the file again:

```
f.read()
```

a ValueError is raised:

```
ValueError: I/O operation on closed file.
```

Python will attempt to close files automatically when they are no longer needed, but it is best practice to explicitly close them to reduce memory usage. We've seen this kind of situation before when discussing database connections in Chapter 13, "Errors and Exceptions." Files, just like database connections, must be closed with some sort of closing or teardown statement. To do this, we might use a try/finally pattern:

```
f = open('15_test.txt', 'r')
try:
    print(f.read())
finally:
    f.close()
```

This ensures that the file is always closed even if an error is raised when the file is read.[1] When working with files, it's extremely common to simplify this pattern by using a *with statement*:

```
with open('15_test.txt', 'r') as f:
    print(f.read())
```

The with statement assigns the file object returned value from open('15_test.txt', 'r') to the variable declared after the keyword as, in this case, the variable f. Any lines indented under the with statement can use the opened file object f. Outdenting will automatically close the file object, even if an error is thrown inside the with statement.

For example, executing this cell in a Jupyter notebook file (which raises a ZeroDivisionError):

```
f = open('15_test.txt', 'r')
1/0
f.close()
```

followed by this cell:

```
f.read()
```

allows us to read the file. The file did not get closed.

---

[1] It's worth noting that if an error is raised and causes the Python program to exit, the file will be cleaned up and closed automatically because the software that requested it is no longer running. However, errors raised in Python programs running in Jupyter do not cause Python to exit in the same way. Jupyter is always running until the kernel is explicitly closed or restarted, and any raised errors are caught behind the scenes and displayed nicely under the cell that raised them.

However, executing this cell:

```
with open('15_test.txt', 'r') as f:
    1/0
```

followed by this:

```
f.read()
```

will result in a ValueError because we are attempting to read a file that has already been closed.

MORE ABOUT *WITH* STATEMENTS

Although one of the most common uses of with statements is to handle files, they are extremely useful in a variety of Python applications. Behind the scenes, the with statement calls the methods __enter__ and __exit__ on the specified object. These methods can be easily implemented in any class:

```
class SetupAndTeardown:
    def __init__(self):
        print('Instantiating')

    def __enter__(self):
        print('Setup')

    def __exit__(self, exc_type, exc_value, traceback):
        print('Teardown')
```

We can use new SetupAndTeardown class in a with statement:

```
with SetupAndTeardown() as st:
    print('Doing some stuff')
```

This prints the following lines:

```
Instantiating
Setup
Doing some stuff
Teardown
```

The __enter__ method is executed before the block of code under the with statement is run. After the with statement block, the __exit__ method is executed.

The __exit__ method also contains three arguments that normally have the value None but are populated if an exception was raised while executing the code under the with statement. These can be printed in the __exit__ method:

```
def __exit__(self, exc_type, exc_value, traceback):
    print(exc_type)
    print(exc_value)
    print(traceback)
    print('Teardown')
```

continues

continued

Now, if a ZeroDivisionError is raised in the with block:

```
with SetupAndTeardown() as st:
    print(1/0)
```

this will print out information about the error:

```
Instantiating
Setup
<class 'ZeroDivisionError'>
division by zero
<traceback object at 0x107103180>
Teardown
```

Note that the error will still be raised after this information is printed. Using a with statement does not necessarily catch or suppress any errors; it merely ensures that any teardown is handled before the program exits.

To suppress errors (similar to surrounding with a try/except), return True from the __exit__ method:

```
def __exit__(self, exc_type, exc_value, traceback):
    print(exc_type)
    return True
```

This will prevent the error from propagating.

When working with very long files, you may not want to load their entire contents into memory at once. You can read one line at a time with the method readline:

```
with open('15_test.txt', 'r') as f:
    print(f.readline())
    print(f.readline())
```

This prints only the first two lines of the file:

```
And Now for Something Completely Different

Monty Python and the Holy Grail
```

The file object has a sort of internal "bookmark," a file position, that keeps track of what has been read and what hasn't. Calling the same method, readline(), twice in a row will result in different lines. This is commonly used in conjunction with a while statement to process all the lines of a file:

```
with open('15_test.txt', 'r') as f:
    while line := f.readline():
        print(line)
```

This uses a walrus operator (:=) to assign the value of f.readline() to the variable line and also check that there's still another line to print. After readline has returned the last line, subsequent calls to it will return an empty string. The empty string evaluates to a Boolean False, which causes the while loop to exit.

The method `readlines` (note the pluralization) reads all lines as a list:

```
with open('15_test.txt', 'r') as f:
    print(f.readlines())
```

This produces the following list:

```
['And Now for Something Completely Different\n', 'Monty Python and the Holy Grail\n',
"Monty Python's Life of Brian\n", 'Monty Python Live at the Hollywood Bowl\n', "Monty
Python's The Meaning of Life"]
```

Each line in the list (also, each line produced by `readline`) still contains the newline character (\n) following it. On Windows, each line will contain a return and newline character (\r\n). It's very common to want to remove these, which can be done using `strip`:

```
with open('15_test.txt', 'r') as f:
    lines = [l.strip() for l in f.readlines()]
```

You can also read the entire text with `read` and `split` on the newline character:

```
with open('15_test.txt', 'r') as f:
    lines = f.read().split('\n')
```

Of course, on Windows, where lines are separated by \r\n, this isn't the cleanest solution and will result in an extra \r at the end of your lines. Python has a solution for this, which is `splitlines`:

```
with open('15_test.txt', 'r') as f:
    lines = f.read().splitlines()
```

The string method `splitlines` handles both the \n and \r\n cases smoothly, making the code operating system agnostic. Although there may be multiple ways to accomplish the same task in Python, one of them often rises to the top as the preferred option. As always, the preferred method may only be obvious at first if you're Dutch.

WRITING FILES

You can write to a file using a syntax that is very similar to reading from a file:

```
with open('15_new.txt', 'w') as f:
    f.write('Some text')
```

Here, we provide the `open` function the name of the file we want to write to, along with the string `'w'`, which opens the file for writing. If the file `15_new.txt` exists, it will be overwritten with the string `'Some text'`. If it does not exist, it will be created and the string `'Some text'` will be written to it.

We can write two lines in two separate with statements:

```
with open('15_new.txt', 'w') as f:
    f.write('Some text')

with open('15_new.txt', 'w') as f:
    f.write('Some other text')
```

However, you may be disappointed by the result. If you open the file, it displays only the text:

```
Some other text
```

By default, each open function using the 'w' argument to open the file for writing will completely overwrite the contents of the file. Only the text from the last write statement ('Some other text') appears in the file. To write multiple strings to the file across multiple file openings, you must open the file in *append mode*, using the mode string 'a':

```
with open('15_new.txt', 'a') as f:
    f.write('Some text')

with open('15_new.txt', 'a') as f:
    f.write('Some other text')
```

If you open the file, you'll find that it took its instructions very literally:

```
Some textSome other text
```

The method writelines can write multiple lines at once, but still requires that a line separator like '\n' be added to each line to prevent them from running together:

```
with open('15_new.txt', 'w') as f:
    lines = ['Some text\n', 'Some other text\n']
    f.writelines(lines)
```

Note that, in this example, the file is being opened in 'w' mode, rather than 'a' mode, causing it to overwrite any previously existing contents.

One might expect that, if a file can be written to, it can also be read. This is not necessarily the case:

```
with open('15_new.txt', 'a') as f:
    f.read()
```

Opening the file in 'a' mode and attempting to read it will raise an error:

```
UnsupportedOperation: not readable
```

There are six modes that text files can be opened in for reading and writing (non-text files, interpreted as binary files, have different modes, which will be discussed later). These six modes are identical to those used for the underlying C programming language.

In C, a structure called a *file handle*, or just "handle," acts as an interface between the programming language and the underlying file object in the operating system. This handle is analogous to the file object in Python. It contains a bookmark pointing to a position within the file.

A description of each mode of opening files, based on the C documentation, is as follows:

'r'   Open the file for reading only. The handle is positioned at the beginning of the file.

'r+'   Open the file for reading and writing. The handle is positioned at the beginning of the file.

'w'   Open the file for writing only. Truncate any existing file, or create new file if it doesn't exist. The handle is positioned at the beginning of the file.

'w+'   Open the file for reading and writing. Truncate any existing file, or create new file if it doesn't exist. The handle is positioned at the beginning of the file.

'a' Open the file for writing only. The handle is positioned at the end of the file. Subsequent writes will be appended to the file.

'a+' Open the file for reading and writing. The handle is positioned at the end of the file. Subsequent writes will be appended to the file.

In practice, it is somewhat unusual to need the mode w+. Any mode with a w in it will truncate the text as soon as the file is opened, so this will always be an empty string:

```
with open('15_new.txt', 'w+') as f:
    print(f.read())
```

Also, if you've just written text to the file, you should already know what's in it. It's the string you just wrote! In theory, though, if you really wanted to, I suppose you could write this:

```
with open('15_new.txt', 'w+') as f:
    f.write('This is some new text')
    print(f'File contents are: {f.read()}')
```

Although it might seem glaringly obvious what this code will do—so obvious that elucidation really isn't necessary—just for the sake of superfluous verbosity, here is the output:

```
File contents are:
```

That's right; f.read() returns an empty string. If this isn't what you expected, consider the file position reference that Python uses to keep track of where you are within the file.

When first opened, the file is truncated and the file position is set to position 0 (the only option, really) within the file. After writing, the file position is moved to the end of the newly written text. When f.read() is called, it returns all the text from the current file position to the end of the file, which is an empty string.

We can show this by using the seek method, which resets the file position:

```
with open('15_new.txt', 'w+') as f:
    f.write('This is some new text')
    f.seek(0)
    print(f'File contents are: {f.read()}')
```

This prints:

```
File contents are: This is some new text
```

Modifying the file position using seek is probably not something you want to do regularly, and it can have unintended consequences. Using it in a writer will cause you to overwrite existing text:

```
with open('15_new.txt', 'w+') as f:
    f.write('This is some new text')
    f.seek(0)
    print(f'File contents are: {f.read()}')
    f.seek(0)
    f.write('Spam')
    f.seek(0)
    print(f'File contents are now: {f.read()}')
```

This prints:

```
File contents are: This is some new text
File contents are now: Spam is some new text
```

BINARY FILES

So far, we've been reading and writing text files. However, Python can work with any file type using byte data. Doing this is very similar to working with text files—simply add a `'b'` to the file mode:

```
with open('15_logo.jpg', 'rb') as f:
    print(f.read()[0:10])
```

This opens an image file, `15_logo.jpg` in `'rb'` ("read binary") mode, then prints the first 10 bytes of it:

```
b'\xff\xd8\xff\xe0\x00\x10JFIF'
```

This is six sets of hexadecimal characters (e.g., `\xe0`) followed by four ASCII characters: `JFIF`. This is because, if the byte is representable as an ASCII character, Python will automatically display its ASCII representation rather than its hexadecimal representation. This is useful in many situations, especially when dealing with file types that may contain (at least partially) ASCII data or headers. However, when dealing with JPEGs (which do not contain ASCII characters) these 10 bytes might be better represented as:

```
b'\xff\xd8\xff\xe0\x00\x10\x4A\x46\x49\x46'
```

Regardless of how they're represented when printed, the Python type that is returned by `f.read()` is a bytes object. Data read from any file that is opened using the mode `'rb'` or `'rb+'` will be read as a bytes object rather than a string.

Similarly, the data written to files that are opened in bytes mode must be "bytes-like"—usually bytes or `bytearray`. This will raise a `TypeError`:

```
with open('15_new.txt', 'wb') as f:
    f.write('asdf')
```

This will not:

```
with open('15_new.txt', 'wb') as f:
    f.write('asdf'.encode('utf-8'))
```

Writing bytes provides the freedom to write any type of data for any purpose, usually in a very compact form. For example, hex color codes[2] are usually represented with six ASCII characters. If we were storing a series of color codes in a file designed for human readability, we might even write something to the file like this:

```
#FF0000, #FFA500, #FFFF00, #008000, #0000FF, #800080
```

This is 52 characters, which would require a file size of 52 bytes to store. Of course, we could always compress it like this:

```
FF0000FFA500FFFF000080000000FF800080
```

---

[2] Hex color codes, also known as HTML colors or web colors, are represented with six hexadecimal characters, usually prefixed with a hash symbol. For example, a nice shade of neutral light green would be #9bc4a5. The first two characters (9b, or 155 in decimal) are the red component of the color. The next two (c4, or 196 in decimal) are the green component of the color. The last two (a5, or 165 in decimal) are the blue component of the color. Higher numbers make lighter colors, up to #FFFFFF, which is white. Lower numbers make darker colors, where #000000 is black.

This requires that the program reading the file knows that it represents hex color codes and be able to break the string up into segments that are six characters long. But there's a way we can reduce even this smaller size by half.

Each pair of hexadecimal characters (A5, for example) represents a single byte of data. We should be able to store each color in only 3 bytes, rather than 6, simply by storing it as bytes data instead of ASCII characters.

There are a few steps that need to be considered in order to accomplish this task. Strings like FF0000FFA500FFF... can be broken up into sets of two characters each for processing by using the itertools module.

The itertools module contains a variety of useful utilities that simplify common looping, grouping, and list iterating tasks. One function we can use here is batched. It takes, as arguments, an iterable sequence, and the length of chunks that sequence should be split into. It returns an iterator that yields tuples of requested size. For example:

```
from itertools import batched

hex_pairs = 'FF0000FFA500FFFF000080000000FF800080'
list(batched(hex_pairs, 2))
```

This code converts the iterator to a list that looks like this:

```
[('F', 'F'),
 ('0', '0'),
 ('0', '0'),
 ...
]
```

Also recall that the constructor of the integer class, int, can be used to convert hexadecimal strings to integers. For example, int('FF', 16) returns the integer 255. In addition, the integer method to_bytes converts integers to bytes objects.

With all of this in mind, we can write a short program that will take a string hex_pairs, and write as bytes to a file 15_colors.col (because we're essentially inventing a new file type, we can use any extension we want, and .col is a good one for color files):

```
from itertools import batched

def hex_pair_to_bytes(hex_pair):
    hex_str = ''.join(hex_pair)
    dec_number = int(hex_str, 16)
    return dec_number.to_bytes()

def hex_to_bytes(hex_pairs):
    hex_pairs = list(batched(hex_pairs, 2))
    with open('15_colors.col', 'ab') as f:
        for pair in hex_pairs:
            f.write(hex_pair_to_bytes(pair))


hex_pairs = 'FF0000FFA500FFFF000080000000FF800080'
hex_to_bytes(hex_pairs)
```

After the file is written, it should be exactly 18 bytes on disk—half the size of its ASCII equivalent. We can check the file's contents by reading it:

```
with open('15_colors.col', 'rb') as f:
    print(f.read())
```

This shows the ASCII colors we stored, written as bytes:

```
b'\xff\x00\x00\xff\xa5\x00…'
```

BUFFERING DATA

In computer science, a buffer is a temporary storage area for data, often used when you're dealing with large quantities of it. You can process or read the part of the data that you need when you need it, without loading everything in memory at once.

For example, when you stream a movie online, you're dealing with buffered data. You can start watching the movie when only a small part of it has been downloaded and discard it from memory as you watch it. In this way, only a minute or two of the film might be loaded in memory or "buffered" at any given time. Any pre-downloaded data also serves as protection against momentary internet outages, as long as your average internet speed is able to compensate and fill the buffer back up when connectivity is regained.

Buffers allow us to load only the data we need, when we need it, often making our lives more efficient and convenient without us realizing that any buffering is happening at all.

Every time you open, read, or write to a file with Python, you are dealing with a buffer. This can be seen when opening a binary file:

```
with open('15_colors.col', 'rb') as f:
    print(type(f))
```

This prints:

```
<class '_io.BufferedReader'>
```

Text files are handled with a different class:

```
with open('15_new.txt', 'w') as f:
    print(type(f))
```

This prints:

```
<class '_io.TextIOWrapper'>
```

Although it doesn't have the word "Buffered" in the name, the Python documentation for `TextIOWrapper` reads:

> *A buffered text stream providing higher-level access to a* `BufferedIOBase` *buffered binary stream. It inherits from* `TextIOBase`.

Every file reader and writer is simply a buffered stream of data. The reason why is obvious in the case of file readers—you may not want to load the entire file into memory at once, and it makes sense to load data only as it's actively needed.

In the case of file writers, it's important to understand that writing to files is an expensive process when compared to writing to memory. If multiple writes are made (especially many small writes), it makes sense to save these into a memory buffer and only write to the file once in a while, or when the file is closed.

We can see this in action by opening a new file, doing many small writes to it, and then leaving it open:

```
f = open('15_buffering.txt', 'a')
for i in range(100):
    f.write(str(i))
```

You should see this file created immediately. File creation itself is not buffered but happens when the file is opened. However, if you open the file (with a text editor), you should see that it's empty, as if none of the writes occurred at all. Close the file, both in the software you opened it with and in Python:

```
f.close()
```

and see that it's now populated with 012345678910...

As an alternative to closing the file, you can *flush* the buffer and write its contents to the file with the flush method:

```
# empty the file
with open('15_buffering.txt', 'w'):
    pass

f = open('15_buffering.txt', 'w', buffering=1)
for i in range(100):
    f.write(str(i))
    f.flush()
```

This takes much longer to run than the previous example, although the runtimes of both are still in milliseconds. The flush method allows you to view the written contents of the file before it's closed and regardless of the buffer size.

The default buffer size, in bytes, can be viewed with the io module:

```
import io
io.DEFAULT_BUFFER_SIZE
```

Typically, it's 4096 or 8192 bytes long. This is a lot of buffer compared to the short examples we've been working with in this chapter. In the number writing example earlier, only 190 bytes are written in total. This means that the file will effectively only be written to when it's closed (at which point the buffer must be cleared and the file written to), rather than when we call f.write.

The default buffer size can be overridden by passing the buffering keyword argument to the open function. However, this argument only affects files opened in binary mode. Because any file (including text files) can be opened to and written in binary mode, this isn't too much of a hurdle:

```
# empty the file
with open('15_buffering.txt', 'w'):
    pass

f = open('15_buffering.txt', 'wb', buffering=3)
for i in range(100):
    f.write(str(i).encode('utf-8'))
```

By setting the buffer size to 3 KB, you should see that all but the last two characters (99) get written to the file until it is closed.

Although buffers are important to understand because they may occasionally cause mysterious effects, you will likely want to leave them and their settings alone the vast majority of the time.

CREATING AND DELETING FILES AND DIRECTORIES

In the Python documentation, the os module is titled "Miscellaneous operating system interfaces." True to its description, it contains tools for working with environment variables, processes, terminals, and directories (among many other things!).

It's easy to make a directory using the os module:

```
import os

os.mkdir('some_directory')
```

The name mkdir comes from the Unix command, which is also in use by most operating systems today. You can try it out yourself if you'd like to create a new directory from the terminal:

```
$ mkdir another_directory
```

Back to Python, the os.mkdir function also allows you to pass in a complete path to create the new directory:

```
os.mkdir('some_directory/level1')
```

However, it can only create one new directory (the last one in the path) at a time. If multiple new directories are required along the way, you need to use the function makedirs. Note that this is spelled makedirs and *not* "mkdirs." With this function, you can create an entire hierarchy of directories easily:

```
os.makedirs('some_directory/level1/level2/level3/level4/level5')
```

The rmdir function, also named after the Unix rmdir, removes directories, but only if they're empty:

```
os.rmdir('some_directory')
```

Trying to remove some_directory after it's been populated results in an error:

```
OSError: [Errno 66] Directory not empty: 'some_directory'
```

It does work, however, on the empty directory level5:

```
os.rmdir('some_directory/level1/level2/level3/level4/level5')
```

Once that directory has been removed, the level4 directory is now empty. We can then remove all the directories in a systematic way:

```
os.rmdir('some_directory/level1/level2/level3/level4')
os.rmdir('some_directory/level1/level2/level3')
os.rmdir('some_directory/level1/level2')
os.rmdir('some_directory/level1')
```

Although this works, it's not very practical if you want to remove large directory structures. In practice, It's more convenient to use the `shutil` module for high-level file operations. The `shutil` module allows you to perform bulk actions on files and directories such as removing an entire directory structure or "tree":

```
import shutil
shutil.rmtree('some_directory')
```

This should be used with caution, as it will remove directories that contain both other directories and other files. If you'd like to see what you're going to delete before you call `shutil.rmtree`, you can use `os.listdir`:

```
os.mkdir('some_directory')
with open('some_directory/another_file.txt', 'w') as f:
    pass

os.mkdir('some_directory/another_directory')

os.listdir('some_directory')
```

This creates a directory, `some_directory`, which contains both a file `another_file.txt` and a directory, `another_directory`. When `os.listdir` is called, it returns a list containing the strings:

```
['another_directory', 'another_file.txt']
```

Although, in this case, they're well named and the file has a file extension (although not all files have file extensions), it's not strictly possible to tell just from this list which string refers to a file and which refers to a directory. For this, `os.path.isfile` and `os.path.isdirectory` come in handy:

```
for name in os.listdir('some_directory'):
    if os.path.isdir(f'some_directory/{name}'):
        print(f'{name} is a directory')
    elif os.path.isfile(f'some_directory/{name}'):
        print(f'{name} is a file')
    else:
        print(f'{name} does not exist')
```

Note that, unlike most other functions in the `os` module, `isdir` and `isfile` do not raise any errors if the entity doesn't exist—they simply return `False`. This has a certain sort of logic to it. A name that doesn't exist will be both "not a file" and also "not a directory."

If you don't want to remove a whole directory of items using `shutil.rmtree`, you can remove an individual file using `os.remove`:

```
# create file
with open('to_be_removed.txt', 'w') as f:
    pass

# remove file
os.remove('to_be_removed.txt')
```

This `remove` function will raise a `FileNotFoundError` if the file doesn't exist, so it needs to be created first. If there's ever doubt about whether or not the file exists, `os.path.exists` works well as a wrapper:

```
if os.path.exists('to_be_removed.txt'):
    os.remove('to_be_removed.txt')
```

SERIALIZING, DESERIALIZING, AND PICKLING DATA

Although files are slower to write to and read from, they do have a distinct advantage over memory: They persist. When programs crash or your computer restarts, files will be there waiting patiently. In addition, files can be easily shared between processes and applications on the same computer, or even transferred to other computers.

Transferring data via files is easy enough. One way to do this is to store the data in the JSON format.[3] Any Python dictionary can be converted to JSON with the `json` module's `json.dumps` function:

```
import json

data = {
    'foo': 1,
    'bar': 2,
    'spam': ['spam', 'spam', 'spam']
}

json.dumps(data)
```

The function `json.dumps` converts Python data structures to a string (`dumps` stands for *dump string*). The previous code sample returns the JSON-formatted string:

```
{"foo": 1, "bar": 2, "spam": ["spam", "spam", "spam"]}
```

And, of course, once you have a string, you can write it to a file:

```
with open('data.json', 'w') as f:
    f.write(json.dumps(data))
```

The `json` module contains another function, `json.loads` (*load string*) that performs the opposite task and loads JSON-formatted strings as Python dictionary objects. By reading the file and loading it, we get our original data dictionary back:

```
with open('data.json', 'r') as f:
    data = json.loads(f.read())

print(f'Data is now type: {type(data)}')
print(data)
```

---

[3] JSON stands for JavaScript Object Notation. Although its name derived from its original use in JavaScript APIs, it's a bit of a misnomer today as JSON is a language-agnostic format.

The JSON format resembles Python dictionaries and lists. All strings are enclosed in double quotes (single quotes cannot be used). JSON name-value pairs (also called objects) are surrounded with curly brackets, similar to Python dictionaries. JSON arrays are surrounded with square brackets, similar to Python lists. Inside these data structures are individual values, which can be of the type number, string, Boolean (lowercase values `true` or `false`), or `null` (similar to a Python None).

It's important to stress that this data is a Python dictionary, not a JSON-formatted string:

```
Data is now type: <class 'dict'>
{'foo': 1, 'bar': 2, 'spam': ['spam', 'spam', 'spam']}
```

The act of taking an object (in this case, a dictionary), converting it to a writable data format (JSON), and persisting it (to a file) is called *serialization* in computer science. The act of taking that file and turning it back into an object is called *deserialization*.

Dictionaries are easy to serialize and deserialize in this way because of their similarities to JSON. A Python dictionary that contains only basic data types (strings, Booleans, integers, lists, etc.) will always be easily convertible to a JSON string, and vice versa.

What if we wanted to serialize and deserialize another object—a User object, for example?

```
class User:
    def __init__(self, name):
        self.name = name
        self.email = email
```

One way might be to write both to_json and from_json methods that can be used to serialize and deserialize the object:

```
class User:
    def __init__(self, name, email):
        self.name = name
        self.email = email

    def to_json(self):
        return json.dumps(
            {
                'name': self.name,
                'email': self.email
            })

    @staticmethod
    def from_json(data):
        data = json.loads(data)
        return User(data['name'], data['email'])
```

Not only does this work, but it's often an excellent approach to the problem. The resulting JSON files are both lightweight and easily read. In addition, the to_json and from_json methods can be used to transmit data over an API (more about APIs in Chapter 20, "REST APIs and Flask").

The following lines create a new user, serialize that data to JSON (at which point it can be written to a file or sent through some other non-Python means), and then deserialize it to a copy of the User object:

```
u = User('Alice', 'alice@unlockingpython.com')
data = u.to_json()
new_u = User.from_json(data)
print(new_u.name)
print(new_u.email)
```

There's another approach to this problem that works for any type of Python object and doesn't require writing any custom to_json or from_json methods. The pickle module, also part of the standard library, contains tools for writing Python objects directly to binary files, which can then be read in as a Python object again.

To write an object to a file, first open a file in binary mode, in preparation for the pickle module to write bytes data to it. Technically, any file extension can be used, but .pkl or .pickle is traditional. Then, write the data with pickle.dump:

```
import pickle

u = User('Alice', 'alice@unlockingpython.com')

with open('alice.pkl, 'wb') as f:
    pickle.dump(u, f)
```

The data can be read again with pickle.load:

```
with open('alice.pkl', 'rb') as f:
    new_u = pickle.load(f)
```

If you want to do something else with the data, such as send it over a network, you can use pickle.dumps (with an s) and pickle.loads to write the data to a bytes object, rather than to a file:

```
u = User('Alice', 'alice@unlockingpython.com')
data = pickle.dumps(u)
new_u = pickle.loads(data)
```

Note that the Python process loading the data back into a User object from a pickle file must have the definition for the User class. If you were to send the alice.pkl file, or the pickled bytes data, to a friend who then attempts to load it without knowing what the User class is, they will get an error like this:

```
AttributeError: Can't get attribute 'User' on <module '__main__'>
```

Of course you can always send your friend the User class as a separate file, but this takes away some of the elegance and convenience of using Pickle in the first place. Depending on the situation, you might also package your User class into a library which your friend can install and then import to get access to the User class definition.

Another solution is to package the User class definition alongside the data for the alice class instance. This is not possible with pickle, but can be done with other third-party libraries such as dill (https://pypi.org/project/dill).

There are many considerations to make when deciding how to store and transmit your Python objects. If the objects are large or you have a large number of them, file and data size may be a concern. In our example, the User object required 54 bytes as a JSON file and 91 bytes as a pickle file. However, it is not always the case that JSON files are smaller than binary files—far from it, especially when large objects with non-string data are involved!

JSON files are, of course, human-readable, but also require custom serialization and deserialization methods to get them into that readable state. If you have objects associated with more complex data fields, such as data structures, datetimes, and other custom objects, writing methods to convert them to JSON may be a significant consideration.

EXERCISES

1. For each of the following pieces of code, predict if they will run successfully or raise an error. You can double-check in Python if you're unsure:

   a.
   ```
   with open('test.txt', 'a') as f:
       f.write('line 1\n')
       f.write('line 2\n')
       f.read()
   ```

   b.
   ```
   with open('test.txt', 'w+') as f:
       f.write('line 1\n')
       f.write('line 2\n')
       f.read()
   ```

   c.
   ```
   with open('test.txt', 'r+') as f:
       f.write('line 1')
   ```

   d.
   ```
   with open('test.txt', 'w+') as f:
       f.write('line 1')
   f.read()
   ```

2. Read the file `15_colors.col`, generated from the string `FF0000FFA500FFFF000080000000F` `F800080` (this string and code that generates it is included in the exercise files) and convert it back into pretty-printed hex codes of this form:

   ```
   #FF0000, #FFA500, etc.
   ```

3. Write a function, `remove_directory`, that performs the same action as `shutil.rmtree`, using only functions from the `os` module. When a valid directory path is passed to the function `remove_directory`, it should empty it of all files and directories if it's not already empty, and then remove it with `os.rmdir`.

   Remember that any directories within the target directory can have files and directories of their own. The structure you are deleting may be several levels deep! You may want to consider a recursive solution.

4. In Chapter 10, "Functions," exercise problem 4, we covered the concept of run-length encoding and wrote the functions `encode` and `decode` in order to compress ASCII art. Working solutions for the `encode` and `decode` functions are provided in the exercise files for you to use:

   ```
   def encode(data_str):
       encoded_data = []
       count = 0
       last_char = data_str[0]
       for char in data_str:
           if char != last_char: # encountered a new character!
               encoded_data.append((last_char, count))
               count = 0
   ```

```
            last_char = char
        count += 1
    encoded_data.append((last_char, count))
    return encoded_data

def decode(encoded_data):
    data_str = ''
    for char, count in encoded_data:
        data_str += char * count
    return data_str
```

Use these, or your own solution, these to read the file `15_ascii.txt` (which is 2,754 bytes in size), compress it using the encode function, and write the result to a binary file `15_ascii.bin`.

Consider the minimum amount of information needed to be written to the binary file. You will probably want to write a single character, followed by an 8-bit number, followed by another character, followed by another 8-bit number, etc. What is the resulting size of this file?

Finally, write a function that reads the file back in and decompresses it using the decode function. Check that the decompressed version looks the same as the original!

16

Logging

Logs are ubiquitous in computing. They help monitor program performance, troubleshoot failures, and (hopefully) provide reassurance that all is well. Without logs, our programs would be a black box with no way to peer inside.

The overwhelming majority of logs in production applications are never read by humans. They are stored and eventually discarded. But they can also serve as an alert to problems as they arise and a record of the events that led up to that problem.

Previously, we've used the `print` function to add "logs" to our code and let us know what's going on. Print statements are a kind of logging. They even have some more advanced features in common with logging systems. For example, you can pass a filename to print, which will cause all printed output to be written to that file:

```
with open('test.txt', 'w') as f:
    print('Hello, World!', file=f)
```

However, this is about the extent of the `print` function's flexibility. Compared to the Python logging module, `print` statements are extremely limited. In general, a well-designed logging system does the following:

➤ Allows for centralized control over logging parameters

➤ Makes it easy for programmers to add metadata to logs

➤ Allows for filtering by *log level* and other parameters

➤ Allows for flexible viewing in a variety of applications

In this chapter, we'll look at the many ways that logs can be used, stored, and styled to make your Python applications a little more verbose.

THE *LOGGING* MODULE

The `logging` module, part of the Python standard library, may appear very similar in functionality to the `print` function at first glance:

```
import logging

logger = logging.getLogger()
logger.warning('Some warning message')
```

This prints (or, rather, logs) the message Some warning message. If you're running this from the exercise files in Jupyter Lab, you'll see that it logs the message with a pink background. This pink background style is not a default with the logging module, but is applied to all warning messages by the Jupyter Lab software itself. In other software, such as Visual Studio, you should see the message printed out with default styling.

The logger object obtained from logging.getLogger(), as you might suspect, can be reused and log all sorts of messages. There are five different log levels that can be used, including Warning, seen in the previous example. The following list describes each level, from least to most important or severe:

> **Debug:** Very verbose logs that are usually only looked at to diagnose an issue with the software.

> **Info:** Less detailed than Debug but still records normal operation of the software. For example, it may record when a program is entering a particular state, but may not record the value of every variable in that state.

> **Warning:** Records unexpected situations that do not result in errors or failures. Generally, individual warnings do not need to be addressed, although changes in warnings, or rising rates of warnings may be worth looking into since they suggest a symptom of an underlying issue.

> **Error:** Records errors that result in missing data or lost functionality of the application. The application can recover and continue to work around it, but users may experience less-than-ideal behavior.

> **Critical:** Records serious errors that indicate a complete loss of core functionality, or perhaps fatal errors that prevent the application from continuing altogether.

If you've programmed in other languages or dealt with other types of logging before, these levels should seem familiar. Most programming languages have very similar log levels, although you might see variations like Warn instead of Warning or Fatal instead of (or in addition to) Critical. You may also see the addition of a Trace level that is more detailed than Debug.

Regardless of the exact names or number of levels, common to all of these systems is the concept of "order of importance." If you ask to display all the error logs, there is an assumption that you will *also* want to view critical logs. If you are viewing debug logs (the least important and most verbose logs), what you actually want is all of the logs regardless of level. In general, if you request logs at a certain level, you are actually requesting all logs at that level or higher.

Using the same logger object that we used to log the warning earlier, we can create logs for any of these logging levels:

```
logger.debug('A debug log')
logger.info('An info log')
logger.warning('A warning log')
logger.error('An error log')
logger.critical('A critical log!!!')
```

If these five logging lines are run, you may be surprised to see that only the warning, error, and critical logs are displayed:

```
A warning log
An error log
A critical log!!!
```

This is because, by default, the log level is set to Warning in Python. Only logs of level Warning and greater are displayed. We can change this by using the `basicConfig` method on the `logging` module:

```
logging.basicConfig(level=logging.DEBUG)
```

Now, if you rerun the logging calls, all five messages will be displayed:

```
DEBUG:root:A debug log
INFO:root:An info log
WARNING:root:A warning log
ERROR:root:An error log
CRITICAL:root:A critical log!!!
```

Instead of being displayed with the message only, the log level and logger name (in this case, the default name `root`) are prefixed to the message, separated by semicolons. This is because `basicConfig` provides default log formatting, which can also be modified. We will discuss log formatting in greater detail later in this chapter.

Note that `basicConfig` can only be called once per program execution, and subsequent calls will be ignored. You can run this line in the same Jupyter notebook file:

```
logging.basicConfig(level=logging.CRITICAL)
```

However, it will have no effect on which logs are displayed. To change the log level, you will need to restart the Python kernel and call `basicConfig` with the new log level. This may seem like a clunky oversight, but it's important to keep in mind that the `logging` module wasn't designed to be experimented within an iPython notebook. It was designed to perform coordinated logging across many files in a package.

To simulate a more realistic logging scenario, I've created a package called `lumberjack`[1] inside the directory `16_logging` in the exercise files. It has the following structure:

```
lumberjack
        __init__.py
        forest.py
        tree.py
        lumberjack.py
```

Inside `tree.py` are several classes. Two of these, `TreeStatus` and `TreeSpecies`, define various constants used by the `Tree` class:

```
class TreeStatus:
    STANDING = 'standing'
    CUT = 'cut'

class TreeSpecies:
    DOUGLAS_FIR = 'Douglas Fir'
    WESTERN_HEMLOCK = 'Western Hemlock'
    SITKA_SPRUCE = 'Sitka Spruce'
```

---

[1] Suggested listening while using this package is Monty Python's "Lumberjack Song."

The Tree class itself has a species type, a status (either standing or cut) and two methods, cut and grow:

```
class Tree:
    def __init__(self, species, height=1):
        self.species = species
        self.status = TreeStatus.STANDING
        self.height = height

    def cut(self):
        self.status = TreeStatus.CUT
        self.height = 0

    def grow(self):
        if self.status == TreeStatus.STANDING:
            self.height += 1
```

The file forest.py contains only the class Forest, which defines a collection of trees. It has two methods, grow and plant, which allow those trees to be modified:

```
from lumberjack.tree import Tree

class Forest:
    def __init__(self, trees):
        self.trees = trees

    def grow(self):
        [t.grow() for t in self.trees]

    def plant(self, species):
        self.trees.append(Tree(species))
```

Finally, the Lumberjack class in lumberjack.py represents a particular employee of a logging operation who is directly responsible for cutting down trees. They are assigned a name and a forest to work at, and have only a single method, cut_trees:

```
class Lumberjack:
    def __init__(self, name, forest):
        self.name = name
        self.forest = forest

    def cut_trees(self, min_height=30, num_trees=5):
        trees_cut = 0
        for t in self.forest.trees:
            if trees_cut >= num_trees:
                return
            if t.height >= min_height:
                t.cut()
                trees_cut += 1
```

We can add logging to this package, starting with the __init__.py file:

```
import logging

logging.basicConfig(level=logging.DEBUG)
logger = logging.getLogger(__name__)
logger.debug('Importing package')
```

This sets the log level to `logging.DEBUG` and creates a new `logger` object named with the Python variable `__name__`. In the `__init__` file of any package, `__name__` will have the value of the package name, in this case, `"lumberjack"`.

We can create a file in the `16_logging` directory called `do_logging.py`, which contains only the `import` statement for the `lumberjack` package:

```
import lumberjack
```

When this is run from the command line:

```
$ python do_logging.py
```

it displays the log:

```
DEBUG:lumberjack:Importing package
```

The log name `root`, seen earlier, has been replaced by the package name `lumberjack`. The name of the logger is not just for decorative purposes, but it determines the structure and hierarchy of the loggers themselves. The `getLogger` method ensures that loggers are created and connected appropriately based on the name that gets passed in.

In fact, if two loggers share the same name, then `getLogger` will return the same class instance for both. This can be seen using Python's `id` function, which returns a unique integer ID for each object. We can rewrite `__init__.py` to have two loggers, one retrieved using `__name__` (which is `'lumberjack'`), another one explicitly using the string `'lumberjack'`:

```
logger1 = logging.getLogger(__name__)
print(f'ID of logger1: {id(logger1)}')

logger2 = logging.getLogger('lumberjack')
print(f'ID of logger2: {id(logger1)}')
```

This prints two identical IDs, showing that these are the exact same object:[2]

```
ID of logger1: 4379775280
ID of logger2: 4379775280
```

We can add a new logger to the `forest.py` file as well:

```
import logging
from lumberjack.tree import Tree

logger = logging.getLogger(__name__)

class Forest:
    def __init__(self, trees):
        self.trees = trees
        logger.info(f'Initialized forest with {len(self.trees)} trees')
```

---

[2] This type of software design, or "pattern," where an object is retrieved in multiple places and it's the exact same object, is called the *singleton pattern*. The singleton pattern can be very handy if you want to have only one of a particular object floating around and also want to hide all the messy details of how that happens from the user.

In this case, the value of __name__ that gets passed to the getLogger method is lumberjack .forest. Back in our do_logging.py file, we can initialize a new Forest class with several trees:

```
from lumberjack.forest import Forest
from lumberjack.tree import Tree, TreeSpecies

forest = Forest([
    Tree(TreeSpecies.DOUGLAS_FIR),
    Tree(TreeSpecies.SITKA_SPRUCE),
    Tree(TreeSpecies.WESTERN_HEMLOCK),
])
```

This results in the logs:

```
DEBUG:lumberjack:Importing package
INFO:lumberjack.forest:Initialized forest with 3 trees
```

It's common to initialize a new logger variable at the top of each Python file in a package or other large project using this line:

```
logger = logging.getLogger(__name__)
```

Each file gets its own distinct logger, which is connected to all the other loggers only through internal mechanics of the logging module itself. For example, recall that the default log level of the logging module is Warning, which hides Debug and Info logs. However, setting the log level in __init__.py:

```
import logging

logging.basicConfig(level=logging.DEBUG)
```

also sets that log level everywhere else the logging module is imported, including in forest.py. This allows the info log to be displayed:

```
INFO:lumberjack.forest:Initialized forest with 3 trees
```

In the next two sections, we'll look at other properties that get passed between seemingly disconnected logger objects in different files. Understanding and using these features correctly will help you create logging systems that are both powerful and easy-to-use.

HANDLERS

A *log handler* is an object that controls the recording of logs. It contains information about where logs should be written to, which levels should be written, and how those logs should be formatted. If a handler isn't provided for your logger, the "handler of last resort" (logging.lastResort, introduced in Python 3.2) is used. This handler provides minimal formatting and logs only warnings or higher.

We can create a new handler in __init__.py that writes all logs to a file, lumberjack.log:

```
logging.basicConfig(level=logging.DEBUG)
file_handler = logging.FileHandler('lumberjack.log')
file_handler.setLevel(logging.DEBUG)
```

Although logs can have any file extension you want, they traditionally have a .log extension. Also note that we're setting the global log level using basicConfig to logging.DEBUG. Without this global setting in place, the Debug and Info log levels would be ignored by the handler.

On their own, log handlers don't do anything. They must be added to a specific logger:

```
logger = logging.getLogger(__name__)
logger.addHandler(file_handler)
logger.debug('Importing package')
```

Now, if you run do_logging.py from the previous section, you'll see that the file lumberjack.log gets created with two logs inside it:

```
Importing package
Initialized forest with 3 trees
```

Although the handler was only added to the logger object in __init__.py, logs from forest.py (Initialized forest with 3 trees) also get recorded to the file. This is because the forest logger has the name lumberjack.forest and is therefore considered part of the lumberjack logging hierarchy. Any handlers added to the parent logger, lumberjack, will be used by loggers that have names prefixed with lumberjack.

We can see this in action by changing the name of the logger in forest.py:

```
logger = logging.getLogger('nothing_to_do_with_lumberjacks')
```

If this is done, and do_logging.py is rerun, then both logs will print to the terminal, courtesy of the "handler of last resort":

```
DEBUG:lumberjack:Importing package
INFO:nothing_to_do_with_lumberjacks:Initialized forest with 3 trees
```

However, only one log will appear in lumberjack.log from the file handler we manually created and added to the lumberjack logger:

```
Importing package
```

To stop the handler of last resort from being used, you must provide another handler to replace it globally. Although we did provide another handler to our logger object in __init__.py, this did not replace the global handler. You can replace the global handler by providing at least one other handler to the handlers keyword argument in the basicConfig function:

```
import logging
import sys

stream_handler = logging.StreamHandler(sys.stdout)
stream_handler.setLevel(logging.WARNING)

logging.basicConfig(level=logging.DEBUG, handlers=[stream_handler])
```

Here, we're setting the handler to write to sys.stdout (*standard output*), which is an output stream that data can be written to. This is the default output stream that the print function uses, and it is what writes data to the terminal.

Alternatively, you can use sys.stderr (*standard error*), an output stream that the handler of last resort uses for all log levels. This is what all logs we've seen previously in the terminal were written with, although the styling for both standard error and standard output is the same in the terminal. This is why all log messages in Jupyter notebooks have a pink background by default—all messages written to standard error in Jupyter are styled with that background to differentiate them from standard output messages.

In addition to the output stream, the new `stream_handler` has its log level set to `logging.WARNING`, which means that only Warning, Error, or Critical log levels will be handled by it. This means that only those Warning and higher logs will be shown in the terminal (standard output), but all other logs will be written to a file by the `file_handler`.

To see this in action, let's add warning log to the `tree.py` constructor when an unknown species string is passed:

```python
logger = logging.getLogger(__name__)

class Tree:
    def __init__(self, species: str, height:int=1):
        self.species = species
        if self.species not in [
            TreeSpecies.DOUGLAS_FIR,
            TreeSpecies.WESTERN_HEMLOCK,
            TreeSpecies.SITKA_SPRUCE]:
            logger.warning(f'Unknown tree species: {self.species}')

        self.status:str = TreeStatus.STANDING
        self.height = height
```

Then in `do_logging.py`, we create a forest with an invasive species:

```python
from lumberjack.forest import Forest
from lumberjack.tree import Tree, TreeSpecies

forest = Forest([
    Tree(TreeSpecies.DOUGLAS_FIR),
    Tree(TreeSpecies.SITKA_SPRUCE),
    Tree(TreeSpecies.WESTERN_HEMLOCK),
    Tree('Horse Chestnut'),
])
```

Finally, in `__init__.py`, this is the full code for our two different logging handlers:

```python
import logging
import sys

stream_handler = logging.StreamHandler(sys.stdout)
stream_handler.setLevel(logging.WARNING)

logging.basicConfig(level=logging.DEBUG, handlers=[stream_handler])
file_handler = logging.FileHandler('lumberjack.log')
file_handler.setLevel(logging.DEBUG)

logger = logging.getLogger(__name__)
logger.addHandler(file_handler)

logger.debug('Importing package')
```

When `do_logging.py` is run, only the warning is displayed in the terminal:

```
WARNING:lumberjack.tree:Unknown tree species: Horse Chestnut
```

However, all logs are displayed in the file `lumberjack.log`:

```
Importing package
Unknown tree species: Horse Chestnut
Initialized forest with 4 trees
```

There are some obvious formatting differences between the logs these two handlers are creating, of course. The handler passed to `basicConfig` is still using the default format, whereas `file_handler` is writing only the log message. In the next section, we'll look at log styling and creating custom formats to clean these up and make them beautiful (or at least more readable).

FORMATTING

Logging formatters determine the structure of your logs. A simple way to modify the format is to provide a formatting string to the `basicConfig` function:

```
format_str = '%(levelname)s:%(created)f:%(message)s'
logging.basicConfig(level=logging.DEBUG, format=format_str)
```

These format strings contain keywords surrounded with `%()`, followed by a letter (`s`, `d`, or `f`) indicating whether the value is a string, digit, or float. This particular format string creates logs with the log level name, epoch time, and message all separated by colons:

```
DEBUG:1724641379.062120:Initializing package
INFO:1724641379.063527:Initialized forest with 3 trees
```

If the epoch times aren't readable enough, you can use `%(asctime)s`, along with, optionally, a date format string as described in Chapter 8, "Other Types of Objects":

```
format_str = '%(levelname)s:%(asctime)s:%(message)s'
logging.basicConfig(
    level=logging.DEBUG,
    format=format_str,
    datefmt='%m/%d/%Y %H:%M:%S'
)
```

Any date format string passed to the keyword argument `datefmt` will be used to format the date string used by `asctime`.

The complete list of available formatting strings can be found in the Python documentation at `https://docs.python.org/3/library/logging.html#logrecord-attributes`. Here are a few of the more commonly used ones:

➤ `%(asctime)s`: Human-readable datetime format.

➤ `%(created)f`: Float epoch time.

➤ `%(filename)s`: The name of the file the log originated from. Often, each file will get its own named logger, although this might not always be the case or there may be some reason you want to see the filename instead.

➤ `%(levelname)s`: Name of log level.

➤ `%(lineno)d`: Line in the file where the log originated from.

➤ `%(msg)`: Perhaps the most important part of the log, the message.

➤ `%(name)`: Name of the logger.

While the `basicConfig` function applies its settings to every log produced by the logging module, there may be situations where you want finer-grained control over the style of your logs. In this case, you can create `Formatter` objects that can be used with handlers:

```
formatter = logging.Formatter('%(asctime)s - %(name)s - %(levelname)s -
%(message)s')

file_handler = logging.FileHandler('lumberjack.log')
file_handler.setFormatter(formatter)
file_handler.setLevel(logging.DEBUG)

logger = logging.getLogger(__name__)
logger.addHandler(file_handler)
```

This uses the formatting string `'%(asctime)s - %(name)s - %(levelname)s - %(message)s'`, which provides a little whitespace to make logs more readable:

```
2024-08-27 14:01:51,448 - lumberjack - DEBUG - Importing package
2024-08-27 14:01:51,450 - lumberjack.tree - WARNING - Unknown tree species:
Horse Chestnut
2024-08-27 14:01:51,450 - lumberjack.forest - INFO - Initialized forest
with 4 trees
```

The `Formatter` class also takes the optional argument `datefmt` used to customize the date string:

```
formatter = logging.Formatter(
    '%(asctime)s - %(name)s - %(levelname)s - %(message)s',
    datefmt='%m/%d/%Y %H:%M:%S'
    )
```

This produces logs like:

```
08/27/2024 14:06:19 - lumberjack - DEBUG - Importing package
```

There may be times when you want application-specific information formatted in the logs. To do this, simply choose a name for that information and add it into the format string as if it exists. As an example, we can add a logger above the `Lumberjack` class definition in `lumberjack.py` and provide a format string that contains `%(ljname)s` for the lumberjack's name:

```
import logging
import sys

logger = logging.getLogger(__name__)
formatter = logging.Formatter(
    '%(asctime)s - Lumberjack %(ljname)s - %(levelname)s - %(message)s',
    datefmt='%m/%d/%Y %H:%M:%S'
)

handler = logging.StreamHandler(sys.stdout)
handler.setLevel(logging.INFO)
handler.setFormatter(formatter)
logger.addHandler(handler)
```

Make sure that the name you choose in the formatting string doesn't conflict with existing formatting string keywords. Here, we're using ljname instead of just name, which refers to the name of the logger.

Now, each time the logger is used, a dictionary can be passed containing the definitions for these extra formatting strings. This is passed in the keyword argument extra. Here is the Lumberjack class with several info logs:

```python
class Lumberjack:
    def __init__(self, name, forest):
        self.name = name
        self.forest = forest
        logger.info('Initialized', extra={'ljname': self.name})

    def cut_trees(self, min_height=30, num_trees=5):
        logger.info(
            f'Cutting {num_trees} trees of height {min_height}',
            extra={'ljname': self.name}
        )
        trees_cut = 0
        for t in self.forest.trees:
            if trees_cut >= num_trees:
                break
            if t.height >= min_height:
                t.cut()
                trees_cut += 1
        logger.info(f'Cut {trees_cut} trees', extra={'ljname': self.name})
```

Back in do_logging.py, we create two lumberjacks, Alice and Bob, that are provided with a name string, the forest of four trees created earlier, and then cut (or at least attempt to cut) two trees each:

```python
alice = Lumberjack('Alice', forest)
bob = Lumberjack('Bob', forest)
# Grow the forest before cutting
[forest.grow() for _ in range(0, 30)]
alice.cut_trees(num_trees=2, min_height=20)
bob.cut_trees(num_trees=2, min_height=40)
```

The command-line logs now read as follows:

```
WARNING:lumberjack.tree:Unknown tree species: Horse Chestnut
08/27/2024 14:24:21 - Lumberjack Alice - INFO - Initialized
08/27/2024 14:24:21 - Lumberjack Bob - INFO - Initialized
08/27/2024 14:24:21 - Lumberjack Alice - INFO - Cutting 2 trees of height 20
08/27/2024 14:24:21 - Lumberjack Alice - INFO - Cut 2 trees
08/27/2024 14:24:21 - Lumberjack Bob - INFO - Cutting 2 trees of height 40
08/27/2024 14:24:21 - Lumberjack Bob - INFO - Cut 0 trees
```

Of course, passing this dictionary of data each time you log something is a little annoying. It also violates one of the core principles of software engineering: "Don't Repeat Yourself." As an alternative to writing this information every time you want to log something, you can use the LoggerAdapter class.

A LoggerAdapter is essentially a wrapper around a logger that behaves very similarly to the logger that it wraps. However, it also contains additional contextual information, alleviating the need for that information to be explicitly passed every time a log is made.

For example, each instance of the Lumberjack class can contain its own LoggerAdapter instance, which carries the instance's name:

```
class Lumberjack:
    def __init__(self, name, forest):
        self.name = name
        self.forest = forest
        self.logger = logging.LoggerAdapter(logger, {'ljname': self.name})
        self.logger.info('Initialized')
```

Although we're calling this logger self.logger, it's actually a LoggerAdapter instance. This distinction is not especially important for the user, as it can be used exactly like the logger that it wraps. Now, instead of writing logs like this:

```
logger.info(
            f'Cutting {num_trees} trees of height {min_height}',
            extra={'ljname': self.name}
            )
```

any logging done in the Lumberjack class should be written like this:

```
self.logger.info(f'Cutting {num_trees} of height {min_height}')
```

This results in the same logs as before:

```
08/27/2024 14:24:21 - Lumberjack Alice - INFO - Initialized
08/27/2024 14:24:21 - Lumberjack Bob - INFO - Initialized
08/27/2024 14:24:21 - Lumberjack Alice - INFO - Cutting 2 trees of height 20
```

EXERCISES

1. Add a warning log if insufficient trees are available for the lumberjack to chop in lumberjack.py.

2. Create a global Formatter and a Handler, passed into basicConfig in the __init__.py file, that formats all error or critical logs in red. Test it out by creating some error logs—for example, changing the warning in the Lumberjack class if no trees are available to cut to an error instead.

3. Create a global Formatter and a Handler, passed into basicConfig in the __init__.py file, that formats critical logs in red (or multiple colors) surrounded by some attention-grabbing ASCII art, like:

```
#####################
#
#    <YOUR LOG HERE>
#
# ##################
```

Also include the error formatter from problem 3 so that multiple handlers and formatters are used.

Generate a critical log to test this, such as a critical log if there are no more uncut trees left in the forest.

4. Write a function called get_forest that returns a Forest object containing a list of some default trees (decide on your own assortment of trees for this one, which are hard-coded in get_forest).

When get_forest is called the first time, it will return a new Forest instance. If it is called multiple times in the same Python program, it will return the same Forest instance it returned before. That is, it implements the Singleton pattern (https://en.wikipedia.org/wiki/Singleton_pattern).

After doing this, you may consider updating the Lumberjack constructor to this:

```
class Lumberjack:
    def __init__(self, name):
        self.name = name
        self.forest = get_forest()
```

By doing this, all Lumberjack instances will necessarily be assigned to the same Forest.

17

Threads and Processes

Previously, all our programs have been executed step by step in a single thread of execution. Each line is executed in a state that is determined by the previous lines. The programs operated in a single pool of memory so that any variables and data could easily be shared.

In this chapter, we'll explore asynchronous and multithreaded programming so that lines of your program can execute in parallel with each other, rather than one at a time. This means that many of the things that were previously taken for granted (such as every line of a program having a particular deterministic order of execution) are no longer valid assumptions.

Because of this, the techniques in this chapter may be somewhat challenging, particularly if you have little experience with them in other programming languages. However, they are essential for writing efficient code in certain situations, such as:

- ➤ Programs waiting idly for a result before continuing
- ➤ Multiple requests being handled at once (such as on a web server)
- ➤ Large and time-consuming computations being done on a machine dedicated to this task

HOW THREADS AND PROCESSES WORK

Before diving into the code, it's important to understand a bit about how computers execute instructions. Everything your computer does must be submitted as an instruction to the processor.

Every time you press a key on the keyboard, it creates an instruction that must be processed. Applications like a Python program generate lots of instructions that must all be dealt with. You might be running dozens of applications at any given time, all with streams of instructions being submitted to the processor.

Each of these instructions is assigned to a processor by the computer's *scheduler*. A scheduler is a low-level process that queues instructions for execution based on many factors, such as the order they were added in, their priority, and how busy each processor currently is.

Each physical processor on your computer can execute a single process at a time. In general, each application on your computer runs in a single process. When you run a Python program (including a Jupyter Lab server), it runs in its own process.

The scheduler allows processes to run and pauses them when another process has priority. When that other process has finished, the scheduler is responsible for loading the prior process's data state and resuming execution.

A process can contain multiple threads. A thread is a sequential set of instructions within a process. You can think of a thread as a single piece of linear code being executed. A process can switch between multiple threads—it might execute a line from thread 1, thread 2, thread 3, and back to thread 1 again, all within the same slot of time the scheduler allocates for it on a physical processor.

All threads running within a process share that process's memory. That is, all the threads will have access to the same objects, variables, and loaded data. This makes it fast and easy for a process to switch between its threads. Each process operates in its own allocated memory space, and memory is not shared between multiple processes. It is more expensive to switch between processes than it is to switch between threads.

If you haven't worked with processes and threads before, this information may seem a little abstract. However, there are many concrete considerations that need to be made when using threads and processes (and their associated tools like locks and queues) in your code. After a few examples in this chapter, the differences, interactions, and uses of threads and processes should become clear.

THREADING MODULE

Here are three different functions, each of which takes time to execute when it's called, for various reasons:

```python
import urllib
import time
import math

def do_get_website():
    r = urllib.request.urlopen('https://unlockingpython.com/')
    return r.getcode()

def do_sleep():
    time.sleep(0.5)

def do_calculation():
    for i in range(0, 10000000):
        math.sin(i)
```

The function do_get_website uses urllib, part of the Python standard library. The urllib package contains functions for making web requests and fetching data from remote servers. In this case, we're making a request to unlockingpython.com and returning the HTTP status code from that request (which is, hopefully, a 200). We'll see urllib again, as well as other libraries for making web requests, in Chapter 22, "Web Scraping and Scrapy."

The function `do_sleep` calls `time.sleep` for half a second, during which time nothing is happening. The function `do_calculation`, in contrast, does quite a lot of things in the (approximately) half a second it takes to run on my computer.

We can print the amount of time that a function takes to run using the following function:

```
def print_function_time(func):
    start = time.time()
    func()
    print(f'{func.__name__}: {time.time() - start}')
```

If called like this:

```
print_function_time(do_sleep)
```

it prints a message like this:

```
do_sleep: 0.5034749507904053
```

Here, the execution of `time.sleep` itself takes `0.5` seconds, but there is additional overhead wrapping it that takes another 3–4 milliseconds. We can also write a function that calls `do_sleep` multiple times in a row, and then time that function:

```
def do_sleep_multiple():
    for _ in range(5):
        do_sleep()


print_function_time(do_sleep_multiple)
```

As expected, if `do_sleep` is called five times in a row, it will take a little over 2.5 seconds to run:

```
do_sleep_multiple: 2.5233500003814697
```

This is because each execution of `do_sleep` must finish before the next one can start. These `do_sleep` executions are being called sequentially. However, using the `threading` module, we can effectively run them in parallel:

```
import threading

t1 = threading.Thread(target=do_sleep)
t2 = threading.Thread(target=do_sleep)

t1.start()
t2.start()

t1.join()
t2.join()
```

This creates two threads, called `t1` and `t2`. Each thread executes a function provided with the keyword argument `target`. In this case, both threads have the target `do_sleep`.

Simply instantiating the thread does nothing. In order to actually execute it, we need to call the `start` method. The `start` method is *non-blocking*. That is, program execution does not pause (or "block") and wait on the line `t1.start()` for the thread to finish its execution. If we were to put a `print` statement after calling the `start` methods, it would print immediately:

```
t1.start()
t2.start()
print('Started the threads')
```

In order to wait for the threads to finish, the `join` method is used. This `join` method is *blocking*. If we were to put a `print` statement after it, we'd see a slight delay in printing while `time.sleep` is running:

```
t1.join()
t2.join()
print('Joined the threads')
```

If this delay isn't clear, try increasing the half second of sleep in the `do_sleep` function to several seconds for a more dramatic effect.

The advantage of using threads, of course, is that this "sleeping time" can effectively be done in parallel. We can examine this effect using the `print_function_time` method used previously:

```
t1 = threading.Thread(target=print_function_time, args=(do_sleep,))
t2 = threading.Thread(target=print_function_time, args=(do_sleep,))
t1.start()
t2.start()
t1.join()
t2.join()
```

Here, the target is the function `print_function_time`, and the argument `do_sleep` (the function we want to time the execution of) is passed using the `args` keyword argument. Because `args` is a tuple containing only a single item, make sure to write a comma after `do_sleep` to indicate that it is a tuple data structure and not simply parentheses surrounding a value.

Executing this takes approximately half a second, and the `print` statements report that each thread takes half a second to run:

```
do_sleep: 0.504033088684082do_sleep: 0.5035300254821777
```

Note that the two `print` statements are printing on the same line (although this may not happen or happen only intermittently depending on your operating system and computer). This is because, behind the scenes, the newline character following the message is being sent to the terminal in a separate instruction. The two messages, printed in separated threads, may be sent to the terminal in quick succession before their newlines are sent. This results in two messages concatenated to each other in a single line, followed by two newline characters in a row.

Like many operations in Python, the `print` function is considered to not be *thread-safe*. That is, running it from multiple threads at the same time may lead to incorrect behavior. This doesn't mean we can't use `print` statements in multithreaded programs; however, special care needs to be taken to ensure thread safety.

More information about writing thread-safe programs can be found in the following sections on queues and locking. Until then, the output might look a little funny.

Timing each thread in our program is useful, but to show that our threads are working and decreasing runtime effectively we also need to measure the execution time of the entire program. We can create a function called `do_sleep_threads`, which creates an arbitrary number of threads executing `print_function_time`. The function `print_function_time`, in turn, executes the `do_sleep` function passed into it:

```
def do_sleep_threads(num_threads=5):
    threads = [
        threading.Thread(target=print_function_time, args=(do_sleep,))
        for i in range(num_threads)
    ]
    [t.start() for t in threads]
    [t.join() for t in threads]
```

This function can be wrapped in a timer itself so that the entire process of creating the threads, starting them, and then joining them is timed:

```
print_function_time(do_sleep_threads)
```

When run, this creates output like this:

```
do_sleep: 0.5049021244049072do_sleep: 0.5048871040344238
do_sleep: 0.5050952434539795
do_sleep: 0.5065779685974121

do_sleep: 0.5059530735015869
do_sleep_threads: 0.5093050003051758
```

We can see that the total execution time of do_sleep_threads is only slightly longer (by about 3 milliseconds) than the execution time of the longest-running thread. Without threading, we would expect this to take a little over 2.5 seconds to complete.

Writing a similar function, do_get_website_threads, for the corresponding function do_get_website, has similar results:

```
do_get_website: 0.06455397605895996
do_get_website: 0.06277871131896973
do_get_website: 0.06604790687561035
do_get_website: 0.09793782234191895
do_get_website: 0.09963083267211914
do_get_website_threads: 0.11292290687561035
```

Writing and running the function do_calculation_threads appears to follow the same pattern at first glance:

```
def do_calculation_threads(num_threads=5):
    threads = [
        threading.Thread(
            target=print_function_time,
            args=(do_calculation,)
        )
        for i in range(num_threads)
    ]
    [t.start() for t in threads]
    [t.join() for t in threads]

print_function_time(do_calculation_threads)
```

Each thread takes a little over 2.5 seconds to run with a total runtime of 2.75 seconds:

```
do_calculation: 2.5484988689422607
do_calculation: 2.584764003753662
do_calculation: 2.694783926010132
do_calculation: 2.64986515045166
do_calculation: 2.6715378761291504
do_calculation_threads: 2.7532739639282227
```

However, recall that when we ran a single threaded instance of the `do_calculation` function, as shown in this line:

```
print_function_time(do_calculation_threads)
```

it took only half a second to run:

```
do_calculation: 0.555372953414917
```

Running five instances of `do_calculation` at once requires approximately 2.5 seconds for each of them to complete, leading to no net decrease in runtime unlike with the `do_get_website` and `do_sleep` functions. This is because `do_calculation` requires actual work during its runtime. The scheduler keeps the processor busy with `math.sin` operations on each of the five threads, meaning only a fifth of the previously available processing time can be devoted to a single thread. When five of these threads execute in parallel they take five times as long to run.

Waiting for a web server to return its content or waiting for a certain time to be reached (as with `time.sleep`) requires very little processing power and can be done in parallel on multiple threads within the same process.

It's clear that threads can speed up some applications by making more efficient use of limited resources. However, this increase in speed isn't always guaranteed. In fact, the mere cost of instantiating and managing the threads can have a net-negative impact on runtime in some scenarios!

In addition, multithreading requires careful consideration in order to appropriately structure code and make it thread-safe. In the next two sections, we'll look at two tools, queues and locks, which can help do just that.

LOCKING

Previously, we saw examples of Python's `print` function demonstrating non-thread-safe behavior. This happens when two messages from separate threads or processes write data to `stdout` at the same time, resulting in messages being printed to the same line, followed by multiple newline characters in a row:

```
do_sleep: 0.5049021244049072do_sleep: 0.5048871040344238

do_sleep: 0.5059530735015869
```

To fix this, we need to acquire a *lock*, which prevents other threads from executing while a particular operation is being performed. After the non-thread-safe operation has completed, the lock can be released and operations in other threads can be executed.

This is similar to the real-world lockout-tagout procedure (`https://en.wikipedia.org/wiki/Lockout%E2%80%93tagout`) used in equipment maintenance. A worker, or multiple workers, will literally lock a piece of equipment such that it cannot be turned on. This is done in situations where turning a machine on may result in injury or death—for example, during maintenance. The workers hold the keys to these locks while maintenance is being done, and then unlock, or release them when it is safe to resume normal operations again.

The following demonstrates the use of a lock to block other threads from executing during the thread-unsafe portion of code in the function sleep_and_print:

```python
def sleep_and_print(lock):
    time.sleep(0.5)
    lock.acquire()
    print('Done sleeping!')
    lock.release()

def do_sleep_and_print_threads(num_threads=5):
    lock = threading.Lock()
    threads = [
        threading.Thread(target=sleep_and_print, args=(lock,))
        for i in range(num_threads)
    ]
    [t.start() for t in threads]
    [t.join() for t in threads]

do_sleep_and_print_threads()
```

The lock object, lock, is instantiated in the function do_sleep_and_print_threads and is passed as an argument to each thread for use in the function sleep_and_print. It's important that each thread use the same lock object, which is managed in some central location outside the threads themselves.

The method acquire is used to "acquire a lock" so that the thread that called acquire is blocking and no other threads can execute until the release method is called, releasing the lock.

It's important that locks be used only to surround specific lines of code that have non-thread-safe behavior. Locks should be released as soon as it is safe to do so. Although you *can* surround the entirety of a program being executed in a separate thread with a single lock (that would be very thread-safe!), doing so would be equivalent to not using any separate threads at all. In fact, it would be worse, now that you have all this extra overhead keeping track of your locks and threads.

Instead of explicitly calling lock.acquire() and lock.release(), we can also use a with statement to handle locks:

```python
def sleep_and_print(lock):
    time.sleep(0.5)
    with lock:
        print('Done sleeping!')
```

This approach has another benefit as well. If an exception is thrown between when lock.acquire() is called and when lock.release() is called, the lock will never be released and no other threads will be able to execute. Granted, it's relatively unlikely that a print function will throw an exception. However, we can still demonstrate this effect by commenting out the lock.release() line in the original version of sleep_and_print so that the lock is acquired but never released:

```python
def sleep_and_print(lock):
    time.sleep(0.5)
    lock.acquire()
    print('Done sleeping!')
    # lock.release()
```

If this is done and the function `do_sleep_and_print_threads` is run again, only the first line will ever print:

```
Done sleeping!
```

The lock will never release, the program will hang, and you'll need to take action to interrupt the process, either by pressing the square "Interrupt this kernel" button in Jupyter Lab or pressing Ctrl+C in the terminal.

In general, it's better to use locks in conjunction with a `with` statement, rather than acquiring and releasing with the `acquire` and `release` methods.

We can rewrite the function `print_function_time` to use a lock around the `print` statement so that it is thread-safe:

```
def print_function_time(func, lock=threading.Lock()):
    start = time.time()
    func()
    with lock.acquire():
        print(f'{func.__name__}: {time.time() - start}')
```

There are cases where we don't need or want to use a lock when `print_function_time` is called because there are no other threads executing simultaneously—all other threads have been joined outside the function. For this reason, the `lock` argument is a keyword argument with a supplied value of `threading.Lock()`, which creates a new lock. By creating a new lock and using it only one time inside the function, we're effectively locking nothing (if nothing else can share the lock, it's useless to lock). However, using a one-time lock does make the function a little shorter and easier to read.

We can use this rewritten `print_function_time` in conjunction with `do_sleep_threads`, which previously demonstrated incorrect print behavior:

```
def do_sleep_threads(num_threads=5):
    threads = [
        threading.Thread(target=print_function_time, args=(do_sleep,))
        for i in range(num_threads)
    ]
    [t.start() for t in threads]
    [t.join() for t in threads]

print_function_time(do_sleep_threads)
```

This results in cleaner printed messages, with each one getting its own line like it's supposed to. In addition, we can verify that the runtime is approximately the same as it was before, with no significant delays due to locking:

```
do_sleep: 0.5042147636413574
do_sleep: 0.5044667720794678
do_sleep: 0.5052378177642822
do_sleep: 0.5038330554962158
do_sleep: 0.5055201053619385
do_sleep_threads: 0.5093989372253418
```

Although locking has the potential to hurt performance, or even cause programs to hang if used incorrectly, it is also often necessary to ensure that parallel computations maintain predictable and desired behavior.

QUEUES

One of the major challenges when working with multiple threads in Python is handling communication and workloads across the threads. Queues are handy objects that solve many of these problems in a thread-safe way.

Queue objects can be created by importing the queue module and instantiating one of its classes: Queue, LifoQueue, PriorityQueue, or SimpleQueue. Here, we're going to use SimpleQueue, which provides basic queue functionality:

```
import queue

q = queue.SimpleQueue()
```

An essential feature of a queue is the ability to add and remove objects to and from it. We can do just that with the SimpleQueue:

```
q.put('thing 1')
q.put('thing 2')
print(q.get())
print(q.get())
```

This prints:

```
thing 1
thing 2
```

The SimpleQueue is what's known as a first in/first out, or *FIFO queue*. The first thing to be added to the queue ('thing 1') is the first thing to be removed from it, and the newest additions ('thing 2') are removed last. This is in contrast to the last in/first out, or *LIFO queue*, where the oldest items are removed last.

If we attempt to remove an item from the empty queue, the program hangs as execution is blocked until an item is added to the queue:

```
q.get()
```

This can be fixed by adding a timeout keyword argument to the get method:

```
q.get(timeout=5)
```

The fact that the get method hangs until something is added to the in-memory queue is a strong indicator of the queue's intended use case in multithreaded applications. Without the possibility of other threads adding items, this blocking feature in the get method is useless. However, if you do want to turn it off, you can always set blocking to False:

```
q.get(block=False)
```

Note that if a timeout is reached or block is set to False and the queue is empty, an Empty exception will be raised.

Queues are great for storing work that other threads can pick up as they're able to. For example, we might have a queue containing websites that need to be scraped. We can simulate work being added to this queue over time by writing a function, add_urls, that adds a new domain name to a work queue, q_work, every two seconds:

```python
def add_urls(q_work):
    urls_list = [
            'https://unlockingpython.com',
            'https://google.com',
            'https://apple.com',
            'https://ryanemitchell.com'
    ]
    while len(urls_list):
        q_work.put(urls_list.pop())
        time.sleep(2)
```

Then, write a function, fetch_urls, that gets URLs from the work queue and prints the HTTP status code of the response:

```python
def fetch_urls(q_work):
    try:
        while url := q_work.get(timeout=5):
            r = urllib.request.urlopen(url)
            print(f'url: {url}, status code: {r.getcode()}')
    except Empty:
        print('Done')
```

Here, a timeout of 5 seconds is being passed to the get method on q_work. The Empty exception is being handled, which nicely terminates the thread if no new items are picked up from the queue within 5 seconds.

Finally, we can create two threads that get URLs off the queue and fetch their data, and a single thread that adds new URLs to the queue:

```python
q_work = SimpleQueue()

threads = [
    threading.Thread(target=fetch_urls, args=(q_work,)),
    threading.Thread(target=fetch_urls, args=(q_work,)),
    threading.Thread(target=add_urls, args=(q_work,))
]

[t.start() for t in threads]
[t.join() for t in threads]
```

This produces the followed printed messages:

```
url: https://ryanemitchell.com, status code: 200
url: https://apple.com, status code: 200
url: https://google.com, status code: 200
url: https://unlockingpython.com, status code: 200
Done
Done
```

MULTIPROCESSING MODULE

The `multiprocessing` module has a very similar syntax to the `threading` module. Recall the function `do_calculation`:

```
def do_calculation():
    for i in range(0, 10000000):
        math.sin(i)
```

The following runs two instances of this function in two separate processes:

```
import multiprocessing

p1 = multiprocessing.Process(target=print_function_time, args=(do_calculation,))
p2 = multiprocessing.Process(target=print_function_time, args=(do_calculation,))
p1.start()
p2.start()
p1.join()
p2.join()
```

This results in output like this:

```
do_calculation: 0.5675208568572998
do_calculation: 0.5701651573181152
```

It's important to note that this usage of the Python `multiprocessing` module will not work inside a Jupyter notebook. If you want to run this code, you must write it in a `.py` file and run it from the command line. Alternatively, you can use the `multiprocess` module.

The `multiprocess` module can be installed with `pip`:

```
$ pip install multiprocess
```

It has the same usage as the standard multiprocessing module:

```
import multiprocess

p1 = multiprocess.Process(target=print_function_time, args=(do_calculation,))
p2 = multiprocess.Process(target=print_function_time, args=(do_calculation,))
p1.start()
p2.start()
p1.join()
p2.join()
```

For the following code samples, I will assume you have an `import` statement like one of the following:

```
from multiprocessing import Process # Use for .py files

from multiprocess import Process  # Use for iPython notebooks
```

That is, all code samples will simply use the `Process` class, regardless of which module it's imported from.

The following function, do_calculation_processes, is very similar to do_calculation_threads in the previous section:

```
def do_calculation_processes(num_threads=5):
    processes = [
        Process(
            target=print_function_time,
            args=(do_calculation,)
        ) for i in range(num_times)
    ]   [p.start() for p in processes]
    [p.join() for p in processes]
```

It instantiates a number of processes running the do_calculation function, starts them, and then joins them. By timing the entire function, we can see a marked reduction in runtime over the 2.75 seconds that do_calculation_threads required:

```
print_function_time(do_calculation_processes)
```

This prints output like:

```
do_calculation: 0.5750401020050049do_calculation: 0.593463659286499

do_calculation: 0.5878500938415527
do_calculation: 0.5956990718841553
do_calculation: 0.6083760261535645
do_calculation_processes: 0.6313052177429199
```

Of course, this still has the same problem that threads had in that the print statements are writing on top of each other. To fix this, we can use the multiprocessing lock object.

Ideally, processes are able to run independently of each other and locks shouldn't be required. It is more common for threads to communicate with each other, but less common to have collaboration between processes. However, there may be situations in which this dependency is necessary, such as when multiple processes are writing to the same output file. You may want to ensure that a process is able to start and finish its output to the file without that output being interrupted by another process doing the same thing.

The syntax for acquiring and releasing a lock across multiple processes is very similar to the syntax for doing it across multiple threads. Import the Lock class from either multiprocessing or multiprocess, depending on which library you're using:

```
from multiprocessing import Lock
from multiprocess import Lock
```

Then pass the lock to the function being run in parallel:

```
def print_function_time(func, lock=Lock()):
    start = time.time()
    func()
    with lock:
        print(f'{func.__name__}: {time.time() - start}')

def do_sleep_processes(num_processes=5):
    lock = Lock()
    processes = [
        Process(
            target=print_function_time,
```

```
            args=(do_calculation, lock)
        )
        for i in range(num_processes)
    ]
    [p.start() for p in processes]
    [p.join() for p in processes]

print_function_time(do_sleep_processes)
```

Obviously, the number of processes that a computer can truly run in parallel is not infinite. It's limited by the number of physical cores, physical CPUs, how many other applications and processes are currently running, and how much processing time those applications are requiring. As the value of the argument num_processes increases, the total runtime of the function do_calculation_processes will also increase.

However, given that multiple processes use processing power more effectively when and where it's available on the computer, what is the downside of always using multiprocessing instead of multithreading just in case there's some additional runtime advantage to be gleaned?

There are additional costs associated with creating and destroying an entire process as opposed to a comparatively cheaper thread. Beyond that, concrete architectural decisions need to be made for retrieving and/or storing the results of computations.

Recall that the function do_get_website returns the HTTP status code from the web server:

```
def do_get_website():
    r = urllib.request.urlopen('http://www.unlockingpython.com/')
    return r.getcode()
```

How might we collect a list of these status codes across threads and processes? It might seem like we would be able to return the output from the join method of all these threads to get a list of status codes:

```
def do_get_website_threads(num_processes=5):
    threads = [
        threading.Thread(target=do_get_website)
        for i in range(num_processes)
    ]
    [t.start() for t in threads]
    return [t.join() for t in threads]

do_get_website_threads()
```

Unfortunately, this does not work. The return value of the join method is always None:

```
[None, None, None, None, None]
```

However, recall that these threads do share memory. This means that modifying an object in one thread will modify that object across all threads. We can demonstrate this by modifying the do_get_websites function to add the status code to a global list status_codes, rather than returning the value:

```
status_codes = []

def do_get_website(lock):
    global status_codes
    r = urllib.request.urlopen('http://www.unlockingpython.com/')
```

```
    with lock:
        status_codes.append(r.getcode())

def do_get_website_threads(num_processes=5):
    lock = threading.Lock()
    threads = [
        threading.Thread(target=do_get_website, args=(lock,))
        for i in range(num_processes)
    ]
    [t.start() for t in threads]
    return [t.join() for t in threads]

do_get_website_threads()
print(status_codes)
```

Because modifying lists is not a thread-safe operation, we must use a lock to ensure the list is written to correctly.

Printing status_codes results in a list of (hopefully) 200 statuses:

```
[200, 200, 200, 200, 200]
```

It might be tempting to try something similar across multiple processes. Change threading.Thread to multiprocess.Process and threading.Lock to multiprocess.Lock. This code will run and even go out and fetch the websites, but the list of status_codes will be empty:

```
[]
```

To check what's going on, we can even print a message announcing the addition of the new status code in the do_get_website function:

```
def do_get_website(lock):
    global status_codes
    r = urllib.request.urlopen('http://www.unlockingpython.com/')
    with lock:
        print(f'Adding {r.status} to status_codes')
        status_codes.append(r.getcode())
```

This cheerfully prints that the status code has been added, but the list status_codes, printed at the very end, still remains empty:

```
Adding 200 to status_codes
Adding 200 to status_codes
Adding 200 to status_codes
Adding 200 to status_codes
Adding 200 to status_codes
[]
```

This is because each process has its own memory space allocated, each with its own copy of the status_codes list. Each copy of the list is destroyed along with the process after it finishes execution.

To capture the output of a process, you must store the output outside the process itself. This might be in a file written to disk, in a database, as a request to a completely different application running in its own memory (such as Redis), or as a request to a remote web server that does something with the data.

You can also use the Python class SharedMemory to—exactly like its name implies—share memory across processes:

```
from multiprocess.shared_memory import SharedMemory

sm = SharedMemory(size=1024, create=True)
```

This creates a SharedMemory object 1,024 bytes (one kilobyte) long. The data in it is represented by a bytearray, with each value in it initialized to 0. The data is stored in the buf attribute and can be accessed and modified accordingly:

```
sm.buf[0] = 200
print(sm.buf[0])
```

This sets the value of the first byte to 200 and then prints that same value.

Shared memory must be explicitly closed. Even stopping the Python program (or restarting Jupyter, as the case may be) will not deallocate the memory and release it back for use. On some operating systems, this can be accomplished with the close method alone. On other operating systems, you must also call unlink to release the memory. It's a good idea to call both, for safety:

```
sm.close()
sm.unlink()
```

In the following example, we can use multiple processes to set random integers between 0 and 255 (anything larger would be greater than a byte) at the provided indices in the shared memory:

```
import random

def do_set_random(sm, i):
    sm.buf[i] = random.randint(0, 255)

def do_set_random_processes(sm, num_processes=5):
    processes = [
        multiprocess.Process(target=do_set_random, args=(sm, i))
        for i in range(num_processes)
    ]
    [p.start() for p in processes]
    return [p.join() for p in processes]

sm = SharedMemory(size=1024, create=True)
try:
    num = 10
    do_set_random_processes(sm, num_processes=num)
    print([int(sm.buf[i]) for i in range(0, num)])
finally:
    sm.close()
    sm.unlink()
```

A try/finally statement is used to ensure that both close and unlink are called on the SharedMemory object, sm.

The function do_generate_random takes in a SharedMemory object and an integer, i, representing the index to set the randomly generated number at. Running this prints output like the following:

```
[66, 4, 69, 178, 220, 194, 224, 35, 197, 216]
```

Of course, passing around specific indices for a function to update is a pain. What would be nicer is if we could simply append items to a list, without regard to which predetermined "order" everything should go in. For this, we have ShareableList.

If you don't want to deal with managing bytes and want a little more user-friendliness in your shared memory, you can also use ShareableList. A ShareableList works very similarly to SharedMemory:

```
from multiprocess.shared_memory import ShareableList

sl = ShareableList([0, 0, 0, 0])
sl[0] = 'spam'
sl[1] = 3.14159
sl[2] = 123456
print(sl)

sl.shm.close()
sl.shm.unlink()
```

This initializes a ShareableList containing four zeros, sets the values to various types of data, prints it, and then closes and unlinks the list using the shm (underlying SharedMemory instance) attribute.

Although the syntax is, in some ways, similar to the native Python list, the ShareableList is important in several different ways. Like SharedMemory, the entire size of the list must be declared upfront. You cannot append to the list or increase the size afterward. Also, it cannot store more complex data structures like dictionaries or other lists.

When working with more complex Python data structures across multiple processes in shared memory, it is common to use the pickle library, discussed in Chapter 15, "Working with Files," to serialize and deserialize data to and from bytes objects. This allows you to, say, take a dictionary, serialize it into bytes, store it into shared memory, and then do the opposite to read the dictionary again in a different process.

Recall also in Chapter 15 that we used the int method to_bytes to convert integers to a bytes array. The following converts the number 500 to bytes and then back again using the to_bytes and from_bytes methods:

```
data = int.to_bytes(500, 2)
int.from_bytes(data)
```

If the number being converted is 255 or less, only 1 byte of data will be returned even though we allow for 2 bytes to be used by to_bytes with the second argument, 2. By passing byteorder='little' to the function, we can force 2 bytes to be always returned by asking, essentially, for a zero-padded byte format. This is similar to asking for zero-padded months of the year (January is 01, February is 02, etc.), which always takes up two integers.

Two bytes of data can store all positive integers up to, and including, 65,535. This is plenty to represent the length of memory, in bytes, being used by a reasonably sized pickled object. If we create a SharedMemory instance where the first 2 bytes represents the size of the object, and the rest of the memory contains the object (with some number of empty unused bytes following it), we should be able to effectively pass Python objects back and forth between processes.

We can write new functions write_object and read_object, which use this system to pickle and write objects to shared memory and then read them back from shared memory:

```python
def read_object(sm):
    bytes_size = int.from_bytes(sm.buf[0:2], byteorder='little')
    bytes_data = sm.buf[2:2 + bytes_size]
    return pickle.loads(bytes_data)

def write_object(sm, obj):
    bytes_data = pickle.dumps(obj)
    bytes_size = len(bytes_data)
    sm.buf[0:2] = int.to_bytes(bytes_size, 2, byteorder='little')
    sm.buf[2:2 + bytes_size] = bytes_data
```

Because we are performing several operations in a row on the shared memory object, it is necessary to use a lock to ensure that multiple processes are not trying to read and write at the same time.

The function do_append_random_processes takes in a SharedMemory instance, creates a new lock, and then passes sm and lock to the function do_append_random.

The function do_append_random gets a random integer, then uses the lock to read a shared native Python list object, append the number, and write it back to shared memory:

```python
def do_append_random(sm, lock):
    random_int = random.randint(0, 256)
    with lock:
        shared_list = read_object(sm)
        shared_list.append(random_int)
        write_object(sm, shared_list)

def do_append_random_processes(sm, num_processes=5):
    lock = multiprocess.Lock()
    processes = [
        multiprocess.Process(target=do_append_random, args=(sm, lock))
        for i in range(num_processes)
    ]
    [p.start() for p in processes]
    [p.join() for p in processes]
    return get_object(sm)
```

To use the function do_append_random_processes, simply create a new SharedMemory instance, write an empty array to it, and ensure that it's closed.

```python
sm = SharedMemory(size=1024, create=True)
# write an empty list to the shared memory
write_object(sm, [])
try:
    num = 10
    random_nums = do_append_random_processes(sm, num_processes=num)
    print(random_nums)

finally:
    sm.close()
    sm.unlink()
```

This prints a native Python list like this:

```
[153, 26, 107, 161, 87, 65, 100, 158, 166, 197]
```

In these examples, the function `random.randint` is a stand-in for a process that takes a long time, particularly one that might require a great deal of computational power. With the amount of careful planning and overhead required to manage multiple processes communicating with each other using native Python objects, it's important to make sure that doing so is necessary, or at least more efficient than some other method.

EXERCISES

1. When the function `do_sleep_threads` was run without locking, we saw that the `print` statements interfered with each other, leading to printed output appearing incorrectly on the same line. When the function `do_get_website_threads` is run, this happens more rarely. Explain why this is.

2. Create a new queue and add a number of dictionaries to it that have the following form:

   ```
   {'timestamp': time.time(), 'data': random.randint(0, 100)}
   ```

   where `time` and `random` are the built-in Python modules.

   Then, retrieve items from the queue and print what the data is and how long each item had been sitting in the queue.

3. Create a function, `write_uuids_to_file`, that writes UUID (universally unique identifier) strings to a file. Use the `uuid` module to do this:

   ```
   from uuid import uuid4

   str(uuid4())
   ```

   When called, the function `write_uuids_to_file` should write five UUID strings on a single line, separated by commas. Each time a UUID is written, it should be written in a separate `write` statement to the file. That is, each time the function is called, five separate writes to the file are made.

   After finishing, a newline should be written to the end of the file so that when `write_uuids_to_file` is called again, the UUIDs will be written on a new line.

   Create 10 new processes that have the target `write_uuids_to_file`. Start and join the processes and observe the file. Did the processes interfere with each other?

4. Add locking to the function `write_uuids_to_file` so that writes cannot be made by two processes at the same time while UUIDs are being written in the function call. Delete or clear the contents of the file, run the 10 processes again, and observe the contents of the file.

5. Create a work queue, `q_work` and populate it with 100 UUIDs. Change the lock object used previously in `write_uuids_to_file` to a thread-locking object. Rewrite `write_uuids_to_file` so that it gets UUIDs from `q_work` and only exits when `q_work` contains no more UUIDs.

   Run `write_uuids_to_file` in several threads.

18

Databases

Fundamentally, databases are just files with fancy applications designed to read little bits of the files at a time. These fancy applications are called *database management systems* (DBMSs), and the syntax used to specify the bits of the files you want to read is called a *query language*.

Many popular databases today are *relational databases*. These are databases that have tables (similar to spreadsheet tables) containing rows and columns. Crucially, some of the columns in these tables are ID columns that relate to other tables. For example, a User table might have a user_type_id column that relates to a table of user types.

user_id	first_name	last_name	username	user_type_id
1	Alice	Acevedo	alice123	2
2	Bob	Brown	bobby_brown	3

user_type_id	name	monthly_cost
1	admin	0
2	free	0
3	premium	10

There are many different relational databases commonly used with Python:

➤ **MySQL:** Currently the most popular free DBMS

➤ **Postgres:** Another very popular free DBMS

➤ **Microsoft SQL Server:** Popular proprietary DBMS

➤ **Snowflake:** Proprietary DBMS designed for bulk data operations and data warehousing

➤ **SQLite:** Free DBMS ideal for local development and lightweight applications

Although popular and useful, not all databases are relational databases. Databases that are not relational are often called NoSQL databases. These are usually key-value store databases such as Redis, MongoDB, and DynamoDB.

Key-value stores work a bit like dictionaries in Python. The database contains some number of unique keys that point to data or documents. When provided with a key, the database is very quick to retrieve the data associated with it.

NoSQL databases are great at storing and retrieving large documents, loosely structured documents, or documents with widely varying structures. However, they're not usually as good as relational databases when it comes to tasks like getting statistics or summaries across large swaths of data, or getting sets of filtered data.

In this chapter, we will be focusing on relational databases, although many of the concepts are applicable to NoSQL databases as well.

When you're working with relational databases in Python, it makes very little difference which DBMS you decide to use. The interfaces used to connect Python to the database software are very similar from database to database. For example, the methods you would use to send a query to and retrieve data from a Postgres database are identical to the methods you would use for a MySQL database. This is because of the Python Database API Specification (https://peps.python.org/pep-0249) used to standardize the method names between database packages in Python.

INSTALLING AND USING SQLite

Although there are many excellent free relational databases available, they are often difficult to install and require configuration and management steps that change frequently and are highly dependent on the user's operating system.

It would be a tremendous waste of time to try and write OS-agnostic and future-proof instructions for installing, say, MySQL or Postgres. It would also be a tremendous waste of your time to read these instructions and attempt to implement them for complex software you may have no use for outside of this book. Fortunately, this is exactly the sort of problem that *SQLite* was created to solve.

SQLite is a lightweight database management software that is easy to install and that has a query syntax very similar to other relational database software. Because of this, it makes an excellent teaching tool.

In this chapter, we'll be working with SQLite, a database application written in the C programming language, designed for lightweight development and local applications. This is not a database where you store millions of records for all users of an application, but you might store local application settings for a single user on that user's computer.

Installing SQLite

SQLite is managed through a command-line tool, sqlite3. The 3 refers to the current major version of SQLite. This tool is required to interact with SQLite from the command line but, importantly, it is not required to use SQLite from Python.

SQLite3 comes with Python automatically. Not only is the Python interface to the software, the sqlite3 library, part of the Python standard library, but the underlying database software itself is installed with Python. However, it can be handy to see and work with SQLite tables from the command line during development, so I recommend installing the SQLite command-line tool.

On macOS, the easiest way to install the SQLite command-line tool is to use Homebrew. Homebrew, mentioned briefly in Chapter 4 "Installing and Running Python," is an excellent management tool for command-line software on macOS. Homebrew can be installed according to the instructions found at https://brew.sh. Once Homebrew is installed, you can use it to install sqlite3 with the following command:

```
$ brew install sqlite3
```

Test your installation with the sqlite3 command, and it should take you to the SQLite command prompt:

```
$ sqlite3
SQLite version 3.43.2 2023-10-10 13:08:14
Enter ".help" for usage hints.
Connected to a transient in-memory database.
Use ".open FILENAME" to reopen on a persistent database.
sqlite>
```

On Windows, the installation is slightly more complicated. You must download the executable files and add them to your environment variables.

Download the binaries from the SQLite downloads page: www.sqlite.org/download.html. On this page, under the Windows binaries, download the package sqllite-tools, described as "A bundle of command-line tools for managing SQLite database files."

Unzip the file once it's downloaded. This file should unzip into a directory containing three files:

➤ sqldiff

➤ sqlite3_analyzer

➤ sqlite3

It doesn't matter where you save these files, but ideally, they'd be somewhere near the root of the directory structure like C:\sqlite\.

Finally, tell Windows where the executable binaries have been saved to and that you'd like to execute then when you type sqlite3 in the command line. This can be done by adding a new environment variable. Choose System ⇨ About ⇨ System Info ⇨ Advanced System Settings ⇨ Environment Variables. Alternatively, you can search for **Environment variables** in the Start menu.

Click the New button to add a new environment variable. Call it **sqlite3** and provide the value **C:\sqlite\sqlite3** (depending, of course, on where you saved your downloaded files). Open a new Power Shell terminal to verify the installation using this command:

```
$ sqlite3
```

On Linux, SQLite is likely already installed. If not, you can use this:

```
$ sudo apt install sqlite3
```

Or you can download the binaries from www.sqlite.org/download.html and add them to the bin directory.

Using SQLite

Each DBMS installed on a server can hold multiple *databases*. Each database holds multiple tables. In order to create a table, you must first create a database to hold that table. To create a database, most of the time we'd use a query like this:

```
CREATE DATABASE unlocking-python;
```

This will create a new database called unlocking-python in just about every relational database application. With SQLite, however, each database is stored in a separate .db file, which needs to be explicitly named from the command line when starting SQLite.

To create a database in SQLite, type this:

```
$ sqlite3 unlocking-python.db
```

This will create the file unlocking-python.db, which holds all the data for that database, and start the SQLite command prompt. This new database is empty and ready to be populated with tables. We can create a table to store users of an application with a CREATE TABLE statement:

```
sqlite> CREATE TABLE User(
    user_id INTEGER PRIMARY KEY AUTOINCREMENT,
    first_name VARCHAR(32),
    last_name VARCHAR(32),
    username VARCHAR(32),
    email VARCHAR(64),
    last_login DATETIME DEFAULT CURRENT_TIMESTAMP
);
```

Although long, this statement details the schema, or data structure, for the table. To avoid mistyping it, I recommend that you paste it into the terminal from the exercise files where all SQL statements, including this one, can be found.

To see all tables in the current SQLite database, you can use the .tables command:

```
sqlite> .tables
```

This prints a list containing only the User table:

```
User
```

To see the schema for any table, use the .schema command followed by that table's name:

```
sqlite> .schema User
```

This prints out the original CREATE TABLE statement used to create the table.

To remove the table (and, of course, any data inside of it) use the DROP TABLE query:

```
sqlite> DROP TABLE User
```

As we work with SQL queries in the next section, it will be helpful to have some data in the table for the queries to return. This can be accomplished using an INSERT statement (make sure to re-create the User table if you just dropped it!):

```
INSERT INTO User
    (first_name, last_name, username, email, last_login)
VALUES
    ('Alice', 'Acevedo', 'alice123', 'a@example.com', '2024-01-01 12:00:00'),
    ('Bob', 'Brown', 'bobby_brown', 'b@example.com', '2024-02-01 12:00:00'),
    ('Charlie', 'Clark', 'chuck', 'c@example.com', '2024-03-01 12:00:00');
```

This inserts three records for users Alice, Bob, and Charlie. The second line (indented after `INSERT INTO User`) details the columns we're going to be defining values for. This is useful if you want to use the default values for certain columns. In this case, we're not specifying any values for the `user_id` column.

Because the `user_id` column was defined as an `AUTOINCREMENT` column in the `CREATE TABLE` statement earlier, it will be populated with an integer value, starting with 1, that is *auto-incremented*. This means that the first record will contain an ID of 1, the second record will have an ID of 2, etc. Each time a new record is created, the database gives it an ID that is 1 greater than the last ID in the table. The IDs are incremented automatically, or auto-incremented.

The data in the User table then looks like this:

user_id	first_name	last_name	username	email	last_login
1	Alice	Acevedo	alice123	a@example .com	2024-01-01 12:00:00
2	Bob	Brown	bobby_brown	b@example .com	2024-02-01 12:00:00
3	Charlie	Clark	chuck	c@example .com	2024-03-01 12:00:00

QUERY LANGUAGE SYNTAX

Most relational databases use a query language called SQL[1] (Structured Query Language). This is a standardized language that allows you to select, filter, and aggregate data in relational databases.

For example, in each one of the five DBMSs listed at the beginning of this chapter, the syntax to query the `User` table looks like this:

```
SELECT * FROM User WHERE first_name = 'Alice';
```

This selects all records from the `User` table where the `first_name` column contains the string `'Alice'`. Here, the asterisk represents a sort of wildcard that gets all available data in the table. We can also request a specific set of columns by name:

```
SELECT first_name, last_name, email FROM User WHERE first_name = 'Alice';
```

---

[1] There exists some mixed opinions about how to pronounce "SQL." Officially, MySQL is pronounced "My ess que ell" rather than "my sequel" (`https://dev.mysql.com/doc/refman/8.4/en/what-is-mysql.html`). In practice, no one will care that much about how you pronounce it. On the other hand, Microsoft's SQL Server is universally pronounced "sequel server" and saying anything else would be odd.

The query language itself, SQL, is officially pronounced "ess que ell," but most people pronounce it "sequel." So, there you go. My advice is to use whatever pronunciation your boss uses.

Explicitly selecting columns rather than using an asterisk is considered best practice, especially when writing production SQL queries. This practice clarifies which columns are actually required by the query making it easier for database administrators to, among other things, rename or remove unused table columns with confidence . Avoiding asterisks also reduces the amount of data transferred over the network by returning only the fields needed.

That being said, we will be using asterisks frequently in this chapter for the sake of brevity. Using asterisks is also great to do during development, when writing exploratory queries, or when learning about SQL syntax like you're doing now. Just keep in mind that it's best to replace asterisks with actual column names before going to production.

While SQL is standardized by ANSI, there are slight variations between DBMSs. For example, in Snowflake, MySQL, SQLite, and Postgres, you can select 10 records from the User table like this:

```
SELECT TOP(10) * FROM User;
```

In Microsoft's SQL Server, you use this syntax:

```
SELECT * FROM User LIMIT 10;
```

The words SELECT, FROM, and LIMIT here are all *SQL keywords*. They are not names of tables, values like 10, or string constants, but actions that the query is performing. Although these keywords are case-insensitive, it is common to write them in all caps as a matter of style.

In general, SQL queries are less case-sensitive than most other programming languages. For example, a table named User can be queried as USER or uSeR and work just fine (although it might cause your code reviewers some anxiety). In general, only the first letter of table names should be capitalized.

Table names should also be singular. We call the tables User and Usertype, not Users and Usertypes. If you bring these tables into a database management system other than SQLite, you should be careful, however, as USER is a reserved keyword in many DBMSs. It is used as a keyword by the software along with other words, a list of which can be found here: https://en.wikipedia.org/wiki/List_of_SQL_reserved_words. A list of SQLite reserved words can be found here: https://sqlite.org/lang_keywords.html.

The rules for case sensitivity in string comparisons (getting records where first_name is 'Alice' or first name is 'ALICE') differs depending on which DBMS you're using, but these queries are also usually case insensitive.

Earlier, we saw a simple query that fetched records where the first name was Alice. Filters using a WHERE statement can also get more complex:

```
SELECT * FROM User
WHERE (
    first_name = 'Alice'
    OR last_name LIKE 'B%'
    OR email LIKE 'c@%.com'
)
AND last_login > '2024-01-01 00:00:00';
```

This returns all three of the records. The LIKE statement searches for strings by a pattern, where the % symbol acts as a wildcard operator that can be used at any position, or at multiple positions, in the string pattern.

In addition to retrieving data from a single table, data can be retrieved across multiple tables in the database. To see this in action, let's create a new table called Usertype that contains different types of User accounts:

```
CREATE TABLE Usertype(
    user_type_id INTEGER PRIMARY KEY AUTOINCREMENT,
    name VARCHAR(32),
    monthly_cost INTEGER
);
```

then insert some records in it:

```
INSERT INTO Usertype (name, monthly_cost)
VALUES
    ('admin', 0),
    ('free', 0),
    ('premium', 10)
```

We can add a new column to the User table called user_type_id using an ALTER TABLE statement:

```
ALTER TABLE User ADD COLUMN user_type_id INT;
```

Finally, update the existing records in the User table so that the new user_type_id column is populated with various user types:

```
UPDATE User SET user_type_id = 3 WHERE first_name = 'Alice';
UPDATE User SET user_type_id = 2 WHERE first_name = 'Bob';
UPDATE User SET user_type_id = 2 WHERE first_name = 'Charlie';
```

Now the unlocking-python database contains two tables: User and Usertype. The User table contains a column, user_type_id, which points to a record in Usertype. We can retrieve data across both tables using a JOIN statement:

```
SELECT * FROM User JOIN Usertype ON User.user_type_id = Usertype.user_type_id;
```

This query matches records in User with matching records in Usertype based on the user_type_id column in both tables. This results in the returned data:

```
1|Alice|Acevedo|alice123|a@example.com|2024-01-01 12:00:00|3|3|premium|10
2|Bob|Brown|bobby_brown|b@example.com|2024-02-01 12:00:00|2|2|free|0
3|Charlie|Clark|chuck|c@example.com|2024-03-01 12:00:00|2|2|free|0
```

Note that, when multiple tables are involved, there will be ambiguity if two tables have a column with the same name. Therefore, the column should be referred to using its table name as well, such as User.user_type_id rather than just user_type_id.

Although not strictly necessary for columns that are not ambiguous (such as first_name in the User table), it's best practice to write the full name any time multiple tables are involved.

Writing the full name each time might get cumbersome, particularly for queries that have lots of references to column names, like this one:

```
SELECT
    User.first_name, User.last_name, Usertype.name
FROM
    User JOIN Usertype ON User.user_type_id = Usertype.user_type_id
WHERE
    User.email = 'a@example.com';
```

To make this a little more elegant, we can provide *aliases* for the table names in the query. An alias is a temporary name for a table that is declared and used only within a single query:

```
SELECT
    u.first_name, u.last_name, ut.name
FROM
    User u JOIN Usertype ut ON u.user_type_id = ut.user_type_id
WHERE
    u.email = 'a@example.com';
```

The statement User u JOIN Usertype ut both introduces the two tables and provides the aliases u and ut for them that can be used elsewhere in the query.

USING SQLite WITH PYTHON

Most databases require installing a third-party package, often called a *connector*, to communicate with that database in Python. Here are the pip install statements to install packages for MySQL, Snowflake, Postgres, and SQL Server, respectively:

```
$ pip install mysql-connector-python
$ pip install snowflake-connector-python
$ pip install psycopg2
$ pip install mssql
```

And their corresponding import statements in Python:

```
from mysql import connector
from snowflake import connector
from psycopg2 import connect
from pymssql import connect
```

Thanks to the Python Database API Specification (https://peps.python.org/pep-0249), all database connectors work in essentially the same way. The methods that you'll see here for the SQLite connector will also be found for those other database connection objects. The nice thing about SQLite, however, is that you don't need to install anything.

The SQLite package, sqlite3, is part of the Python standard library. It can be used to connect to the database unlocking-python like this:

```
from sqlite3 import connect

conn = connect('unlocking-python.db')
```

Unlike other database connectors, sqlite3.connect does not require credentials like a username and password to connect to the database. This is because SQLite does not use credentials, instead relying on the operating system's file permissions to either allow or deny access to the database file.

Because SQLite always runs locally, the connection also does not require information about the location of the server or data, beyond the name of the SQLite database file, 'unlocking-python.db'. Compare this to the information required for a typical Postgres connection:

```
import psycopg2

conn = psycopg2.connect(
    user='postgres',
    password='pass',
    host='127.0.0.1',
    port='5432',
    database='unlocking-python'
)
```

It's important to note that, even though the way it's called is slightly different, the method name, connect, is still the same. They also both return database connection objects, conn, that behave in much the same way, and have the same methods available to them.

Connections cannot be used to fetch data directly, but they can return a cursor object:

```
cur = conn.cursor()
```

A database cursor is an object that allows us to traverse records and keep track of where it is in the dataset while we do it. It's a bit like the file object from Chapter 15, "Working with Files."

To execute a string query, use the cursor's execute method:

```
cur.execute('SELECT * FROM User')
```

This does not return the results of the query, in much the same way that opening a text file in Python does not immediately return the contents of that file. The records must be explicitly asked for:

```
cur.fetchone()
```

This fetches the first result of the query, resulting in the following tuple:

```
(1, 'Alice', 'Acevedo', 'alice123', 'a@example.com', '2024-01-01 12:00:00', 3)
```

We can also fetch all the results at once:

```
cur.fetchall()
```

When this is called on the same cursor that just returned the Alice record with fetchone, it will return a list containing only the last two records (remember that Alice has already been fetched):

```
[(2, 'Bob', 'Brown', 'bobby_brown', 'b@example.com', '2024-02-01 12:00:00', 2),
 (3, 'Charlie', 'Clark', 'chuck', 'c@example.com', '2024-03-01 12:00:00', 2)]
```

If you want to fetch a list containing only a certain number of records at a time, you can use the fetchmany method:

```
cur.execute('SELECT * FROM User')
cur.fetchmany(2)
```

This returns the first two records:

```
[(1, 'Alice', 'Acevedo', 'alice123', 'a@example.com', '2024-01-01 12:00:00', 3),
 (2, 'Bob', 'Brown', 'bobby_brown', 'b@example.com', '2024-02-01 12:00:00', 2)]
```

Each time fetchmany is called on the same cursor, it will continue to attempt to fetch two records at a time. The next time it is called, only one record is left:

```
[(3, 'Charlie', 'Clark', 'chuck', 'c@example.com', '2024-03-01 12:00:00', 2)]
```

If it is called again, an empty array will be returned.

Calling execute and a fetch method (`fetchone`, `fetchmany`, `fetchall`) on a cursor object can read data, but it cannot be used to modify the database in any way. The following executes without an error:

```
cur.execute(
'''
INSERT INTO User (
    first_name, last_name, username, email, last_login, user_type_id)
VALUES
    ('Daria', 'Dorgendorffer', 'daria', 'd@example.com', '2024-04-01 12:00:00', 1);
''' )
```

If you use that same cursor object to fetch all records from the User table, you'll see that a fourth record does apparently get added:

```
cur.execute('SELECT * FROM User')
cur.fetchall()
```

This returns the original three records, plus a new one:

```
(4, 'Daria', 'Dorgendorffer', 'daria', @example.com', '2024-04-01 12:00:00', 1)
```

However, if you go to the terminal and inspect the database outside of Python, you'll see that only the original three records are present. There's a disagreement between this cursor object and, well, every other source.

In addition to keeping track of where it's at in the dataset, like a virtual bookmark, the cursor keeps track of the "state" of the dataset. If data is added (such as with the INSERT statement), the cursor keeps track of that additional data without actually storing anything in the underlying database. So when we go back and ask the cursor what data is in the database, the cursor cheerfully sends us four records back when that last record doesn't actually exist.

To persist changes to the database, use the `commit` method:

```
conn.commit()
```

Note that this `commit` method is on the *connection*, not the cursor. This commits the current state back to the database, at which point you'll be able to see the new user. Forgetting to commit changes to the database is a common source of bugs, and one where errors may not even be thrown if something is wrong. It's important to analyze all SQL queries to determine if they're reading data, or making changes, and act appropriately.

Another common source of bugs is a *connection leak*. Every time a connection to the database is made, like the one created in Python when the `sqlite3.connect` method is called, a small amount of memory is allocated for that connection. Databases usually also have limits, called connection limits, on the number of open connections they can have. Once this limit is reached, no new connections can be made.

For this reason, it's important to make sure your connections are closed when you're done using them:

```
conn.close()
```

Connections can be more safely managed using try/finally statements or by using connections only within a with block:

```
import sqlite3
with sqlite3.connect('unlocking-python.db') as conn:
    cur = conn.cursor()
    res = cur.execute('SELECT * FROM Users')
    print(res.fetchall())
```

Object Relational Mapping

An *object relational mapper* (ORM) is a tool that transforms data from the database into usable Python objects, and vice versa. They are often used to interface with the database in a clean way, without having to worry about writing queries or persisting changes every time you use an object.

There are many popular ORMs for Python, such as SQLAlchemy, PeeWee, and Django. Although Django is a web framework and not primarily an ORM, it does have very easy to use ORM functionality that we will be working with in Chapter 21, "Django."

In theory, the goal of an ORM is very simple. Move the data from the database into a Python object and back again, keeping the data in the database and the Python objects you're working with more or less in sync.

In practice, general-purpose ORMs designed for any number of situations they might encounter in enterprise applications tend to get, well, complex. For the purposes of understanding ORMs quickly, it's often easier to build them from scratch.

Regardless of whether you use an ORM system like SQLAlchemy or write your own, you will need to create new Python classes for the objects that the database data represents. In this case, we can create a User class:

```
class User:
    def __init__(self, data):
        pass
```

Here, the argument data represents a tuple of data retrieved from the database. However, we need to decide the order this data will be returned in so that the User class attributes can be initialized from it. To do this, we need to write the data selection query:

```
USER_SELECT_QUERY = '''
SELECT
    u.user_id,
    u.first_name,
    u.last_name,
    u.username,
    u.email,
    u.last_login,
    ut.name,
    ut.user_type_id,
    ut.monthly_cost
FROM
    User u JOIN Usertype ut ON u.user_type_id = ut.user_type_id
'''
```

Here, we're defining the fields and the particular order they will be fetched in. This query is assigned to the constant variable USER_SELECT_QUERY because, with the addition of optional WHERE clauses at the end, it can be reused by multiple methods that want to fetch data. This will ensure that the order of the fields being sent to the User class does not change. Now that this field order is defined, we can write the constructor in the User class:

```
class User:
    def __init__(self, data):
        self.user_id = data[0]
        self.first_name = data[1]
        self.last_name = data[2]
        self.username = data[3]
        self.email = data[4]
        self.last_login = data[5]
        self.usertype_name = data[6]
        self.usertype_id = data[7]
        self.usertype_monthly_cost = data[8]
```

Now we need to create a class that handles business logic for doing the mapping in our ORM. This class should be responsible only for User objects in an SQLite database. We can call it, appropriately, SQLiteUserMapper:

```
class SQLiteUserMapper:
    def __init__(self, conn):
        self.conn = conn

    def get_all_users(self):
        cur = self.conn.cursor()
        cur.execute(USER_SELECT_QUERY)
        return [User(d) for d in cur.fetchall()]

    def get_user_by_id(self, user_id):
        cur = self.conn.cursor()
        cur.execute(f'{USER_SELECT_QUERY} WHERE user_id = {user_id}')
        return User(cur.fetchone())
```

The SQLiteUserMapper is initialized with a database connection, self.conn, which it uses to create temporary cursor objects as needed. It has two methods: get_all_users, which returns a list of all users in the table, and get_user_by_id, which returns a single User matching the ID passed to it as an argument. Both methods use the same USER_SELECT_QUERY for the needed queries.

We can create a new SQLiteUserMapper with a connection object:

```
conn = sqlite3.connect('unlocking-python.db')
mapper = SQLiteUserMapper(conn)
```

Here, the new connection is assigned to the variable conn so that it can be closed when the mapper is no longer needed. In general, it's good practice to require that the code entity that opened the connection is also responsible for closing it. Rather than relying on the SQLiteUserMapper object to close the connection, the connection should be closed outside the mapper.

This mapper can be used to fetch a single user:

```
user = mapper.get_user_by_id(1)
print(f'Got user {user.first_name} {user.last_name}')
```

This prints:

```
Got user Alice Acevedo
```

Using the same mapper object, we can fetch all users in the database:

```
users = mapper.get_all_users()
for u in users:
    print(f'Got user {u.first_name} {u.last_name}')
```

This prints:

```
Got user Alice Acevedo
Got user Bob Brown
Got user Charlie Clark
Got user Daria Dorgendorffer
```

So far, our ORM is great at fetching data, but this is only half the job of an ORM. It also needs to write data back to the database. An easy way to keep everything in sync is to write a generic method that will update the database with every modifiable value in the object:

```
def commit(self, u):
    cur = self.conn.cursor()
    update_query = f'''
    UPDATE User SET
        first_name = {u.first_name},
        last_name = {u.last_name},
        username = {u.username},
        email = {u.email},
        last_login = {u.last_login},
        user_type_id = {u.user_type_id}
    WHERE user_id = {u.user_id}
    '''
    cur.execute(update_query)
    self.conn.commit()
    return self.get_user_by_id(u.user_id)
```

Note that this method is not capable of modifying the user_id of the user. This number is assigned by the database when the user is created and should never change.

The commit method does allow you to update the user_type_id, but does not update the user type name or monthly cost, which should be done through a more specific tool to manage user types. That is, you can reassign a user to have a different user type, but you cannot modify information about the user types themselves.

When the commit method returns the user object it, importantly, does not return the object that was passed into it. It retrieves a new one from the database based on the user ID. This is useful for two reasons. First, it helps detect any errors that may have occurred during the update. If a field wasn't updated, or perhaps was modified by a different process running at the same time, this will be easier to recognize and fix. Secondly, it re-fetches the user type name and monthly cost based on the user type ID, which may have changed.

We can test this out by fetching a User, updating their user type ID, committing the change, and then printing the name of the new user type:

```
bob = mapper.get_user_by_id(2)
print(f'{bob.first_name} has the {bob.usertype_name} membership')
bob.user_type_id = 3
bob = mapper.commit(bob)
print(f'{bob.first_name} has the {bob.usertype_name} membership')
```

This prints:

```
Bob has the free membership
Bob has the premium membership
```

EXERCISES

1. Design two tables that hold social media post and comment data. Call these tables `Posts` and `Comments`. The `Comments` table should have a `post_id` (the ID of the post being commented on). Both tables should have a `user_id` column that points to the `User` table.

2. Design a table that holds following/follower relationships between users. You should be able to write a query that gets a user's followers, and also a query that gets a list of users they follow.

3. Add a method to the `SQLiteUserMapper` that updates `last_login` to the current timestamp. This method should take only the user object as an argument and use the `datetime` package to get the current timestamp.

4. Create a mapper class for `Usertype`, that allows us to make changes to the name and monthly costs of the `Usertype`.

5. Rewrite the `User` and `SQLiteUserMapper` classes to use a `Usertype` class, rather than storing the user type data as flat attributes in the `User` class. That is, the `User` class should have an attribute, `self.usertype`, which points to a `UserType` object.

19

Unit Testing

If debugging is the process of removing software bugs, then programming must be the process of putting them in.

—EDSGER DIJKSTRA

Most of what I learned during my high school programming internships happened during the interviews. These interviews are when senior software engineers show off by testing the mettle and cleverness of teenagers with ridiculous questions, before hiring them to write mindless code that will be forgotten about by October.

One interview question stuck with me: "How do you know when you're done testing a software application?"

The answer, of course, is that "done testing" is simply not a thing. It's the pot of gold at the end of the rainbow, the Buddhist ideal of being free from earthly passions, and seeing a "No Vacancy" sign at Hilbert's Hotel.[1]

Unfortunately, I wasn't very clever all those years ago and mostly responded to the interviewer with a lot of variations on "You're done testing when you don't see any bugs" before melting into a pool of adolescent anxiety. This foreshadowed my career in professional software engineering, but not professional software testing. Oddly, they still offered me a job writing tests, which I accepted.

---

[1] The mathematician David Hilbert introduced a famous thought experiment in 1925, in his lecture "Über das Unendliche" ("About the Infinite"). In it, he proposed a hotel containing an infinite number of rooms, but populated by an infinite number of guests so that each room was full. Despite the hotel being full, the arrival of a new guest is not a problem. The hotel manager simply asks everyone to move into their current room number plus 1. The guest in room 1 moves to room 2, room 2 to room 3, etc. Finally, room 1 is empty and ready for the new guest.

If an *infinite* number of prospective new guests arrive, this is also not a problem. Each existing guest simply moves to their current room number times 2. Room 1 moves to room 2, room 2 to room 4, etc. Then there are an infinite number of odd-numbered rooms for the new guests to move into.

Another answer to this question is that you're done testing when the company says you are. In some companies, this might be as soon as you're done writing code (the "move fast and break things" philosophy). Other companies maintain extensive repositories of testing programs, large QA teams, and rigorous product release life cycles.

Although there are many types of tests, the ones that software engineers are most often responsible for writing and maintaining are called *unit tests*. These are small, low-level tests, each of which makes an assertion about a single unit of functionality in the software. These tests are narrow in their scope so that, if a unit test fails, it should be very easy to fix the error with only minimal follow-up debugging.

Unit tests should not test anything larger than a single method or function, with some functions and methods having many unit tests, each one asserting something about a different aspect of their logic.

In this chapter, we will use Python's unit testing framework, `unittest`, and look at strategies and best practices for writing these tests.

DIFFERENT TYPES OF TESTING

The focus of this chapter is on unit testing because these are the tests that software engineers are most frequently asked to write. However, in the software quality assurance industry, unit testing is only one small part of the testing ecosystem.

Although you may not be asked to write these other tests, familiarizing yourself with them and understanding how all the parts work together may help you write more focused and purposeful unit tests. At the very least, you may have a newfound appreciation for the complexities of QA and be driven to write more reliable code for your co-workers in that department!

Integration Tests   A single integration test covers a swath of functionality, usually a single feature of the application. For instance, it may test that a user record is ultimately updated in the database when an API endpoint receives a form submission. Integration tests span multiple services and may verify connectivity between those services.

Functional Tests   Functional tests are similar to integration tests in that they (at least usually) test a larger amount of code than a unit test. However, functional tests test against assertions received from business stakeholders. They often focus on actions the user takes and the precise results received back, checking that those results match business requirements.

End-to-End Tests   End-to-end tests are very complex tests that, as their name implies, test the entire system from the front to the back. For web applications, end-to-end tests may use browser automation tools to manipulate the website and check the responses coming back from the interface.

Because of the development and maintenance costs of automated end-to-end tests (they are often fragile), these tests are often done manually.

continues

continued

Acceptance Tests   Acceptance tests are similar to end-to-end tests but, like functional tests, focus on meeting business requirements. These are called "acceptance" tests because they're often performed as a last check before accepting the changes and pushing a new version to production.

Performance Tests   Performance tests measure software's ability to perform under a load. Often, performance tests measure the response time for a request or action. They may also place a large workload on a system, mimicking hundreds or thousands of simultaneous users, and verify that it can respond and successfully handle the load.

Although performance tests can have any scope, they are usually larger in scope, similar to an integration or end-to-end test.

Smoke Tests   These are manual tests that quickly ensure that all major functionality looks correct. They may take place when new, often major, changes are pushed. Smoke tests are usually performed manually. The tester might validate the software by logging in, checking that it loads correctly, and going through a few key features. Smoke tests do not provide full coverage, but they are a good sanity check to make sure things aren't falling over and crashing.

THE UNIT TESTING FRAMEWORK

Python's unit testing framework, `unittest`, is heavily based on the syntax of other major unit testing frameworks and will seem familiar if you've written tests in other languages.

Each individual unit test is written as a method within a class that extends `unittest.TestCase`. Each unit test contains one or more *assertions*, which can either pass (the assertion is true) or fail (the assertion is false).

Here is an example of a unit test confirming that 5 + 2 is 7:

```python
import unittest

class TestMath(unittest.TestCase):

    def test_5_plus_2(self):
        seven = 5 + 2
        self.assertEqual(seven, 7)
```

Importantly, the test method `test_5_plus_2` begins with the word `test`. Because `TestCase` classes can also contain non-test methods, all test methods must start with the word `test` to be picked up by the `unittest` framework. All tests can be run by adding the line outside of the class:

```python
unittest.main()
```

This line runs all unit tests, in classes extending `unittest.TestCase`, that have been defined in the currently running Python process.

Generally, when writing unit tests using the `unittest` framework, each class containing tests will go into its own Python file. In the case of the exercise files accompanying this book, the test class `TestMath` is in `19_test_math.py`.

Test files are run from the command line. Because these files may be imported as modules as well, it's important to prevent the tests from running when executed in anything other than the __main__ namespace. To this end, a protective wrapper is usually added at the bottom of each file:

```
if __name__ == '__main__':
    unittest.main()
```

This allows you to run the file with:

```
$ python 19_test_math.py
```

resulting in the following output:

```
.
-------------------------------------------------------------------
Ran 1 test in 0.000s

OK
```

Because it was designed to be triggered from the command line, running unit tests from inside a Jupyter notebook file is somewhat tricky. One complicating factor is that the unittest framework takes optional command-line arguments, which can be accessed using sys.argv:

```
import sys
sys.argv
```

When you're running Jupyter Lab, this sys.argv value is populated with Jupyter's system arguments instead of ones designed for unittest. This results in errors when the unit tests use the value of sys.argv and access unknown command-line arguments intended for Jupyter.

In addition, the unittest framework calls sys.exit() after finishing its run, which does not work as well inside Jupyter Lab. Although the tests will still run, it results in a confusing warning:

```
UserWarning: To exit: use 'exit', 'quit', or Ctrl-D.
```

To eliminate both issues, you can pass custom arguments as the keyword argument argv and set the keyword argument exit to False:

```
unittest.main(argv=[''], exit=False)
```

This will run all unit tests in a Jupyter notebook file. This line is equivalent to calling:

```
if __name__ == '__main__':
    unittest.main()
```

in a .py file and running it from the command line.

Although checking that 5 + 2 is equal to 7 is a good way to ensure the foundations of mathematics aren't collapsing (or that your computer hasn't malfunctioned), unit tests are best when they're testing some potentially buggy outside piece of code. For the unit test examples in this chapter, we'll use the Deck class from Chapter 11, "Classes":

```
class Deck:
    SUITS = ['SPADES', 'HEARTS', 'DIAMONDS', 'CLUBS']
    FACES = ['A', '2', '3', '4', '5', '6', '7', '8', '9', '10', 'J', 'Q', 'K']
```

```
    def __init__(self):
        self.cards = [(f, s) for s in self.SUITS for f in self.FACES]

    def shuffle(self):
        random.shuffle(self.cards)

    def deal(self, num):
        if len(self.cards) < num:
            print(f'Not enough cards to deal {num} cards')
        else:
            dealt = self.cards[0:num]
            self.cards = self.cards[num:]
            return dealt
```

In addition to a constructor, this class has two methods: `shuffle` and `deal`, which unit tests can be written for. Earlier, we saw the `assertEquals` method. This can be used to test that a deck is created with exactly 52 cards:

```
class TestDeck(unittest.TestCase):
    def test_52_cards(self):
        deck = Deck()
        self.assertEqual(len(deck.cards), 52)
```

There is also a corresponding `assertNotEquals` method. This can be used to test that a deck is shuffled:

```
    def test_shuffle(self):
        deck = Deck()
        cards_before = str(deck.cards)
        deck.shuffle()
        self.assertNotEqual(cards_before, str(deck.cards))
```

Sometimes unit tests are written very verbosely, with many assertions in a row, starting simple and building up to more complex assertions. This is a matter of personal style, but also convenient in case of test failure. You'll know exactly what went wrong when something fails!

```
class TestDeck(unittest.TestCase):
    def test_cards(self):
        deck = Deck()
        self.assertIsNotNone(deck.cards)
        self.assertIsInstance(deck.cards, list)
        self.assertNotIsInstance(deck.cards, set)
        self.assertIn(('A', 'SPADES'), deck.cards)
        self.assertEqual(len(deck.cards), 52)

unittest.main(argv=[''], exit=False)
```

A variety of `assert` methods are used here. Although it's best to use the specific `assert` method for the situation, it's worth noting that all of these can also be rewritten using only `assertTrue`:

```
        self.assertTrue(deck.cards is not None)
        self.assertTrue(type(deck.cards) == list)
        self.assertTrue(type(deck.cards) != set)
        self.assertTrue(('A', 'SPADES') in deck.cards)
        self.assertTrue(len(deck.cards) == 52)
```

Although `assertTrue` can be used for every test, the error message it gives often leaves something to be desired. For example, if we check the length of the deck of cards against 51 instead of 52, the error message produced by the `assertEqual` method is:

```
    self.assertEqual(len(deck.cards), 51)
AssertionError: 52 != 51
```

whereas `assertTrue` produces:

```
    self.assertTrue(len(deck.cards) == 51)
AssertionError: False is not true
```

For additional clarity, an optional message can be passed using the `msg` keyword argument, which will be printed only if the assertion fails:

```
    self.assertEqual(len(deck.cards), 52, msg='Decks should contain 52 cards')
```

By modifying the `FACES` list in the `Deck` class and removing the value `'K'`, only 48 cards will be created when a new deck instance is instantiated, simulating a bug:

```
FACES = ['A', '2', '3', '4', '5', '6', '7', '8', '9', '10', 'J', 'Q']
```

Running the test again produces the more verbose test failure:

```
AssertionError: 48 != 52 : Decks should contain 52 cards
```

SETTING UP AND TEARING DOWN

Perhaps the most important rule of writing unit tests is that each unit test is completely independent. That is, the success of a test should not rely on another test running beforehand, or a particular order of tests being run.

These tests may pass technically, but they fail philosophically:

```
class TestDeck(unittest.TestCase):
    deck = Deck()

    def test_one(self):
        self.deck.cards[0] = ('foo', 'bar')
        self.assertEqual(len(self.deck.cards), 52)

    def test_two(self):
        self.assertEqual(self.deck.cards[0], ('foo', 'bar'))
```

The unit test `test_two` relies on `test_one` setting the first card to `('foo', 'bar')` in order for it to pass.

Granted, if the code remains the same, the unit tests should run in the same deterministic order every time. However, code not changing in unit tests is a big ask. Unit tests are frequently added and removed. In fact, it's so common to skip individual tests that a decorator was created specifically for that purpose:

```
@unittest.skip('This will cause test_two to fail')
def test_one(self):
    self.deck.cards[0] = ('foo', 'bar')
    self.assertEqual(len(self.deck.cards), 52)
```

Now, you might accept my advice without protest and, at this very moment, are mentally promising to be a good programmer and always write independent unit tests. However, I caution you that it's very easy to *accidentally* write dependent unit tests, leading to confusing bugs. Modifying a class attribute shared between tests, like self.deck, is not always as obvious as it was in the earlier example.

Creating any required objects for tests as attributes of that test class (such as self.deck) carries the risk of dependency between unit tests if those objects are modified. However, writing this object creation over and over again inside each test method is tedious and carries the risk of accidentally writing inconsistent setups.

The way to ensure that each test gets a fresh and standardized new test environment is to do any dependency creation in setUp and tearDown methods:

```python
class TestDeck(unittest.TestCase):
    def setUp(self):
        self.deck = Deck()

    def tearDown(self):
        pass

    def test_52_cards(self):
        self.assertEqual(len(self.deck.cards), 52)

    def test_shuffle(self):
        cards_before = str(self.deck.cards)
        self.deck.shuffle()
        self.assertNotEqual(cards_before, str(self.deck.cards))

unittest.main(argv=[''], exit=False)
```

The method setUp runs before each test, and tearDown runs after each test. In this example, the setUp method creates a new Deck instance, eliminating the need to repeat the line deck = Deck() at the beginning of every unit test.

As testing setup becomes more complicated, this practice also ensures that every test starts with the same infrastructure and removes the possibility of accidentally skipped steps. For example, we could create a suite of unit tests that run tests on a deck consisting of only three specific cards, re-created for us before each test:

```python
class TestDeck(unittest.TestCase):

    def setUp(self):
        self.deck = Deck()
        self.deck.cards = [
            ('5', 'SPADES'),
            ('6', 'SPADES'),
            ('7', 'SPADES')
        ]
```

Of course, our card deck doesn't require any special teardown, so the tearDown method in TestDeck is empty and present only for the sake of example. However, if you need to close a connection or a file, this would be a convenient place to do it, as it's guaranteed to run (as long as `setUp` succeeds) even if an exception is thrown from within the unit test.

While you should be very careful when using these to avoid creating dependencies between tests, the `unittest` framework also provides the methods `setUpClass` and `tearDownClass`. These are run before and after the entire class of tests:

```
class TestDeck(unittest.TestCase):

    @classmethod
    def setUpClass(cls):
        print('This will run once, before tests')

    @classmethod
    def tearDownClass(cls):
        print('This will run once, after tests')

    def setUp(self):
        print('setup')
        self.deck = Deck()

    def test_52_cards(self):
        self.assertEqual(len(self.deck.cards), 52)

    def test_shuffle(self):
        cards_before = str(self.deck.cards)
        self.deck.shuffle()
        self.assertNotEqual(cards_before, str(self.deck.cards))
```

Because they are class methods that are not tied to a particular instance of `TestDeck`, both `setUpClass` and `tearDownClass` must be decorated with the `@classmethod` decorator and provided with a `cls` argument. When run, these tests print:

```
This will run once, before tests
TestDeck setup
TestDeck setup
This will run once, after tests
```

MOCKING METHODS

A deck of playing cards has four suits and 13 faces. Let's say you want to write a test that asserts the value and order of every card in the deck to ensure that the deck creation is working as expected. Not only is 52 a lot of cards to exhaustively list inside a test, but any changes to the order of the SUITS and FACES lists will result in a failed test, even though the deck is still valid as a deck of playing cards.

Ideally, we'd test the *behavior* of the methods rather than the exact production values they're using. Of course, we could dynamically generate the list and write a unit test like this:

```
def test_cards(self):
    expected_cards = [(f, s) for s in Deck.SUITS for f in Deck.FACES]
    self.assertEqual(self.deck.cards, expected_cards)
```

However, this is essentially just copying the code inside of the Deck class itself:

```
def __init__(self):
    self.cards = [(f, s) for s in self.SUITS for f in self.FACES]
```

Copying and pasting code into a unit test from the method it tests is dangerous. Not only are we not actually testing that logic (because the output of two identical pieces of code will always be the same), but it appears, superficially, that we do have a test written for it, which will lead to a false sense of security.

Unit tests should not be a place where we simply copy and paste business logic and call it a day, but they should demonstrate the behavior or expected result in a more hard-coded (or at least a different) way.

To test card-creation behavior without listing 52 different cards, we can *mock* aspects of a class to limit or modify its data or behavior.[2]

For example, we can, inside a unit test, temporarily mock methods in the Deck class to provide it with a smaller and more controllable set of suits and faces to create itself from. This makes it reasonable to assert the value of every card and also control the order those cards should appear in.

To do this, we create a slightly different version of the Deck class that has the methods get_suits and get_faces rather than holding these values as class attributes:

```
class Deck:
    def __init__(self):
        self.cards = [(f, s) for s in self.get_suits() for f in self.get_faces()]

    def get_suits(self):
        return ['SPADES', 'HEARTS', 'DIAMONDS', 'CLUBS']

    def get_faces(self):
        return ['A', '2', '3', '4', '5', '6', '7', '8', '9', '10', 'J', 'Q', 'K']
```

Methods like these, called getters, were discussed in Chapter 11, "Classes." There are different opinions on whether it's appropriate to modify your code to serve the purposes of a particular unit test, like we did here. In general, making code more verbose and flexible, whether for a unit test or some other purpose, is a good thing. There may be times, of course, when you find yourself spiraling down a rabbit hole and ultimately make the code worse. It's important for software engineers to learn to recognize these situations, take a step back, and rethink their unit testing approach.

Adding the methods get_suits and get_faces allows us to use the MagicMock class to write unit tests that use different versions of these methods that return different values:

```
from unittest.mock import MagicMock
```

You may also see the class unittest.mock.Mock used in various unit testing examples outside this book. MagicMock extends the class Mock and adds a bit of syntactic sugar, so it can do everything

---

[2] In software engineering (and, to some extent, engineering in general), "mock" can be used as a verb meaning to simulate something with a simplified model (we're not making fun of it!). Stubbing is very similar to mocking, as in "Let's stub this function." To "stub" a function, you might define it and leave it blank, or with a simple return value, in order to continue development and come back to fill in the rest of the function later. Mocking a function is generally done during testing, when you take a fully defined function and substitute a simpler version in a controlled fashion.

`Mock` can do, and more. You can use whichever class you want, but I will be using `MagicMock` in the examples in this book.

Whether you use `Mock` or `MagicMock`, the methods `get_suits` and `get_faces` can be mocked in the test class's `setUp` method in the same way:

```
class TestDeck(unittest.TestCase):
    def setUp(self):
        self.deck = Deck()
        self.deck.get_suits = MagicMock(return_value=['JAVA', 'RUBY'])
        self.deck.get_faces = MagicMock(return_value=['A', '2', '3'])
        self.deck.__init__()
```

A new deck instance, `self.deck` is created before each test. The deck instance's methods are set to a new `MagicMock` object with specified return values. Note that, after the deck is instantiated and the methods set to mock objects, we must explicitly call `self.deck.__init__()` again to update the cards using the new values.

After `self.deck` is created and configured, it can be used and tested as usual. There are a few other testing features enabled by the use of mock objects as well:

```
def test_card_count(self):
    self.deck.get_suits.assert_called()
    self.deck.get_faces.assert_called()
    self.assertEqual(len(self.deck.cards), 6)
    self.assertEqual(self.deck.cards, [
        ('A', 'JAVA'),
        ('2', 'JAVA'),
        ('3', 'JAVA'),
        ('A', 'RUBY'),
        ('2', 'RUBY'),
        ('3', 'RUBY')
    ])
```

`MagicMock` objects keep track of their calls and enable assertions about those calls. The most basic assertions are `assert_called` and `assert_not_called`. You can also make assertions about the exact arguments a function was called with, which we will see later in `assert_called_with`.

After asserting that both `get_suits` and `get_faces` were called, we assert that the number of cards in the deck is 6 and, finally, what their exact values are.

It's safe to say that instance methods are more common in Python than class methods; therefore, it's more common to mock instance methods in tests. However, because the card suits and faces can be better represented as *class* attributes rather than instance attributes (they do not change from deck to deck), our `Deck` class can also, and perhaps more accurately, be written like this:

```
class Deck:
    def __init__(self):
        self.cards = [(f, s) for s in self.get_suits() for f in self.get_faces()]

    @classmethod
    def get_suits(cls):
        return ['SPADES', 'HEARTS', 'DIAMONDS', 'CLUBS']

    @classmethod
    def get_faces(cls):
        return ['A', '2', '3', '4', '5', '6', '7', '8', '9', '10', 'J', 'Q', 'K']
```

This simplifies the `setUp` method:

```
class TestDeck(unittest.TestCase):
    def setUp(self):
        Deck.get_suits = MagicMock(return_value=['JAVA', 'RUBY'])
        Deck.get_faces = MagicMock(return_value=['A', '2', '3'])
        self.deck = Deck()
```

The test method `test_card_count` remains unchanged, as all class methods can be called like instance methods.

Next, let's add a couple familiar methods to the `Deck` class: `shuffle` and `deal`:

```
class Deck:
...

    def shuffle(self):
        random.shuffle(self.cards)

    def deal(self, num, shuffle=False):
        if shuffle:
            self.shuffle()
        if len(self.cards) < num:
            print(f'Not enough cards to deal {num} cards')
        else:
            dealt = self.cards[0:num]
            self.cards = self.cards[num:]
            return dealt
```

The `deal` method takes two arguments: `num`, the number of cards to deal, and `shuffle`, a Boolean, whether the deck should be shuffled before dealing. Finally, here's the standalone function (function outside the `Deck` class) we'll be testing:

```
def get_poker_hand(deck):
    return deck.deal(5, shuffle=True)
```

The test for this is straightforward. Mock the `deal` method and assert that it was called once, with the correct arguments:

```
class TestDeck(unittest.TestCase):
    def setUp(self):
        self.deck = Deck()
        self.deck.deal = MagicMock()

    def test_get_poker_hand(self):
        get_poker_hand(self.deck)
        self.deck.deal.assert_called_once()
        self.deck.deal.assert_called_with(5, shuffle=True)
```

It's important to note that the `Deck.deal` method is not actually executed in this test. The `MagicMock` instance that we replaced it with on the `self.deck` instance is executed. Therefore, the `shuffle` method is never called, and the following assertion passes:

```
            self.assertEqual(
                self.deck.cards[0:3],
                [('A', 'SPADES'), ('2', 'SPADES'), ('3', 'SPADES')]
            )
```

Additionally, if we set `shuffle` itself to a `MagicMock` object in the `setUp` method:

```
self.deck.shuffle = MagicMock()
```

the following assertion also passes:

```
self.deck.shuffle.assert_not_called()
```

As a reminder, unit testing tests one thing at a time. This also means that it should test one *layer* of code at a time. If we're testing `get_poker_hand`, we should not also be making assertions about business logic inside the `deal` method, even though `deal` might be called by `get_poker_hand`.

MOCKING WITH SIDE EFFECTS

The number of ways a deck of cards can be ordered is approximately 8 followed by 67 zeroes. That's a very big number. Not only is it larger than the estimated number of grains of sand on Earth, but it is about 2^{47} times larger than the number of grains of sand on Earth.[3]

What is the probability that a deck could be shuffled and end up in its original configuration? Well, it's technically not zero. So, it is possible that this assertion in the `test_shuffle` unit test in the previous section could fail, even though the code is working perfectly:

```
self.assertNotEqual(cards_before, str(deck.cards))
```

More realistically, however, we may want to add assertions to our unit tests that depend on having a hard-coded shuffle order. Because the `shuffle` method doesn't return anything, we can't accomplish this by mocking a function with a return value. We must mock it with, essentially, another method. To do this, we can use the `side_effect` argument.

First, we must define the function that will replace the `shuffle` method:

```
def mock_shuffle(self):
    self.cards.reverse()
```

Although this looks like a method, it is actually a standalone function outside the `Deck` class with an argument called `self`. Any algorithm could be used here to modify the order of the cards, although I chose to reverse the list simply because `reverse` is a convenient function that operates on the list in place, just like the original `shuffle` method.

We could also write a `mock_shuffle` function that creates a new list with a hard-coded order and assigns it to `self.cards`, but this is technically different behavior than the `shuffle` method (creating and assigning a new list versus operating on the list in place) and may have unintended consequences in the unit tests.

---

[3] According to one estimate of sand on Earth's beaches: www.scientificamerican.com/article/do-stars-outnumber-the-sands-of-earths-beaches. The number of card permutations can be calculated exactly as 52 factorial.

With the `mock_shuffle` function written, we can use it in our test `setUp`:

```python
class TestDeck(unittest.TestCase):
    def setUp(self):
        self.deck = Deck()
        self.deck.shuffle = MagicMock(
            side_effect=lambda: mock_shuffle(self.deck)
        )
```

Normally, `MagicMock` will call any function passed to `side_effect` with the same arguments that the original function was called with. In this case, we would expect that the deck instance would be passed `mock_shuffle`, just like the deck instance is passed to `shuffle`. However, `MagicMock` behaves a bit differently with instance arguments, and we must manually pass `self.deck` in using a lambda function.

Finally, we write the unit test:

```python
    def test_deal_with_shuffle(self):
        hand = self.deck.deal(3, shuffle=True)
        self.deck.shuffle.assert_called_once()
        self.assertEqual(hand, [
            ('K', 'CLUBS'),
            ('Q', 'CLUBS'),
            ('J', 'CLUBS'),
        ])

        self.assertEqual(self.deck.cards[0:3], [
            ('10', 'CLUBS'),
            ('9', 'CLUBS'),
            ('8', 'CLUBS'),
        ])
```

Because `self.deck.shuffle` is a mock object, we have access to all the `assert` methods about its calls, such as `assert_called_once`. We can also test the value of `self.deck.cards` and the returned hand to ensure that their values are correct, given the known shuffle order.

It's good practice to test all use cases of a function. Part of this is making sure that every line of code in the function being tested is covered by the test cases. To this end, we should test the reverse case of `test_deal_with_shuffle` and write a function where the shuffle is not requested:

```python
    def test_deal_without_shuffle(self):
        hand = self.deck.deal(3, shuffle=False)
        self.deck.shuffle.assert_not_called()
        self.assertEqual(hand, [
            ('A', 'SPADES'),
            ('2', 'SPADES'),
            ('3', 'SPADES'),
        ])

        self.assertEqual(self.deck.cards[0:3], [
            ('4', 'SPADES'),
            ('5', 'SPADES'),
            ('6', 'SPADES'),
        ])
```

Here, `assert_not_called` is used and we confirm that the cards are returned in their original order.

Exceptions can also be passed to `side_effect`, which will cause an exception to be raised when the function is called. This is handy for testing error handling without needing to more realistically create the conditions that cause that error to be raised.

Here, I'm creating an exception `CannotDeal`, something that might be thrown by the `deal` method:

```
class CannotDeal(Exception):
    def __init__(self, msg='Just cannot deal right now', *args, **kwargs):
        super().__init__(msg, *args, **kwargs)
```

No need to update the `Deck` class at all to experiment with this functionality of MagicMock—simply add it as a side effect in the test:

```
class TestDeck(unittest.TestCase):

    def setUp(self):
        self.deck = Deck()

    def test_cannot_deal_is_raised(self):
        self.deck.deal = MagicMock(side_effect=CannotDeal)
        self.assertRaises(CannotDeal, self.deck.deal, 3, shuffle=True)
```

Although we could add the mock with side effect in `setUp`, I'm choosing to add it in the individual unit test so that other unit tests in other classes can still use the `deal` method.

The method `assertRaises` checks that a particular error is raised when a function is called. The syntax for this `assert` statement might seem odd at first. Something like this might be more natural:

```
self.assertRaises(CannotDeal, self.deck.deal(3, shuffle=True))
```

The problem is that if we call `self.deck.deal(3, shuffle=True)` in the test, it will simply raise an uncaught exception and the test will fail. The function must be called carefully, surrounded with a `try`/`except` statement, by `assertRaises`. This is why we pass the function and its arguments separately to be called later.

MagicMock provides an enormous amount of flexibility and power when writing tests. It allows you to, in extreme cases, spend more time writing tests than you spend writing regular code. Well-built test suites that cover the full functionality of your application are invaluable for improving the reliability of a codebase.

On the other hand, you may also be done with testing when you don't see any bugs.

PART IV
Python Frameworks

20

REST APIs and Flask

Without *application programming interfaces* (APIs), software as we know it couldn't exist. APIs between operating systems and the software applications running on them allow for modern personal computing. The internet is essentially millions of tiny programs (web applications, routers, DNS servers) glued together by APIs.

Whenever one program wants to share information with another program, an API is required. The API defines how information will be shared and what that information means. In a literal sense, any file that can be opened by multiple programs, such as a JPEG, is an API. The JPEG file format conveys information about what the software should display, and that information can be modified and shared by any software that understands the JPEG file format.

In practice, very few would refer to JPEGs as an "API." In fact, if no other context is given, when a programmer talks about "APIs" they're usually referring specifically to *REST APIs* (Representational State Transfer APIs) over *HTTP* (Hypertext Transfer Protocol).

The "Representational State Transfer" aspect of REST APIs doesn't refer to a particular technology or language, per se, but a software architecture style. Software that follows this philosophy is designed to be modular, stateless (little stored information or "state," everything needed is transmitted in each call), and scalable.

"REST" isn't especially important to the concept of "REST APIs," however, as REST APIs have outgrown their namesake and now mostly refer to any web API that uses HTTP and sends JSON formatted results (or results with some other standardized formatting, such as XML). Because of this, I will simply refer to REST APIs as "APIs" or "web APIs" from here on out.

HTTP AND APIs

When you make a request for a website, such as www.example.com, you're making a request to a web server to fetch the contents of a specific file (in this case, an HTML file) and send it back to you. Your browser renders the resulting file as an HTML web page and may request additional assets, such as images, based on what the web page says it requires to be viewed properly.

When we request to "get" the contents of a file, we are making a *GET* request over HTTP. Similarly, when we send data to a server we are making a *POST* request.[1] GET and POST are called HTTP *methods*, and, although there are several methods defined by the HTTP specification, GET and POST are the ones encountered most frequently. You are either requesting data (GET) or sending it (POST).

When we make a GET request to a server, the server examines the URL to see which file it should return. In the case of www.example.com, the server returns the file index.html. The fact that this file is named index is simply a convention that most web servers use. The index.html file is the home-page of the website. It's what gets returned when the root domain is requested.

We can also request a specific file:

```
www.example.com/hello.html
```

This is a request to the server to return the file hello.html, if it exists. If it doesn't exist, the server will return an HTTP error. Even if you haven't spent any time working with web servers or APIs, you'll likely recognize this HTTP error: 404 page not found.

You can also make a request to return data in a subdirectory on the server:

```
www.example.com/somefolder/hello.html
```

Just like the previous URL, the first part of the URL contains the domain name, example.com. This is followed by the path /somefolder/hello.html, which tells the web server that the file hello.html in the directory somefolder is being requested.

But web servers don't have to just return hard-coded files that exist in their filesystem in response to a request. They can return anything! A web server is simply a program running on a computer that does things in response to requests. Web servers can return dynamically generated files, store the request data and return nothing, or pass the request on to another server and return that server's response.

Programs running on a web server that do things in response to HTTP requests are called web applications. Web servers that simply return files are web applications, as are those that do more interesting things.

As a silly example, a GET request to a URL like this:

```
www.example.com/mywebapp/ryan
```

may get the string "ryan" from the URL path and return a dynamically generated HTML page that says "Hello, ryan!"

In this example, the web application is like a function that receives the string argument "ryan" and in the URL path as a path parameter. It then returns an HTML web page. We don't know what this argument is called inside the web application function (what the variable name is), but let's call it name.

Although it's possible to pass information in the URL path like what was described in this scenario, and it does happen, it's more convenient to pass information as *GET parameters* (also called URL parameters or query parameters) in the URL:

```
http://example.com/mywebapp?name=ryan
```

---

[1] GET is not an acronym, but all HTTP methods are capitalized by convention.

The question mark (?) at the end of the URL indicates the end of the URL path, where the GET parameters start. The parameters themselves are key-value pairs of the form key=value and, in the case of multiple parameters, are separated by ampersands (&). Multiple GET parameters look like this:

```
http://example.com/mywebapp?first_name=Ryan&last_name=Mitchell&title=Ms
```

Path parameters and GET parameters aren't the only ways to send data in a request. HTTP requests also contain headers, or metadata about the request. *Headers* take the form of key-value pairs (called "header fields") and describe things like the content type being sent, the content types that will be accepted, the user's preferred language, and what web browser they're using.

In Chapter 2, "Programming Tools," we looked at web browser developer tools and how to use them to view network requests. I recommend that you open your developer tools again in this chapter, and in the next few, as we get into web development and web scraping. Your browser's developer tools are invaluable for examining requests and seeing where your data comes from.

In particular, you can use them to view the request and response headers of each network request by going to the Network tab and clicking on a request to view its details. A network request for a JavaScript file, script.js, can be seen in Figure 20.1.

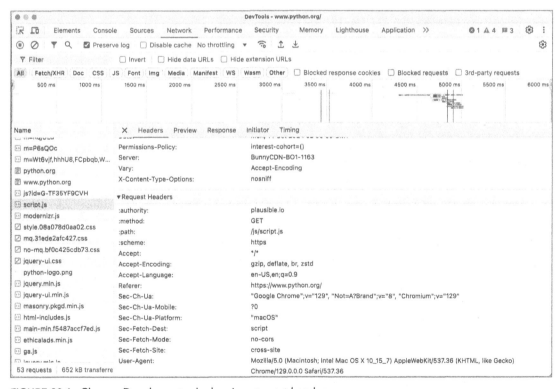

FIGURE 20.1: Chrome Developer tools showing request headers

These HTTP headers will become especially important later in this chapter when we modify the cookie field.

The HTTP requests and responses we've discussed so far are not APIs. Recall that APIs involve machines talking to machines, and, generally, machines do not want to view HTML pages. We need data that's designed for other programs, rather than humans, and that data format of choice for web APIs is JSON.[2]

You learned a bit about the JSON data format in Chapter 15, "Working with Files." APIs receive requests and return JSON objects. Here's an example of a GET request to an API:

```
http://example.com/users?user_id=123
```

Here, the path we're reaching is /users and the method we're using is GET. This indicates that we're probably retrieving some user data (like good code, good APIs are usually self-explanatory!). Then, we provide the API with a user_id of 123, fetching a particular user with that ID. This might return a JSON blob like the following:

```
{
    "id": 123,
    "first_name": "Ryan",
    "last_name": "Mitchell",
    "friend_ids": [234, 345, 456],
    "latest_post": {
        "title": "Hello, there!",
        "content": "Here is some post content",
        "timestamp": "2024-10-31 12:34:56.000Z"
    }
}
```

APIs often provide a variety of paths (or "endpoints") that allow users to filter and search data. Full-featured APIs act a bit like database queries, providing access to the data in just about any way you want to consume it. Let's look at some other examples of imaginary API queries:

```
http://example.com/users?first_name=Alice
```

This might be a search query, returning a list of all users whose first name is Alice. It's common to also add sort options onto queries:

```
http://example.com/users?first_name=Alice&sortby=last_name&sortorder=desc
```

Here, we're getting a list of all users with the first name "Alice" sorted, in descending order, by their last name.

In addition to receiving data, being able to send data to a web server using the HTTP POST method is vital to many web applications. Every time you write a social media post, send an email in your browser, or upload a file, you're making a POST request.

A POST request requires both a URL and a body. The *body* consists of data, usually JSON formatted, with the data being posted to the server. For example:

```
http://example.com/comment
```

```
{
    "post_id": 456,
    "content": "What an insightful post!",
    "user_id": 123
}
```

---

[2] I say "data format of choice" because this is the most popular format for modern APIs. APIs might also return data in XML, CSV, or some other format. Technically, there are no rules that enforce using the JSON format, and APIs are free to return data in any format they choose. However, JSON is far and away the most popular!

Here, we're submitting a comment on a social media post. The body of the API request contains the post ID, 456, our user ID (so that the website knows who authored it), 123, and, of course, the post content.

POST requests can also contain GET parameters or even use data from the URL path. For example:

```
http://example.com/post/123/comment?secrettracker=8675309


{
    "content": "What an insightful post!",
    "user_id": 123
}
```

The path /post/123/comment indicates that we're creating a comment on the post with ID 123. A secret tracker number is passed as a GET parameter, which may aid in tracking user actions for analytics or marketing purposes. The user_id and comment content are passed in the POST body.

With so many ways of passing data in HTTP from one server to the other, it's important to pay attention to your API structures as you write them to make sure that API routes are consistent and usable. For instance, passing a large amount of text content (such as a post or comment) may not be ideal as a GET parameter. URLs are limited to 2,048 characters, but most users find URLs even approaching that length to be obnoxious.

As we write web applications and APIs in Python, we'll discuss additional best practices and techniques for keeping your interfaces clean and usable.

GETTING STARTED WITH FLASK APPLICATIONS

Flask is an extremely popular and well-supported Python web framework. While it can build full websites and web applications with user interfaces, it is particularly well suited to API development. You can install it with pip:

```
$ pip install Flask
```

Although a capital F is used to install Flask according to the official instructions, pip is case-insensitive. Feel free to use an uppercase or lowercase f or even this:

```
$ pip install fLaSk
```

Because we will be developing web applications that live on running web servers in this chapter, we cannot work from within a Jupyter notebook. This is because Jupyter Lab is, itself, already a web application living on a running web server. Instead, all code for this chapter can be found within the directory 20_flask in the exercise files.

The basic goal of any web application is to receive a request and do something with it, usually by sending back some dynamic content. A basic Flask application looks like this:

```
from flask import Flask

app = Flask(__name__)

@app.route('hello')
def hello_world():
    return 'Hello, World!'
```

You can find this code in the file `20_flask/hello.py` in the exercise files for this chapter.

The variable `app` is our Flask application, and it is used to create a decorator `@app.route`. This decorator contains the URL path (`/hello`) we are mapping to the Python function `hello_world`. This is the function that will ultimately handle requests sent to that path, do something with them, and return a response.

In web app development, when a URL path is mapped to a particular function for handling requests to that path, that is called a *route*. We are defining a new API route using the decorator `@app.route`.

The function that handles the request is often called an *endpoint*. You might also hear URLs or paths referred to as "endpoints," depending on the context.

The term `endpoint` is somewhat philosophical. It refers to the logic that returns a response. If multiple URL paths map to the same response-returning logic, they are said to be the same endpoint. Different routes may also map to the same endpoint.

In our simple Flask application, the path `/hello` is mapped to an endpoint that returns the response `"Hello, World!"`. We can see this in action by running the server using the command:

```
$ flask --app hello run
```

Here, we're providing the module name for our application using the `--app` flag. The file is named `hello.py` and the module name is `hello`, so the command is `--app hello`.

This runs a small development server on your computer at `http://127.0.0.1:5000`. This development server also comes with a serious warning:

```
WARNING: This is a development server. Do not use it in a production deployment.
Use a production WSGI server instead.
```

The server that comes with Flask is suitable for local development purposes only. If you're happy with your application and want it released to the world, you will need to consult resources outside this book to do that. The official Flask documentation for deploying applications can be found at `https://flask.palletsprojects.com/en/3.0.x/deploying`.

Once the server is running, you can navigate to the path we provided to the decorator: `http://127.0.0.1:5000/hello` to view the output, which hopefully looks like this:

Hello, World!

This is not a very interesting web application we've built, but it is technically a web application!

A homepage is the content that is returned when no URL path is specified — that is, when the path is empty. We can add a homepage for our web app by creating a new route and endpoint:

```
@app.route('/')
def home():
    return '''
    <html>
        <head>
            <title>My cool new web app</title>
        </head>
        <body>
            <h1>Spanish Inquisition</h1>
```

```
        <p>
            In the early years of the 16th century, to combat the rising tide of
    religious unorthodoxy, the Pope gave Cardinal Ximinez of Spain leave to move
    without let or hindrance throughout the land, in a reign of violence, terror and
    torture that makes a smashing film. This was the Spanish Inquisition...
        </p>
    </body>
</html>
'''
```

When you make changes to the code in your Flask application, you will need to stop and start the web server again to see those changes appear. After restarting the web server and navigating to `http://127.0.0.1:5000`, you should see some HTML content. This is still a static page, but at least it's more interesting than plain text.

To make dynamic content, we need to get information passed in from the user and add that information to the response. Let's create a basic profile page for a social media website that displays the user's name. That name will be passed in as GET parameters in the URL, like this:

```
http://127.0.0.1:5000/profile?first_name=Ryan&last_name=Mitchell
```

To use the value of any GET parameter in the URL, we can use Flask's `request` object:

```python
from flask import request

@app.route('/profile')
def profile():
    name = f'{request.args.get("first_name")} {request.args.get("last_name")}'
    return f'<html><body><h1>{name}</h1></body></html>'
```

A dictionary of all GET parameters for the current request is contained in `request.args`, which makes it easy to use in the response data. Again, make sure you restart the Flask server from the terminal before checking for changes.

Of course, it's not guaranteed that the GET parameters `first_name` and `last_name` will be present in the request. If they're not provided by the user, the page will read None None. This isn't the worst result in the world, but it might be useful to give some sort of error message to help us and other developers debug the page later.

We can return any HTTP exception in Flask using the *Werkzeug* library, which is installed with Flask:

```python
from werkzeug.exceptions import BadRequest
```

In this case we'll raise a Bad Request, which has the HTTP error code 400. Simply check for the presence of both `first_name` and `last_name` values and return a new `BadRequest` instance, with an optional error message, if they're not present:

```python
@app.route('/profile')
def profile():
    if not (request.args.get('first_name') and request.args.get('last_name')):
        return BadRequest('Missing required parameters first_name and last_name')
    name = f'{request.args.get("first_name")} {request.args.get("last_name")}'
    return f'<html><body><h1>{name}</h1></body></html>'
```

When the page at `http://127.0.0.1:5000/profile` is visited without any parameters present, it displays this:

Bad Request
Both first_name and last_name are required

A complete list of HTTP exceptions in the Werkzeug library can be found at `https://werkzeug.palletsprojects.com/en/3.0.x/exceptions`. Some popular ones are `NotFound`, `NotAuthorized`, and `InternalServerError`.[3] Note that an `InternalServerError` will also be returned automatically by Flask if any of the endpoints raise uncaught exceptions.

In addition to GET parameters, Flask can use path parameters in endpoints. Path parameters are variables passed into the URL path itself, as in:

```
http://127.0.0.1:5000/profile/ryan/mitchell
```

The `profile_path` function uses path parameters of this form:

```
@app.route('/profile/<firstname>/<lastname>')
def profile_path(firstname, lastname):
    return f'<html><body><h1>{firstname} {lastname}</h1></body></html>'
```

In this case, two path parameters, `firstname` and `lastname`, are indicated inside the route string in the `@app.route` decorator using less than and greater signs. The variable names used in the path are then passed as arguments to the `profile_path` function where they can be used to return a response.

APIs IN FLASK

In the previous section, our web application returned text or HTML data designed for human consumption. Now we need to return JSON to make these APIs suitable for machine consumption.

Here's a very useful API endpoint that provides the factorial of the given number, `num`, for any machines that might need to consume such information:

```
import math

@app.route('/factorial')
def factorial():
    num = int(request.args.get('num', 0))
    return {
        'factorial': math.factorial(num),
        'num': num
    }
```

---

[3] My personal favorite is HTTP error code 418, `ImATeapot` (`https://datatracker.ietf.org/doc/html/rfc2324`), which should be used if the coffee pot you are sending an HTTP request to is actually a teapot.

This was created as an April Fools' Day joke by a publication called Request For Comments (RFC), which usually publishes more serious internet standards, such as the standard for HTTP itself. Unlike many of the RFC's April Fools' Day jokes (`www.cs.hmc.edu/~awooster/joke_rfcs.html`), HTTP error code 418 didn't just get a couple of laughs and get forgotten—it started getting implemented into software that generated and displayed error codes, such as web browsers, web applications, and, yes, the Werkzeug library.

Although its status as an "official" HTTP error code is complicated, 418 continues to receive widespread support. As vocal 418 supporter Shane Brunswick says on his website (`http://save418.com`): "It's a reminder that the underlying processes of computers are still made by humans."

This returns a set of JSON key-value pairs. Here's another endpoint that returns a list of all numbers less than the given number, num:

```
@app.route('/lessthan')
def lessthan():
    num = int(request.args.get('num', 0))
    return [i for i in range(num)]
```

Although I've stressed previously that Python objects are not JSON strings, Flask allows us to return a dictionary or list and converts it automatically to JSON-formatted data. Prior to 2019, this required explicitly wrapping any returned Python objects in the `Flask.jsonify` function, like this:

```
return jsonify({
    'factorial': math.factorial(num),
    'num': num
})
```

However, using `jsonify` directly is no longer necessary as Flask calls it for us behind the scenes. It's worth noting, however, that `jsonify` uses the Python `json` package to convert Python objects to JSON. If you're dealing with a JSON object that cannot be deserialized to JSON by `json.dumps`, you will need to explicitly write a deserialization function for it or use a third-party library to handle turning the object into JSON.

We've seen the request object before, when working with arguments passed in a request. While it's technically possible to write a Flask application without `request`, it's basically a requirement to use when writing APIs, so you should import both `Flask` and `request` with a single import:

```
from Flask import Flask, request
```

The `request` object represents the current HTTP request being handled by the application. Although a Flask application running on a server is capable of handling multiple requests simultaneously (using multiple threads or processes, depending on the configuration), this `request` instance is guaranteed to represent only one request — the one being handled by the server in the thread or process you are writing for.

The request object has many useful attributes, including these:

➤ **args:** We've seen this before. This contains any arguments passed into the query string.

➤ **method:** The HTTP method of the request. If an endpoint accepts multiple methods (such as both GET and POST), this is what you check to see which method you're dealing with.

➤ **headers:** An `EnvironHeaders` object, which contains all headers as key-value pairs. You can access headers with the get method—for example, `request.headers.get('cookie')`.

➤ **cookies:** A dictionary-like object (technically an `ImmutableMultiDict`) containing all cookies parsed from the cookie string.

The `request` object also contains the following attributes that will give you data sent in the body of a POST request in various formats:

➤ **data:** A bytes object containing the posted data, regardless of its type

➤ **json:** Python object containing JSON data

➤ **form:** Python object containing form data

➤ **files:** File data uploaded from a form

One request header that you may need to pay attention to is Content-Type. This is modified by Flask automatically when a response is sent. Your browser will receive a content type of text/html when HTML is sent and application/json when JSON data is sent. However, when requests are being sent by your browser with posted data, you may need to change the headers manually.

Although our browsers send POST queries all the time when interacting with web applications (such as when we're submitting a form), it is difficult to write and trigger a POST request in the same way we can enter a URL into the URL bar and trigger a GET request. For POST requests, most API developers use a browser extension specifically for API testing and development.

You can get a REST API testing browser extension from your browser's extension catalog by searching for **REST API tester** or similar. For Chrome, which is my web browser of choice, I prefer the Talend API Tester (see Figure 20.2), although they all work similarly.

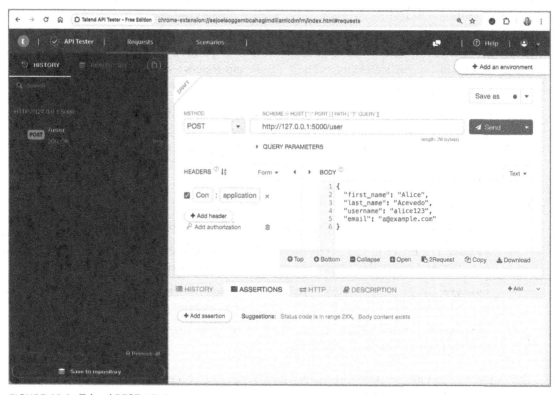

FIGURE 20.2: Talend REST API Tester

A suitable API tester needs to have a place to put the request URL, a way to change the HTTP method, a way to add and remove headers, and the ability to send JSON in the POST body.

To send POST data to APIs using an API tester, make sure that your headers correctly reflect the data being sent. You can test this by using your API tester to send POST data to http://127.0.0.1:5000/headers when running the hello.py file.

In the next sections, we will be writing and testing many Flask APIs that accept POST requests and use the JSON body associated with that request.

DATABASES

In Chapter 18, "Databases," we looked at reading from and writing to databases with Python. Databases are used to persist data in most modern web applications. In this section, we'll use SQLite to create an API that searches, filters, and creates user records in a database.

First, we'll use the following table definition, found in 20_flask/user_app.py in the exercise files:

```
CREATE TABLE Users(
    user_id INTEGER PRIMARY KEY AUTOINCREMENT,
    first_name VARCHAR(32),
    last_name VARCHAR(32),
    username VARCHAR(32),
    email VARCHAR(64),
    password_hash VARCHAR(32),
    last_login DATETIME DEFAULT CURRENT_TIMESTAMP
);
```

You will also want to run the INSERT statement found in this file to insert our friends Alice, Bob, Charlie, and Daria from Chapter 18. After this data is set up, writing the endpoint to fetch user data by user_id should be straightforward:

```
@app.route('/user', methods=['GET'])
def get_user_by_id():
    with sqlite3.connect('unlocking-python.db') as conn:
        cur = conn.cursor()
        fetch_query = f'''
            SELECT
                user_id, first_name, last_name, username, email, last_login
            FROM Users
            WHERE user_id = {request.args.get('user_id')}
        '''
        cur.execute(fetch_query)
        return cur.fetchall()
```

We can now send a request like http://127.0.0.1:5000/user?user_id=1 and get back the user Alice. Unfortunately, we can also abuse this endpoint to get back a list of all users:

```
http://127.0.0.1:5000/user?user_id=1%20OR%201=1
```

The `%20` here is a URL-encoded space character. This translates to a user ID of `"1 OR 1=1"`. When this string is put directly into the WHERE clause of the select query, it becomes:

```
SELECT
    user_id, first_name, last_name, username, email, last_login
FROM Users
WHERE user_id = 1 OR 1=1
```

When this query is executed, the WHERE statement always evaluates to True and it returns all records in the Users table. This type of attack is called an *SQL injection attack*. This might seem like a trivial or innocuous example, but attacks like this allow hackers to access user accounts and reveal secret information. They're also easily preventable.

The following allows only a single value to be passed in and will escape any SQL query language that is injected:

```
fetch_query = f'''
    SELECT
        user_id, first_name, last_name, username, email, last_login
    FROM Users
    WHERE user_id = ?
'''
cur.execute(fetch_query, (request.args.get('user_id'),))
```

The question mark (`?`) in the query is a *parameter marker*. Different SQL libraries allow different styles of parameter markers. A complete list of parameter marker styles can be found in PEP 249 (`https://peps.python.org/pep-0249/#paramstyle`).

Using a parameter marker tells your SQL library that you are expecting a single value to be passed in at that location, and it prevents any SQL from being injected.

Some also use Python "percent formatting" to create query strings:

```
user_id = int(request.args.get('user_id'))
fetch_query = '''
    SELECT
        user_id, first_name, last_name, username, email, last_login
    FROM Users
    WHERE user_id = %d
''' % (str(user_id,))

cur.execute(fetch_query)
```

Because this doesn't depend on the SQL library at all but is a Python string function, it can be used regardless of what kind of database you're using. It uses three parameter markers: `%s` (string), `%d` (integer number), and `%f` (float number) to insert data. Because of this parameter type system, we must convert the URL parameter value (which will always come in as a string) to an integer before formatting it with the query.

Unfortunately, using percent formatting or other types of Python string formatting like this can leave your applications vulnerable to injection attacks. Providing a user ID of `1; DROP TABLE Users;` might cause some damage if the query interpreter executes this successfully as two statements. In general, it is safer to use the parameter styles provided by the SQL library, such as qmark, rather than generating your own SQL query strings.

Using the browser-based API tester installed in the previous section, we can start writing API endpoints in Flask that use the POST method. First, we need to let Flask know that this endpoint should accept POST requests:

```
@app.route('/user', methods=['POST'])
```

By default, Flask APIs only accept requests using the GET method. Note that the methods argument is a list, meaning endpoints can accept multiple methods. Sometimes logic can change based on the method used in a particular request. For this, you can use request.method. For example:

```
if request.method == 'GET':
    user_id = request.args.get('user_id')
else:
    ...
```

As a general rule, HTTP requests using GET should fetch information. HTTP requests using POST to create information. Therefore, if we want to create new users, we need to use the POST method. The create_user function uses the JSON-formatted POST body of a request and does just that:

```
@app.route('/user', methods=['POST'])
def create_user():
    with sqlite3.connect('unlocking-python.db') as conn:
        cur = conn.cursor()
        data = request.json
            insert_query = '''
            INSERT INTO Users (
                first_name, last_name, username, email
            )
            VALUES
            (?, ?, ?, ?)
            '''
        cur.execute(insert_query, (
            data.get('first_name'),
            data.get('last_name'),
            data.get('username'),
            data.get('email')
        ))
        conn.commit()
        return { 'id': cur.lastrowid }
```

There are a few ways to get POST data out of a request. The first, request.data, contains binary data regardless of the request type. This is useful for handling file uploads, for example.

For form submissions, you can use request.form to get form values as a dictionary. In create_user, we're using request.json, which parses the JSON body and returns it as a Python dictionary or list.

Next, the insert query is created using the percent formatter to insert a new User record with the string fields first_name, last_name, username, and email. Because we are inserting new data we need to call conn.commit() to commit this modification.

Finally, there is a useful attribute of the database connection cursor called lastrowid. This contains the value of the most recently generated ID by that cursor. That is, if the cursor inserts a new record into a table that has an AUTOINCREMENT column like in the Users table:

```
user_id INTEGER PRIMARY KEY AUTOINCREMENT
```

the value lastrowid will be set to that latest ID.

Especially in high-traffic databases, this is not only an *easy* way to get the ID for the last inserted record, but it's the only feasible way to do it at all. Even if we write a separate query to fetch the most recently created user, there's no guarantee that another record won't be written between the time our new user was created and when we fetch its ID, returning the ID of a completely different user.

AUTHENTICATION

The Users table in this chapter has a column that didn't exist in the similar table from Chapter 18:

```
password_hash VARCHAR(32),
```

A *hash function*, in computer science, is a function that can take data of any size and map it to a fixed-size value. This fixed-size value is called a *hash*. A simple example of a hash function is a modulo operation:

```
123456 % 10 = 6
```

No matter how big the value on the left is, "modulo 10" means that it will always map, or "hash," to a single digit, in this case, 6. If we want our hashes to be longer, we can also use `% 100` or `% 1000`. This is because using a modulus of 100 will give us the remainder after dividing a number by 100, which will provide numbers up to three digits long. The modulus of 1,000 will, of course, provide numbers up to four digits long.

It's also important to note that if you have the hash, 6, there's no way of telling what the original value was. It could have been 106, 31415926, or simply 6.

These properties make hash functions extremely useful for handling passwords and authentication in web apps. Rather than storing the original passwords in the database, web applications use very complex and secure hash functions (no, not a modulo!) that turn a password like `Top_S3cret!1` into the 64-character string:

```
d1909bc868a1854855590dee3739bc4f9a1695d7bddce9976e26d2ef372aafcb
```

This 64 character hash is what's stored in the database and the original plain-text password is discarded. Even if an attacker gains access to the database, there's no way to turn that hash back into the original password.[4]

When a user tries to log in with their password, you can simply turn that entered password into a hash and compare that hash against the one stored in the database. If the hashes match, the password was correct. If the hashes don't match, the password was incorrect.

---

[4] There is an important caveat to this. There are a limited number of common hashing algorithms in the world. This means that hackers can take millions of known plain-text passwords, run each password through all the common hashing algorithms, and store each hash in a database. When they find a hash like `d1909bc8...`, they can look up that value in their database to see if `Top_S3cret!1` happened to be one of the passwords that they processed. These databases are called "rainbow tables."

One easy way to prevent these rainbow table attacks is to use what's called a "salt." Simply take the plain-text password, add some random data to the end that only you know (the salt), and hash that entire password+salt before inserting it into the database. Unless the attackers know your salt and can create new rainbow tables for only your database, the hashes cannot be resolved back to their original passwords.

Knowing the hash, but not the actual password, also means that we're unable to provide the user with their password even when they ask for it. This is one reason why websites have a "password reset" button, but not many of them have a "get my password" button.

We can implement a simple, but secure, login system in our User application. First, we need to update every record in the User table to have a populated `password_hash` field.

Note that, in production, one should never update their User table such that all records have the same default password. In a worst-case scenario where all user records need their passwords reset, unique randomly generated passwords should be created for each user, the user gets notified of the new password (usually via email), and the plain-text password is discarded. With that in mind, this will update every record in the Users table so that they all have the password `password`:

```
UPDATE User SET
password_hash='5e884898da28047151d0e56f8dc6292773603d0d6aabbdd62a11ef721d1542d8'
```

This hash, `'5e884898...'`, is the UTF-8 representation of the string `"password"` using the popular hashing algorithm SHA256. This hashing algorithm was chosen because it can be generated using the Python standard library. If you are creating a production application, I recommend using a more secure and complex hashing algorithm such as Argon2 or Bcrypt, which can also be easily generated using third-party Python packages.

As usual, this SQL query can be found in the `user_app.py` file in the exercise files.

This `login` function is somewhat longer than the code samples we've seen in the past, but, when broken down, is not very complicated:

```python
from werkzeug.exceptions import BadRequest, Unauthorized
import hashlib


@app.route('/login', methods=['POST'])
def login():
    data = request.json
    username = data.get('username')
    password = data.get('password')
    if not username or not password:
        return BadRequest('Must provide username and password to log in')

    password_hash = hashlib.sha256(password.encode('utf-8')).hexdigest()
    match_query = f'''
        SELECT user_id FROM Users
        WHERE username = ?
        AND password_hash = ?
    '''
    with sqlite3.connect('unlocking-python.db') as conn:
        cur = conn.cursor()
        cur.execute(match_query, (username, password_hash))
        user_id = cur.fetchone()
        if user_id:
            user_id = user_id[0]
            session = create_session(user_id, conn)
            resp = make_response({'id': user_id})
            resp.set_cookie('session_id', session)
            return resp
    return Unauthorized('Authentication failed')
```

You can test this endpoint using the URL `http://127.0.0.1:5000/login` with the POST body:

```
{
  "username": "alice123",
  "password": "password"
}
```

The first thing `login` does is get the username and password from the POST body. If they don't exist, or they're empty strings, a `BadRequest` exception is returned to the user.

Then, the SHA256 algorithm is used to get a hash string:

```
hashlib.sha256(password.encode('utf-8')).hexdigest()
```

Although we might speak and think about hashing algorithms as if they're strings being transformed into strings, it's important to remember that they're simply data (bytes) being hashed into data. Because of this, Python's `hashlib.sha256` function accepts a `bytes` object, which can be created using `str.encode`, and returns a `sha256` hash object, which can be converted into a hexadecimal representation of its bytes using the `hexdigest` method.

Once the password has been hashed, we can declare the login successful if both the username and password hash match a record in the database. If a record is found, we return the `user_id`.

So, after the user has successfully "logged in," what happens? Right now, nothing. There is nothing that keeps them logged in, no record of successful authentication, no special data they can access. This API is a one-time thumbs up that they gave us the correct password and that's it. To keep them logged in, we need a *session*.

SESSIONS

When you log into a website, you remain logged into that site across multiple browser tabs. You may even be able to close the browser entirely, reopen it, and still be logged in. The only way for you to log into that website is through the website itself—you cannot visit a third-party site or application and have them log in for you. This is all accomplished with sessions.

Information like "Is this user logged in and, if so, who are they logged in as?" is stored as session data. Session data is secure. It cannot be read by third parties and it cannot be written by third parties. If your web application sees that a particular value is stored in the session, you can be guaranteed that your application was the one that generated and wrote that value.

On the client (user) side, session data is stored in *cookies* in the web browser. A cookie is a small piece of data that is stored and managed by the web browser and is associated with a single domain name. Cookies are stored as a series of key-value pairs. Whenever an HTTP request is made for a URL, the browser sends any stored cookies associated with the URL's domain as part of the HTTP headers in that request.

Cookies store items you have in a shopping cart, which ad you click on that brings you to a site, and how many pages you visit. Unlike sessions, general cookie data is not secret nor guaranteed to be created by that website or domain itself. Users can modify and write their own cookie data for any domain. However, sessions, which are stored inside cookies, are not modifiable (at least not without being rendered invalid) by anyone else.

There are many ways to write a user session mechanism that keeps track of users who are authenticated, as well as any data associated with those users. Flask even has its own session tool: https://flask.palletsprojects.com/en/3.0.x/api/#sessions.

To use sessions in Flask, start by importing session and adding a secret key to the top of your file:

```
from flask import Flask, request, session

app.secret_key = 'CHANGE_ME'
```

This secret key is used for encrypting and signing cookies, and should be set to a long random string, similar to a password. This is done to ensure that the only one able to create valid cookies is your application. If you get a user with session data containing, say, a username, you can be confident that your application was the one that set that username, not some other application or the user themselves.

Using a strong secret key allows you to set user information after a successful login and assume that anyone with their user information in the session is successfully authenticated.

Next, simply set and retrieve data using the session object:

```
@app.route('/set-session-data', methods=['GET'])
def set_session_data():
    data = request.args.get('data')
    session['data'] = data
    return f'Set session data: {data}'

@app.route('/get-session-data', methods=['GET'])
def get_session_data():
    if 'data' not in session:
        return 'No session data set'
    return f'Session data is: {session['data']}'
```

This defines two endpoints at http://127.0.0.1:5000/set-session-data and http://127.0.0.1:5000/get-session-data. The first, set-session-data, can be visited with query parameters like ?data=foo, which will store the value foo under the key data in that user's session. Then, when visiting the page http://127.0.0.1:5000/get-session-data, it will display:

Session data is: foo

If you open an incognito window or clear your cookies and revisit the same page, you should see this:

No session data set

I don't usually like reinventing the wheel, and Flask's built-in session mechanism is great and easy to implement. However, there are many ways to use and implement sessions, and I'd like to explore one other method of doing it. Writing a session-handling system also brings together multiple concepts in API development and practice using Flask.

One way of securely setting and reading sessions, without the risk of data being modified by another application and without using secret keys, is to store the data yourself. These sessions have *session IDs*. These are very long random strings that are stored either in a database or in memory and are associated with the user ID of the logged-in user. The session ID is also sent to the user to store in their browser. Whenever a user requests some data, they provide the session ID with their request.

Let's write a session system that allows users to log in and keeps them logged in and authenticated while browsing the website. To keep users logged in as part of our User API system, we first need to create a Session table:

```
CREATE TABLE Session(
    user_id INTEGER PRIMARY KEY,
    session_id VARCHAR(32),
    expiration_date DATETIME
);
```

The user_id is the primary key in the Session table, which means that user_id is a unique column—each user can have only one session (even if that session is expired). Although there are many ways to implement this system, for simplicity of development, let's assume that each user has exactly one session record. Because no user can have *zero* session records, we must run a query that populates the Session table with empty records for all users:

```
INSERT INTO Session (user_id)
    SELECT user_id FROM Users;
```

Now, when a user logs in, we must create a new session ID, store it with an appropriate expiration date, and return that session id to the user so they can set it in their cookies.

To do this, we can create a function called create_session:

```
import uuid
from datetime import datetime, timedelta

def create_session(user_id, conn):
    session_id = uuid.uuid1().hex
    session_query = f'''
        UPDATE Session
        SET session_id = ?, expiration_date = ?
        WHERE user_id = ?
    '''
    print(session_query)
    cur = conn.cursor()
    cur.execute(session_query, (
        session_id,
        datetime.today() + timedelta(days=1),
        int(user_id),
    ))
    return session_id
```

This function does not have an API route, but is a utility called by other functions, such as login. To promote connection reuse, a database connection is passed to create_session by the calling function, rather than it creating its own.

To create the session ID, create_session uses the Python uuid library. *UUIDs* are called universally unique identifiers for a reason. They are essentially very large random numbers that are guaranteed to be unique regardless of how many of them you have stored in your database. This allows us to look up a user_id based only on the session ID they provide us, regardless of how many other users we have.

The session expiration date is set, arbitrarily, at one day from the current date. This forces users to log in and generate a new session ID every 24 hours. The timedelta function from the Python datetime library is used to generate a timestamp one day in the future. This date object can be passed directly to SQLite3 and is converted to a string appropriately.

Finally, the query to update the Session table is executed and the generated session ID is returned.

The login function has additional responsibilities as well. If a user enters the correct password, the function must get a new session ID from create_session and set that session ID in a cookie:

```
from flask import make_response
def login():

    ...

        if user_id:
            user_id = user_id[0]
            session = create_session(user_id, conn)
            resp = make_response({'id': user_id})
            resp.set_cookie('session_id', session)
            return resp
```

If all you want to do in the request is return string data like HTML or JSON, you can return the string like we've been doing. However, Flask's make_response function is useful for modifying headers, HTTP status codes, and other properties. Here, we're setting the cookie and adding the session ID with the key session_id.

Now that we can set a session ID when a user logs in, we need to be able to read that session ID and recognize that user as being authenticated. To do that, I've created a utility function called authorize_request, which takes a connection, conn, as an argument, and determines whether the current request is from an authenticated user. If the user is authenticated it returns the user_id.

```
def authorize_request(conn):
    session_id = request.cookies.get('session_id')
    if not session_id:
        return None
    authorize_query = f'''
    SELECT user_id FROM Sessions
    WHERE session_id = ?
    AND expiration_date > CURRENT_TIMESTAMP
    '''
    cur = conn.cursor()
    cur.execute(authorize_query, (session_id,))
    user_id = cur.fetchone()
    if user_id:
        return user_id[0]
    return None
```

Recall that the session ID was set in the cookie under the key session_id. Now, we retrieve the session_id from the cookie and use it to query the database for a user_id. We need to check the expiration date as well, only retrieving sessions where expiration_date is greater than (in the future, relative to) the current timestamp.

We can set up a simple API endpoint, `whoami`, which uses the `authorize_request` function to return the `user_id` of logged-in users:

```
@app.route('/whoami')
def whoami():
    with sqlite3.connect('unlocking-python.db') as conn:
        return {'user_id': authorize_request(conn)}
```

To see this in action, make a POST request to `http://127.0.0.1/login` with valid credentials of this form:

```
{
  "username": "<username>",
  "password": "password"
}
```

where *<username>* is the username of any user in the database (assuming the default password of `password` is still set for all users). Then visit `http://127.0.0.1/whoami` to see a response containing that user's ID.

TEMPLATES

Flask is a tool for creating both JSON APIs and HTML websites. Previously, we saw examples where endpoints returned dynamically generated HTML (as trivial as the dynamic attributes were). However, returning HTML strings generated in this way is not a particularly scalable or robust solution.

Flask templates allow for HTML pages to be kept in their own files, apart from Python code. Rather than reinvent the wheel, Flask uses the template language *Jinja2*, which allows you to insert data, insert HTML blocks from other templates, loop through lists, and do simple control flow based on the parameters passed to the template.

To demonstrate this templating language, let's construct a basic HTML page showing information about the logged-in user.

By default, Flask looks for templates in the `templates` directory. The following template is in the exercise files at `20_flask/templates/profile.html`:

```
<html>
    <head>
        <title>User Profile</title>
    </head>
    <body>
        <h3>Profile Page</h3>
        First name: {{ user.first_name }}<br/>
        Last name: {{ user.last_name }}<br/>
        Email: {{ user.email }}<br/>
        Username: {{ user.username }}<br/>
    </body>
</html>
```

The double curly brackets (`{{ }}`) indicate a variable inserted into the template. In this case, we are passing a User object with various attributes into the template. The User class is straightforward and designed to be constructed from a tuple of data retrieved from the database:

```
class User:
    def __init__(self, data):
        self.first_name = data[0]
        self.last_name = data[1]
        self.username = data[2]
        self.email = data[3]
```

Tying this all together, we have the Flask endpoint, `profile`:

```
from flask import render_template

@app.route('/profile', methods=['GET'])
def profile():
    with sqlite3.connect('unlocking-python.db') as conn:
        user_id = authorize_request(conn)
        if not user_id:
            return Unauthorized('Need to log in')
        user_query = f'''
            SELECT first_name, last_name, username, email
            FROM Users
            WHERE user_id = ?
        '''
        cur = conn.cursor()
        cur.execute(user_query, (int(user_id),))
        user = User(cur.fetchone())
    return render_template('profile.html', user=user)
```

This fetches the `user_id` for the currently logged-in user using `authorize_request` and returns an HTTP error if no user is logged in. Using that `user_id`, it retrieves profile information from the database and initializes a new `User` instance. Finally, it passes `user` to the `render_template` function along with the template's filename (`profile.html`) and returns the result as the HTTP response.

One of the nice features of Flask templates is template blocks. We can make putting together new web pages easy by defining header, footer, and base template HTML files in the `templates` directory.

header.html:

```
<h1>A Website for Users</h1>
```

footer.html:

```
<span>Copyright 2024 ACME Social Co.<span>
```

base.html:

```
<html>
    <head>
        <title>Site for Users</title>
        <style>
            div {
                    margin: 20px 0px;
                }
        </style>
    </head>
    <body>
        <div class="header">
            {% include "header.html" %}
```

```
        </div>
        <div class="content">
        {% block content %} {% endblock %}
        </div>
        <div class="footer">
        {% include "footer.html" %}
        </div>
    </body>
</html>
```

In the Flask template language, anything surrounded by curly brackets and percent signs ({% %}) is called a *tag*. Tags contain bits of programming logic and can be used to import templates, evaluate statements, and execute loops and other control flow.

Both the header and footer are required by base.html and referenced inside the {% include %} tags, which show where they will be placed inside the base template.

An additional {% block %} tag defines a new block called content, which is a placeholder for content defined in templates that extend the base template. This is where individual page content will go when the base template is used.

Finally, we create profile.html, which extends the base template and defines its content block between {% block content %} and {% endblock %} tags:

```
{% extends 'base.html' %}
{% block content %}
        <h3>Profile Page</h3>
        First name: {{ user.first_name }}<br/>
        Last name: {{ user.last_name }}<br/>
        Email: {{ user.email }}<br/>
        Username: {{ user.username }}<br/>
{% endblock %}
```

Restart the Flask server and reload http://127.0.0.1:5000/profile to see the new profile page with a header and footer.

In the next chapter, we will be working with another popular web framework called Django. Although Django and Flask do, technically, use different template engines to parse and render their templates, they have a very similar syntax. In fact, the techniques we've used with Flask templates here are directly applicable to Django templates as well.

If you want to build web applications with Flask, I recommend that you also read the next chapter about Django. Not only will you learn more about the common Flask and Django template syntax, but you might discover that your application is better suited for the more complex web application framework.

21

Django

Django is a large open source web framework, with contributors all around the world. Like Flask, it can be used to create simple APIs. Unlike Flask, it has a built-in user authentication and management system that can be configured from an admin GUI. Out-of-the-box, Django is designed to create complex user-facing web applications.

Development began on Django in 2003 by two programmers, Adrian Holovaty and Simon Willison. They were working at the Kansas newspaper *Lawrence Journal-World*, which at the time was using a PHP content management system. Holovaty and Willison created Django out of a desire to rewrite the newspaper's website in Python. While they initially created a content management system specific to their own website, it gradually became more generalized and abstract until it was published as an open source project by the newspaper in 2005.

Today, many large and popular websites use Django, including Instagram, Pinterest, YouTube, and Dropbox. Ironically, in 2018 the *Lawrence Journal-World* re-created its website again and switched it to WordPress, a PHP content management system.

The *Django Software Foundation* (DSF) is a nonprofit organization that supports the Django project. Like the Python Software Foundation, the DSF's mission is to promote the development and use of Django.

The DSF organizes local meetup groups in many cities around the world (www.djangoproject .com/community/local), hosts online forums for Django discussions, and awards recognition and prizes to volunteers who have made outstanding contributions to the community.

The Django framework is designed around the concept of projects that contain multiple apps. Each app is an independent module responsible for a feature or related set of features within the project. For example, an app might add the ability to create blog posts with comments on those blog posts. A larger app might provide complete e-commerce functionality, and a smaller app might generate neat drop-down menus or a color picker.

Good Django apps are self-contained, and information is not directly passed between apps. Ideally, you should be able to delete an app from a project and have that project continue to operate normally (albeit without the specific functionality provided by the app).

Another nice feature of Django is that it comes prepopulated with apps that provide functionality for user accounts, security groups, and an admin interface to help configure and manage the website.

Although Django does have a GUI and some nice low- or no-code features, it still requires Python programming and an understanding of its major components to use effectively.

INSTALLING DJANGO AND STARTING DJANGO

As usual, Django can be installed with `pip`:

```
$ pip install Django
```

After Django is installed, you will need to use its command-line tool, `django-admin`, to create a new project. The project we'll be building in this chapter has already been created in the directory `21_django` in the exercise files. If you want to follow along and create your own project, feel free to create a different directory, navigate to it, and follow the directions from there.

To create a new project, type the following:

```
$ django-admin startproject unlockingpython .
```

This creates the project, `unlockingpython`, in the current directory. In it, you should see the following files and directories:

- ➤ `manage.py`
- ➤ `unlockingpython`
    - ➤ `__init__.py`
    - ➤ `asgi.py`
    - ➤ `settings.py`
    - ➤ `urls.py`
    - ➤ `wsgi.py`

The `manage.py` file has many useful utilities in it that allow you to run and manage your project. Although we used the `django-admin` command to create default files for new projects and apps, `manage.py` is used to run and modify projects and apps that have already been created.

Now that we have a new, unmodified Django project, you can run the server using this:

```
$ python manage.py runserver
```

Ignore the warnings that pop up when the server starts. We will fix those later, but for now, just check that the default Django page, as shown in Figure 21.1, appears at `http://127.0.0.1:8000`.

If you navigate to, for example, `http://127.0.0.1:8000/asdf`, you will see an error page for a 404 error. The error page contains this text:

Using the URLconf defined in unlockingpython.urls, Django tried these URL patterns, in this order:

admin/
The current path, asdf, didn't match any of these.

FIGURE 21.1: The Django welcome page shows after installation.

This is a strangely helpful message for an error page on the internet. It tells you exactly what you did wrong and why, and it gives you hints about what you can do to fix it. This page is helpful because of a line in `unlockingpython/settings.py`:

```
DEBUG = True
```

In general, `DEBUG` should be set to `True` when developing locally (unless you're testing user-facing error pages!) and set to `False` in production.

It's important to set `DEBUG` to `False` in production for a couple of reasons. First, most users will be confused if they get debugging information. It's much nicer to say "the page wasn't found" and leave it at that. Second, the debug pages may reveal previously hidden vulnerabilities in your Django application to attackers. In theory, your application should be secure even if this debugging information is made public! However, mistakes do happen, and it's best not to have a convenient way for attackers to see vulnerabilities if they do exist.

On the debug page at `http://127.0.0.1:8000/asdf`, or whichever nonexistent URL you choose, you'll notice that the only available path in the application is `/admin`. If you navigate to `http://127.0.0.1:8000/admin`, you'll see the login page for the admin interface, which we will be using later.

The server, admin interface, and all of these defaults belong to the Django *project*. Some of this functionality is inherent to all Django projects; other functionality is driven by apps installed by default, such as `django.contrib.admin` which powers the admin interface. To see how apps add features to a Django project, let's create a new app called `testapp`:

```
$ django-admin startapp testapp
```

This generates default files for the new app:

- ➤ __init__.py
- ➤ admin.py
- ➤ apps.py
- ➤ migrations
    - ➤ __init__.py
- ➤ models.py
- ➤ tests.py
- ➤ views.py

There are two important files to note here, and one directory that's not here but that we'll need to create later. The two files are models.py and views.py, and the directory we need to create is called templates.

Django is based on an *MVT (Model-View-Template) architecture*.[1] Many other programming frameworks use variations on MVT, with the most popular paradigm being MVC, or Model-View-Controller.[2] Regardless of what the three entities are called, they all work in much the same way. Here's how it works in Django:

- ➤ **Model:** Defines the objects (classes) used by the project or application. Defines the attributes for each object. For example, a model defines a User object having the fields first_name and last_name.

- ➤ **View:** Defines the business logic of handling HTTP requests. Is able to serialize data into models, bundle them with a template, and return them as an HTTP response. Handles logic for tasks like authentication and authorization.

- ➤ **Template:** Takes data handed to it from the view and renders it as HTML, putting each field into its appropriate place.

---

[1] Because the order of these entities is arbitrary, Django's MVT is also commonly called the MTV (Music Television) architecture.

[2] Variations on MVC include MVP, MVA, MVVM, and various other MV* acronyms.

Also, I was kidding about the Music Television thing in the previous footnote. Unfortunately, the Dire Straits were not pining over programming architectures when they said, "I want my MTV." In all seriousness, if you've used MVC you may have a preconception about what "views" are. It's worth noting that Django *views* are actually equivalent to MVC *controllers*. MVC *views* are equivalent to Django *templates*.

Because the acronym "MVT" is readily recognized by programmers as a type of "MV*" architecture, that acronym is commonly used. However, because MVC views are Django templates and MVC controllers are Django views, the acronym "MTV" is also commonly used because it lines up with its MVC equivalents.

There does not seem to be a strong preference in the Django community or in the official documentation, so use whichever one you feel like. "VTM," "TVM," "TMV," and "VMT" are definitely not accepted, though.

Let's take a look at the views file. To do this, I recommend that you open the project and its applications in Visual Studio Code or another IDE. Open the file `testapp/views.py`. You'll see that it's populated with the following:

```
from django.shortcuts import render

# Create your views here.
```

The imported `render` function is used to render templates, which we don't have yet but will be using soon. For now, you can replace the entire contents of the file with the following:

```
from django.http import HttpResponse

def hello(request):
    return HttpResponse('Hello, world!')
```

This might seem somewhat reminiscent of our first Flask endpoint, which took in a request and simply returned the response `Hello, world!`. What's missing is a decorator tying the `hello` function to a particular URL path. Instead of a decorator, Django has its own way of tying URL paths to functions that generate an HTTP response.

Inside `unlockingpython/urls.py` there is a list called `urlpatterns`. This list manages which URL paths are associated with which view functions. Import the `testapp` application and add a new entry for the path `'hello'` associating it with the function `testapp.views.hello`:

```
import testapp.views

urlpatterns = [
    path('admin/', admin.site.urls),
    path('hello', testapp.views.hello )
]
```

Restarting the server is not necessary as, unlike in Flask, changes are picked up automatically. Navigate to `http://127.0.0.1:8000/hello`, where you should see the text:

Hello, world!

Returning raw text using `HttpResponse` from a Django view is not very common. Let's add a template to make things pretty with HTML. To do this, make a new directory in your app called templates. This is where Django will look for any template files. Then, create a new file `hello.html` at `testapp/templates/hello.html`.

Inside this new template file, write some HTML with a single variable, `name`:

```
Hello, {{name}}!
```

Just like in Flask, variables in Django templates are surrounded by double curly brackets (`{{ }}`).

Now we can use the `render` function that was imported by default in the `views.py` file, and return the template after a dictionary of values has been applied to it:

```
from django.shortcuts import render

def hello_template(request):
    return render(request, 'testapp/profile.html', {'name': 'world'})
```

Note that I'm returning this rendered template in a new function, `hello_template`, which can be found in an already-made app in the exercise files.

In `unlockingpython/urls.py` write the corresponding path:

```
path('hello_template',testapp.views.hello_template),
```

When you visit `http://127.0.0.1:8000/hello_template`, however, there is a `TemplateDoes NotExist` error, as Django is unable to find the template. In the error message, it details a list of all the places it looked for the template, which should be the admin and auth apps installed by default in the Django library directory.

To fix this missing template error, we need to "install" the app and tell Django it should search in that app's directory for resources when running the project.

In the previous example, when we returned `HttpResponse('Hello, world!')`, Django had everything it needed to handle that request. In `unlockingpython/urls.py`, we explicitly imported the view and referenced the function as `testapp.views.hello`. The secret here is that the `hello` function didn't need to be in a `views.py` file or even in an app at all! That function could have been in any random place, as long as we import and reference it correctly in `urls.py`.

We need to register `testapp` as an actual application so Django knows things like "where to find its templates." To do this, go to `settings.py` in the project directory (`unlockingpython/settings.py`). There, you'll find a list called `INSTALLED_APPS`:

```
INSTALLED_APPS = [
    'django.contrib.admin',
    'django.contrib.auth',
    'django.contrib.contenttypes',
    'django.contrib.sessions',
    'django.contrib.messages',
    'django.contrib.staticfiles',
]
```

Add the string app name `'testapp'` to this list. This is the only step for installing the application. Again, no restarting or rebuilding is required. If you refresh the page `http://127.0.0.1:8000/hello_template`, you should see the HTML template you created.

GET parameters, passed in as key-value pairs after the question marks in URLs, can be accessed through the `GET` attribute on the `request` object:

```
def hello_url_params(request):
    name = request.GET.get('name', 'world')
    return render(request, 'hello.html', {'name': name})
```

Here, I'm passing in a default value of `'world'` if the `name` field doesn't exist. Add the new function `hello_url_params` in the URLs list in `urls.py`:

```
path('hello_url_params', testapp.views.hello_url_params),
```

Then, if you visit the URL `http://127.0.0.1:8000/hello_url_params?name=ryan`, it results in the text `'Hello, ryan!'` printed to the page.

Finally, we have path parameters, such as `http://127.0.0.1:8000/hello_path_params/ryan`. These are not retrieved from the `request` object but are passed into the view directly as arguments:

```
def hello_path_params(request, name):
    return render(request, 'hello.html', {'name': name})
```

The function argument name gets associated with data in the URL path using the following path parameter syntax in `urls.py`:

```
path('hello_path_params/<str:name>', testapp.views.hello_path_params),
```

Path parameters are surrounded by angle brackets (`<>`) with their type (in this case, `str`) followed by a colon and the variable name. Multiple path parameters can be passed to the view function as multiple arguments. For example:

```
path('hello/<str:first_name>/<str:last_name>', testapp.views.hello_path_params),
```

would be passed to the `view` function with this definition:

```
def hello(request, first_name, last_name):
```

Although we've seen some features in Django that weren't in Flask (such as the concept of separate projects and apps), the framework might not seem entirely un-Flask-like. Django takes requests, it does a little business logic, it returns responses, and it uses templates (if provided). This is exactly what Flask did.

However, Django is not simply a Flask alternative or API-creation tool. Next, we'll look at some additional basic uses of the Django framework that show its power and flexibility for creating full-fledged web applications.

DATABASES AND MIGRATIONS

By default, Django uses an SQLite database in the local project directory. This makes it easy to develop the application locally. In fact, you don't ever really need to worry about database infrastructure at all until the application goes to production, and you need something that can handle higher traffic (such as MySQL).

During development, many changes might be made to the database schema. You might add and remove tables/objects and add and remove fields within those objects. To keep track of these changes, and even revert them if necessary, Django tracks all modifications to the database schema in files called *migrations*.

Migrations are associated with apps only. A Django project itself does not have migrations, but apps within the project have them. Migrations are sets of files that must be applied (run on the database) one at a time, in the order they were created, to build the structure of the database that the application requires. When a change is made (such as converting a table's field from an integer to a string), a new migration file is added.

When a new Django project is first created, no database exists and no migrations have been applied. This doesn't mean that no migrations *exist*. Recall the list of INSTALLED_APPS in `settings.py`. Many of these apps require database changes. However, on a brand-new project, none of the migrations have yet been applied.

To apply all migrations that have not yet been applied to the database, run this command:

```
$ python manage.py migrate
```

This command produces output like this:

```
Applying contenttypes.0001_initial... OK
Applying auth.0001_initial... OK
Applying admin.0001_initial... OK
Applying admin.0002_logentry_remove_auto_add... OK
```

This is applying necessary database changes for the default Django apps `contenttypes`, `auth`, and `admin`.

After the `makemigrations` command has been run, you should see a new SQLite database file in the project directory, which you can access:

```
$ sqlite3 db.sqlite3
```

The following SQLite command will show a list of all tables:

```
> .table
```

You should see a list of Django project tables, which are managed by the migration function itself, such as `django_content_type` and `django_migrations`. You will also see app-specific tables for the authentication app such as `auth_user` and `auth_permission`.

All models get their own database table. To demonstrate this, we can create a new migration for a new database table simply by adding a model to our Django app, `testapp`. In the `testapp/models.py` file, create a new class, TestModel:

```
from django.db import models

class TestModel(models.Model):
    some_name = models.CharField(max_length=32)
    some_number = models.IntegerField()
```

Models will be discussed in greater depth later in this chapter. For now, just know that Django models contain static fields that describe what type of data that field holds and how it should be stored in the database. In this case, we have a `CharField` (string), and an `IntegerField` (integer).

After this model is written, we need to generate the migration file that will put it in the database. Run the `makemigrations` command:

```
$ python manage.py makemigrations
```

which produces this output:

```
Migrations for 'testapp':
  testapp/migrations/0001_initial.py
    - Create model TestModel
```

Running this command also creates a new directory at `testapp/migrations`. Inside this is the first migration file, `0001_initial.py`. If you look inside this file, you won't find SQL commands but a Django description of the model in the form of a `Migration` object:

```
class Migration(migrations.Migration):

    initial = True

    dependencies = [
    ]
```

```
        operations = [
            migrations.CreateModel(
                name='TestModel',
                fields=[
                    ('id', models.BigAutoField(auto_created=True, primary_key=True,
    serialize=False, verbose_name='ID')),
                    ('some_name', models.CharField(max_length=32)),
                    ('some_number', models.IntegerField()),
                ],
            ),
        ]
```

Django migrations track, not SQL statements, but models and changes to them. Each `Migration` object is converted to an SQL statement by Django before applying it to the database. Occasionally, a table may be written or modified in a way that you weren't expecting, or you want to see the generated SQL before actually applying the migration in case it's not what you want. You can do this using the `sqlmigrate` command:

```
$ python3 manage.py sqlmigrate testapp 0001
```

Here, the name of the app the migration belongs to is `testapp` and the index of the migration we want translated to SQL is `0001`.

After the migrations are generated from the app models using the `makemigrations` command, you need to apply them, just like we applied the initial migrations for the default Django apps:

```
$ python manage.py migrate
```

This applies the migration for our new model:

```
    Applying testapp.0001_initial... OK
```

Back in the SQLite command prompt, use the `.table` query to see the newly created table `testapp_testmodel`. You can describe this table with `.schema`:

```
> .schema testapp_testmodel
```

This produces the same SQL statement seen with the `sqlmigrate` command:

```
CREATE TABLE IF NOT EXISTS "testapp_testmodel" (
    "id" integer NOT NULL PRIMARY KEY AUTOINCREMENT,
    "some_name" varchar(32) NOT NULL,
    "some_number" integer NOT NULL
);
```

DJANGO ADMIN INTERFACE

Earlier, you saw the login page for the Django admin interface at `http://127.0.0.1:8000/admin`. There are two things you need to do before you can actually log in and access the admin interface. The first is to run the migrations for the auth and admin apps, according to the instructions in the previous section. The second is to create credentials for an admin user account:

```
$ python manage.py createsuperuser
```

This will start an account-creation terminal dialog. For the sake of example, I will be using the username admin and the password password:

```
Username (leave blank to use 'rmitchell'): admin
Email address:
Password:
Password (again):
This password is too common.
Bypass password validation and create user anyway? [y/N]: y
Superuser created successfully.
```

The email address can be left blank.

It's critical to use a secure admin password on web apps that will be made public. However, for local development, the password password will be fine. Press Y to bypass Django's warning about the insecure password.

After you've created the account, go back to http://127.0.0.1:8000/admin to log in.

The admin interface allows you to do many useful things out-of-the-box. You can change the admin password, add and modify users, and add and modify security groups for those users.

Click the Add link in the Users row to add a new user. This will take you to the page http://127.0.0.1:8000/admin/auth/user/add/, where you can add a new user with basic information. Create a new user, "Alice," with a strong password.

After the user Alice is created, you will be taken to a page to edit Alice's details. This page will also provide information about the hashed password, including the algorithm and salt used to hash it (see Figure 21.2).

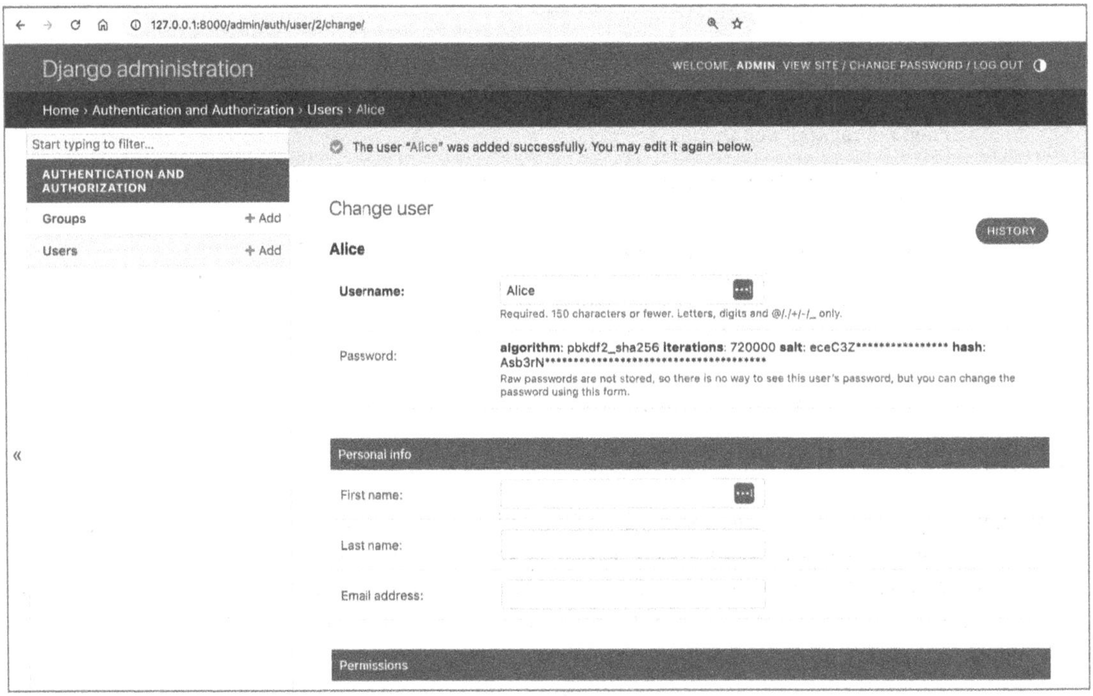

FIGURE 21.2: The Django admin interface allows you to edit user details.

Populate any first and last name for Alice. Create a couple other users as well! In the next section, we will create a new app that displays data from these users.

MODELS

Previously, we created a simple model called `TestModel` in the `testapp` app. Now, we're going to create a model called `Post` in a new application, `posts`. Eventually, this application will allow users to create and publish posts, like they would on a social media website.

Create the app using the `django-admin startapp` command:

```
django-admin startapp posts
```

Next, navigate to the newly created `posts/models.py` file and add the `Post` model:

```
from django.db import models
from django.contrib.auth.models import User

class Post(models.Model):
    user = models.ForeignKey(User, on_delete=models.CASCADE)
    title = models.CharField(max_length=120)
    content = models.TextField()
    created = models.DateTimeField(auto_now_add=True)
```

There are a few new content types we haven't seen yet. `CharField` and `TextField` represent different types of data, although both are "strings," according to Python. A `CharField` stores data of a specific maximum length and is often used for holding names, titles, and other limited text. The `TextField`, in contrast, holds arbitrary text strings with no database limit.

Although, technically, you could use `TextField` every time you want a string and ignore the existence of `CharField` entirely, using both as appropriate will help make your databases more efficient.

The `DateTimeField`, just like it sounds, holds datetimes. I'm providing the argument `auto_now_add=True` to populate each post with the current datetime on creation.

The `ForeignKey` field requires some discussion. Because users write posts, each post is associated with a `User` object. In the database, this is represented by an integer user ID stored in the post table. Sure, we could make this field an integer:

```
user_id = models.IntegerField()
```

This would work, but it would require a great deal of manual effort to maintain the features that Django handles for us when the foreign key field is used. When objects are related to each other (like with users authoring posts) it's always better to register that relationship using a `ForeignKey` field.

One feature that the `ForeignKey` field makes easier is deletions. Most apps that allow users to create new data also allow them to delete that data. Even if that data is not actually removed from the database, there must be some indicator that it was deleted and we must be able to "hide" that data from being shown in the application.

There are other issues to consider with deletion as well. If a user has posts associated with their account and that user account is removed from the database, what happens to their posts? There is no right answer to this question, but there can be very *wrong* answers. One wrong answer would be to do nothing to the posts, keep them associated with the nonexistent user ID, and force every SQL query that fetches posts to check if the post's user actually exists. That is not a good or sustainable solution.

Django has six strategies for handling the deletions of models that have foreign key constraints. In the case of users and posts, here is what would happen in each case:

➤ **CASCADE:** Delete any posts associated with the user being deleted.

➤ **PROTECT:** Do not allow the user to be deleted if it is associated with posts. In the admin GUI, attempting to delete a protected entity will result in an error message.

➤ **SET_NULL:** Keep the post, but sets the user_id to NULL in the database.

➤ **SET_DEFAULT:** Keep the post, and sets the user_id to some default value, perhaps 0 (which is not a valid user_id). This is a somewhat questionable design decision, but I've seen worse.

➤ **SET:** Set the user_id to a value determined by a function that passed into SET.

➤ **DO_NOTHING:** Take no action and leave the user_id in place.

We are able to create users in Django's admin interface because the User model is a model just like any other model. Models can be created and managed from the admin interface. However, our TestModel model in the testapp app was not available for management because it wasn't "registered" with the admin interface first. To register the Post model, write the following in posts/admin.py:

```
from django.contrib import admin
from posts import models

class PostAdmin(admin.ModelAdmin):
    # Changes what's displayed on the Admin site
    list_display = ('title',)

admin.site.register(models.Post, PostAdmin)
```

The PostAdmin class contains static attributes that define how these objects can be viewed and managed in the admin interface. Here, when Post objects are displayed as a list in the admin interface, we're updating the list_display attribute so that the title string is used for identification. Without this line, , posts will be displayed as "post (1)," "post (2)," etc.

Next, install the app in settings.py:

```
INSTALLED_APPS = [
    ...
    # my apps
    'testapp'
    'posts'
]
```

Finally, make migrations and migrate:

```
$ python manage.py makemigrations
$ python manage.py migrate
```

After the new migration has been applied, you can check the SQLite database:

```
$ sqlite3 db.sqlite3
```

Use the SQLite query .table to see a list of tables, including the newly created posts_post. All Django table names consist of the app name followed by the model name separated by an underscore.

After you've verified that the data infrastructure is in place, refresh the admin interface at http://127.0.0.1:8000/admin. You should now see an option to add and change Posts. Click Add to add a new post.

Another advantage to using the ForeignKey field over a numeric field to store user IDs is that Django can provide a list of valid Users to choose from when creating a new post, rather than requiring you to write in a number (which may or may not actually be a valid user ID!). Clicking the + button next to the User field also lets you create a new User on the fly in a pop-up window (see Figure 21.3).

I encourage you to create a few posts (use Lorem Ipsum text[3] if you lack inspiration) for Alice, the admin user, and any other users you've created. In the next section, we'll be working with templates to display these posts.

FIGURE 21.3: You can add instances of custom models through the Django admin interface.

---

[3] "Lorem ipsum" is placeholder text, commonly used since the 1960's, in graphic and web design. You use lorem ipsum when text is needed, but it doesn't need to mean anything. The first sentence reads: "Lorem ipsum dolor sit amet, consectetur adipiscing elit, sed do eiusmod tempor incididunt ut labore et dolore magna aliqua."

MORE VIEWS AND TEMPLATES

Previously, we worked with views that extract data from a request and return it directly as a response. Now, we're going to the database to fetch additional data for a response.

Unlike with Flask, you don't need to write your own database connectors, Django provides them automatically with the Model class. The following view, in posts/views.py, retrieves all posts currently in the database and sends them to a template:

```
def all_posts(request):
    posts = Post.objects.all()
    return render(request, 'posts.html', {'posts': posts})
```

The method call Post.objects.all() retrieves all the posts via the static attribute on the class, Post.objects. In Django, every model has a *Manager* as a static attribute called object. The manager is the interface to the database, and it can be thought of as the table where the models reside (in this case, the posts_post table).

The all method on the Manager, as you might assume, fetches all the objects in the table. We can fill out a simple template in posts.html to test this:

```
{% extends 'base.html' %}
    {% block content %}
        <h2>Posts:</h2>
        {% for post in posts %}
        <div class="post">
            <h3>{{post.title}}</h3>
            <span class="post-created-date">{{post.created}}</span>
            <span class="post-text">
                {{post.text}}
            </span>
        </div>
    {% endfor %}
{% endblock %}
```

Recall that the Flask template language mostly works in Django, and vice versa. Here, I've created a set of HTML files very similar to what we had in Chapter 20, "REST APIs and Flask," with base.html including header.html and footer.html. The content block, defined in posts.html, extends base.html.

The important part, of course, is the tag {% for post in posts %}. This for loop looks a bit like Python syntax (for post in posts), but it's important to note that these templates can't control logic with whitespace (indenting and outdenting) like Python can. The templates are nicely indented here, but they don't have to be. This is why the endfor tag is important. It defines where the end of the for loop is, so that only the things in between the for tag and the endfor tag are considered part of the loop.

Inside the for loop we get access to all the attributes in the Post model: title, text, and created (the date the post was created). We can use any HTML tags to surround these, which can be styled with CSS.

Finally, we add this path to urlpatterns in unlockingpython/urls.py:

```
path('posts', posts.views.all_posts)
```

Navigate to http://127.0.0.1/posts, and you should see a list of all the posts you created in the admin interface.

Back in the views, you can also use a model's Manager to get data by attribute:

```
def profile(request):
    posts = Post.objects.filter(user=request.user)
    return render(request, 'posts.html', {'posts': posts})
```

The User object associated with the request is passed in as request.user every time a request is made by a user who is logged into the site. No need to look things up in a session table or deserialize data and create User objects yourself—Django does it for you.

The Manager's filter method accepts keyword arguments for all attributes of a model. In this case, we're filtering Posts by the user who is currently logged in and making the request.

Add this path to urls.py:

```
path('profile', posts.views.profile)
```

Navigate to 127.0.0.1/profile, and you should see a page with only your (admin) posts.

A page that shows posts for a specific user. not just the logged-in user, can be made using path parameters. This line in urls.py captures a user ID as a path parameter in the URL and sends it to the view function profile_by_id as the argument user_id:

```
path('profile/<int:user_id>', posts.views.profile_by_id)
```

Then it's used by the view:

```
def profile_by_id(request, user_id):
    posts = Post.objects.filter(user=user_id)
    return render(request, 'posts.html', {'posts': posts})
```

Notice that we're not passing the User object in to filter this time but simply the integer user_id. This also works! Again, the magic of defining the Post model using a ForeignKey field is that Django automatically associates the user_id with the User object, and both are acceptable.

Let's make a profile page, profile.html, that contains information about the User object, rather than just a list of posts. First, we know that both the posts.html and profile.html pages will contain a list of posts. It might be convenient to pull out just the HTML that formats a single post into its own file, post.html (note the singular post):

```
<div class="post">
    <h3>{{post.title}}</h3>
    <span class="post-created-date">{{post.created}}</span>
    <span class="post-text">
        {{post.text}}
    </span>
</div>
```

Then, we can include this post template in the parent `profile.html`:

```
{% extends 'base.html' %}
    {% block content %}
        {% if user.first_name and user.last_name %}
            <h2> {{user.first_name}} {{user.last_name}}
        {% else %}
                <h2>{{user.username}}</h2>
        {% endif %}
        {% for post in posts %}
            {% include "post.html" %}
        {% endfor %}
    {% endblock %}
```

The `profile.html` template contains additional logic for displaying the user's name using the `{% if %}`, `{% else %}`, and `{% endif %}` tags. If `first_name` and `last_name` are populated (like you might have done in the admin interface with the Alice user), then they are displayed. Otherwise, we display the username, which must be populated for every user.

You can switch over to this new profile template simply by updating the `profile` function in the view. Change the template name and pass in the `User` object:

```
def profile(request):
    posts = Post.objects.filter(user=request.user)
    return render(request, 'profile.html', {
        'posts': posts,
        'user': request.user
        })
```

In the case of the `profile_by_id` function, there is no `User` object, only a `user_id`. We could get a `User` object from the first post in the list of posts by that user:

```
def profile_by_id(request, user_id):
    posts = Post.objects.filter(user=user_id)
    user = posts[0]
    return render(request, 'profile.html', {
        'posts': posts,
        'user': user
        })
```

This works for users who have posts but will break if no posts are returned. It also has a little bit of "code smell." A much cleaner way to do this is to get it from the `User Manager`:

```
from django.contrib.auth.models import User

def profile_by_id(request, user_id):
    posts = Post.objects.filter(user=user_id)
    user = User.objects.get(id=user_id)
    return render(request, 'profile.html', {
        'posts': posts,
        'user': user
        })
```

Unlike filter, the got method returns one, and exactly one, object when it's called. It will raise an exception if multiple items match the criteria it was given or if no objects are found. For this reason, it's best to use it for unique attributes (such as user ID or username) where you're certain the user exists.

In this case, of course, we're not certain the user exists. An old profile URL could be used, or someone might be manually changing the URL ID to an invalid one. Rather than a rendered response, we can return a Django HTTP error:

```
from django.http import HttpResponseNotFound

def profile_by_id(request, user_id):
    posts = Post.objects.filter(user=user_id)

    try:
        user = User.objects.get(id=user_id)
    except User.DoesNotExist as e:
        return HttpResponseNotFound(f'User not found')

    return render(request, 'profile.html', {
        'posts': posts,
        'user': user
        })
```

This excepts the User.DoesNotExist exception, which, yes, is an Exception class inside the model. This isn't anything special about the User model itself. The Post model we created also has a DoesNotExist exception. Although Django models can be declared with just a few lines, each one automatically has a plethora of objects, classes, and attributes associated with it.

With this new view, the URL http://127.0.0.1:8000/profile/2 should display the profile for Alice, and http://127.0.0.1:8000/profile/100 should (unless you've gone overboard with user creation) display the text "User not found."

MORE RESOURCES

This chapter was a whirlwind look at how Django projects and apps fit together, as well as just a few of the framework's powerful features. Although I hope you now have a feel for what it's like working with Django, I'll be the first to admit that one chapter is not going to be enough to go out and write an enterprise web application.

If you'd like to learn more, the official Django tutorial (https://docs.djangoproject.com/en/5.1/intro) is an excellent place to start. It covers important topics such as forms and object creation, static file management, testing, and more.

From there, the Django topic guides (https://docs.djangoproject.com/en/5.1/topics) cover most major Django topics and can point you to the right places in the documentation for further learning.

If you want a readable guide to working with more advanced features, such as security groups and third-party Django plug-ins, I recommend *Django in Action*, by Christopher Trudeau (Manning, 2024).

22

Web Scraping and Scrapy

In the previous two chapters, we've used our web browsers to send requests and receive responses from Python applications running on a server. These requests might be generated by entering an address into the URL bar or using an extension to create POST requests, or they might be triggered by the web application itself inside the browser to load additional resources.

However, web browsers aren't the only things that can send HTTP requests and receive HTTP responses. Web browsers are simply software written in a programming language (usually C++). Any piece of software, including software written in Python, can make and receive HTTP requests.

Traditionally, websites are designed to be viewed and used by humans through a web browser. Writing Python code that bypasses the browser entirely and that can automate loading and interacting with websites opens lots of new and exciting ways for using the internet.

For example, you can write a Python program that navigates to a store's website and records the price of every item they sell. This program can run frequently and track the prices of various items over time.

You might create a Python program that collects contact information, sales leads, or product reviews. These programs can collect this data from a single website, multiple websites, or even crawl the wider internet, making requests to any domain name and URL path they come across.

These programs are called *web scrapers* because they scrape (or collect) data from the internet.

The following makes a GET request to https://unlockingpython.com and then prints the resulting HTML:

```
from urllib3 import request

r = request('GET', 'https://unlockingpython.com')
print(r.status)
print(r.data.decode('utf-8'))
```

The `urllib3` package is part of the Python standard library and can send and receive any HTTP request. However, the third-party *requests* library (`pip install requests`) is arguably more popular:

```
import requests

r = requests.get('https://unlockingpython.com')
print(r.status_code)
print(r.text)
```

In addition to "web scrapers," you may also hear the terms "web crawlers" and "web bots," or simply "bots." Web crawlers collect data from the web by traversing websites through page links. They hop from page to page, using any hyperlinks they find on the page to tell them where to go next. All web crawlers are also web scrapers, but not all scrapers do crawling (some use a hard-coded list of pages, for example).

Bots often collect data, but they can also post data. Bots may spam sites with comments and posts advertising products. They may interact with social media sites. They might purchase products or manipulate a web app (e.g., an airline's flight search form) to find price information.

INSTALLING AND USING SCRAPY

Scrapy is a popular web scraping framework that, since 2011, has been maintained by Zyte, a web scraping services company.[1] Although Zyte uses Scrapy heavily in its product offerings, the Scrapy library itself is completely free with few signs of its corporate associations.

Scrapy can be installed with `pip`. Because it is dependent on a large number of somewhat finnicky packages and specific version numbers of those packages, it's strongly recommended that you install Scrapy in a virtual environment:

```
$ python -m venv scrapy
$ source scrapy/bin/activate
$ pip install Scrapy
```

Remember that virtual environments can be deactivated at any time with the `deactivate` command:

```
$ deactivate
```

To re-activate the virtual environment, simply navigate to where it was created (where the `scrapy` directory is) and activate it again:

```
$ source scrapy/bin/activate
```

Similar to Django projects containing multiple apps, Scrapy has the concept of a project that contains multiple *spiders*.[2] The Scrapy project we are about to create, `articles`, can be found in the directory `22_scrapy` in the exercise files accompanying this book. You can create your own version of it using the instructions in this chapter.

---

[1] Zyte sells APIs that automate or simplify some aspects of web scraping and offers scraping hosting plans. This is a popular business model, and many companies, such as ScrapingBee, Apify, Octoparse, and ScraperAPI offer similar services.

[2] If the name "spider" sounds odd to you, consider the fact that spiders "crawl" across "webs."

To create a new project with Scrapy, use the scrapy command, installed with the Python package:

```
$ scrapy startproject articles
```

In this scraper, we will be collecting data from Wikipedia articles.[3] Importantly, this project is *not* called wikipedia, after the website we're scraping data from, but articles, because that's the type of data we're collecting. Spiders, inside the project, are associated with specific websites and domain names, but projects themselves should not be.

The structure of the newly created Scrapy project looks like this:

- ➤ scrapy.cfg
- ➤ articles
  - ➤ __init__.py
  - ➤ items.py
  - ➤ middlewares.py
  - ➤ pipelines.py
  - ➤ settings.py
  - ➤ spiders
- ➤ __init__.py

Each of these files is initialized with some basic code to get started, but it still requires a spider for the project to do anything. A new spider can be created with scrapy genspider:

```
$ scrapy genspider wiki wikipedia.org
```

Here, wiki is the name of the spider and wikipedia.org is the domain name it's targeting. When initialized, the new spider, at articles/spiders/wiki.py, looks like this:

```
import scrapy

class WikiSpider(scrapy.Spider):
    name = "wiki"
    allowed_domains = ["wikipedia.org"]
    start_urls = ["https://wikipedia.org"]

    def parse(self, response):
        pass
```

---

[3] Wikipedia is an excellent website for web scraping examples. It is stable and rarely changes, and it has a large variety of pages to choose from. However, if you need data from Wikipedia for any serious purpose, I would urge you to use their API instead: www.mediawiki.org/wiki/API:Main_page. Not only is this a more efficient way to get Wikipedia data, but it's less load on Wikipedia's server, which is paid for through donations.

Also, speaking of server loads, please do not run any of the Wikipedia web scrapers in this book excessively, especially when we get to crawlers that can run indefinitely. Wikipedia is a fantastic organization that endeavors to make knowledge freely accessible to the world. It does not need more web crawlers spamming it for no purpose.

The class, WikiSpider, extends scrapy.Spider. The scrapy.Spider class contains many attributes and methods for you to define in the child class, if desired, but only a few of them are included by default here.

The name attribute can be any string you want, but it must be unique within the project. The attribute allowed_domains isn't used yet but will be used in the future to determine whether a link on the page can be followed. For now, WikiSpider will simply load the URLs in the list start_urls.

We can see this scraper in action by filling in the parse method with something slightly more interesting:

```
def parse(self, response):
    print(f'Response is: {response}')
```

then modifying start_urls to contain a list of article pages:

```
start_urls = [
    'https://en.wikipedia.org/wiki/Python_(programming_language)',
    'https://en.wikipedia.org/wiki/Monty_Python',
    'https://en.wikipedia.org/wiki/Pythonidae'
    ]
```

Finally, we run the spider with scrapy:

```
$ scrapy runspider articles/spiders/wiki.py
```

This produces a tremendous amount of output, especially considering the relatively small amount of actual effort put into the spider so far. Remember that Scrapy is taking care of a lot of boilerplate and extra functionality behind the scenes. The output that we're interested in is this:

```
2024-10-29 21:34:00 [scrapy.core.engine] DEBUG: Crawled (200) <GET https://www
.wikipedia.org/> (referer: None)
Response is: <200 https://www.wikipedia.org/>
```

The response object passed to the parse method is HtmlResponse, a class from the Scrapy package, very similar to the Response object from the requests library. In the next section, we'll look at parsing the HTML from this HtmlResponse object in order to extract specific data from the page.

PARSING HTML

In previous chapters, we've encountered simple HTML documents, generated by web applications, such as this document:

```
<html>
    <head>
        <title>My cool new web app</title>
    </head>
    <body>
        <h1>Spanish Inquisition</h1>
        <p>
        In the early years of the 16th century, to combat the rising tide of
religious unorthodoxy, the Pope gave Cardinal Ximinez of Spain leave to move
without let or hindrance throughout the land, in a reign of violence, terror and
torture that makes a smashing film. This was the Spanish Inquisition...
        </p>
    </body>
</html>
```

Each item surrounded by angle brackets, such as <h1>, <head>, and <html>, are called *tags*. The tags determine how the document is structured and how it is displayed by the browser.

Tags have opening tags (such as the paragraph tag, <p>) followed by closing tags with a backslash in them (</p>). These opening and closing tags generally surround some text or other content, which gets the formatting and styles of that tag applied to it.

For example, the <h1> and </h1> tags surround the text "Spanish Inquisition," which is formatted in large bold text as a header for the document. The <h1> tag is the largest HTML header. Smaller headers can be created as well, using the <h2>, <h3>, <h4>, <h5> and <h6> tags:

```
<h2>Slightly smaller than h1</h2>
<h4>Even smaller</h4>
<h6>The smallest header</h6>
```

Everything within the <head> tags at the top of the document is not displayed in the main content window of the browser. This <head> section contains things like the web page's title, usually displayed in the browser tab. It also contains additional styling information or links to style documents, called *CSS (Cascading Style Sheets)*.

CSS markup references groups of HTML tags and contains instructions for styling them. For example,

```
h1 {
    color: red;
    text-decoration: underline;
}
```

turns all header text within <h1> tags red and underlines it.

In a CSS document, the reference to the HTML tag that the styles get applied to, h1 in the previous example, is called the *CSS selector*. Often, you want these selectors to be very specific. You may want to apply styles to content in one tag that do not get applied to content surrounded by another tag, even if the tags are the same. For example, in this document,

```
<p>This a paragraph of text</p>
<p>This is another paragraph of text</p>
```

we may want to apply different styles to the first paragraph than are applied to the second paragraph. In situations like this, HTML attributes can be used to differentiate the tags:

```
<p class="first">This a paragraph of text</p>
<p class="second">This is another paragraph of text</p>
```

Here, we've defined *class attributes* for the HTML. These class attributes have the values "first" and "second". We can write CSS to select these tags individually in the following way:

```
p.first {
    color: red;
}

p.second {
    color: blue;
}
```

The dot notation p.first selects all <p> tags with a class attribute containing the value "first".

We can also select tags based on which other tags they are nested in. Take, for example, this HTML document:

```
<span class="some-text">Here's some text up here</span>
<div class="footer">
    <span class="some-text">Copyright 2025</span>
</div>
```

The following CSS will style only the Copyright 2025 text inside the footer:

```
div.footer span.some-text {
    font-weight: bold;
}
```

The space between div.footer and span.some-text indicates that it selects nested tags. Only span.some-text tags that are a child of div.footer tags will be selected.

If we want to style the content in both of the span.some-text tags in this document, you can simply use the span.some-text selector by itself:

```
span.some-text {...}
```

In addition to the HTML attribute class, the id attribute is often used to differentiate HTML tags:

```
<span id="main-title">Some Title</span>
<p class="content">Lorem ipsum</p>
<p class="content">dolor sit amet</p>
```

Where multiple tags can have the same value for their class attribute (in this case, two tags have the class value "content"), the id value must be unique within the HTML document (no other tags can have the id "main-title"). The id value uniquely identifies the HTML tag.

Just like a dot (.) is used to indicate a class attribute value, CSS selectors use a hash (#) to indicate an id attribute value. The CSS selector for a span tag with an id of main-title is span#main-title.

It's also worth noting that the tag name itself is not required in a CSS selector. For example, here are tags with three different tag names but the same class value:

```
<p class="content">Some text in paragraph tags</p>
<span class="content">Some text in span tags</span>
<div class="content">Some text in division (div) tags</div>
```

You can style the content of all three of them with the CSS:

```
.content {
    font-size: 10px;
}
```

The CSS selector syntax, with its dots, hashes, and spaces, is excellent for selecting HTML tags. That is why it's commonly used in any situation where things in an HTML document need to be identified or selected. In Scrapy, we can use it to extract specific content from a page.

Back to our Scrapy spider, we can use the `css` method on the `response` object to extract data from the HTML page in the response:

```
def parse(self, response):
    title = response.css('h1#firstHeading').extract_first()
    last_updated = response.css('li#footer-info-lastmod').extract_first()
    print(f'URL: {response.url}')
    print(f'Title: {title}')
    print(f'Last Updated: {last_updated}')
```

Because multiple HTML tags can be returned from each selection, the method `extract_first` must be used to specify that we want the first tag only.

As usual, run the spider with this:

```
$ scrapy runspider articles/spiders/wiki.py
```

This produces output like the following:

```
URL: https://en.wikipedia.org/wiki/Monty_Python
Title: <span class="mw-page-title-main">Monty Python</span>
Last Updated: <li id="footer-info-lastmod"> This page was last edited on 27 October
2024, at 20:53<span class="anonymous-show"> (UTC)</span>.</li>
```

Notice that the HTML tags are included with the text content. We're not extracting `Monty Python` specifically; we're extracting the full string `<span class="mw-page-title-main">Monty Python</span>`.

To deal with this, you can add `::text` to the CSS selector, to specify that you want the inner text, rather than the full tag selected:

```
    title = response.css('h1#firstHeading::text').extract_first()
    last_updated = response.css('li#footer-info-lastmod::text').extract_first()
```

This produces the somewhat cleaner output:

```
Title: Python (programming language)
Last Updated:  This page was last edited on 29 October 2024, at 21:47
```

Notice, however that the time zone information `"UTC) "` was removed from the "last updated" text. This is because the time zone was surrounded by its own `<span>` tags. Adding `::text` to the selector returns *only* the text inside the tag and removes any child tags, including tags that might contain additional text content.

If you want to "strip" the HTML tags from the content rather than remove them, preserving their child content, there are several techniques you can use. One popular and effective way to do this is to use a different library altogether for parsing and extracting HTML: *BeautifulSoup*.

BeautifulSoup, like Scrapy, supports CSS selectors, but it has a nicer user interface for working with HTML data as well as additional functionality for extracting text content. BeautifulSoup can be installed with `pip`:

```
$ pip install beautifulsoup4
```

After it's installed, import it into your Scrapy spider and use the text from the `response` object to create a `BeautifulSoup` object:

```
from bs4 import BeautifulSoup

class WikiSpider(scrapy.Spider):
    ...
    def parse(self, response):
        soup = BeautifulSoup(response.text, 'lxml')
```

The attribute `response.text` contains a string with all the HTML in our Wikipedia article, which can be passed to the `BeautifulSoup` class. The string `'lxml'` indicates the parser library that BeautifulSoup should use for interpreting the HTML.

Different parsing algorithms work at different speeds and have various levels for "forgiveness" for badly formatted HTML pages (which occur frequently on the internet!). Although a comparison of these various methods is outside the scope of this book, `lxml` is a good one to use that balances speed and flexibility nicely.

With BeautifulSoup imported and being used to create the `soup` object, we can rewrite the data extraction:

```
    def parse(self, response):
        soup = BeautifulSoup(response.text, 'lxml')
        title = soup.select_one('h1#firstHeading').get_text()
        last_updated = soup.select_one('li#footer-info-lastmod').get_text()
        print(f'URL: {response.url}')
        print(f'Title: {title}')
        print(f'Last Updated: {last_updated}')
```

The method `select_one` gets the first tag selected by the CSS selector. The `get_text` method acts on the selected `BeautifulSoup` element and extracts all the text, including any text in child tags (effectively stripping out the tags) and returns the string.

Running the spider now results in output like this:

```
URL: https://en.wikipedia.org/wiki/Monty_Python
Title: Monty Python
Last Updated:  This page was last edited on 27 October 2024, at 20:53 (UTC).
```

We can further refine the " `last edited`" text string using plain old Python:

```
        last_updated = soup.select_one('li#footer-info-lastmod').get_text()
        last_updated = last_updated.replace('This page was last edited on ', '')
        last_updated = last_updated.replace(', at', '')
        last_updated = last_updated.replace('.', '').strip()
```

This removes the repeating text `This page was last edited on`, the string "`, at`" between the date and the time, and finally strips all punctuation and whitespace from the beginning and end of the string. This results in cleaned date and time strings like this:

```
27 October 2024 20:53 (UTC)
```

Another data cleaning challenge can be found in the text content of Wikipedia articles. Article content is found inside the `div.mw-content-ltr` tags and contains many images, sidebars, tables, and other data in addition to text. However, these non-text elements are contained in `<div>`, `<table>`, and `<figure>` tags, whereas the text is contained in `<p>` tags.

The following lines can be added to the `parse` method in our `WikiSpider` class to get relatively clean text data from each Wikipedia article:

```
paras = soup.select('div.mw-content-ltr p')
text = '\n'.join([p.get_text() for p in paras])
```

This uses the BeautifulSoup method `select` to get all elements matching the CSS selector `div.mw-content-ltr p` as a list. The text is extracted from each of these paragraph elements using the `get_text` method and joined with newlines into a single string.

Although printing collected data to the terminal is fun, in the next section we're going to look at putting this data into Scrapy objects that will keep it organized and make it more useful.

ITEMS

Scrapy items, as you might suspect, are kept in the `items.py` file in your Scrapy project. Scrapy even creates a stub `Item` for you with the name of your project (in this case, Articles):

```
import scrapy


class ArticlesItem(scrapy.Item):
    # define the fields for your item here like:
    # name = scrapy.Field()
    pass
```

Let's change the name of `ArticlesItem` to the singular `ArticleItem`. Then, add the four fields `url`, `title`, `text`, and `last_updated` to make it more useful:

```
class ArticleItem(scrapy.Item):
    url = scrapy.Field()
    title = scrapy.Field()
    text = scrapy.Field()
    last_updated = scrapy.Field()
```

These Scrapy items are very similar to Django models. However, unlike Django models with many different field types (`IntegerField`, `TextField`, etc.) Scrapy only has a single field type: `Field`.

Once the `ArticleItem` class is defined, it can be used in the `parse` method of the `WikiSpider` class:

```
def parse(self, response):
    soup = BeautifulSoup(response.text, 'lxml')
    article = ArticleItem()
    article['url'] = response.url
    article['title'] = soup.select_one('h1#firstHeading').get_text()

    last_updated = soup.select_one('li#footer-info-lastmod').get_text()
    last_updated = last_updated.replace('This page was last edited on ', '')
    last_updated = last_updated.replace(', at', '')
    article['last_updated'] = last_updated.strip('. ')

    paras = soup.select('div.mw-content-ltr p')
    article['text'] = '\n'.join([p.get_text() for p in paras])

    return article
```

Instead of saving the data into variables, printing those variables, and returning nothing, we are adding the data to our new `ArticleItem` object. Another difference from Django models: Scrapy items are very similar to dictionaries. Attributes must be set and accessed using Python dictionary syntax, `article['url']`, rather than as attributes on the object using the dot notation, `article.url`.

Run the spider again and you'll see data in the `ArticleItem` printed as a dictionary:

```
{'last_updated': '11 October 2024 14:11\xa0(UTC)',
 'text': <article text here>,
 'title': 'Monty Python',
 'url': 'https://en.wikipedia.org/wiki/Monty_Python'}
```

If the article text is too long and interferes with your ability to read and make sense of the terminal logs, feel free to limit the length using the string slicing syntax. This limits the text to the first 100 characters:

```
article['text'] = '\n'.join([p.get_text() for p in paras])[0:100]
```

Although items might seem like barely more than fancy dictionaries at first glance, they are critical for using Scrapy effectively. Scrapy has many ways of exporting data, all of which depend on that data being passed in items. Data processing, also, as we'll see with item pipelines later in this chapter, uses the `Item` class.

If you want to generate a CSV file from your scraped data during a run, it's as easy as this:

```
$ scrapy runspider articles/spiders/wiki.py -o articles.csv -t csv
```

The `-o`, or output, command flag specifies a filename, `articles.csv`, where the data is stored. The `-t` flag specifies the type or format of data, in this case, CSV.

If CSV doesn't meet your needs, data can also be exported as JSON or XML:

```
$ scrapy runspider articleItems.py -o articles.json -t json
$ scrapy runspider articleItems.py -o articles.xml -t xml
```

These files contain all item data returned by the `parse` method in the spider, or parsing methods named as callbacks, as we'll see in crawlers.

CRAWLING WITH SCRAPY

Scraping the same three articles over and over again sure has been fun, but the real advantages of using a framework like Scrapy comes when you start to crawl.

Crawling the web, in theory, is easy. Scrape each page, look for links to other pages, and follow those links to scrape those pages and look for links as well. Keep following links and scraping for new links until you've crawled through the whole website (or the whole internet, if you're following external links).

Links are easy enough to find in HTML pages. The link tag looks like this:

```
Click <a href="https://example.com">here</a> to go to the website.
```

The `<a>` tag, also called an anchor tag or anchor link, was one of the first HTML elements in the original HTML specification. It contains the attribute `href`, which stands for hyperlink reference.

This href attribute value is the URL that the hyperlinked text is linked to. In the example above, the word here is the hyperlinked text and is linked to the URL https://example.com.

Although web crawling through these `<a>` tags is easy in theory, it can be tricky in practice. Consider that, if we were to write a web crawler that traversed Wikipedia articles, it would need to do the following things:

➤ Extract all links on the HTML page (`<a>` tags with the href attribute).

➤ For each link, determine if it's internal (part of the wikipedia.org domain) or external.

➤ For each internal link, determine if it's another article page, or a non-article page (such as an "About Wikipedia" page) that we don't want to follow.

➤ For each internal link that we want to scrape, determine if we've *already* scraped it.

➤ If we still want to scrape this link, add it to a queue for scraping.

➤ Pop a URL off the queue, scrape the page, and repeat by finding all links on the page.

As you might imagine, the code to write this gets complicated quickly. Fortunately, Scrapy takes care of nearly all of this for you. To create a new crawler, use the genspider command from earlier:

```
scrapy genspider -t crawl wikicrawler wikipedia.org
```

By passing -t crawl to the genspider command, Scrapy uses the CrawlSpider template to create a new default spider:

```
import scrapy
from scrapy.linkextractors import LinkExtractor
from scrapy.spiders import CrawlSpider, Rule

class WikicrawlerSpider(CrawlSpider):
    name = "wikicrawler"
    allowed_domains = ["wikipedia.org"]
    start_urls = ["https://wikipedia.org"]

    rules = (
        Rule(LinkExtractor(allow=r"Items/"), callback="parse_item", follow=True),
    )

    def parse_item(self, response):
        ...
```

This looks similar to the Spider template used previously, with two major differences. First, the spider now extends scrapy.CrawlSpider rather than scrapy.Spider. Also, it has a new attribute: rules.

Scrapy crawlers use this tuple of rules, in conjunction with the allowed_domains, to determine whether a link should be added to the queue to be crawled. Three arguments are commonly passed to the Rule class:

➤ **link_extractor:** This is a keyword argument in the Rule class, although it is written as a positional argument in the crawl template. It takes a LinkExtractor object, which defines a pattern or regular expression that will be used to match with links on the page.

➤ **callback:** Can be either a string function name or a callable function object. This is the function that will be called with the `response` object for responses at links that match with the `link_extractor`.

➤ **follow:** A Boolean, indicating whether we should continue to follow links on pages that match with the `link_extractor`. If set to `False`, then page data will be extracted with the callback function, but no links found on the page will be evaluated or added to the queue.

The order of `Rule` objects in the `rules` tuple is important. If a link matches to multiple rules, then the first matching rule decides how to handle the link.

In order to write a crawler that traverses Wikipedia articles, we need to understand what Wikipedia article links look like. Here are the `href` values from a few `<a>` tags that link to articles:

```
wiki/Guido_van_Rossum
wiki/Zen_of_Python
wiki/C%2B%2B
```

Here are a few links that are not Wikipedia articles, but other informational or utility pages:

```
wiki/Wikipedia:About
/w/index.php?title=Foobar&action=edit
/wiki/Wikipedia:Help_desk
```

As a general rule, Wikipedia article links start with `wiki/` and do not contain colons (`:`) in them.

In Chapter 12, "Writing Cleaner Code," regular expressions were briefly mentioned, along with the Python regular expression package `re`. Here is a situation where regular expressions will come in handy. If you choose to write your own regular expressions to match links, I recommend using a tool like pythex (`https://pythex.org/`) to test your regular expressions, particularly as you're learning.

Otherwise, you can simply take my word for it that the following regular expression will match all links that start with `wiki/` and do not contain colons:

```
(wiki/)((?!:).)*$
```

The `WikicrawlerSpider` class then looks like this:

```
from scrapy.linkextractors import LinkExtractor
from scrapy.spiders import CrawlSpider, Rule

class WikicrawlerSpider(CrawlSpider):
    name = "wikicrawler"
    allowed_domains = ["wikipedia.org"]
    start_urls = ['https://en.wikipedia.org/wiki/Benevolent_dictator_for_life']

    rules = (
        Rule(
            LinkExtractor(allow='(wiki/)((?!:).)*$'),
            callback=parse,
            follow=True
        ),
    )
```

It also includes the parse method (used as the callback for our only rule) taken directly from the original WikiSpider class. In fact, we could even add this line to WikicrawlerSpider, which would eliminate the need to repeat code:

```
from articles.spiders.wiki import WikiSpider

class WikicrawlerSpider(CrawlSpider):
    ...
    parse = WikiSpider.parse
```

Run the crawler in the usual way:

```
$ scrapy runspider wikicrawler.py
```

Unlike the WikiSpider, this crawler will have to be stopped manually by pressing Ctrl+C in the terminal. Alternatively, you can provide a maximum number of items, or pages for the spider to crawl before closing:

```
$ scrapy runspider wikicrawler.py -s CLOSESPIDER_PAGECOUNT=10
```

The -s allows you to pass in optional settings for the crawler to use. Settings can also be set in the settings.py file. Adding this line anywhere in settings.py will stop the crawler after 10 pages:

```
CLOSESPIDER_PAGECOUNT = 10
```

The settings.py file contains many configuration options for your spider or crawler. One particularly interesting one is ROBOTSTXT_OBEY:

```
# Obey robots.txt rules
ROBOTSTXT_OBEY = True
```

The robots.txt file is part of the *Robots Exclusion Protocol* and is a document found at the root of most domains. For example, https://wikipedia.org/robots.txt contains Wikipedia's robots.txt file.

The Robots Exclusion Protocol defines a way for websites to tell bots and web scrapers which pages they can scrape and which pages they can't. For example, Wikipedia might want scrapers to stay away from editing or login pages.

However, this standard isn't enforced by anyone —the robots.txt file relies on voluntary compliance. While Scrapy crawlers, by default, ignore pages that are blocked in robots.txt, changing this behavior is as easy as this:

```
ROBOTSTXT_OBEY = False
```

In the next section, we'll come back to settings.py again for configuring pipelines. Because the Scrapy settings file is used for so many things and pops up in so many of Scrapy's features, I recommend browsing the documentation's complete list of available Scrapy settings to gain familiarity with the framework:

https://docs.scrapy.org/en/2.11/topics/settings.html#built-in-settings-reference

ITEM PIPELINES

Like most good Python frameworks, Scrapy places heavy emphasis on the modularity and reusability of components. The spiders collect data, but it makes sense to have separate components for cleaning and writing data to its destination.

In addition, because Scrapy is a web scraping framework, it makes a lot of requests to web servers that can take entire seconds to get a response back from. That's a lot of time spent waiting around. Rather than twiddle its thumbs, Scrapy attempts to do other things while waiting, such as clean previously received data.

To make Scrapy projects fast and efficient, any processing done after the data is collected should, ideally, be moved into item pipelines. All pipelines are defined in the pipelines.py file. By default the pipelines.py file in new Scrapy projects looks like this:

```
# Define your item pipelines here
#
# Don't forget to add your pipeline to the ITEM_PIPELINES setting
# See: https://docs.scrapy.org/en/latest/topics/item-pipeline.html

# useful for handling different item types with a single interface
from itemadapter import ItemAdapter

class ArticlesPipeline:
    def process_item(self, item, spider):
        return item
```

The settings for these pipelines are commented out in the settings.py file:

```
# Configure item pipelines
# See https://docs.scrapy.org/en/latest/topics/item-pipeline.html
#ITEM_PIPELINES = {
#    "articles.pipelines.ArticlesPipeline": 300,
#}
```

Uncomment by removing the hashes in front of the last three lines only so that the ITEM_PIPELINES dictionary is defined. This dictionary contains, as keys, all the pipeline classes that should be run. The values of the dictionary are numbers that determine the run order of the pipelines. Traditionally, these values range from 0 to 1000, but, technically, any integer will work. Pipelines with lower values are executed first; pipelines with higher values are executed last.

To see item pipelines in action, let's remove the data cleaning code from the parse methods in our WikiSpider and WikicrawlerSpider classes so that they only collect data from the BeautifulSoup object and pass it on:

```
def parse(self, response):
    soup = BeautifulSoup(response.text, 'lxml')
    article = ArticleItem()
    article['url'] = response.url
    article['title'] = soup.select_one('h1#firstHeading').get_text()
    article['last_updated'] = soup.select_one('li#footer-info-lastmod').get_text()
    article['text'] = soup.select('div.mw-content-ltr p')
    return article
```

Then, in pipelines.py, create two classes. The first class, LastUpdatedPipeline, cleans the last_updated string. The class TextPipeline cleans article text.

```
import re

class LastUpdatedPipeline:
    def process_item(self, item, spider):
        item['last_updated'] = item['last_updated'].replace(
            'This page was last edited on ', '')
        item['last_updated'] = item['last_updated'].replace(', at', '')
        item['last_updated'] = item['last_updated'].strip('. ')

        return item

class TextPipeline:
    def process_item(self, item, spider):
        item['text'] = [p.get_text() for p in item['text']]
        item['text'] = '\n'.join(item['text'])
        item['text'] = re.sub(r'\[[0-9]+\]', '', item['text'])

        return item
```

Article text can be messy, and there are many other cleaning tasks and formatting we can do here. To make things a little more interesting, I added a new statement that removes in-text citations of the form [123] using the re.sub function.

Once you have data cleaning how you like it, add the new classes to the settings.py file:

```
ITEM_PIPELINES = {
    "articles.pipelines.LastUpdatedPipeline": 300,
    "articles.pipelines.TextPipeline": 200,
}
```

With a value of 200, TextPipeline will be run first, followed by LastUpdatedPipeline.

Notice that there's nothing we can configure that sends only items returned by WikiSpider or by WikicrawlerSpider to specific pipelines. A single spider class can also contain multiple parsing methods capable of generating different types of items. We might be collecting records of both article edits and user account information in addition to article text, for example. How does Scrapy decide which pipelines are responsible for which types of items? Well, it doesn't.

The pipelines defined in settings.py are run for every collected item, regardless of its type or which spider file collected it.

Although this might seem like an oversight, it's designed to encourage you to design Scrapy projects and write processing code in a clean and modular way. If you have a very fundamentally different type of data you're collecting, you may want to create a new Scrapy project for it.

There may still be cases, however, where it's necessary to have different sets of pipelines for different spiders. To do this, you can add custom settings to each spider using the `custom_settings` class attribute:

```
class WikiSpider(scrapy.Spider):
    custom_settings = {
        'ITEM_PIPELINES': {
            'articles.pipelines.TextPipeline': 200
        }
    }
```

Any setting in `settings.py` can be overridden using `custom_settings` within the spider class. Now when WikiSpider is run, the `last_updated` text will no longer be cleaned. When WikicrawlerSpider is run, it will get its pipelines from the `settings.py` file and run both pipeline classes.

23

Data Analysis with NumPy and Pandas

Data science and machine learning are trendy fields, with many fancy software programs that make it easy to do advanced things quickly. However, much is lost when these tools are used without an understanding of the principles they are based on.

But you don't have to take my word for it. According to ChatGPT:[1]

Even with advanced tools that automate many aspects of data science, understanding the fundamentals ensures you can critically evaluate the results and make informed decisions about model choices, assumptions, and data quality. Without this foundational knowledge, it's easy to misuse tools, overlook potential biases, or misinterpret outcomes, leading to flawed analyses.

I couldn't have said it better myself.

Python is, easily, the most popular programming language for data science. It's easy to learn,[2] has an elegant syntax that lends itself to data processing, is popular in academia, and has many third-party data science libraries written for it.

Data science and machine learning are, obviously, huge topics. Reading two chapters on them is probably not enough to go out and work at a FAANG company building machine learning (ML) models.[3] However, an understanding of the tools and techniques is useful regardless of which technology path you take.

As a software engineer, you may be asked to do some of the following:

➤   Write reports that contain data and visualizations.

➤   Ensure that the existing data in a database can support a requested feature of an application.

---

[1] ChatGPT 4o mini, with the prompt: "Write two sentences about why learning data science fundamentals is still important when there are so many tools that 'do data science for you.'"

[2] But takes a lifetime to master!

[3] You'd be surprised, though.

➤ Monitor application performance.

➤ Analyze and quantify increases or decreases in application performance and hypothesize about the factors that drive it.

In this chapter, we'll look at two libraries used in scientific computing and data analysis: NumPy and Pandas. In the next chapter, we'll continue our data science exploration with two more tools used in data science and machine learning: Matplotlib and scikit-learn.

These four libraries, combined with Jupyter notebooks, are the go-to tools in both academia and industry for data scientists around the world.

To install Pandas, you can use `pip`:

```
$ pip install pandas
```

Because NumPy is a requirement of Pandas, you do not need to install NumPy separately.

Traditionally, NumPy and Pandas are imported as `np` and `pd`, respectively:

```
import numpy as np
import pandas as pd
```

This convention is so ubiquitous that you may see example code online containing `np` and `pd` without explicitly naming these libraries. It's simply understood that they are NumPy and Pandas. This is also the convention we will use in this book.

NUMPY ARRAYS

NumPy holds data in arrays. An array is similar to a list in Python. In fact, in many other programming languages, the "list structure" is called an array.

This is an example of a NumPy array:

```
>>> a = np.array([1,2,3,4])
```

Elements from arrays can be accessed using the list slicing syntax:

```
>>> a[2]
3
>>> a[0:3]
array([1, 2, 3])
```

Notice that an `array` object is returned when multiple elements are captured by the slice. In fact, even the individual elements inside the array are converted to a NumPy datatype:

```
>>> type(a[2])
numpy.int64
```

While NumPy arrays might feel superficially similar to Python lists and primitive objects, it's important to remember that they're very different entities. Their attributes and methods, and the attributes and methods of the elements they contain, are NumPy-specific. Arrays are fundamentally different from lists in many ways, as you'll see shortly.

Like Python lists, NumPy arrays can contain other arrays as elements (and those child arrays can contain arrays of their own, and so on). This allows us to have multidimensional arrays. In Python, the following is a valid list:

```
b = [[1,2], [3,4,5]]
```

However, this will result in an error when we try to convert it to a NumPy array:

```
np.array([[1,2], [3,4,5]])
```

Unless you're the sort of person who uses the word "inhomogeneous" regularly, the error message is somewhat opaque:

```
ValueError: setting an array element with a sequence. The requested array has an
inhomogeneous shape after 1 dimensions. The detected shape was (2,) + inhomogeneous
part.
```

Here, inhomogeneous (from Greek, "not same kind") simply means that the elements in the array do not have the same length. The length of [1,2] is different from the length of [3,4,5]. This difference in length occurs along the second dimension. Hence the message

```
"inhomogeneous shape after 1 dimensions."
```

NumPy is a mathematics library, and two-dimensional arrays represent mathematical matrices. Matrices must be perfect rectangles. The following is a valid matrix:

$$1 \quad 2 \quad 3$$
$$4 \quad 5 \quad 6$$

This is mathematical nonsense:

$$1 \quad 2$$
$$3 \quad 4 \quad 5$$

Because all NumPy arrays are guaranteed to be homogeneous (all elements in the same dimension have the same length), a useful classification for arrays is their *shape*. The shape of an array is its size in each dimension, represented as a tuple. In the case of a one-dimensional array that is four elements long, its shape is a tuple containing only the value 4:

```
>>> a.shape
(4,)
```

For two-dimensional matrices, NumPy follows the convention in mathematics, where an m × n matrix contains m rows (vertical direction) and n columns (horizontal direction). This is an example of a 3 × 4 matrix:

```
>>> b = np.array([
    [1,2,3,4],
    [5,6,7,8],
    [9,10,11,12]
])
>>> b.shape

(3, 4)
```

As you might expect, NumPy arrays can go beyond just one and two-dimensional objects. You can create NumPy arrays representing arbitrary multidimensional matrices. For example, three dimensions can be represented as:

```
>>> c = np.array([
    [[1, 2], [3,4]],
    [[5,6], [7,8]],
    [[9,10], [11,12]],
])
>>> c.shape
(3, 2, 2)
```

Although four dimensions are beyond the scope of this book, astute readers will probably get the picture.

In addition to homogeneity of size, another key property of NumPy arrays is that every element must be the same type. Fortunately, NumPy handles much of this conversion for us. Here's an array that we've seen before:

```
>>> a = np.array([1,2,3,4])
>>> a
array([1, 2, 3, 4])
>>> type(a[0])
numpy.int64
```

Replacing the last element with the string `"four"` results in a different type of array:

```
>>> a = np.array([1,2,3,'four'])
>>> a
array(['1', '2', '3', 'four'], dtype='<U21')
>>> type(a[0])
numpy.str_
```

The `dtype` attribute is the data type of each element in the array. In this case, it's a Unicode string where each element has 21 bytes allocated to it. You can also see that each element, even the former integers, are now surrounded by quotes indicating that they are strings.

Similarly, adding a single float value to an array of integers will cause all elements to be floats, with decimal points displayed after each element:

```
>>> np.array([1,2,3,4.0])
array([1., 2., 3., 4.])
```

Adding a `None` value does something a bit different, however:

```
>>> a = np.array([1,2,3,None])
>>> a
array([1, 2, 3, None], dtype=object)
>>> type(a[0])
int
>>> type(a[3])
NoneType
```

Because NumPy has no way of converting these to the same type, it essentially "gives up" and declares them to be `objects` of some sort. Rather than storing the values of every element in the same location in a row in memory, it only stores pointers to the elements. The actual values live elsewhere, and the NumPy array contains memory addresses for their locations.

In situations where having a None value in an array is important, it's better to use the NumPy equivalent, np.nan ("not a number"):

```
>>> a = np.array([1,2,3,np.nan])
>>> type(a[0])
numpy.float64
>>> type(a[3])
numpy.float64
```

This np.nan is, in the NumPy library, a float. To be clear, it's not a native Python float, but a special type in the NumPy library, called float64. Using it allows NumPy to store all numeric values in the same location, making operations more efficient.

Efficient operations can be extremely important when the number of calculations grows. NumPy arrays often store thousands or even millions of elements, and NumPy is designed to execute statements that perform operations across every element. For example:

```
>>> x = np.array([1,2,3,4,5])
>>> np.sin(x)
array([ 0.84147098,  0.90929743,  0.14112001, -0.7568025 , -0.95892427])
```

This performs the sine operation (np.sin) on every element in the array. Similarly, operations can be performed across multidimensional matrices:

```
>>> c = np.array([[1 * np.pi, 2 * np.pi], [2.5 * np.pi, 1.5 * np.pi]])
>>> np.round(np.sin(c))
array([[ 0., -0.],
       [ 1., -1.]])
```

This uses the constant np.pi to initialize a two-dimensional array, then performs the np.sin and np.round operations to get a two-dimensional result.

NumPy is a powerful math framework with advanced linear algebra and scientific computing functionality. However, it is commonly used today in conjunction with other frameworks that are built on top of it, such as Pandas and scikit-learn.

PANDAS DATAFRAMES

The Pandas library is centered around a single data structure, the *DataFrame*. The DataFrame is a powerful and flexible data structure that, at times, seems like it has more in common with an Excel spreadsheet than the Python data structures we usually deal with.

You can create a DataFrame directly using the DataFrame class:

```
df = pd.DataFrame(
    [['one', 1], ['two', 2], ['three', 3]],
    columns=['name', 'value']
)
```

Both native Python data structures and NumPy arrays can be passed in as data. Columns names are optional, but if they're not supplied, integers starting with 0 will be used as column names. Because you will frequently reference column names as you work with DataFrames, it's best to come up with something short and meaningful.

Although DataFrames can be used in any Python code, they work especially well in Jupyter notebooks. When returned from a notebook cell, they have an attractive formatted display that makes them easy to view.

Subsets of the DataFrame can be viewed using the head method, as shown in Figure 23.1. By default, the head method returns up to the first five rows of a DataFrame as a new DataFrame object. You can also pass an integer number of rows to return to head as an argument. When used in a notebook, head is a great way to get a summary of DataFrames quickly.

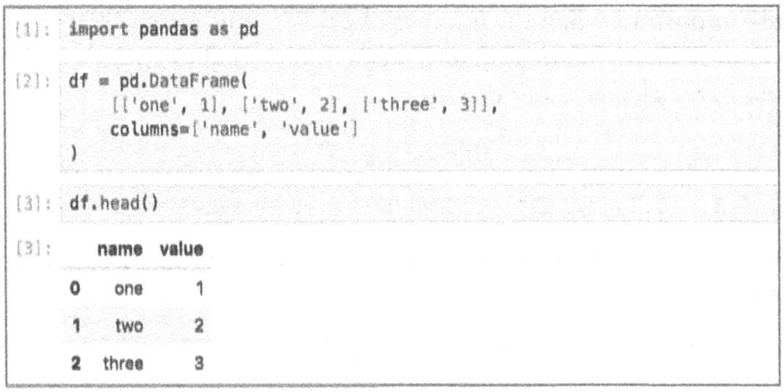

```
[1]: import pandas as pd

[2]: df = pd.DataFrame(
        [['one', 1], ['two', 2], ['three', 3]],
        columns=['name', 'value']
     )

[3]: df.head()

[3]:    name  value
     0  one     1
     1  two     2
     2  three   3
```

FIGURE 23.1: Pandas DataFrames display in a readable way, which makes them ideal for viewing and presenting data.

Learning about DataFrames is easier when they contain more interesting data. One source of interesting data is from Kaggle (https://kaggle.com). Kaggle is a platform for learning about data science and competing in data science model building. It hosts many excellent open source datasets that are made freely available for experimentation and discovery.

One such dataset is "Real Estate Data London 2024" (www.kaggle.com/datasets/ kanchana1990/real-estate-data-london-2024). This dataset contains, as of this writing, 1,109 London properties, each with a text description, various size measurements, and price, among other fields. It is freely available to download as a CSV file, and, once downloaded, can be loaded as a CSV file using the Pandas read_csv function, which returns a DataFrame from CSV files.

```
df = pd.read_csv('23_real_estate.csv')
df.head()
```

	addedOn	title	descrip tionHtml	property Type	sizeSqF eetMax	bed rooms	bath rooms	listing Update Reason	price
0	10/10/2024	8 bedroom house for sale in Winnington Road, H...	This magnifi cent home, set behind security gat...	House	16749.0	8.0	8.0	new	£24,950,000
1	Reduced on 24/10/2024	7 bedroom house for sale in Brick Street, Mayf...	In the heart of exclusive Mayfair, this majest...	House	12960.0	7.0	7.0	price_ reduced	£29,500,000
2	Reduced on 22/02/2024	6 bedroom terraced house for sale in Chester S...	A freehold home that gives you every thing you...	Terraced	6952.0	6.0	6.0	price_ reduced	£25,000,000
3	08/04/2024	6 bedroom detached house for sale in Winningto...	A magnifi cent bespoke residence set behind sec...	Detached	16749.0	6.0	6.0	new	£24,950,000
4	Reduced on 11/07/2023	8 bedroom detached house for sale in St. John'...	With its village like ambiance, elegant regenc...	Detached	10241.0	8.0	10.0	price_ reduced	£24,950,000

A DataFrame is an ordered collection of columns. Each column has a type and an array of data associated with it. The fields `addedOn`, `title`, `descriptionHtml`, `propertyType`, `listingUpdateReason`, and `price` are strings. The fields `sizeSqFeetmax`, `bedrooms`, and `bathrooms` are floats.

Although "half bath" is a common real estate term and the `bathrooms` column is a float type, fractional bathrooms are not present in this data. The reason it's a float and not an integer is because, like `sizeSqFeetmax` and `bedrooms`, some of this data is missing and populated with `pd.nan`. This forces the entire column to become a float.

The underlying data in DataFrames is stored in NumPy arrays. You can see this by accessing each column of data in the DataFrame using dot notation. These columns are Pandas `Series` objects, while the values they hold are NumPy arrays:

```
print(type(df.title))
print(type(df.title.values))
```

```
<class 'pandas.core.series.Series'>
<class 'numpy.ndarray'>
```

One important part of DataFrame anatomy is the *index*. Every Pandas DataFrame has at least one index that is used to locate data quickly. The index is displayed as the leftmost column with bold values. If an index isn't provided, Pandas will dynamically generate one with ascending integers.

Indexes usually contain unique (non-duplicated) values. Pandas does not actually require that indexes be unique, but having unique indexes does provide performance gains, particularly in larger tables.

You can provide the name of a column to use as an index when loading the data:

```
df = pd.read_csv('23_real_estate.csv', index_col='sizeSqFeetMax')
```

This sets the index of the DataFrame to the column `sizeSqFeetMax` and eliminates the need for the default index. In practice, of course, `sizeSqFeetMax` would likely not make a good index because this column does not contain unique values. You can also set the index using the `set_index` method on existing DataFrames:

```
df = pd.read_csv('23_real_estate.csv')
df.set_index('sizeSqFeetMax', inplace=True)
```

The keyword argument `inplace` is set to `True` to indicate that we want to update the existing DataFrame rather than returning a copy containing the new index.

To create a new dynamically generated integer index and treat any existing indexes as regular columns, use the method `reset_index`:

```
df = pd.read_csv('23_real_estate.csv', index_col='sizeSqFeetMax')
df.reset_index(inplace=True)
```

Note that this does not discriminate between its own dynamically generated index and "actual data" that was loaded. If you call it repeatedly, you'll end up with old indexes containing ascending integers mixed in with data columns. In general, you want to update DataFrame indexes sparingly, and with caution.

In addition to the data values, column names are also indexed. You can view the column names of a DataFrame using the `columns` attribute:

```
df.columns
```

```
Index(['sizeSqFeetMax', 'addedOn', 'title', 'descriptionHtml',
'propertyType',
       'bedrooms', 'bathrooms', 'listingUpdateReason', 'price'],
      dtype='object')
```

This returns a Pandas `Index` object, which provides an index on top of the string column names. Although it might seem a little silly with just nine columns, keep in mind that DataFrames can get very large, and some might contain so many columns that an index provides a significant performance value.

Digging into the index, we find our old friend, the NumPy array:

```
df.columns.values
```

```
array(['sizeSqFeetMax', 'addedOn', 'title', 'descriptionHtml',
       'propertyType', 'bedrooms', 'bathrooms', 'listingUpdateReason',
       'price'], dtype=object)
```

While NumPy arrays provide efficient memory management and faster operations (in most cases) than standard Python, DataFrame indexes provide a layer of efficiency on top of that for some operations on large datasets.

CLEANING

If you remember nothing else about data science after reading this book, remember this one thing: Data science involves a lot of data cleaning. Data scientists spend a huge amount of time cleaning and parsing text, formatting numbers, and wrestling multiple data sources into alignment with each other. It's not all glamour and writing AI prompts. Sometimes, it's removing punctuation and figuring out how to convert currency.

In this section, we'll continue with the "Real Estate Data London 2024" dataset used previously. The cleaned version of the dataset produced in this section will also be used throughout the rest of this chapter and the next. A clean dataset is just too valuable a thing to waste.

```
df = pd.read_csv('23_real_estate.csv')
df.head()
```

London real estate is expensive. It might be interesting to see exactly *how* expensive it can get. To sort values by the `price` column in the dataset, use the `sort_values` method:

```
df.sort_values(by='price', inplace=True, ascending=True)
df.head()
```

This should rearrange the data in place with the cheapest properties first and the most expensive ones last. Unfortunately, because the values in the `price` column are strings, it doesn't have quite the desired effect. The first price is POA (a real estate term meaning "price on application" or "price on asking"), which is reasonable. The next lowest prices are all prices that happen to start with a 1.

The `tail` method can be used to inspect the end of a DataFrame, just like `head` is used to inspect the beginning:

```
df.tail()
```

This shows us that the last rows in the DataFrame have prices that start with a 9 (such as £9,950,000) but are not actually the highest price, given that, previously, we saw prices of £24,950,000 and £29,500,000.

This can be solved by cleaning the price strings and converting them, if possible, to an integer. We write a simple price cleaning function:

```
def price_cleaner(price):
    price = price.replace('£', '').replace(',', '')
    try:
        return int(price)
    except:
        print(f'Could not process {price}')
        return np.nan
```

Then, we use the `apply` method on the `price` column to apply that function to every item, sort the values again, and view:

```
df.price = df.price.apply(price_cleaner)
df.sort_values(by='price', inplace=True, ascending=True)
df.head()
```

This shows that the cheapest property is £315,000 and the most expensive (seen using the `tail` method) is an eye-watering £80,000,000.

Pandas `Series` objects are iterable. This is useful for examining data more closely. The `descriptionHtml` column is truncated in each cell, but we can view the first 10 records in full by iterating over and printing each one:

```
for description in df.head(10).descriptionHtml:
    print('\n')
    print(description)
```

Here the `head` method is used with an argument of 10 to return only the first 10 rows.

The description column contains HTML data, although it appears that the only HTML tag in use is `<br />`. We can remove this using:

```
def description_cleaner(description):
    return description.replace('<br />', '\n')
df.descriptionHtml = df.descriptionHtml.apply(description_cleaner)
```

With cleaning functions that consist of a single statement, a Lambda function can be used instead:

```
df.descriptionHtml = df.descriptionHtml.apply(lambda d: d.replace('<br />', '\n'))
```

After cleaning this, we may want to examine additional records to ensure that we didn't miss anything in cleaning. The Python slicing syntax can be used with DataFrames to get a subset of rows:

```
for description in df[10:20].descriptionHtml:
    print('\n')
    print(description)
```

This reveals opening and closing tags for `<b>`, `<div>`, `<strong>`, and more. Theoretically, we could make an exhaustive list of every HTML tag encountered and simply remove them. However, we may get additional data in the future with HTML tags that we haven't seen.

Alternatively, we could use regular expressions to remove everything between a < character and a > character, which would strip all properly formatted HTML tags. Something like this would work:

```
import re

html_regex = re.compile(r'<.*?>')
def description_cleaner(description):
    return html_regex.sub('', description)

df.descriptionHtml = df.descriptionHtml.apply(description_cleaner)
```

This regular expression matches on an opening < character, searches until it finds a closing > character, and using the sub method, removes <, >, and everything in between them.

But this leaves the possibility of *improperly* formatted HTML getting through. We have no idea how these HTML documents are created. They may, in fact, be handwritten by real estate agents who are prone to typos in their tags. In addition, something as simple as the use of greater than or less than signs in normal writing ("Buyer will need to show > £1,000,000 in assets") may cause issues.

For situations in which HTML is more complex, I recommend using BeautifulSoup to remove it. Discussed in Chapter 22, "Web Scraping and Scrapy," BeautifulSoup can be used in a simple function to strip HTML tags:

```
def description_cleaner(description):
    return BeautifulSoup(description).get_text()
```

Although the BeautifulSoup solution is robust, maintainable, and clean, it does have a speed disadvantage. If your HTML is relatively simple, and your application is not high stakes (it's fine if a few records get mangled here and there), you may consider sticking with regular expressions or even just the replace method.

It may also be worth timing both operations across a representative set of records in order to inform your decision:

```
import time

html_regex = re.compile(r'<.*?>')
def description_cleaner_regex(description):
    return html_regex.sub('', description)

def description_cleaner_bs(description):
    return BeautifulSoup(description).get_text()

df = pd.read_csv('23_real_estate.csv')
start = time.time()
df.descriptionHtml = df.descriptionHtml.apply(description_cleaner_regex)
print(f'Regex cleaning took {time.time() - start} seconds')

df = pd.read_csv('23_real_estate.csv')
df.descriptionHtml = df.descriptionHtml.apply(description_cleaner_bs)
print(f'BeautifulSoup cleaning took {time.time() - start} seconds')
```

This prints:

```
Regex cleaning took 0.006099224090576172 seconds
BeautifulSoup  cleaning took 0.15406513214111328 seconds
```

BeautifulSoup is 25 times slower than using regular expressions for these descriptions. If you're processing millions of records in a speed-critical operation, you may want to reconsider using BeautifulSoup in favor of regular expressions. However, over our thousand or so records, taking the extra milliseconds to ensure the data is reliably cleaned is a good trade-off.

The titles in the dataset are interesting. They have a similar pattern:

```
4 bedroom apartment for sale in 22 Hanover Square, London, W1S 1JA, W1S
7 bedroom town house for sale in Whistler Square, London, SW1W
6 bedroom house for sale in Whistler Square, Chelsea Barracks, London, SW1W, United
Kingdom, SW1W
```

In fact, they all have the format "*<bedroom number>* bedroom *<property type>* for sale in *<location>*." Although the bedroom number and property type are already available in the data, the location or the property is absent. If you're doing an analysis of housing costs, this location data may be useful. We may also be able to use bedrooms and property type data from the title to fill in any missing data or flag discrepancies.

To create several new columns from a single DataFrame column, we can use the `apply` method again:

```
def title_parser(row):
    try:
        data, row['location'] = row['title'].split(' for sale in ')
        row['bedrooms_title'], row['property_type_title'] = data.split(' bedroom ')
        row['bedrooms_title'] = int(row['bedrooms_title'])
        return row
    except:
        print(f'Non-standard title: {row['title']}')

df = df.apply(title_parser, axis=1)
```

Passing `axis=1` to the `apply` method allows you to perform operations on the entire row, rather than just a single value in it. The row argument passed to the function is the Pandas `Series` object from that row in the DataFrame. We can then update any columns we want in the row, as well as add new columns entirely. Make sure to return the argument `row` from the parsing function, as well as update the original DataFrame with the return value from the `apply` method.

The `title_parser` function splits titles of the form "*<bedroom number>* bedroom *<property type>* for sale in *<location>*" and extracts the number of bedrooms, property type, and location. If the title doesn't match the expected format, a `Non-standard title:` message is printed and any values in the new columns (`location`, `bedrooms_title`, `property_type_title`) that haven't been set yet will have a value of `None` for that row.

Finally, the `added_on` column in the dataset contains strings with dates of the format <month>/<day>/<year>. Let's extract the string dates from this column to NumPy `datetime` objects in a new column.

Some values contain only a date string, and other records have an apparently reduced price and state `Reduced on <month>/<day>/<year>`. For our purposes, we can remove the `Reduced on` or any other text surrounding the date string and simply extract the date.

Other values in this column say things like `Reduced today` or `Added yesterday` and don't mention a specific date. As of this writing, the last update date for the dataset is given as November 6, 2024, so we will use the date `06/11/2024` as a substitute for `today` and the date `05/11/2024` as a substitute for `yesterday`.

The function `date_str_cleaner` handles missing dates; removes the text `Added`, `Reduced`, and `on`; and substitutes the correct dates for `yesterday` and `today`:

```
def date_str_cleaner(date_str):
    if pd.isna(date_str):
        return None

    date_str = date_str.replace('Added', '').replace('Reduced', '').
replace('on', '')
    date_str = date_str.replace('today', '06/11/2024')
    date_str = date_str.replace('yesterday', '05/11/2024')
    date_str = date_str.strip()
    return date_str
```

We can create a new `date` column in our DataFrame using a two-step process where, first, `date_str_cleaner` is applied to get a clean date string. Then, the Pandas function `to_datetime` is used on the `Series` to convert all values to a date string using a format of `'%d/%m/%Y'`:

```
df['date'] = df.addedOn.apply(date_str_cleaner)
df['date'] = pd.to_datetime(df.date, format='%d/%m/%Y')
```

With the dates converted to `datetime` objects, they can be safely sorted and used chronologically.

Currently, there's a bit of conflict between the column names from the data like `propertyType` and the snake case column names we're creating, like `property_type_title`. To rename columns, use the `rename` method:

```
df.rename(columns={
    'descriptionHtml': 'description',
    'propertyType': 'property_type',
    'sizeSqFeetMax': 'sq_feet',
    'listingUpdateReason': 'listing_update_reason'
}, inplace=True)
```

Very rarely are you presented with a pristine dataset where all columns are readily useful for data science operations. In the vast majority of cases, at least a little titivation is required. The process of cleaning is also often our first peek at how complete the dataset is and what fun anomalies it might contain.

In the next section, we'll continue this initial analysis of the data and find out how to start exploring and quantifying it more thoroughly.

FILTERING AND QUERYING

Although using the `head` method to view a few initial rows of a DataFrame is a great way to get a sense of the data's format, it's simply no way to really explore it. For that, you need to be able to search and select the rows using specific parameters.

Pandas DataFrames can be queried using their own query language, a modified version of Python syntax. The DataFrame `query` method returns a new DataFrame containing all the rows that match the provided query:

```
df.query('price < 1000000')
```

It's important to stress that, although we are querying based only on the price in the dataframe, all data colums for all rows matching the query, not just the price data, will be returned. In this case, we get back a DataFrame containing the 28 records of properties worth less than £1,000,000.

Boolean operators can be used in queries as well. This retrieves the eight cheap properties with at least three bedrooms:

```
df.query('price < 1000000 and bedrooms >= 3')
```

And this retrieves the 16 cheap properties with at least three bedrooms or two bathrooms:

```
len(df.query('price < 1000000 and (bedrooms >= 3 or bathrooms >= 2)'))
```

And, finally, the five very expensive penthouses:

```
df.query('price > 20000000 and property_type == "Penthouse"')
```

Another way of selecting DataFrame data is by using bracket notation. The bracket syntax is somewhat more difficult to read, but also more flexible than the query language syntax.

Here are the same four queries translated into bracket notation:

```
df[df['price'] < 1000000]
df[(df['price'] < 1000000) & (df['bedrooms'] >= 3)]
df[(df['price'] < 1000000) & ((df['bedrooms'] >= 3) | (df['bathrooms'] >= 2))]
df[(df['price'] > 20000000) & (df['property_type'] == 'Penthouse')]
```

Earlier, we used the dot notation `df.price` to access the `Series` object representing the `price` column. Another way of writing this is with the bracket notation `df['price']`. While the dot notation is arguably nicer-looking, using brackets is handy if your DataFrame contains column names with spaces or special characters in them, like `df['column name with spaces']`.

Boolean comparisons performed on a `Series` return a `Series` of Boolean values. The comparison `df['price'] > 20000000` returns a `Series` with the corresponding truth value at each index in the DataFrame:

```
74      False
484     False
850     False
241     False
753     False
        . . .
43       True
45       True
44       True
46       True
882     False
Name: price, Length: 1019, dtype: bool
```

When we pass this `Series` of Boolean values into the DataFrame with square brackets, it is used as a "mask" to decide which values will be returned in a new DataFrame and which won't:

```
prices_to_be_returned_mask = df['price'] > 20000000
df[prices_to_be_returned_mask]
```

If you're struggling to understand the bracket syntax for filtering DataFrames, it can help to view it as "applied masks," rather than a query language similar to the one the `query` method uses. What makes this syntax powerful is that Pandas has many ways of creating these Boolean masks. Any method on a `Series` that produces a Boolean result can be used to create a DataFrame mask. For example,

```
df[df['property_type'].isin(['Apartment', 'Flat'])]
```

selects all properties that are described as either "Apartment" or "Flat." This one selects all properties containing the word "charming" in the description:

```
df[df['description'].str.contains('charming', na=False)]
```

Because some of the descriptions are empty, we need to pass na=False as an argument to provide a default value for empty descriptions. Otherwise, the `contains` method returns np.nan instead of a Boolean for that description. This causes an error when we try to use the `Series` as a DataFrame mask, as masks must contain only `True` or `False` values, not np.nan.

In addition to selecting a subset of rows using a mask of Boolean values, we can pass in a list of column name strings to select a subset of DataFrame columns. For example,

```
df[['sq_feet', 'bedrooms', 'bathrooms', 'price']]
```

creates a DataFrame containing only the numeric columns sq_feet, bedrooms, bathrooms, and price. This can be useful for narrowing down the data that you're looking at when doing initial data analysis. In addition, the columns in the new DataFrame will be ordered according to the provided list, so this is a great way to get two columns side-by-side for comparison.

Column selection and row selection can also be chained together to create new DataFrames with a subset of the original data:

```
df[df['property_type'] == 'Penthouse'][['price']]
```

This results in a DataFrame of penthouses containing only one column, the price.

Be careful when getting a DataFrame containing only a single column with this syntax, as it can easily be confused with this line:

```
df[df['property_type'] == 'Penthouse']['price']
```

This does not select using the list of lists, [['price']], but a list containing a single string ['price']. The second example, with a list containing a single string, will return a `Series` object representing the price column. The first example, with a list of lists, will return a DataFrame.

GROUPING AND AGGREGATING

Data aggregation is when we go from simply viewing data to performing operations on the data and synthesizing it to generate potentially novel insights.

Aggregations on a DataFrame are equivalent to a GROUP BY operation in SQL syntax. It partitions the data into groups, based on some criteria, and performs some operation across the values in each group to summarize the data within them.

Examples of questions that aggregations and grouping can answer, in our dataset:

➤ What is the total property value of all penthouses? All apartments?

➤ What is the average price by number of bedrooms?

➤ What is the average number of bedrooms by number of bathrooms (average number of bedrooms for 1 bathroom, 2 bathrooms, etc.)?

➤ How many bedrooms does the property with the most bedrooms have, for each of the property types?

If our London real estate DataFrame were an SQL table called real_estate, we might write an operation to get the average price of each property type like this:

```
SELECT property_type, AVG(price) FROM real_estate GROUP BY property_type
```

Here, we're grouping the data by property_type and selecting the average price from within each property type group. Because there are 19 unique property types in the dataset, there will be 19 rows returned.

In Pandas, we do something similar:

```
df.groupby(['property_type']).agg({
    'price': 'mean'
})
```

This calls two methods in succession. The first is groupby, which creates a Pandas DataFrameGroupBy object. This DataFrameGroupBy can be aggregated into a new DataFrame using the agg method, which takes a dictionary of columns and aggregating functions or strings. This new DataFrame has 19 rows, the first five of which are:

property_type	price
Apartment	9.946726e+06
Block of Apartments	1.093750e+07
Character Property	6.500000e+05
Detached	1.167687e+07
Duplex	1.129160e+07

It's important to note that the property_type column is not just another data column, but an index. Because DataFrames are required to have an index of some sort, and this grouped column is guaranteed to contain unique values, it is set as the index by the aggregating function.

The string `'mean'` passed to the aggregating function, corresponds to the function `np.mean`. Any NumPy function that takes in an array and returns a value can be used here. For example:

```
df.groupby(['property_type']).agg({
    'price': 'std'
})
```

The string `'std'` corresponds to the function `np.std` and calculates the standard deviation of property values for each property type.

Multiple columns can be aggregated and returned in the DataFrame by passing multiple key-value pairs to the dictionary:

```
df.groupby(['property_type']).agg({
    'price': 'mean',
    'bathrooms': 'max',
    'bedrooms': 'max'
})
```

Multiple types of aggregations can also be done on a single column. For example, both the average and standard deviation might be useful when examining prices in various property categories:

```
df.groupby(['property_type']).agg({
    'price': ['mean', 'std']
})
```

This results in a DataFrame with hierarchical columns, where the `price` column has two columns under it: mean and std, as shown in Figure 23.2. You can also see this for yourself by using the `head` method on the DataFrame returned by the grouping.

```
[260]: df_grouped = df.groupby(['property_type']).agg({
           'price': ['mean', 'std']
       })
       df_grouped.head()

[260]:                              price
                           mean            std
       property_type

            Apartment  9.946726e+06    5.792350e+06
 Block of Apartments  1.093750e+07    4.942903e+06
  Character Property  6.500000e+05             NaN
             Detached  1.167687e+07    5.891813e+06
               Duplex  1.129160e+07    5.819055e+06
```

FIGURE 23.2: Hierarchical columns show multiple column names (mean, std) below a single parent column (price).

The `columns` attribute of this DataFrame is represented as a `MultiIndex` object:

```
MultiIndex([('price', 'mean'),
            ('price',  'std')],
           )
```

Using these hierarchical or multilevel indexes is somewhat outside the scope of this book, although many examples of their usage can be found in the Pandas documentation: https://pandas.pydata.org/docs/user_guide/advanced.html.

If you want to flatten these columns to get back to a simple list of columns, you can use the following:

```
df_grouped.columns = ['_'.join(col).strip() for col in df_grouped.columns.values]
```

This will flatten all columns and rename them to the values in the hierarchy separated by underscores. In the case of this example, the new column names will be price_mean and price_std.

DataFrame groupings can also contain multiple columns. For example, if we wanted to analyze all possible combinations of bathroom and bedroom counts we could make the following aggregation:

```
df.groupby(['bedrooms', 'bathrooms']).agg({
    'price': 'mean',
    'sq_feet': 'mean'
})
```

This results in a DataFrame that contains two columns in its index, bedroom count and bathroom count, and two columns of data representing the average (mean) price and square footage for each combination of bedrooms and bathrooms.

If you're not satisfied with the NumPy-provided math functions for your aggregations, you can supply your own as well. The following creates a DataFrame with a column representing the first property type encountered for each group:

```
def first(s):
    return s.iloc[0]

df.groupby(['bedrooms', 'bathrooms']).agg({
    'price': 'mean',
    'sq_feet': 'mean',
    'property_type': first
})
```

The functions used in aggregations must accept a Pandas Series object as their argument. The function first uses the iloc (index location) attribute of the Series to access the value of an element by index location. Using a Series object s, the value s.iloc[0] is the first element.

Cleaning, formatting, querying, and aggregating data are essential skills for any data scientist (or software engineer looking to dabble in data science once in a while). Although it may not be glamorous, simply cleaning the data can often be the bulk of the work.

In the next chapter, we'll take this data and look at some methods to visualize it and make predictions based on it.

24

Machine Learning with Matplotlib and Scikit-Learn

In the previous chapter, we viewed, cleaned, and did some basic data analysis with NumPy and Pandas using data from London real estate listings. In this chapter, we'll continue with that same dataset.

First, we'll use Matplotlib, a plotting and visualization library, to view the data and look for trends and outliers. Then we'll use scikit-learn to train machine learning models on the data and analyze the performance of those models.

Scikit-learn comes with its own datasets that, while based on real-world data, have nice correlations and patterns that make them popular as "toy datasets." A complete list of datasets is available here: https://scikit-learn.org/1.5/datasets/toy_dataset.html.

Each toy dataset can be loaded as a Pandas DataFrame in the following way:

```
from sklearn.datasets import load_iris

iris = load_iris()
df_iris = pd.DataFrame(data=iris.data, columns=iris.feature_names)
```

"Iris" is perhaps the most famous dataset in data science and is based on measurements of iris flowers taken in 1936. It is excellent for practicing clustering and classification. The "diabetes" dataset (load_diabetes) is also very famous and is useful for regression problems.

Of course, these toy datasets are part of a carefully curated collection because each of them is clean and easy to use. To learn how to really work with data, you often want data that is a little messier. For datasets like these, I highly recommend that you go to Kaggle (https://kaggle.com), Data.gov (https://data.gov), Google Cloud Public Datasets (https://cloud.google.com/datasets), or another one of the plentiful sources of free and open source datasets. You never know—you might just discover something new!

Many data cleaning functions were developed in the last chapter to format and extract data from various columns of the London real estate dataset. I won't reproduce them here (you can always go back a few pages), but the primary functions we're interested in are:

➤ `price_cleaner`

➤ `description_cleaner`

➤ `title_parser`

➤ `date_str_cleaner`

It can be handy, when building models, to get a fresh and clean copy of the dataset you're working with easily. The function `get_clean_df` will be used throughout this chapter to do just that:

```python
def get_clean_df():
    df = pd.read_csv('23_real_estate.csv')
    df.descriptionHtml = df.descriptionHtml.apply(description_cleaner)
    df.price = df.price.apply(price_cleaner)
    df['date'] = df.addedOn.apply(date_str_cleaner)
    df['date'] = pd.to_datetime(df.date, format='%d/%m/%Y')

    df = df.apply(title_parser, axis=1)

    return df.rename(columns={
        'descriptionHtml': 'description',
        'propertyType': 'property_type',
        'sizeSqFeetMax': 'sq_feet',
        'listingUpdateReason': 'listing_update_reason',
        'addedOn': 'added_on'
    })
```

This function reads the raw data downloaded from Kaggle and combines each step of the cleaning process we developed. It is, of course, included in the Jupyter notebook file for this chapter and will be used throughout.

TYPES OF MACHINE LEARNING MODELS

In machine learning, the end result of your efforts is typically a *model*. This model is built, or *trained*, on a large existing dataset and can make determinations or predictions for new data coming in.

For example, we might have a dataset of demographic information for people who made an appointment at a car dealership. This dataset might include information such as age, zip code, gender, and income, as well as whether those people ultimately purchased vehicles. We could then build a model that predicts, based on the demographics of a new potential customer making an appointment, if they will purchase a vehicle.

This kind of model is called a *classification*. It is classifying people into two types: those who purchase a car and those who do not purchase a car.

We might also want to make predictions about what *kind* of car a person will want. Will they want a Ford F-150, a Subaru Outback, or a Chevy Camaro? This is another classification problem, because we are trying to take demographic information and predict if that person belongs to the class of "people who purchase Subaru Outbacks," "people who purchase Camaros," etc.

As you might expect, the more specific or accurate the classification is, the more information you typically need about a person. To predict if someone will purchase a sports car or a minivan, it might be helpful to know how many children they have and the ages of those children, for instance.

Each property of the dataset is called a *feature*. Features might be numeric (how many children), multidimensional (ages of those children), categorical (whether they have children) or something else that might require additional processing, such as a freeform text field where the customer describes what they want in a vehicle. A text field feature might then be turned into multiple features (whether particular makes/models were mentioned, results of a sentiment analysis, length of text, etc.).

If the customer applies for financing for their new vehicle, the car dealership will be interested in whether the customer will make payments on time. This is another classification into "people who make payments on time" and "people who do not make payments on time." Or, more realistically, they may classify the customer into one of several interest rate groups (such as 3.5%, 5%, 12.99%, "do not lend") given the customer's risk of not making payments.

In the United States, the dataset used to determine which of these interest rate classes the potential debtor falls into often contains only one feature: the credit score.

The credit score, an integer ranging from 300 to 850, is itself the output of another type of model. These models are created and maintained by companies that supply consumer reports (Equifax, TransUnion, and Experian). They take many features (number and length of credit accounts, account balances, payment history, etc.) and output a single number: the credit score.

This is not a classification problem; rather, credit scores are created with *regression* models. The output of a classification model is a discrete class, such as gender, preferred car model, or whether a purchase will be made. The output of a regression model is a numeric value.[1] This might be *percent likelihood* of making a purchase, how many minutes of salesperson time it will take to close a single deal, or amount sales will decrease if the dealership cuts its marketing budget.

Both of classification and regression are types of *supervised learning*. To create the models, we must give it data containing all of our features plus the "answer"—the output that those features correctly correspond to in the real world.

If we're classifying people into "purchasers" and "non-purchasers," we must have a set of historical data containing all their demographic features and whether they ultimately made a purchase. If we want to model how the marketing budget impacts sales, we must have historical data points in which the marketing budget was modified and how sales were actually impacted.

Other types of machine learning models use *unsupervised learning*. One popular type of unsupervised ML algorithm is *clustering*, which identifies "clusters" in features of data. These clusters represent areas where the data naturally bunches together, forming a group of similar data points.

---

[1] Theoretically, if you *really* wanted to, a classifier could be used to output a credit score as well. Each number of a credit score, from 300 to 850, could be its own class, for 451 classes (including both 300 and 850) in total. However, this would be an extremely difficult and silly task in practice. The fact that numbers have a sequential order is critical to the concept of regression models. The model knows that "501" is very close to "502" which is relatively close to "510" but very distant from "830." All of this information is completely lost when it comes to classification models, where each class is distinct and unrelated to other classes.

Although these clusters are not named or labeled by the clustering algorithm, we may want to examine these clusters and recognize the patterns that describe them. For example, if we're clustering demographic data of people who visit a car dealership, we may find clusters like "55 plus–year-old men with high incomes who buy sports cars and have grown children" and "35–50-year-old women who enjoy hiking and buy Subarus."

The marketing department of a car dealership may be interested in clustering algorithms to identify new user groups to advertise to. For example, clustering may reveal a large number of 25-to-35-year-old women with high incomes interested in Audis. They may then decide to advertise Audis available for sale through media that caters to that demographic.

Generative AI models, which gained popularity with the public in the early 2020s, are also largely unsupervised. However, they may have some supervised aspects on top of this unsupervised base model.

For example, ChatGPT was built by processing large (very large) amounts of text data and creating an unsupervised model that could generate text similar to what it had already seen. However, for specific or novel problems, you can provide ChatGPT with feedback about its performance, which will be incorporated into a new model for your specific application.

When developing machine learning models, it is important to keep in mind exactly what you want to use your model to accomplish. You can't simply "throw machine learning at it" and expect AI to solve all your problems! The features of your dataset must be gathered, cleaned, and processed into numeric and categorial values. You must decide exactly what kind of output you need, what the output means, and how to make use of it. Models must constantly be evaluated and updated as new information and better algorithms come in.

EXPLORATORY ANALYSIS WITH MATPLOTLIB

Although it can be fun to blindly throw machine learning at a dataset and see what happens, plotting the values first will help you get a better sense of the data, estimate the strength of various correlations, and check for any outliers that might cause problems with the models.

To create a visualization in Matplotlib you need to use the `pyplot` interface. Traditionally, this is imported as `plt`:

```
import matplotlib.pyplot as plt
```

The simplest visualization to make in Matplotlib is a scatter plot which shows the relationship between two features:

```
plt.scatter(df['sq_feet'], df['price'])
```

This shows square feet on the x-axis and price in pound sterling on the y-axis. To make this more obvious, we can add some labels and a title:

```
plt.scatter(df['sq_feet'], df['price'])
plt.xlabel('Square Feet')
plt.ylabel('Pound Sterling')
plt.title('Price vs. Square Feet')
```

The output of this code is shown in Figure 24.1.

```
plt.scatter(df['sq_feet'], df['price'])
plt.xlabel('Square Feet')
plt.ylabel('Pound Sterling')
plt.title('Price vs. Square Feet')

Text(0.5, 1.0, 'Price vs. Square Feet')
```

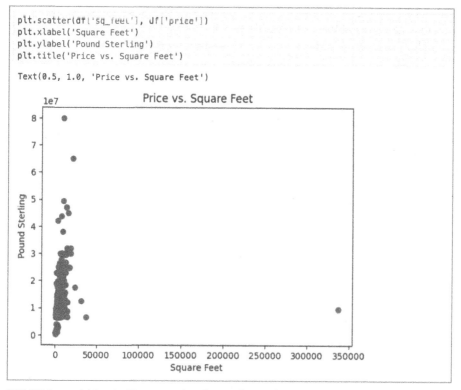

FIGURE 24.1: A Matplotlib scatterplot shows all samples plotted on a graph of price vs. square feet.

This relationship appears to be nearly vertical on the left side of the graph. It's hard to really see what's going on at all. This is because a data point on the right side, an extreme outlier, is distorting the data. This data point, representing a five-bedroom penthouse, appears to be incorrect, as other sources online list it as a relatively modest 3,354 square feet rather than 336,989 square feet.

Outliers can be eliminated from the dataset entirely using a DataFrame query:

```
df = df.query('sq_feet < 250000')
```

Because this property is listed as a five-bedroom penthouse apartment, and not "5 bedroom large office building," I think we can safely eliminate it. To be safe, this filter should be added to the get_clean_df function:

```
def get_clean_df():
    df = pd.read_csv('23_real_estate.csv')
    ...
    df = df.apply(title_parser, axis=1)

    # remove outlier
    df = df.query('sizeSqFeetMax < 250000')

    return df.rename(columns={
        ...
    })
```

For most other purposes, you likely want to "zoom in" on the data by adjusting the axes in Matplotlib, rather than eliminate outliers entirely—especially during earlier exploratory stages. To adjust the axes, use the axis method and pass in a list of values representing the x-axis minimum, x-axis maximum, y-axis minimum, and y-axis maximum:

```
plt.axis([0, 25000, 0, 80000000])
plt.scatter(df['sq_feet'], df['price'])
```

This displays all properties between 0 and 25,000 square feet and priced between 0 and £80,000,000. Although this is a better view of the data, it still looks relatively "blob-like." Many data points are stacked on top of each other, making it difficult to discern patterns. To remedy this, we can shrink the size of the dots themselves and zoom in again on the more crowded parts of the data (see Figure 24.2):

```
plt.axis([0, 15000, 0, 30000000])
plt.xlabel('Square Feet')
plt.ylabel('Pound Sterling')
plt.title('Price vs. Square Feet')
plt.scatter(df['sq_feet'], df['price'], s=1)
```

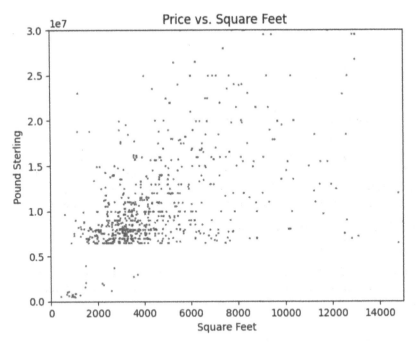

FIGURE 24.2: Shrinking the size of the points and zooming in on the data can help reveal additional trends.

This shows some interesting patterns. There's a loose positive correlation between price and square footage. Also, a strong line at £6,500,000, with very few properties priced below that number. This could be caused by some interesting quirk of the London real estate market or an artifact of the data. Perhaps the data was taken from a website that only deals with properties above £6.5 million with few exceptions, for example.

Although there are 19 unique property types in this dataset, only six of them have more than six records. Those top six comprise 86% of the total dataset. Others, such as "Ground Flat" and "Character Property," have only one record each! The following gets a list of the top six most popular property types, and then creates a new DataFrame, df_ppt, with only properties of those types:

```
property_types = df.groupby('property_type').agg({
    'title': 'count'
}).sort_values(by='title', ascending=False)

popular_property_types = list(property_types.index[0:6])
df_ppt = df[df['property_type'].isin(popular_property_types)]
len(df_ppt)
```

We can use this to create a more focused visualization that displays each of these major property types in a different color. Matplotlib provides a variety of color sets, called *colormaps*, to choose from. They can be viewed here: https://matplotlib.org/stable/gallery/color/colormap_reference.html.

Most Matplotlib colormaps gradually fade from one color to another to display values that are continuous or sequential. For example, a value of 56% is very close to a value of 57% so they will display similarly in the graph but they will both be visually distinct from a value of 3%. "Property types," in contrast, are *categorical*. They should all be visually distinct from each other. To display these property types, we will use the `tab10` colormap, which contains 10 distinct colors.

You can see the full set of RGB color values in a colormap with the `colors` attribute:

```
from matplotlib import colormaps

colormaps['tab10'].colors
```

We want to provide our Matplotlib visualization with an iterable collection (such as a list, Pandas Series, or NumPy array) representing the desired color of each data point. One way to do this is by applying a function to the `property_type` column of our DataFrame. This function takes in a string property type (pt) and returns a corresponding color from `colormaps['tab10'].colors` based on its index in the `popular_property_types` list that we found earlier:

```
colors = df_ppt.property_type.apply(
    lambda pt: colormaps['tab10'].colors[popular_property_types.index(pt)]
)
```

The Pandas Series `colors` can then be passed to our scatterplot using the c keyword argument:

```
plt.scatter(
    df_ppt['sq_feet'],
    df_ppt['price'],
    s=1,
    c=colors,
)
```

Alternatively, we can draw our scatterplot multiple times, one for each color/property type combination:

```
vis_colors = colormaps['tab10'].colors[0:len(popular_property_types)]
for pt, color in zip(popular_property_types, vis_colors):
    df_pt = df.query(f'property_type=="{pt}"')
    plt.scatter(
        df_pt['sq_feet'],
        df_pt['price'],
        s=2,
        color=color,
        label=pt
    )
```

This gets a list of colors, `vis_colors`, representing the six colors that we want to use in the visualization. Then it uses the Python function `zip`[2] to merge the six colors in `vis_colors` with the six property types in `popular_property_types` so that it becomes a list of tuples with the format `(<vis_color>, <property_type>)`.

In each iteration of the `for` loop, we use the `query` method to get a DataFrame, `df_pt`, that contains only the records for the property type we're looking at. Then create the scatter plot with those property type records and color.

In the `scatter` function, I'm also passing in the property type, `pt`, using the `label` keyword argument. This allows us to easily add a legend to the plot. The rest of the code for this visualization adjusts the axes, adds a title and labels, and creates the legend:

```
plt.axis([0, 15000, 6500000, 30000000])
plt.xlabel('Square Feet')
plt.ylabel('Pound Sterling')
plt.title('Price vs. Square Feet')
plt.legend(markerscale=2, loc='upper left')
```

If you're reading the print edition of this book, there is an obvious problem we're about to run into here: The publisher is, very reasonably, unwilling to print a book in full color for the sake of one code example. If you are reading this book in print, you may want to have a quick look at the Jupyter Notebook files with this visualization. But if you're cozy where you are and don't feel like opening a computer, please just use your imagination when looking at Figure 24.3!

Another way to represent this data, and one that can be more easily displayed in grayscale, is to use six separate plots. The following produces a series of six plots (blank and without data) arranged in a 2 by 3 grid:

```
fig, ax = plt.subplots(2, 3)
```

---

[2] The `zip` function is often used in situations like this when two lists need to be iterated through at the same time. It returns a generator which can be used to create a list:

```
letters = ['a', 'b', 'c']
numbers = [1, 2, 3]
list(zip(letters, numbers))
```

This creates the list `[('a', 1), ('b', 2), ('c', 3)]`.

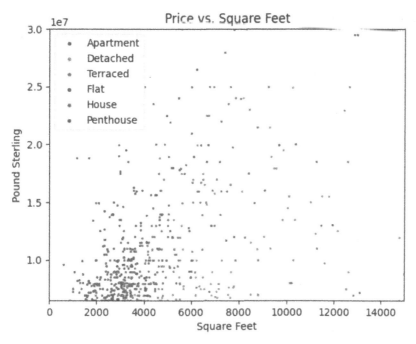

FIGURE 24.3: Adding colors to our scatterplot and zooming in even further shows additional patterns in the data

Two values, `fig` and `ax` are returned. The first, `fig`, represents the Matplotlib `Figure` object, which acts as a container for the multiple subplots. `Figure` represents the area around the subplots and can be used to adjust things like borders and margins that display all of them. The second returned value, `ax`, is a NumPy array containing six Matplotlib `Axes` objects. This NumPy array has the dimensions 2, 3, which mirrors how they are laid out visually in a 2×3 grid. Each `Axes` object represents a single subplot in the figure, with a title, x- and y-axes, tickmarks, and data.

The following is modified from the previous code sample that iterated through the property types and plotted each set of data in a different color. Here instead, we plot each property type on its own `Axes` object:

```
fig, ax = plt.subplots(2, 3, figsize=(16,10))

ax_listing = [ax[0][0], ax[0][1], ax[0][2], ax[1][0], ax[1][1], ax[1][2]]

for pt, ax_item in zip(popular_property_types, ax_listing):
    df_pt = df.query(f'property_type=="{pt}"')
    ax_item.scatter(
        df_pt['sq_feet'],
        df_pt['price'],
        s=2,
        label=pt
    )
    ax_item.axis([0, 15000, 6500000, 30000000])
    ax_item.set_title(pt)
    ax_item.set_xlabel('Square Feet')
    ax_item.set_ylabel('Pound Sterling')
```

This produces the visualization seen in Figure 24.4.

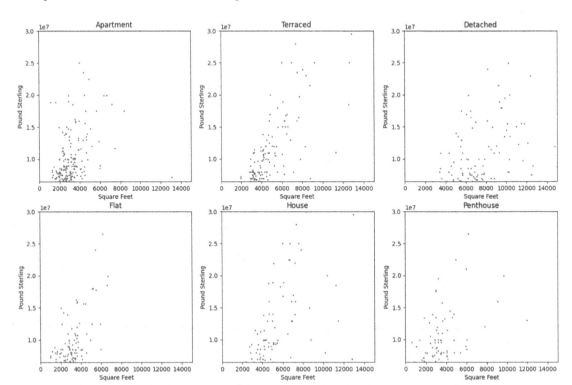

FIGURE 24.4: Subplots can represent multiple dimensions of the same dataset.

The way the list ax_listing is declared isn't particularly elegant but gets the point across. If you are dealing with a large number of subplots, you may want to iterate through each Axes object in a more flexible way using the number of plots in each dimension, rather than typing each one by hand. For small numbers of plots, however, listing each one by its coordinates may be more readable.

Rather than setting the title, axis boundaries, and labels on the entire figure at the end of the iteration, as we did previously, each ax_item gets its own settings. Each property can be adjusted independently. For example, each plot has a different title, the variable pt representing the string property type.

Because there are a lot of components to display in this new figure, it is useful to adjust the size so that everything can fit in. This can be done using the figsize argument passed into plt.subplots. Here, we're passing a figsize of (16, 10), which represents a width of 16 inches and a height of 10 inches. This can be adjusted in conjunction with the dpi (dots per square inch) parameter, if desired, for printing purposes. If you plan to print the figure, it may also be useful to save it to a PNG file, which can be done outside the for loop using the Figure object itself:

```
fig.savefig('london_realestate.png')
```

Regardless of whether you use color to represent the various types of properties or use multiple plots, the visualizations display several trends. Apartments, Flats, and Penthouses cluster with a steep slope, indicating that they are very expensive for the square footage. Linguistically speaking, the difference between a "flat" and an "apartment" is unclear, but it's interesting to note that there are many more expensive "apartments" than "flats."

Detached homes cluster with a shallower slope toward the bottom of the visualization, indicating that they are larger and cheaper. Terraced homes are somewhat in between the two groups, clustered on the diagonal. The "House" group, in purple, appears to exhibit the least-clear trends, and is loosely scattered throughout the Terraced and Detached groups.

Of course, Matplotlib can do far more than scatter plots. A full list of plot types can be seen here: `https://matplotlib.org/stable/plot_types/index.html`. Regardless of the plot type you use, the syntax for creating it remains much the same.

Line plots are commonly used with chronological data, such as our date column, representing the date that the property was added or last price reduced on. We can plot the average price of properties listed/reduced over time by first creating a DataFrame aggregated by month:

```
df = get_clean_df()
df_by_month = df.groupby(pd.PeriodIndex(df['date'], freq='M')).agg({
    'price': 'mean',
    'title': 'count'
})
df_by_month.reset_index(inplace=True)
df_by_month.date = df_by_month.date.apply(lambda d: d.to_timestamp())
df_by_month.rename(columns={'title': 'count'}, inplace=True)
df_by_month.head()
```

This uses the Pandas class `Period` to group the date column by the date period "months" (`freq='M'`) and then aggregate the average price for each month. Both the average price and the count of properties per month are populated in the aggregated DataFrame. Technically, we are getting the count of the `title` column; however, which column is used for the count is unimportant—it will always return the count of rows in that aggregation.

A little bit of finagling is required afterward to reset the index, rename the `count` column, and convert the date column back to a Pandas `datetime` (rather than a `Period` object, which Matplotlib cannot handle). Afterward, the data can be drawn in a line graph using the `plot` function (see Figure 24.5):

```
plt.plot(df_by_month.date, df_by_month['price'])
```

This seems to show at least one outlier that has not been updated in several years. In fact, there is a single property in both 2019 and in 2020, which you may want to consider removing from the dataset:

```
df = get_clean_df()
df.query('date < 20220101')
```

	added_on	title	description	property_type	sq_feet	bed rooms	bath rooms	listing_update_reason	price	date	location	bed rooms_title	property_type_title
313	15/03/2020	4 bedroom penthouse for sale in Bolsover Stree...	Arguably the finest penthouse in Fitzrovia wit...	Penthouse	3176.0	4.0	4.0	new	11000 000.0	2020-03-15	Bolsover Street, Fitzrovia, London, W1W	4.0	pent house
351	01/08/2019	3 bedroom flat for sale in Montrose Place, Bel...	An excep tional three bedroom lateral apart ment...	Flat	3084.0	3.0	3.0	new	11795 000.0	2019-08-01	Montrose Place, Belgravia, London, SW1X	3.0	flat

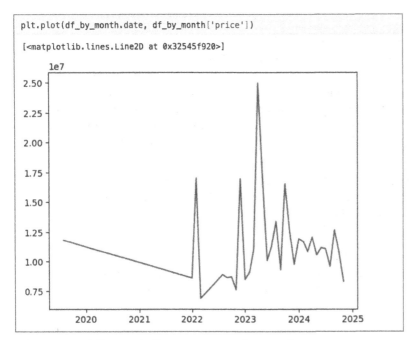

```
plt.plot(df_by_month.date, df_by_month['price'])

[<matplotlib.lines.Line2D at 0x32545f920>]
```

FIGURE 24.5: A line graph displays average price over time.

Large spikes in the price data might be explained by the fact that not very many properties exist within each monthly grouping. The mean price can be more easily swayed if there are fewer properties in the group, leading to "spiky" data rather than clear, smooth trends. It might be good to see the number of properties listed per month to determine if any of these spikes represent real trends, or if they're side effects of a small amount of data:

```
df_by_month = df_by_month.query('date > 20220101')
plt.bar(df_by_month.date, df_by_month['count'], width=20)
```

This displays a bar graph with 31 bars, one for each month in the dataset, starting in February 2022 (the first month that is greater than January 2022). Bar graphs are very similar to line graphs in the types and dimensions of data they can display, but bar graphs are better at displaying discontinuous or categorical data.

BUILDING SUPERVISED MODELS WITH SCIKIT-LEARN

When creating machine learning models, it's important to consider which type of data you will use:

```
df_train = get_clean_df().query('property_type == "Terraced" and price.notna()')
df_train = df_train.query('sq_feet.notna() and bathrooms.notna()')
```

Scikit-learn is a powerful machine learning library with a very simple interface. It's so simple that we can build a machine learning model that estimates the price of, say, "Terraced" properties with just a few lines of code:

```
from sklearn.linear_model import LinearRegression

model = LinearRegression().fit(
    df_train[['sq_feet', 'bedrooms', 'bathrooms']],
    df_train['price']
)
```

The model itself is instantiated with `LinearRegression` and the `fit` method is called with a DataFrame containing features used as inputs (`sq_feet`, `bedrooms`, and `bathrooms`) and a `Series` containing the output feature that will be predicted by the model (`price`).

When `fit` is called, this model is trained on the provided data. Once trained, it can be used to predict the price of new properties, such as a 1,450-square-foot property with three bedrooms and two bathrooms:

```
model.predict([[1450, 3, 2]])
```

Because `predict` is usually used to run the model over multiple records at a time, it takes an iterable containing multiple sets of data from which to make predictions. Here, a list of lists is passed to `predict` containing the values for the single theoretical property. The `predict` method returns a NumPy array of length 1 containing the prediction:

```
array([3747218.93990251])
```

Because we're using a list of lists and not a Pandas DataFrame with labeled columns, there is a warning:

```
UserWarning: X does not have valid feature names
```

This warning can be ignored, although it's good to double-check that the values we're passing in ([[1450, 3, 2]]) correspond correctly with the columns 'sq_feet', 'bedrooms', 'bathrooms' used to train the model.

The algorithm used to create the LinearRegression model is, as you might have guessed, linear regression. *Linear regression* is a simple approach that assumes linear relationships between the features in the dataset and the values they predict. Because it only deals in linear correlations, its models may not be very accurate, depending on the real-world system it's modeling.

We can substitute a different algorithm in for linear regression easily with Scikit-Learn. Here is an example that uses *logistic regression*:

```
from sklearn.linear_model import LogisticRegression

model = LogisticRegression().fit(
    df_train[['sq_feet', 'bedrooms', 'bathrooms']],
    df_train['price']
)
model.predict([[1450, 3, 2]])
```

And here is an algorithm that uses a type of neural network, called a *multilayer perceptron*, to create a model:

```
from sklearn.neural_network import MLPRegressor

model = MLPRegressor().fit(
    df_train[['sq_feet', 'bedrooms', 'bathrooms']],
    df_train['price']
)
model.predict([[1450, 3, 2]])
```

Astute readers may note that the only difference between these examples is the class used to create the model. One of the really nice parts of the scikit-learn library is the consistency of the interfaces between various classes and algorithms. As we work through more examples, keep in mind that the exact algorithm being used is usually unimportant. Every ML algorithm in the scikit-learn library—from simple linear regression to a neural network classification—is instantiated, trained, used, and scored in much the same way.

Of course, just because you *can* plug another algorithm in and run the code doesn't always mean you *should* or that your results will be any good. The estimated price of our 1,450-square-foot house using the linear regression model was £3,747,218. The estimated price using logistic regression was £7,950,000. Given that most of the prices start at £6,500,000, the output of this logistic regression "feels" a little more correct here.

And we'd expect logistic regression to be more correct, right? It uses fancier math and can make more accurate predictions. Of course, we would also expect the MLPRegressor, using a neural network, to be the most accurate of all.

The MLPRegressor model predicts the 1,450-square-foot house in London will cost £6,495. What a bargain!

Clearly, something strange is going on here. When both the LogisticRegressor and MLPRegressor are fit, a warning appears. The warning for the LogisticRegressor reads:

```
ConvergenceWarning: lbfgs failed to converge
```

The warning for the MLPRegressor is similar:

```
ConvergenceWarning: Stochastic Optimizer: Maximum iterations (200) reached and the
optimization hasn't converged yet.
```

Many machine learning algorithms, such as logistic regression and multilayer perceptron regression, use an iterative function that adjusts the parameters of the model in order to reduce the error (amount of training data the model-in-training disagrees with) during each pass. In some cases, however, subsequent iterations do not reliably shrink the error and the "optimal" settings for the parameters are unclear. In these cases, the algorithm fails to converge.

There are several things you can do in this case. The best thing you can do is add more data. Obviously, this is not always possible, and the data is what it is. In these cases, you can also adjust the settings for the algorithm itself. You might use a different method to find convergence or allow additional iterations for the model to converge.

In the case of LogisticRegressor, we can modify the number of iterations performed before the regression gives up on converging by changing the max_iter parameter:

```
model = LogisticRegression(max_iter=10000).fit(
    df_train[['sq_feet', 'bedrooms', 'bathrooms']],
    df_train['price']
)
```

This takes noticeably longer to run and still fails to converge. A good rule of thumb is that if you have relatively few data points (and there are only 140 of them in this subset of the data), throwing more computational power at it won't make your model better. Sometimes, there's just nothing there.

We can also change the mathematical method used to find the logistic regression using the solver parameter:

```
model = LogisticRegression(solver='newton-cholesky').fit(
    df_train[['sq_feet', 'bedrooms', 'bathrooms']],
    df_train['price']
)
```

A complete list of available solvers can be found in the documentation for LogisticRegression (https://scikit-learn.org/dev/modules/generated/sklearn.linear_model .LogisticRegression.html). Changing the solver may allow the algorithm to converge, but convergence doesn't mean the model is necessarily good. In the next section, we'll look at ways to evaluate models for "goodness."

As mentioned before, adding more data to the dataset, if possible, is a good way of improving model performance. You can also add more features (columns) to the existing records. In the previous examples, the data was limited to just "Terraced" properties because that appeared to be the group with the clearest correlation when viewing the data by square footage and price. In theory, that pattern should be easiest to model with a regression algorithm.

However, what if we could include *all* data points along with information about their property type? In theory, this would allow the regression model to find unique "rules" or correlations for each different property type.

Machine learning algorithms in scikit-learn must be provided with numeric data only. A naïve approach for supplying property type information might be to substitute the property type strings for numbers: "Apartment" is 1, "Detached" is 2, "Terraced" is 3, etc. However, this would be a mistake. Property types are categorical data, not ordinal (ordered, numerical) data. If "Apartment" is represented by the number 1, "Detached" and "Penthouse" is 6, the regression algorithm will infer that "Apartment" and "Detached" are very close to each other because the number 1 is close to the number 2, and that "Detached" is a third of a "Penthouse," which is nonsensical.

Instead, use the Pandas function get_dummies to convert categorical data with a limited number of possible values into columns of Boolean values indicating the data belongs to that particular category.

For this, let's use the DataFrame containing only real estate that is a member of the six most popular property types, df_ppt. This was the DataFrame used earlier when creating scatterplot visualizations. These are the first five property types in df_ppt:

```
df_ppt[['property_type']].head()
```

	property_type
0	House
1	House
2	Terraced
3	Detached
4	Detached

The get_dummies function takes a Series as an argument and returns a DataFrame:

```
pd.get_dummies(df_ppt['property_type']).head()
```

	Apartment	Detached	Flat	House	Penthouse	Terraced
0	False	False	False	True	False	False
1	False	False	False	True	False	False
2	False	False	False	False	False	True
3	False	True	False	False	False	False
4	False	True	False	False	False	False

Because Booleans can be interpreted as numerical values (either a 1 or a 0), we have successfully converted categorical data into numerical data that is suitable for use in a regression algorithm.

The full set of filtering and data synthesis steps are as follows:

```
df_train = get_clean_df()
df_train = df[df['property_type'].isin(popular_property_types)]
df_train = df_train.query('price.notna() and sq_feet.notna()')
df_train = df_train.query('bedrooms.notna() and bathrooms.notna()')
df_train = df_train.join(pd.get_dummies(df_train.property_type))
```

We filter the DataFrame to only those records that are one of our six popular property types and remove records that don't contain a listed price, square footage, number of bathrooms, or number of bedrooms. Finally, we use the `join` method to combine the columns in `df_train` with the "dummies" synthesized from the `property_type` column.

This DataFrame can be used for any scikit-learn regression algorithm. Here, we're using it with SVR (Epsilon-Support Vector Regression), which can be computationally intensive but works well with relatively small datasets:

```
from sklearn.svm import SVR

input_cols = [
    'sq_feet',
    'bedrooms',
    'bathrooms',
    'Apartment',
    'Detached',
    'Flat',
    'House',
    'Penthouse',
    'Terraced'
]
model = SVR().fit(df_train[input_cols], df_train['price'])
```

In addition to `sq_feet`, `bedrooms`, and `bathrooms`, all six columns representing the various property types must also be passed into the model.

`LinearRegression`, `LogisticRegression`, `MLPRegressor`, and `SVR` are all types of regression algorithms. They take, as inputs, various numeric values and predict a continuous numeric value (price) as an output. Another type of machine learning model is a classifier. These take various numeric values as inputs and predict a categorical class as an output.

Rather than using the property type and other information to the predict price, as we did with the regressors, we can put price and other information in a classifier to predict the property type!

One popular type of classification algorithm is k-nearest neighbors using scikit-learn's `KNeighborsClassifier`. This algorithm looks at the k nearest (most similar) points to the input data point to be classified and uses a voting mechanism of those known points to provide a best guess for the classification of the new data.

There is no limit to the number of classes (number of property types) we can provide the `KNeighborsClassifier`, but the performance of the model may decrease if there are too many different types of properties. It's critical that the property type be defined, so at the very least we must filter for populated `property_type` strings only:

```
df_train = get_clean_df().query('property_type.notna()')
```

If we want to increase model performance (at the expense of ignoring more niche types of properties, of course), we can also limit this to the six most popular property types:

```
df_train = df[df['property_type'].isin(popular_property_types)]
```

From there, we need to ensure that all the data has populated values for `sq_feet`, `price`, `bedrooms`, and `bathrooms`. Historically, we've done this by filtering:

```
df_train = df_train.query('price.notna() and sq_feet.notna()')
df_train = df_train.query('bedrooms.notna() and bathrooms.notna()')
```

Alternatively, we can also use `fillna` to replace all missing values with a `0`, preserving those records:

```
df_train.fillna(0, inplace=True)
```

Removing records with missing data is ideal for algorithms that view all values on a spectrum and make decisions via a limited number of thresholds. For example, if lower-priced units tend to be flats, but penthouses frequently have unlisted prices, some algorithms may have difficultly differentiating "low price" from a "price of 0." In contrast, k-nearest neighbors makes decisions in many small clusters and has no problem differentiating "low price" and "price of 0" if needed.

For our `KNeighborsClassifier`, let's use data with only the six most popular property types along with filled `0` values where data is missing:

```
df_train = get_clean_df()
df_train = df[df['property_type'].isin(popular_property_types)]
df_train.fillna(0, inplace=True)
```

The syntax for training a classification model is exactly the same as it is for training a regression model:

```
from sklearn.neighbors import KNeighborsClassifier

input_cols = ['bedrooms', 'bathrooms', 'price', 'sq_feet']
model = KNeighborsClassifier().fit(
    df_train[input_cols], df_train['property_type']
)
```

The syntax for making predictions is the same as well. Here, we can use the trained model to predict what type of property we should assign to something with three bedrooms, two bathrooms, 1,400 square feet, and with a price of £8,000,000:

```
model.predict([[3, 2, 5000000, 1400]])
```

One interesting thing we can do with this trained model is run it across the data that it's already been trained on:

```
model.predict(df_train[input_cols])
```

This produces an array of predicted classes:

```
array(['Detached', 'House', 'House', 'Detached', 'Detached', 'House', ...
```

In theory, if the trained model preserved all the information it was trained on and replicated its training data perfectly, it would produce an array that matches the values in df_train['property_type'] exactly. However, it doesn't. In fact, these predicted values match the actual values just over half of the time (which isn't bad considering there are six possible choices!).

Of course, predicting values that the model has already "seen" is cheating if you're trying to ascertain how the model would likely perform in the real world on future data. We would expect the model to score higher when it's predicting data it's already been trained on. However, this score on training data is still important and gives us a useful measurement of other aspects of the model, as well as hints about how to improve it. In the next section, we'll use these scores on training data and evaluate classification models in more detail.

EVALUATING CLASSIFICATION MODELS WITH SCIKIT-LEARN

When we ask a trained classification model for a prediction, that prediction is either right or wrong. The data point we've provided either belongs to the class the model gave us, or it doesn't.

The percentage of data points that a model predicts correctly is called the model's *score*. To be scored correctly, a model must be scored on data it wasn't trained on—data that it hasn't seen before. Otherwise, the best model would simply be one that records every data point it was trained on and returns the known class!

Therefore, in order to judge the performance of models that we build, we need to withhold some data from the training dataset. This data is called *test data*. Typically, datasets are split into both train and test datasets where the training portion accounts for approximately 80% of the data and the test portion is the remaining 20%.

Let's look at an example of this in action with a *binary classification model*, or a classification that consists of only two groups. For this, we want to make a new column in the data, is_reduced, which indicates whether the property has been reduced in price. To do this, we can look for the key word 'Reduced' in the original added_on column:

```
df = get_clean_df()
df = df.query('added_on.notna()')
df['is_reduced'] = df['added_on'].apply(lambda s:'Reduced' in s)
```

There are 299 cases in the dataset where the price has been reduced and 702 cases where it has not been reduced. This is an *imbalanced dataset*. This can cause problems when building and evaluating classification models, because the model may tend to favor the more popular group over the less popular one.

In fact, in extreme cases, models may even choose the more popular group every single time, for example predicting "not reduced" for every property it sees. After all, by using this strategy, the model will have a 70% "success rate" for the data it was trained on!

To combat this, we can create a dataset of balanced positive (reduced price) and negative (no reduced price) samples where each class comprises half the dataset:

```
def get_balanced_samples(df, col_name):
    pos = df.query(f'{col_name} == True')
    neg = df.query(f'{col_name} == False')
    if len(pos) > len(neg):
        pos = pos.sample(len(neg))
    else:
        neg = neg.sample(len(pos))
    return pos, neg

df_pos, df_neg = get_balanced_samples(df, 'is_reduced')
```

The function `get_balanced_samples` is flexibly designed to work with any Boolean column, `col_name`. It returns two datasets of the same length, one where the value in that column is `True` (the pos list) and one where the value is `False` (the neg list). In this case, it returns two samples of length 299, for a total of 598 samples.

We can use the Pandas function `concat` to stack, or concatenate, the two DataFrames back into a single dataset:

```
df = pd.concat([df_pos, df_neg])
```

Next, the scikit-learn function `train_test_split` is used to split the dataset into train and test data:

```
from sklearn.model_selection import train_test_split

df_train, df_test = train_test_split(df, test_size=0.2)
```

The keyword argument `test_size` is set to `0.2`, indicating that the testing set should be 20% of the data and the training set the remaining 80%.

Because this split is random, we will get different datasets each time the function is called. In addition, we may get slightly different numbers of positive (reduced price) and negative (not reduced price) samples in both our test and train dataset, although they should still be approximately 50/50 and not have an impact on the performance.

Next, we create the model and fit it on the training dataset:

```
from sklearn.tree import DecisionTreeClassifier

input_cols = ['bedrooms', 'bathrooms', 'price', 'sq_feet']

dtc = DecisionTreeClassifier().fit(
    df_train[input_cols], df_train['is_reduced']
)
```

The decision tree classifier is a popular classification algorithm that uses simple thresholds to decide which class a sample belongs to. For example, "If the number of bedrooms is 5 or more and the price is less than 10,000,000, then the price has been reduced." Although a full discussion of decision tree creation and exploration is outside the scope of this book, it's worth noting that decisions that make up these trees can be viewed in human-readable form using Matplotlib:

```
from sklearn import tree
import matplotlib.pyplot as plt

tree.plot_tree(dtc, max_depth=1, feature_names=input_cols)
plt.show()
```

Once the model, dtc, has been trained, we can score it using the retained test data:

```
dtc.score(df_test[input_cols], df_test['is_reduced'])
```

The score will vary depending on many random factors, but in one particular run, had a score of 0.6167, or 61.67%. Keep in mind that, because we're working with a balanced dataset, a score of 50% is essentially random chance. A model that gets a score below 50% is actually *worse* than guessing.[3]

One drawback of decision trees is that, unchecked, they can be prone to *overfitting*. Models are overfit when they contain a lot of rules and information that allow them to very closely model the training data that was used, but which don't *actually* help them on new data. Counterintuitively, limiting the ability of models to conform to the training data may improve model performance on new test data.

One easy way to test for overfitting is to score the model on its own training data. Our decision tree model, dtc, had a score of approximately 60% on test data. However, on training data, the score is more like 99%:

```
dtc.score(df_train[input_cols], df_train['is_reduced'])
```

```
0.9895397489539749
```

Performing much better on the training data than the test data indicates that the model is overfit. In fact, performing better at all on the test data than the training data indicates some degree of overfitting, but it is not necessarily a good thing to eliminate overfitting entirely.

One way to reduce the amount of overfitting in a model is to reduce the number of "rules" that the model uses when evaluating data to make a prediction. This can be thought of as the amount of information in, or the complexity of a model.

In a decision tree we can reduce the number of rules it uses, and, therefore, its ability to overfit the training data, by setting the max_depth. The depth of a decision tree is the number of thresholds, or rules, it can chain together before it needs to decide which class it thinks a sample belongs to.

---

[3] When working with models that do not score significantly above 50% (working within very narrow margins), you may occasionally get dips below that threshold when random chance conspires against you. This doesn't mean you've done anything "wrong," but you may need to re-roll the dice a few times to get a better sense of how your model is actually performing.

If you consistently get numbers below this threshold, or numbers that are significantly below this threshold, you may want to double-check that you haven't made a mistake somewhere.

For example, "If the number of bedrooms is 5 or more and the price is less than 10,000,000" contains two thresholds: `bedrooms >= 5` and `price <= 10,000,000`, and might belong to a decision tree with a depth of 2. However, if the decision tree is allowed to grow unchecked, it could, in theory, contain a long series of rules, culminating in a decision that perfectly matches every sample in the dataset.

By setting the maximum depth of the tree, we're forcing the tree to limit itself to only the most generalizable rules that best describe or best fit the data.

Running and scoring the tree again with a `max_depth` of 3, we get a score that is not significantly different from the previous one on the test data:

```
df_train, df_test = train_test_split(df, test_size=0.2)
input_cols = ['bedrooms', 'bathrooms', 'price', 'sq_feet']

dtc = DecisionTreeClassifier(max_depth=3).fit(
    df_train[input_cols], df_train['is_reduced']
)

dtc.score(df_test[input_cols], df_test['is_reduced'])
```

However, its score is very different on the training data:

```
dtc.score(df_train[input_cols], df_train['is_reduced'])
```

0.6276150627615062

This indicates that the model is no longer overfitting the data.

When we decide on a final version of a trained machine learning model and send it to production, we want to be very sure that this trained model will continue to perform well and that we didn't just get lucky with our data when we scored it. When we run our decision tree models multiple times, we get multiple scores.

In the original decision tree, with no `max_depth` set, rerunning the test/train split, fitting, and scoring gives all sorts of scores, from 0.572 to 0.726 over the course of 100 runs. With the `max_depth` set to 3, we get a smaller range of 0.607 to 0.786.

An important measure of a machine learning model is its *variance*, or how consistent its scores are over repeated sampling, fittings, and scorings.

We can write a function, `measure_performance`, which runs test/train splitting, fitting, and scoring in a loop, then reports the average score on the test data, average score on the training data (to check for overfitting), and variance[4] of the test scores:

---

[4] Mathematical variance is a measurement used in statistics. It's a property of groups of numbers (such as groups of scores). If variance is high, then the numbers are wildly different from each other. If variance is low, the numbers are very similar. Variance is related to standard deviation—in fact, variance is simply the standard deviation squared.

Keep in mind that, because model scores are smaller than 1, the standard deviations will also be smaller than 1. This means that the variance will be smaller than the standard deviation. If the standard deviation is .016, the variance will be .016^2 or .000256.

```
def measure_performance(classifier, df, n):
    test_scores = []
    train_scores = []
    for _ in range(n):
        df_train, df_test = train_test_split(df, test_size=0.2)
        classifier.fit(df_train[input_cols], df_train['is_reduced'])
        test_scores.append(
            classifier.score(df_test[input_cols], df_test['is_reduced'])
        )
        train_scores.append(
            classifier.score(df_train[input_cols], df_train['is_reduced'])
        )
    print(f'    test mean: {np.mean(test_scores)}')
    print(f'    train mean: {np.mean(train_scores)}')
    print(f'    test variance: {np.var(test_scores)}')
```

This uses two lists, `test_scores` and `train_scores` to keep track of scores as it goes, then prints the results with an indent for formatting reasons.

This method of repeated sampling from the same dataset, with replacement, is called *bootstrapping* in data science. Bootstrapping is used in many contexts to improve models and also measure their performance with great accuracy.

Using the function `measure_performance`, we can compare the performance of a decision tree model with unlimited depth and the model with a `max_depth` of 3:

```
print('Unlimited Max Depth')
measure_performance(DecisionTreeClassifier(), df, 100)
print('Max Depth 3')
measure_performance(DecisionTreeClassifier(max_depth=3), df, 100)
```

```
Unlimited Max Depth
    test mean: 0.65
    train mean: 0.9889874999999998
    test variance: 0.0012848073067498334
Max Depth 3
    test mean: 0.6956218905472638
    train mean: 0.717525
    test variance: 0.0007932377911437833
```

We see that both the variance in test scores and the mean score on the training data decreased when we limited the depth of the tree. Also, while the first model fit the training data more closely, the second, depth-limited model performed better on the test data.

The tendency of a model to *not* fit training data is called *bias*. The more constrained the model is during training, the less closely it fits the test data, the more bias it has. If we're using a linear regression (which models relationships with straight lines) but our data has curved correlations, our resulting model will have high bias. Limiting the depth our decision tree also increases bias, which decreases the mean score on the test data.

In general, the less closely a model fits the training data, the less variance in scores you will get. This is called the *bias-variance trade-off*. More constrained models follow training data less closely, which makes them less prone to overfitting the random variations in that training data. This causes less variation from model to model.

When working with real-world data, it's important to keep in mind that, sometimes, a score of 69% or 70% may be as good as it's possible to get. There exists a finite amount of "signal" in the dataset and no machine learning algorithm, no matter how fancy or computationally intensive, no matter how carefully balanced the variance and bias, can overcome this theoretical maximum score.

This is why the bias-variance trade-off is a "trade-off." The goal of machine learning is to find a model that falls somewhere in the sweet spot of this trade-off to maximize the score. And, while we're at it, find something reasonably simple and not too computationally intensive. After all, beautiful is better than ugly.

Index